3/18/2007

SEED & BREAD

ONE HUNDRED STUDIES IN POSITIVE BIBLICAL THEOLOGY

BY
OTIS Q. SELLERS

VOLUME

To find a particular **Subject**, locate the **Issue Number** at the bottom of the last page of each four-page Study. Search from back to front.

NUMERICAL INDEX 1 - 100

ALPHABETICAL INDEX 1 - 100

OTHER PUBLICATIONS

By Otis Q. Sellers

SOFTBOUND BOOKLETS AND STUDY MATERIALS

Six Messages on the Resurrection (1943)	.75
God Has Spoken (1943)	.75
The Sabbath and the Sunday Question (1944)	.75
The Dispensation of the Grace of God (1947)	.75
Acts 28:28 - A Dispensational Boundary (1947)	1.00
Satanic Counterfeits (1942)	.75
God's Present Purpose (1953)	.50
The Study of Human Destiny (1955-2nd Ed.)	1.00
The Resurrections (1955)	1.00
The Thousand Year Reign of Christ (1957)	.75
The Interpretation of Phil. 3:20 (1959)	.75
The Enlightenment of Mankind (1960)	.75
Christian Individualism (1961)	.50
The Concluding Days (1962)	.75
The Rich Man and Lazarus (1962-2nd Ed.)	1.50
This I Believe - That Jesus is the Christ (1963)	.50
This Do in Remembrance (1964) 59 pages	1.00
Absent From the Body (1966) 42 pages	1.25
One-A-Day 87 Brief Studies (1976) plastic comb binding	3.75

SEED & BREAD

FOR THE SOWER   ISA. 55:10   FOR THE EATER

BRIEF BIBLICAL MESSAGES FROM

THE WORD OF TRUTH MINISTRY

158 N. Hill Avenue, Pasadena, CA 91106

Otis Q. Sellers, Founder ❖ David R. Hettema, Director

1

YOU NEED A SAVIOR

The basic needs of mankind are usually thought to be food, clothing, and shelter. That these are necessities all will admit, but even after these have been amply supplied, his most basic need still remains. He still has need for a Savior. This need is one to which the human mind gives constant witness. The individual man has been so constructed by the Creator that he cannot have peace of mind, rest of heart, and quietness of spirit until he is linked up with his Creator by means of a divinely provided Savior.

This unfulfilled need of a Savior is the explanation of the constant dissatisfaction of most men, their ceaseless activity, their restlessness of heart, their constant search for pleasure. They try to still the voice of conscience by listening to a thousand other voices. All thoughts of God must be crowded out and replaced by other thoughts. Man ever strives to bring himself to that state of mind which is described in scripture as being: "God is not in all his thoughts." He must create a constant din of activities above which the voice of conscience cannot be heard. For above all else, conscience continually tells man of his need of a Savior. This is your greatest need, your most important need.

There are many reasons why you need a Savior, but the chief one will always be your standing and state in the sight of God. This truth is expressed in simple, easily-understood words spoken by the Apostle Paul when he said of all men in Romans 3:22,23: "There is no difference, for all have sinned and come short of the glory of God." These words become plainer still when we recognize that to "come short" is to *lack*, and that "glory" has to do with *esteem*. For example, the esteem in which we hold a person is the glory we

-1-

will give to him. If we esteem him to be upright and honest, this is the glory we will give him when the occasion arises for us to speak concerning him. Thus Paul's statement literally tells us that there is no difference, all have sinned and are lacking the esteem of God.

The lesson all should learn here is that while we may be highly esteemed by our friends, family, and fellowmen, yet because we are sinners we are lacking the esteem of God. You may be extolled in life or at death as having been a good citizen, good father, and good churchman, but you are still lacking the esteem of God. Your children may esteem you highly as a good mother and your husband may praise you as a good wife, but you are still lacking the esteem of God. Something must be brought into your life, there must be some definite act of yours that will bring you to God's favorable attention that will result in Him esteeming you for what you are and what you have done.

As to what this is there can be no question. Your neglect of the God-appointed Savior must cease. You must appropriate God's great provision for your great need — your need of a Savior. You must be able to stand before Him as a sinner who has a Savior — not a sinner without one. This will cause Him to esteem you as a believer, and you will no longer lack the esteem of God. It is your crying need that you bring yourself to some final dealing with God in regard to this. Truly, you need a Savior.

Another positive reason why you need a Savior is seen in the fact that death is working in you and you are dying. Apart from divine intervention the death that works in you will reach its end and your life will be over and gone. This is a fact that few want to face, and many will not like being reminded of it, but it is an inexorable fact and the death rate is still one apiece. "It is appointed unto men once to die" (Heb. 9:27). In view of this you need a Savior who can rescue you from the fate and fact of death and give you another life to take the place of the one you are using up little by little, day by day.

Those who are advancing in years, who now realize that there is more sand in the bottom of the glass than there is in the top, should give careful thought to this fact. Senior citizens need more than a hobby. They need a Savior. Do you think that within yourself you have power to turn over the glass so that another life will run through again? Do you think that in death you will automatically be given another life to take the place of the one that is used up and gone? Certainly not. You need to make contact with a Savior who is the author and giver of life. To have such a Savior is to have the guarantee of another life. Truly, you need a Savior.

THE SAVIOR YOU NEED

Of course, the Savior you need is the One that God has provided. No one else will do, and even to consider another would be to slander God's provision. The Virgin Mary spoke of "God my Savior" (Luke 1:47), a phrase that tells us that our Savior should be no one less than God Himself. Happy indeed is the one who can say: "Thou art my Father, my God, and the rock of my salvation." We have come to maturity when we can say in truth, "My Savior is my God, and my God is my Savior."

Through the prophet Isaiah, Jehovah declared: "I, even I, am the LORD (Jehovah); and beside Me there is no Savior" (Isa. 43:11). Again He says, "Who hath told it from that time? have not I the LORD (Jehovah)? and there is no God else beside Me; a just God and a Savior; there is none beside Me. Look unto Me, and be ye saved, all the ends of the earth: for I am God, and there is none else" (Isa. 45:21-22). In view of these declarations it is evident that the Savior we need can be no one else and no one less than the mighty God, the Creator, that Jehovah who is seen on every page of the Old Testament and comes to us in the New Testament as the Lord Jesus Christ.

The Savior that will fulfill our need must be the Savior of sinners. "They that are whole need not a physician; but they that are sick. I came not to call the righteous, but sinners to repentance," are the words of the Lord Jesus concerning this. (Luke 5:31). We go to physicians because we are sick and we should fly to the Savior because we are sinners. It is declared in Scripture that "Christ Jesus came into the world to save sinners" (1 Tim. 1:15). Titus speaks of "the great God and our Savior Jesus Christ" (Titus 2:13), not two beings but one. The two titles here are appositional (one defines the other) and should read "the great God even our Savior Jesus Christ." If Jesus Christ is not "the great God", if He is not Jehovah, then He cannot be our Savior since long before this Jehovah declared that there is no Savior except Himself.

The Savior you need is the Lord Jesus Christ. He was born to be a Savior (Luke 2:11); He was sent to be a Savior (1 John 4:14); He is called "God our Savior" (Titus 1:3,4), and in the same sentence He is spoken of as "the Lord Jesus Christ our Savior." Thus our Savior is our God and our God is our Savior.

In receiving the Lord Jesus Christ as our Savior we are not putting our trust in a peasant who lived in Palestine two thousand years ago. We must not form our opinions of Him from one short period of His long history. The "days of His flesh" is not even the place to begin to understand Him. The record God has given to Him and which we are required to believe in order to be saved does not begin with a babe born in Bethlehem. It begins with His first recorded act, "In the beginning God created the heaven and the earth" (Gen. 1:1). This Creator is called the Word (Logos) in John 1:1 and is declared to have done the total work of creation in John 1:3. And it was this Word, this Creator, who was made flesh and dwelt for thirty-three years as a man upon earth. This is our Creator, this is our Lord, this is our Savior — a capable Savior, an all-sufficient Savior, one who is able to save unto the uttermost all who come unto God by Him.

The simplicity of God's plan of salvation for the sinner and the infallibility of the Word of God should result in the conclusion that a sinner can be saved by Jesus Christ, and that the believer in Christ Jesus should know that he is saved. If we have turned from our own works and merit to a complete dependence upon the all-sufficient work and merit of Christ, we should have this knowledge and assurance. If we have put our trust in Him for our salvation, if we have received Him as our Savior, then we must either believe Him to be what He claims to be and do what He claims to do or else believe Him to be incapable and untrue. Remember, salvation depends on the Savior.

Since by the Word of God you have been shown your need of a Savior, and Jesus Christ has been shown to be the Savior you need, then your next step is to make Him your personal Savior. If your mind has been exercised and your heart stirred, consider this to be the work of God's Holy Spirit. You are being helped in a matter that is very dear to the heart of God. Why not deliberately decide that you will believe in God, that you will from this hour forth be a believer in the Lord Jesus Christ? Let this be your confession of faith in Him, and let your first confession of faith be the most important one. This should be the one you make to God, and to Him alone. Public declarations can come later, and they should follow, but your original confession of faith in Jesus Christ should be your personal dealing with God.

As a preparation for this confession I would suggest that you read through the Gospel of John, paying close attention to every occurrence of the word *believe*. You will find it there just as it has been set forth in this message—that to all sinners who need a Savior, Jesus Christ is the Savior you need.

| The SEED and BREAD Bible-Study leaflets are published as often as time and means permit and are sent free to all names on THE WORD OF TRUTH MINISTRY mailing list. Send us your name. There will be no obligation, solicitation, or visitation. Additional copies of any issue available on request. | ISSUE NO. 1 Reprinted June 30, 1998 |

SEED & BREAD

FOR THE SOWER   ISA. 55:10   FOR THE EATER

BRIEF BIBLICAL MESSAGES

FROM

THE WORD OF TRUTH MINISTRY

339 South Orange Drive, Los Angeles, Cal. 90036

Otis Q. Sellers, Bible Teacher

THE LORD JESUS IS JEHOVAH

In order to qualify as a believer in the Lord Jesus Christ one must believe the record God has given of His Son. To believe in the Lord Jesus Christ is to believe what the Bible says concerning Him. The central and most important feature of divine revelation in regard to Him is that the Jehovah of the Old Testament is the Lord Jesus Christ of the New Testament. There is no fact concerning the man Christ Jesus that is declared more emphatically or that is set forth in more detail than that He is Jehovah.

In spite of this preponderance of testimony, a denomination that calls itself "Jehovah's Witnesses" is most aggressive in the denial of this great Biblical fact. However, in their house to house canvassing they seldom come upon one who is familiar with all the facts of scripture bearing on this great truth, and this results in many triumphs for them over these ignorant ones. This situation demands that the facts should be made known, so, "To the law and to the testimony: If they speak not according to this word, it is because there is no light in them." Isa. 8:20.

In examining the evidence the student will need to remember that every time he comes upon the name LORD in the King James Version spelled out in capital letters, that this represents the Hebrew word *Yahweh* which we translate *Jehovah*. He will also need to note that due to an extreme (but mistaken) reverence for the ineffable name "Yahweh" the ancient custodians of the sacred text, the Massorites, substituted in 134 places the name *Adonai*. The Companion Bible gives a complete list of these (Appendix 32). They committed no sin in doing this as it was merely the substitution of one name of God (*Adonai*) for another (*Yahweh*).

In Genesis 15:2,8 Abraham twice called Jehovah (The One who spoke to him) "Lord GOD", which in the Hebrew reads *Adonai Jehovah*. This presents a great difficulty for those who try to tell us that Jehovah refers only to "the Father," and Adonai refers only to "the Son". This bit of misinformation is constantly being thrown out by those whose conversation shows that they have never made a personal study of the Hebrew titles given to the Deity. Even a superficial acquaintance with the use of these names in Scripture would show that such an idea is impossible. Can we deduce from the two passages cited above that two distinct beings or personalities dealt with Abraham? Certainly not! The titles Jehovah and Adonai are so inextricably interwoven that no one with knowledge would think of applying them to two separate beings. They are many times used in combination; the prophet Ezekiel alone does so almost two hundred times.

In Isaiah 6:1-3 the prophet declares:

In the year that king Uzziah died I saw also the Lord sitting upon a throne, high and lifted up, and his train filled the temple. Above it stood the seraphims; each one had six wings; with twain he covered his face, and with twain he covered his feet, and with twain did he fly. And one cried unto another and said, Holy, holy, holy, is the LORD (Jehovah) of hosts; the whole earth is full of his glory.

This vision was so overpowering that it caused Isaiah to cry out: "Woe is me! for I am undone; because I am a man of unclean lips, and I dwell in the midst of a people of unclean lips; for mine eyes have seen the King, the LORD (Jehovah) of hosts." Isa. 6:5.

Thus in verse one the prophet says, "I saw the Lord" *(Adonai)*, and in verse five he says, "Mine eyes have seen the King, the LORD (Jehovah) of hosts." This presents an insuperable difficulty to those who would tell us that these two names represent two different beings, since they show that Jehovah and Adonai are one and the same.

In John 12:38 to 41 a part of this passage is quoted and it is declared that this was a vision of the glory of Christ; "These things said Esaias (Isaiah), when he saw His glory, and spake of Him." (John 12:41).

In Isaiah 40:3 the prophet speaks of the preparation of a path for Jehovah. "Prepare ye the way of the LORD (Jehovah)", are his stirring words. Seven hundred years later John the Baptist adopts this passage, applies it to himself as the forerunner and to the preparation for the public appearance of the Lord Jesus. See Matt. 3:3 and John 1:23. Truly the One whom Isaiah spoke about (Jehovah) is the One who John heralded (Jesus).

Again in Isaiah, in a passage that begins with the majestic words, "Thus saith the LORD (Jehovah) that created the heavens, God (Elohim) that formed the earth and made it" (Isa. 45:18), Jehovah the Creator declares that "unto Me every knee shall bow, every tongue shall swear" (Isa. 45:23). This is a part of His future glory—the honoring of One who repeatedly declares that "My glory will I not give to another" (Isa. 42:8). Yet in Philippians 2:9-11 it is declared of the one who died "the death of the cross";

Wherefore God also hath highly exalted Him, and given Him a name which is above every name: that at the name of Jesus every knee should bow, of things in heaven, and things in earth, and things under the earth; and that every tongue should confess that Jesus Christ is Lord, to the glory of God the Father.

What else can "Lord" mean in this passage except Jehovah? The universal confession that is yet to be made is that Jesus Christ is Jehovah, a confession that is forced upon men by the unveiling of Jesus Christ. Some of us willingly confess this now.

The "Jehovah Witness" people claim that they find their name in Isaiah 43:10,12, and 44:8. If so one would think that these witnesses would be patently familiar with everything declared in these two chapters, also with those chapters which form the context, chapters 42 and 45. However, in conversation with quite a few of them I have found them to be ignorant of this quartet of chapters as a whole and to have very little interest in what is said in them outside of the three small fragments they use for their name. Yet, these four chapters contain some of the greatest declarations to be found in Scripture. Consider these words:

Thus saith God the LORD (Jehovah Elohim), He that created the heavens, and stretched them out, He that spread forth the earth, and that which cometh out of it; He that giveth breath unto the people upon it, and spirit to them that walk therein: I am the LORD (Jehovah): that is My name: and my glory will I not give to another, neither My praise to graven images. Isa. 42:5,8.

Ye are My witnesses, saith the LORD (Jehovah), and My servant whom I have chosen: that ye may know and believe Me, and understand that I am He: before Me there was no God formed, neither shall there be after Me. I, even I, am the LORD (Jehovah); and beside Me there is no Savior. Isa. 43:10-11.

Thus saith the LORD (Jehovah) the King of Israel, and His redeemer the LORD (Jehovah) of hosts: I am the first, and I am the last: and beside Me there is no God. Fear ye not, neither be afraid; have not I told thee from that time and declared it? ye are even My witnesses. Is there a God beside Me? yea, there is no God; I know not any. Isa. 44:6,8.

Thus saith the LORD (Jehovah), thy redeemer, and He that formed -thee from the womb, I am the LORD (Jehovah) that maketh all things; that stretcheth forth the heavens alone, that spreadeth abroad the earth by Myself. Isa. 44:24.

I am the LORD (Jehovah), and there is none else, there is no God beside Me: I girded thee, though thou hast not known Me: That they may know from the rising of the sun, and from the west, that there is none beside Me. I am the LORD (Jehovah) and there is none else. I have made the earth, and created man upon it: I, even My hands have stretched out the heavens, and all their hosts have I commanded. Isa. 45:5,6,12.

Who hath declared this from ancient time? who hath told it from that time? have not I the Lord? and there is no God else beside me; a just God and a Savior; there is none beside Me. Look unto Me, and be ye saved, all the ends of the earth: for I am God and there is none else. I have sworn by Myself, the word is gone out of My mouth in righteousness, and shall not return. That unto me every knee shall bow, every tongue shall swear. Isa. 45:21-23.

The above passages should be read carefully once again noting exactly what Jehovah declares concerning Himself. He declares that He is the Creator of the heavens, the earth, all that comes out of it and man upon it. He declares that He is the maker of all things, that He alone stretched forth the heavens, that He spread abroad the earth by Himself. Words could not be stronger or more explicit in claiming that He acted alone in the creation. Therefore, when we are told by the Spirit of God in John 1:3 that the Word, the very Word who became flesh, made all things and "without Him was not any thing made that was made", only one conclusion is possible. The One set forth as the Creator in Isaiah is the One set forth as Creator in John. Jehovah is Jesus.

Jehovah proclaims that He is the redeemer of Israel, yet in the New Testament redemption is predicated over and over again to the Lord Jesus, the Christ in whom we have redemption through His blood" (Eph. 1:7). Surely Jesus is Jehovah.

It is the word of Jehovah that He alone is God, that there is none beside Him, that there is none like Him, that before Him there was no God formed, neither shall there be after Him. Yet in spite of these declarations the "Jehovah Witnesses" would explain away the explicit statement found in John 1:1 that "the Word was God" by inserting the indefinite article and saying that Jesus was a God. This cannot be true for it results in a second God who is not Jehovah. Jesus and Jehovah are one and the same God.

Jehovah declares three times that beside Him there is no Savior. Isa. 43:11, 45:21, Hos. 13:4. And yet the angels declared at the birth of Jesus that a Savior had been born which is Christ the Lord. These words can mean nothing but "Messiah Jehovah". Jesus cannot be a Savior unless He is Jehovah.

Jehovah declares that He is the "First and the Last". All must agree that there cannot be two firsts and two lasts. How can it be then that the resurrected Jesus declares in Revelation 1:11, 17, 18 that He is "the Alpha and Omega, the First and the Last". There is no way this could possibly be true unless the speaker Himself is Jehovah.

Jehovah declares that there is none like Him, none to whom He can be likened, none equal to Him, Yet the Lord Jesus declared that those who had seen Him had seen the Father, that those who knew Him knew the Father, that men should honor Him even as they honored the Father. John 5:23, 8:19, 14:7,9. Paul declares that Christ Jesus is the image of the invisible God. Not one word of this can be true if Jesus is not Jehovah.

Again, I repeat, there is no fact that is declared more emphatically or that is set forth in more detail than that the Lord Jesus is Jehovah. This is the record God has given. Salvation becomes ours when we believe the record God has given of His Son.

The SEED and BREAD Bible-Study leaflets are published as often as time and means permit and are sent free to all names on THE WORD OF TRUTH MINISTRY mailing list. Send us your name. There will be no obligation, solicitation, or visitation. Additional copies of any issue available on request.   ISSUE NO. 2

SEED & BREAD

FOR THE SOWER   ISA. 55:10   FOR THE EATER

BRIEF BIBLICAL MESSAGES
FROM
THE WORD OF TRUTH MINISTRY
339 South Orange Drive, Los Angeles, Cal. 90036

Otis Q. Sellers, Bible Teacher

THE FATHER AND THE SON

At one point in the ministry of the Lord Jesus He healed a man who had suffered from an infirmity for thirty-eight years. When the man reported this miracle to the rulers of the Jews, they sought to slay Him because He had done this on the sabbath day (John 5:15-16). The answer of Jesus to them was, "My Father worketh hitherto, and I work" (John 5:17). Because of this they sought more fervently to kill him, declaring, "He not only had broken the sabbath, but said also that God was His Father, making Himself equal with God" (John 5:18).

If the Lord Jesus had not meant here what these Jews understood Him to say and to mean, He should and could and would have said, "But this is not what I mean". But He allowed it to stand, thus providing us with a clear attestation regarding His position in the Deity. The Father and the Son are equal.

Those who profess to be Christians are exhorted to grow in grace and in the knowledge of our Lord and Savior Jesus Christ (2 Pet. 3:18). To increase in the knowledge of Him should be the perpetual aim of every believer. But, alas, few ever do this, for the average professing Christian never advances beyond the few rudiments that he learned in childhood, and even these are often erroneous and confused. These need to be corrected, especially those childish ideas that are related to the titles "the Father" and "the Son."

"The Father sent the Son to be the Savior of the world" (1 John 4:14). This declaration is a major item in the record God has given of His Son. However, it seems that most who hear this are inclined to equate it with a man sending his boy to perform some stupendous task. The foolishness of this is seen in the fact that "saving the world" is not a boy's job, not even a man's job. None but God can save the world. There never was but one Savior, and this is the LORD (Jehovah) of the Old Testament revelation. He declares, "I, even I, am the LORD (Jehovah); and beside Me there is no Savior" (Isa. 43:11). In view of this declaration if the Son of God is not God then He cannot qualify as the Savior. We must believe the words of Him who said, "There is no God beside Me; a just God and a Savior; there is none beside Me. Look unto Me and be ye saved, all the ends of the earth: for I am God and there is none else" (Isa. 45:21,22).

We cannot understand the Father and the Son relationship by likening it to a man's relationship with his boy. We need to take to heart God's question, "To whom will ye liken God? or what likeness will ye compare unto Him"(Isa. 40:18)? Also his declaration, "Remember the former things of old: for I am God, and there is none like Me" (Isa. 46:9). If we believe these words then let us cease trying to understand the Father and the Son relationship by likening it to a parent's relationship to a male child.

In the passage that declares that the Father sent the Son to be the Savior of the world, the word for "sent" is *apostellō*. This is not the word ordinarily used when one is sent from one place to another. When *apostellō* is used of a person, it means to commission with full authority to do the task assigned. The word *Father* when used of God always signifies the totality of the Deity or Godhead. It emphasizes the source and sets forth the originator, the arranger, the disposer. When the Son of God appeared upon the earth, He was a projection of the Deity. He came from God and He returned to God (John 13:3). When one laid hold of Him, He laid hold of God. He was the image of the invisible God. We need to realize that God by virtue of His very nature is able to project Himself in any form, to any place, for any purpose and still remain omnipresent and centered in all the universe.

Inasmuch as God likens Himself to a river and to the sea, we need not hesitate to liken Him, in some respects, to the ocean. All oceans have inlets that are usually called gulfs or bays. If we stood on the shore of one of these and asked the question, "Which is greater, the ocean or the bay?" there could be only one answer. From where we stand the ocean is greater. And yet the bay is a projection of the ocean. Draw from it and you will be drawing upon the mighty ocean of which it is an inseparable part. Fill up the bay and the waters will return to the ocean.

This illustration will help us to understand why at one point in His ministry Jesus Christ declared, "My Father is greater than I" (John 14:28). He had charged His disciples with a certain lack of love because of their failure to rejoice at His return to the Father, an event that would signify the end of the time of His humiliation and a departure from the limited and narrow range in the exercise of His attributes. Of course, the source is greater than the outflow when the outflow is limited, and He so declares this.

It has often been said that any creature who would dare to announce that "God is greater than I", would be as guilty of blasphemous folly as the one who would say, "I am equal to God".

To take the place of a man in a hostile world was not a happy experience for the One who assumed this place. In John 6:62 He spoke of the Son of Man ascending where He was before. This refers not just to place but to the position and glory that had previously been His. His words as to the Father being greater referred only to His person in its state at that time. We must not be guilty of taking the language that belongs to the time of His humiliation and using it as an argument against His Deity.

In Genesis 1:1 we are told that, "In the beginning God (Elohim) created the heavens and the earth". In John 1:1 we are told that in the beginning was the Word (Logos) and that the Logos is the Creator of all things (John 1:3). Thus the God who is set forth as the Creator in Genesis 1:1 is the Word (Logos) in John 1:1-3. Then we are told that the Word (Logos) was made flesh and dwelt among us (John 1:14). This is the Lord Jesus Christ. He was the Son of God before He was born in Bethlehem, and He was rich before He was in poverty upon the earth (2 Cor. 8:9). So again it needs to be emphasized that "the days of His flesh" is not the proper point to begin if we are to form a complete and true concept of Him. The "meek and lowly" Jesus is not the entire story.

At one point in His earthly ministry He declared, "I and My Father are One". Many futile attempts have been made to reduce this statement, making it to mean that they are one in purpose, will, and work. And while this is true, it is not what is being declared here. The reference is to power, and the power to protect the sheep is due to the equality between the Father and the Son. "No man shall pluck them out of My hand—no man is able to pluck them out of My Father's hand", were His words that preceded the statement of His Oneness with the Father.

When the sharp ears of His critics and detractors heard Him say, "I and My Father are one", they knew at once what He meant. They took up stones to stone Him, and when He demanded a reason for such action they declared it was because, "Thou, being a man, makest thyself God". John 10:33. This is the second time they have so charged Him. He made Himself to be equal with God (John 5:18), and He made Himself to be God (John 10:33). These are their accusations, but in making them they actually stated what is now our faith in Him. He is equal to God, for He is God, equal to the Father as touching His Godhood, even though for a time inferior to the Father as touching His manhood. Those who try to make complete separations and sharp distinctions between the Father and the Son will lose both in so doing.

No distinction should ever be made as to the honor we give to the Father and to the Son, for it is the directive of God that all should honor the Son even as they honor the Father. John 5:23.

We can make no distinction in their works. What one does the other does. The Father works and the Son responds in harmony. Like two great gears, when one moves the other moves. The Son could do nothing alone. What the Father did, the Son did also. John 5:19.

In our quest for knowledge we make no distinction between the Father and the Son, for to know one is to know the other. "If ye had known Me, ye should have known My Father also." John 8:19.

As to equality of wisdom we make no distinction. "As the Father knoweth Me, even so know I the Father." John 10:15. Imagine a spirit being, an angelic being, or a human being declaring that He knows God as well as God knows Him.

As an object of belief we make no distinction between the Father and the Son. "He that believeth on Me, believeth not on Me, but on Him that sent Me". John 12:44.

As an object of comprehension we make no distinction between the Sender and the one Sent. "He that seeth Me seeth Him that sent Me." John 12:45.

As the words of the Father and the Son we make no distinction, for the Son declares that the Father gave Him directions as to what He should say and speak. John 12:49,50.

As an object for our faith we make no distinction between the Father and the Son, for the Son said, "Ye believe in God, believe also in Me." John 14:1.

As an object of hatred we can make no distinction for He declared, "He that hateth Me hateth My Father also." John 15:23.

As to possessions we make no distinctions. The Father owns nothing that the Son does not own. The Lord Jesus said, "All things that the Father hath are mine: therefore said I, that He shall take of mine, and shall shew it unto you." John 16:15.

As to the source of eternal life we make no distinctions between the Father and the Son. Jesus Christ gives eternal life to all that the Father gives unto Him. Consider John 17:2 and Romans 6:23 The gift of God is eternal life through Jesus Christ our Lord.

These are things we have learned from personal and assiduous study of the Word of God. Therefore it should be no surprise to anyone that we are quite willing with Thomas of old to fall at the feet of the Lord Jesus and say, "My Lord and my God". John 20:28.

If any problems remain let us remember that the Lord Jesus said, "No man knoweth who the Son is, but the Father: and who the Father is, but the Son, and he to whom the Son will reveal Him." Luke 10:22. If any insist that they will believe nothing until they understand it all, they will finish up just as they are now— believing nothing. We declare with the disciple of old, "Lord I believe, help Thou my unbelief." Mark 9:24.

The SEED and BREAD Bible-Study leaflets are published as often as time and means permit and are sent free to all names on THE WORD OF TRUTH MINISTRY mailing list. Send us your name. There will be no obligation, solicitation, or visitation. Additional copies of any issue available on request.   ISSUE NO. 3

SEED & BREAD

FOR THE SOWER   ISA. 55:10   FOR THE EATER

BRIEF BIBLICAL MESSAGES
FROM
THE WORD OF TRUTH MINISTRY
339 South Orange Drive, Los Angeles, Cal. 90036

Otis Q. Sellers, Bible Teacher

INTERPRETATION OF PHILIPPIANS 1:6

The major problem in the interpretation of Phil. 1:6 is found in the words, "will perform it until the day of Jesus Christ." The word *perform* means to do, to carry out. If anyone performs a process *until* a certain time it means that he keeps on doing it up to that point. However, such an idea completely reverses the meaning of the Greek word *epiteleō*, making it to say the exact opposite of what the Holy Spirit intended. This word means to bring through to an end, and it is not right for a translator to cause the Apostle Paul to say in English what he did not say in the Greek.

The Revisers (ERV and ARV) recognized this contradiction and sought to more accurately render the word *epiteleō* by translating it "will perfect it until the day of Jesus Christ," but in so doing they set up an incongruous statement since the words "will perfect" (verb) are not compatible with the word *until (achris.)* One does not perfect a thing until a certain time. I challenge anyone to construct a single sensible sentence in which the words *perfect* (verb) and *until* are used together unless they are cast in the negative.

In his *King James II Version*, Mr. Jay Green attempts to give a more honest rendering of *epiteleō* by translating it, "will finish it until the day of Jesus Christ." But this is a poor use of words as *finish* is also incompatible with *until*. If I ask the contractor when my building will be finished he may answer, "I will finish it next week." If so, he has made himself plain. But if he answers, "I will finish it until next week," his words will not make sense and I will demand a clearer answer.

In Philippians 1:6 we are face to face with the inexorable fact that the word "until" (*achris*) does occur, and that its appearance here gives *epiteleō* a somewhat special meaning not found in any other occurrence.

All the facts concerning *epiteleō* can be easily assembled by anyone who will make the search. The root of this word, which is the real clue to its meaning, is *teleō*. This is found 26 times in the New Testament where it is translated *finish* 8 times, *fulfill* 7, *accomplish*

4, *pay* 2, *perform, expire, go over* and *make an end* one time each. The student will note the idea of finishing or ending in all these translations.

All the recognized authorities define the verb *teleō* by using such terms as "to make an end" (Cremer); "to bring to a close" (Abbott-Smith). In fact the verb *teleō* and the noun *telos*, from which it is derived, so obviously mean the exact opposite of continuing and continuance that it is of no value to belabor this actuality. Just remember that when Jesus Christ said, "It is finished" (John 19:30), He used the word *teleō*.

In the word *epiteleō* we have *teleō* (finish) with the prefix *epi* (on) before it. This prefix is used before so many other words that we can tell from this usage that it is usually an accelerative contribution. And of this we can be sure, a prefix or a suffix does not change the meaning of the root. It may change its force or direction but never its meaning. In *epiteleō* the prefix adds an emphatic note; just as in *epignosis, gnosis* means knowledge and *epignosis* means exact and full knowledge. Since *teleō* means to finish or to end, there is no possible way that *epiteleō* can mean continuance. Yet this is what we have in most translations of Phil 1:6, and this leads me to borrow the words of James (3:10) and say, "My brethren these things ought not so to be."

As to the actual meaning of *epiteleō* the authorities are practically unanimous:

Young: "to make an end of, complete." In his *Critical Comments* he renders it "will end it fully."
Bullinger: "to bring through to an end."
Arndt and Gingrich: "end, bring to an end, finish."
Abbott-Smith: "to complete, accomplish, execute, make an end."
Thayer: "to bring to an end, accomplish, perfect, execute, complete."
Liddell-Scott: "to complete, finish, accomplish."
Bagster's Analytical: "to bring to an end."
Strong: "to fulfill completely; by implication, to terminate."
Vine: "to bring through to an end."

In the *telos* family of words (that is words that contain this root) there are twenty-six members. These words are found 249 times in the New Testament. If an examination is made of every occurrence, it will be found that there is no idea of continuance in any of them. They all denote cessation, accomplishment, and bringing to an end. This is to be expected since this is what the root means.

As an example of this we might take the root *cardi* (Gk. *kardi*) which is found in so many English words, and which everyone knows indicates the heart. No prefixes or suffixes ever change its meaning, neither does any other word with which it may be combined. Thus we have *cardiogram, electrocardiogram, cardiologic, cardiophobia,* and *cardiospasm*. But no matter what comes before it or follows it, it always means the heart.

What would the reader think if he came upon a doctor who twisted this word around until it meant the liver? He would probably put him down as an ignorant quack — which I also am inclined to do when I come upon someone who claims to be a practitioner of the truth, but who takes a Greek word that everyone knows means to end or to finish and twists it around until it means continuance.

Since in this passage the word *achris* (until) regulates the exact meaning of *epiteleō,* deliberate attempts have been made to alter the obvious meaning of this term. This word means until, that is, up to a declared limit, just as it does in the preceding passage (1:5).

When any matter, process, or work is brought to a full end until a certain time, then it is most evident that it has been suspended, and this is exactly what *epiteleō* signifies in this passage. In view of this I would freely translate Philippians 1:6: "Having come to this settled and firm persuasion concerning this very thing, namely that the One having begun a good work in you will be suspending it until the day of Christ Jesus." If any should prefer the wording "will be bringing it to a full end" in place of "will be suspending it" he can have his choice. Both statements are the same.

The future tense here has bothered some, and it has been used by others to claim a continuing work of God. The future tense here is correct. At Acts 28:28 a declaration was made that introduced a new dispensation, but the old one had to be closed out. There was a transitional period of several years that followed Paul's declaration.

The translation set forth above is true to the Greek and it is also true to the truth. The statement has to do with that dispensation (administration) of God that prevailed from the resurrection of Jesus Christ until Paul's announcement in Acts 28:28, the thirty-three years of the Acts period. Read its constitution in Mark 16:15-20 and note how many of these signs have been brought to a full end.

Consider the twelve apostles. These men were destined to sit upon twelve thrones judging the twelve tribes of Israel (Matt. 19:28). This is an explicit promise from the lips of our Lord which if it is not fulfilled to the letter then no other words of His are dependable. Others were promised rule over ten cities or five cities. It is most evident that from the moment that He called these to follow Him that they were in the school of Jesus Christ, being trained for the service they would perform, a training that continued through the entire Acts period. And yet not one of these men has reached this goal. That good work that God began among them has been brought to a full end until the day of Jesus Christ.

According to one of the most important parables of the kingdom of God, and yet the most ignored and neglected, the progress of the kingdom of God was to be in five stages: 1, the blade; 2, the ear; 3, the full grain in the ear; 4, the ripened grain; and, 5, the harvest. Mark 4:26-29. The first two stages of these are already history. In the 33 years of the Acts period the blade stage and the ear stage were manifest realities. The kingdom was no longer proclaimed as coming; it was already there, even if only in its preliminary stages. And yet it never advanced to the "full grain in the ear," when "Jesus shall reign where'er the sun, does his successive journeys run." If we ask, "What happened?" the answer is found in Philippians 1:6. That good work that God began among them has been suspended until the day of Jesus Christ.

Consider the Apostle Paul, a man who possessed divine powers that were so great that men are inclined to think that he never possessed them at all. Read Romans 15:17-19, and consider his miracles of healing in Acts 28:8-9. And yet after Acts 28:28 he was forced to confess that he had left his helper and traveling companion, Trophimus, "at Miletum sick" (2 Tim. 4:20). This plain, honest statement is very near to the final inspired word he ever wrote. The good work that God had been doing through him was also suspended.

This explains more fully his apologetic note in Phil. 1:7, in which he justifies what he has just said concerning them. Translators have not yet been able to decide whether he said, "I have you in my heart," or "Ye have me in your heart." Nevertheless we know what he meant. This statement means far more in the Greek than it does in the English. We have been prone here to make "the heart" the seat of affections and have Paul expressing either his love for them or their love for him. In Greek thought the heart is the seat of the personality, standing for the collective life of the person, which is influenced by everything that affects the life. He is telling them that he is in the same boat they are, or that they are in this together. See also Phil. 1:30.

However, let no one push this to an extreme and say that I believe that everything that God was doing in the Acts period came to an end. This is not true. In the Greek of Phil. 1:10 they were directed to be "testing the things that carry through." And this we do.

The SEED and BREAD Bible-Study leaflets are published as often as time and means permit and are sent free to all names on THE WORD OF TRUTH MINISTRY mailing list. Send us your name. There will be no obligation, solicitation, or visitation. Additional copies of any issue available on request.   ISSUE NO. 4

SEED & BREAD

FOR THE SOWER   ISA. 55:10   FOR THE EATER

BRIEF BIBLICAL MESSAGES

FROM

THE WORD OF TRUTH MINISTRY

339 South Orange Drive, Los Angeles, Cal. 90036

Otis Q. Sellers, Bible Teacher

WHAT DOES *APOSTELLŌ* MEAN?

Even those who know nothing of New Testament Greek will have the feeling that the word *apostellō* is somewhat familiar. And they are right for this is the verb from which comes the adjective *apostolos* which is so often used as a substantive in the New Testament and is usually translated "apostle."

In seeking the true understanding of the thirty-three unique and important years of which the book of Acts is the history, there is no word more important than the Greek verb *apostellō*. This history is "The Acts of the Apostles," and if this word is misunderstood, everything in the Acts period will be thrown out of line. And it is not enough for the student to have some simple definition of this word. He must master it, get inside of it, know all that there is to know concerning it.

This word has been sorely neglected; its true meaning has been clouded; it has been stultified by weak translations and renderings which are mere transliterations. Much truth has been lost because of this. Consideration of a few occurrences will show the importance of this word.

I am not sent *(apostellō)* but unto the lost sheep of the house of Israel. Matt. 15:24.

I must preach the kingdom of God to other cities also for therefore am I sent *(apostellō)*. Luke 4:43.

There was a man sent *(apostellō)* from God. John 1:6.

And He shall send *(apostellō)* Jesus Christ. Acts 3:20.

The word which God sent *(apostellō)* unto the children of Israel. Acts 10:36.

Men and brethren, sons of the stock of Abraham, and whosoever among you feareth God, to you is the word of this salvation sent *(apostellō)*. Acts 13:26.

How shall they preach except they be sent *(apostellō)*. Rom. 10:15.

For Christ sent *(apostellō)* me not to baptize, but to preach the gospel. 1 Cor. 1:17.

The Father sent *(apostellō)* the Son to be the Savior of the World. 1 John 4:14.

A review of these nine passages will show that great and important truths are expressed by this word, and this should exercise our minds to understand this verb as fully as it can be understood.

The word *apostellō* is found 133 times in the New Testament. See *Englishman's Greek Concordance*, page 76, for a complete list. It is translated *send* 110 times, *send forth* 15, *send away* 4, *send out* 2, *put in* 1, and *set* 1 time. Thus it can be seen that the word *send* is used as a translation in all but two occurrences. To some this might seem to settle its meaning, but it does not. The word *send* as a translation of *apostellō* is weak, misleading, and inadequate. It dims the glory of this important word. It holds down much of the truth that the Spirit of God is revealing.

The Greek word that means "to send" is *pempō*. This is found 81 times in the New Testament and is translated "send" in all but two of these. This is the word that can be used of causing to go in any manner. A man's wife now and then will send him to the store or postoffice. The ancient Greek would use the word *pempō* to describe an act such as this, but never the word *apostellō*. A study of the 81 occurrences of *pempō* will bring the realization that this term has to do with what might be described as a physical sending, a causing to go. Any ideas expressed in the passages that are beyond this would have to come from the context, as nothing more than a physical sending is inherent in this word.

The inadequacy of the King James translator's treatment of the words *apostellō* and *apostolos* is seen in the fact that the word *apostle* shows no relationship to the word *sent*. What reader of the English Bible would know that these are father and son? For example in English we have *do* and from this we get *doer* and *doing,* from *play* we get *player* and *playing,* and from *give* we get *giver* and *giving.* Thus the relationship between these words is obvious. But there is no obvious connection between the words *send* and *apostle. Apostellō* is the parent and *apostolos* is the off-spring, and the relationship between these two words should not be obscured. Any rendering that does this is misleading and inadequate.

In one case the translator did preserve the relationship. In John 13:16 *apostolos* is translated "he that is sent". Between "send" and "he that is sent" the relationship is plain. However, *apostellō* and *apostolos* mean far more than "sent" and "a sent one".

Many lexicons follow the example of the King James Version and define *apostellō* as meaning "to send forth" or "to send away from, while the sender remains behind," but some lexicographers have dared to abandon this superficial definition, realizing that those who are the recipients of this action are not always sent from one place to another.

While the lexicons have been consulted, especially Kittel's, no attempt will be made to establish the meaning of this word through them. The meaning of any word in any language is determined by the use of it. It is possible to discover the meaning of any word if it can be seen in a dozen clear sentences. We find the word *apostellō* in 133 sentences and the substantive that is derived from it *(apostolos)* in eighty-one. If the meaning cannot be determined from these occurrences, then there is no way of determining the meaning of any word in any language. Even a dictionary cannot define a word. It can merely report the usage of a word by careful and capable writers. In defining *apostellō* it will be our purpose to do it from the usage made of it by the inspired writers of the New Testament. When all occurrences are examined the following facts stand out.

Apostellō means to commission, in the sense of authorizing and instructing someone to perform a definite task. The ideas of authority and authorizing are always basic in it. A commission can be very simple involving a very small task, or it can be very complex involving great service and responsibilities.

It has been said that the office of Notary Public is the least a man can have under our government. Nevertheless, a Notary Public has been commissioned; he has a commission and is a commissioned one. He is authorized to take acknowledgments of legal papers, which he does under the seal of his office, usually adding a note that his commission expires on a certain date in order to show that it is an active one. The Greeks would use the word *apostellō* to describe the action of the governor that authorized such, and the word *apostolos* to describe the result—a commissioned one.

The word *apostellō* never has to do with the appointment of anyone to an office. It has to do with a service that is to be performed by one authorized. Thus its real meaning is to commission with authority. However, this definition applies only when it is used in connection with men or angels. When it is used in connection with animals or inanimate things it takes on a more limited meaning. When so used it means to authorize, that is, to make freely available. Both meanings of this word are seen in the following passage, where the first reference is to men and the second is to animals.

> And when they drew nigh unto Jerusalem, and were come to Bethphage, unto the mount of Olives, then sent *(apostellō)* Jesus two disciples, saying unto them, Go into the village over against you, and straightway ye shall find an ass tied, and a colt with her: loose them and bring them unto Me. And if any man say ought unto you, ye shall say, The Lord hath need of them; and straightway he will send *(apostellō)* them. Matt. 21:1-3.

Thus two of His diciples are commissioned for what seemed to be a very small task, and for a short time they were commissioned ones *(apostles)*. If anyone questioned their right to take these animals they are to say, "The Lord has need of them" and the owner would authorize the use of these; that is, he would make them freely available.

Thus we see that to grant or allow by proper authority is the meaning of *apostellō* when it is used of animals or inanimate things. This usage is found nine times in the New Testament, and in these passages *apostellō* should read as follows:

Matt. 21:3 — straightway he will *authorize* them
Mark 4:29 — immediately he *authorizes* the sickle
Mark 11:3 — straightway he will *authorize* it
John 9:7 — which is by interpretation, *authorized*
Acts 10:36 — the word He *authorizes* to the sons of Israel
Acts 11:30 — *authorizing* it to the elders
Acts 13:26 — the word of this salvation *authorized*
Acts 28:28 — is *authorized* to the nations
Rev. 1:1 — He *authorized* and signified it

A third meaning of *apostellō*, which is a derived meaning, is to dismiss, to send away, to banish. But this is always an authoritative dismissal or banishment. This is found in five places: Mark 5:10; Mark 12:3,4, 6; John 18:24.

We can now summarize our findings. Commission, authorization, and direction are the ideas inherent in the word *apostellō* when applied to men or to angels. The idea of authorization in the sense of making freely available becomes paramount when it is used of animals or inanimate things. The word *apostolos* should never be hardened into an office to which men are appointed. The word denotes a commission and authorization that is limited in time and is concerned only with the business at hand, not with the status of a person discharging it. A personal commission is the sole ground of being a commissioned one (an apostle). None of those who was commissioned by Jesus Christ ever felt he had attained to an office of indelible or life-time character.

In the house of Cornelius, Peter declared that the word which proclaimed peace through Jesus Christ had been authorized to the sons of Israel (Acts 10:36). In Acts 13:26 Paul emphatically declares that it was to the sons of Abraham and the God-fearing men among them that "the word of this salvation" had been made freely available. Paul was authorized to speak to the Gentiles, but only after it was proclaimed to Israel first. See Rom. 1:16. In Acts 28:28 Paul announces that "the salvation-bringing *message* of God had been made freely available (authorized) to the nations," with the further guarantee that it will get through to them. These words indicate one great and important feature in the dispensational change that took place at Acts 28:28. It became freely available to all when God inspired John to write a record of the Son of God that is without priority or discrimination of any kind.

The SEED and BREAD Bible-Study leaflets are published as often as time and means permit and are sent free to all names on THE WORD OF TRUTH MINISTRY mailing list. Send us your name. There will be no obligation, solicitation, or visitation. Additional copies of any issue available on request.   ISSUE NO. 5

SEED & BREAD

FOR THE SOWER   ISA. 55:10   FOR THE EATER

BRIEF BIBLICAL MESSAGES
FROM
THE WORD OF TRUTH MINISTRY
339 South Orange Drive, Los Angeles, Cal. 90036

Otis Q. Sellers, Bible Teacher

BIBLICAL GIFT OF TONGUES

The Biblical gift of tongues, which was prominent throughout the thirty-three years of which the book of Acts is the history, was the God-given knowledge of a foreign language with the ability to speak it as if it were one's mother tongue. Any claimed experience today that does not live up to the example given in Acts 2 is a human substitute for the divine gift, and when passed off as the Biblical experience it must be condemned as a Satanic delusion.

If this judgment should seem harsh and opinionated, let it be known that it is the considered judgment and studied opinion of one who has loved, believed, read, studied, and taught the Word of God for fifty-two years. The reader can confirm the correctness of this judgment if he will turn to the Bible and judge all claimed personal experiences by what is written there. "To the law and to the testimony: if they speak not according to this word, it is because there is no light in them" (Isa. 8:20). This includes all business men, movie stars, and clergymen. They are not exempt from this test. The one whose mind is filled with the facts of God's word can never accept ecstatic sounds, the utterance of gibberish, head jerking, eye rolling, and other pumped-up manifestations as being things that have a parallel in the sacred scriptures.

In view of the purpose and program of God in the Acts period and the short time allotted for their full accomplishment (Rom. 9:28), the ability to speak in any language that the circumstances required was an absolute imperative. What had to be done could never have been done apart from this. To appreciate this we must consider the situation that then existed.

It was a time of little education and very little travel. Each village usually had its own language or dialect and the people had few outside contacts. If a man traveled a dozen miles he usually came upon a different dialect, and if he went twenty miles he would encounter a different language.

We who live in the United States have a hard time understanding this. We travel 3000 miles from coast to coast and 1500 miles from border to border, and are always able to understand and be understood. I have found one language to be sufficient for a lifetime of work all over this vast land, but in the Acts period one language would have been sufficient for only a few weeks work, if the work were evangelizing.

Missionaries still face this problem today, but there is no gift of instant knowledge of a language to help them in their task as there was in the Acts period. At present in the small country Liberia, the oldest of the self-governing African republics, with an area of 43,000 square miles (about the same as Ohio) and a population of 1,290,000 (about half as many as Chicago, Illinois) there are forty-five languages spoken. The official language, English, is spoken and understood only by the small upper class who have had educational advantages. The Bible (or parts of it) has been translated into only nine of the twelve principal languages. All this makes widespread evangelizing of this little country almost impossible.

A situation somewhat comparable to this existed outside (and even within) Palestine when the disciples assembled on that memorable day of Pentecost. In fact they were faced with the reality that there were seventeen languages and dialects spoken by those whom God intended should hear His message on that day (Acts 2:5, 9-11). These foreign-born Jews had every right to hear the gospel in their own vernacular, just as the 120 had heard it in theirs. And they did! They heard no mutterings, they heard no gibberish, they heard no "ecstatic sounds." They heard God's message in their own language (Acts 2:8, 11).

It was God's program, purpose and intent in the Acts period that every Israelite upon the earth should hear the salvation-bringing word of God and have a clear-cut opportunity to receive or reject the man Jesus as Israel's long-promised Messiah and as a personal Savior. This was the pledge of God, and it was in writing: "But as it is written, To whom He was not spoken of, they shall see: and they that have not heard shall understand" (Rom. 15:21). God made good on this pledge. "And they went forth and preached everywhere, the Lord working with them" (Mark 16:20). "But I say, have they (Israel) not heard? Yes verily, their sound went into all the earth, and their words unto the ends of the world" (Rom. 10:18).

Thus it was that God-commissioned men (apostles), speaking a God-inspired message, performed a humanly impossible task in less than thirty-three years. Every Israelite on earth was covered in some manner, those inside the land and those in the dispersion. And in order to avoid all delays, all misunderstandings, and any need for fallible, human translation, the gospel was always spoken in the pure mother tongue of one for whom it was intended. This was the normal experience of the witnesses. Truly, the "gift of tongues" was a meaningful reality in the Acts period. It was a powerful sign to the unbeliever (1 Cor. 14:22), and it was a miracle worthy of the God who gave men this ability. Shame on those who would today pass off their "bah, bah, bah, glo, glo, glo, ticky, tacky, monee, monee" as being the same as that miracle of God of the Acts dispensation. We reject this human, unintelligible uttering of sounds as being nothing more than a ridiculous human counterfeit.

It was the promise of the Lord Jesus that those believers who were commissioned as witnesses would "speak with new tongues" (Mark 16:17, Acts 1:8). The word "speak" positively means to utter words (not just sounds), to give oral expression to thoughts by means of words, not the repetition of unintelligible gibberish. When we say, "He speaks Spanish", we mean that he expresses himself in the language of the Spanish people. We do not mean that he makes Spanish sounds. The Greek word translated "speak" *(laleō)* is found 295 times in the New Testament. In every occurrence, no exceptions, it means to utter intelligible discourse.

On that day of Pentecost when the ability to speak in a foreign language was first given, there were dwelling at Jerusalem Jews, devout men out of every nation under heaven (Acts 2:5). Among these were found seventeen languages and dialects. These men probably knew some Hebrew, which they seldom used, and of course some Aramaic, depending on how long they had been in Jerusalem. But the language they could speak fluently and understand without difficulty was that of the country in which they were born and where they had long been sojourners. Little wonder then that they were confounded when every one of them heard some member of the 120 disciples speaking in his own language (Acts 2:6). They knew that these men were Galileans, and they asked how it was that they heard every man speaking in the tongues wherein they were born (Acts 2:8). "We do hear them speak in our own tongues the wonderful works of God" (Acts 2:11), is their positive testimony to the nature of this miracle. These are the words of those present on that day, and they settle beyond all doubt what the Biblical gift of speaking in tongues really was.

The modern tongue speakers do not spend much time trying to find what the truth of Acts 2 really is. They impose upon it a theory they have constructed in advance, grab from it a few phrases, and then rush on to 1 Corinthians 14, a chapter concerning which there consists a great lack of understanding and honest interpretation. This serves their purpose admirably, and the unwarranted insertion of the word *unknown* in four passages seems to help them all the more. However, no matter how much they make of 1 Cor. 14 they pay little attention to the words of Paul in it who said, "I had rather speak five words with my understanding, that by my voice I might teach others also, than ten thousand words in an unknown tongue" (1 Cor. 14:19). The modern tongue advocate would much rather make ten thousand unintelligible sounds than to speak five words that make sense, if their zeal for and exaltation of the tongue experience is any indication.

The key to 1 Corinthians 14 is that there were men in Corinth who had an inordinate love of languages, the ones they knew by natural processes and the ones obtained by gift of God. A grammatical and historical study of this chapter will reveal the problem that existed there and that with which Paul is dealing. While the Corinthians addressed in this epistle were Jews so far as their ancestry was concerned (1 Cor. 10:4 demonstrates this and 12:2

does not contradict it), they had adopted many Greek mores, manners, and attitudes. The Greeks worshipped wisdom, their heroes were scholars and philosophers, they sought after wisdom (1:22), loved the enticing words of man's wisdom (2:4), and as a result of following along these lines many of the Corinthian believers were puffed up (4:18, 19).

In the ancient world a knowledge of several languages was a most valuable commodity. It was then, even as today, evidence of learning and knowledge of which one could be justly proud. Of their knowledge of languages some in Corinth were abnormally proud. I will admit that I too would have a sense of pride if I could speak fluent Spanish, and doubly proud if I could also handle French as if it were my own tongue. However, I trust I would always have the grace of humility and never use these tongues to make a display of learning, as some in Corinth were doing.

The Apostle Paul was a linguist extraordinary. We know for sure that he spoke Hebrew (Acts 22:2) and Greek (21:37). Having lived long in Palestine the Aramaic would have been familiar to him, also the Romaic language which we call Latin. Besides these he had knowledge of many God-given languages to meet the needs of his far-flung ministry. These are what he was referring to when he said, "I thank God that I speak with tongues more than you all" (1 Cor. 14:18).

Some in Corinth were using foreign languages when there was no reason for it. They were using these to display knowledge and make a show of wisdom. This is what Paul is rebuking. He states that even though they may be declaring truths never revealed before (secrets), no man understands them (14:2) if they speak in a foreign tongue, that while these built up (edified) themselves they did not build up the ecclesia (14:4). While he wished that they all had command of languages, he would prefer that they prophesied, that is, spoke forth the Word of God (14:5). Even if he came to them speaking in the various languages at his command it was still important that he say something (14:6), and if he did not bring his message in words easy to be understood he would be speaking into the air (14:9). However, if a man did have a truth to declare, and had only one language in which to say it, and this was not a language common to the majority, then let him pray that he may be able to translate (interpret) his message into their language (14:13).

These are the matters that are dealt with in 1 Corinthians 14. There is nothing in this chapter to support the rattling off of unintelligible sounds, and it should not be twisted to do so. The careful Bible student cannot accept this human, pumped-up uttering of sounds as being a Biblical experience. To claim that it is is a Satanic delusion.

The SEED and BREAD Bible-Study leaflets are published as often as time and means permit and are sent free to all names on THE WORD OF TRUTH MINISTRY mailing list. Send us your name. There will be no obligation, solicitation, or visitation. Additional copies of any issue available on request.   ISSUE NO. 6

SEED & BREAD

FOR THE SOWER   ISA. 55:10   FOR THE EATER

BRIEF BIBLICAL MESSAGES

FROM

THE WORD OF TRUTH MINISTRY

339 South Orange Drive, Los Angeles, Cal. 90036

Otis Q. Sellers, Bible Teacher

THE ACTS DISPENSATION

It is my conviction that ninety percent of all the confusion and contradictions that exist in Christendom are the result of ignoring the true character of that thirty-three year period of which the book of Acts is the history. Some are trying to live in this time as if the same administration and divine purpose prevailed today. Others are trying to live with it and spend much of their time denying its true character. And some are assiduously studying the revealed facts in order to know its distinctive character, and thus by contrast know more of God's will and purpose in the present dispensation.

Those who never make a penetrating study of the Word of God will never have any problems, questions, or difficulties in regard to it. They can exist for a lifetime on the few things they learned before they were ten years of age, and they do not want to add anything to the very little they already know. However, the constant reader and diligent student of the Bible who takes to heart what he finds there will discover that he is faced with numerous problems, questions, difficulties, and apparent contradictions. He then will yearn and even pray for the discovery of some major truth that will resolve all of these.

Familiarity with the Bible, a working knowledge of its pages, the ability to turn to any verse that comes to mind, is one of the greatest assets that can be possessed by the believer in Christ Jesus. I give thanks unto God for those circumstances in my life that could hardly produce anything else but a solid acquaintance with the inspired Scriptures. From this I know how precious to the Bible student are those great truths which do so much to make the Word of God a simple revelation of God's truth to His people. After gaining a good degree of familiarity with the New Testament and experiencing great frustration because of inability to find answers to questions, to solve problems, and to resolve the apparent contradictions that increased in number with every reading, I came upon one great idea that did more to make the Bible a living and relevant book than anything I had ever discovered before. This was the recognition of the true character of the Acts period, and of the distinct program and purpose of God during that time. Related to this and in collocation with it is the great truth that Paul's declaration in Acts 28:28 marks a definite change in God's method of dealing with men and that his words there mark an administrational (dispensational) boundary line.

Failure to recognize this great truth makes it impossible to properly understand many portions of the New Testament. This is especially true of the six epistles written by Paul during this period. These are First and Second Thessalonians, First and Second Corinthians, Galatians, and Romans. All these take on the character of the time in which they were written. They contain many eternal truths which are not subject to change, and every word in them is beneficial for teaching, for reproof, for correction, and for instruction in righteousness (2 Tim. 3:16), but they also contain dispensational truths which changed when that dispensation came to an end. For example see 1 Cor. 1:7; 5:5; 5:8; 6:4; 7:8, 27; Romans 1:16 (last clause); Rom. 3:1, 2; Rom. 15:27.

The foundation of the Acts dispensation was laid down by the Lord Jesus in Mark 16:15-18.

And He said unto them, Go ye into all the world, and preach the gospel to every creature. He that believeth and is baptized shall be saved; but he that believeth not shall be damned. And these signs shall follow them that believe; In My name shall they cast out devils; they shall speak with new tongues; they shall take up serpents; and if they drink any deadly thing, it shall not hurt them; they shall lay hands on the sick, and they shall recover.

These are the words that set the character for the Acts period. They were fulfilled to the letter during that time and they describe the normal, daily experiences of those who believed. This is demonstrated by Mark's final words: "And they went forth, and preached everywhere, the Lord working with them, and confirming the word with signs following" (Mark 16:20).

It is a constant trick of exposition to cast doubt upon these passages by saying that they are not found in the two most ancient manuscripts. This is only about one percent of the information available concerning this passage. The same is also true of John 8:1-11 and the entire book of Revelation. Before anyone casts a shred of doubt upon this portion of the Word of God, let them read with care Dean Burgon's monumental work *The Last Twelve Verses of Mark*, (recently reprinted by The Religious Book Discount House).

The chief characteristic of the Acts dispensation was that God-commissioned men went forth at His direction speaking a God-inspired message, each word of which was given to them each time they spoke it (1 Thess. 2:13), and which was always given in the mother tongue of those for whom it was intended. The word they spoke was always confirmed by signs that followed (Heb. 2:4), and when anyone believed his faith was accredited and confirmed by miraculous signs (Mark 16:17). This was the unvarying pattern of the Acts period. It was entirely different from God's method of dealing with men today.

About 650 years before the birth of Christ the prophet Habakkuk, anticipating the dispersion of Israel "among the nations" declared that a time would come when God would work a work of such incredible nature among the dispersed ones that His hearers would not believe it even if He told them of it (Hab. 1:5). His prophecy still awaits its final and definitive fulfillment, yet there can be no doubt but that there was a precursory fulfillment in the Acts period. The words of Paul are proof of this:

Beware therefore, lest that come upon you which is spoken of in the prophets; Behold, ye despisers and wonder and perish: for I work a work in your days, a work in which ye shall in no wise believe, though a man declare it unto you. Acts 13:40, 41.

The Israelites who lived in the Acts period, those in Palestine as well as those scattered among the nations, not only heard what God was doing, they saw what He was doing (Acts 2:33). They were the objects of and the witnesses of a work of God that is unparalleled in human history. Thus that thirty-three year period stands apart and is different from all other periods of divine activity. In view of this the most careful study needs to be given to the divine purposes and activities that made it so unique. This is a sorely neglected study.

It has ever been the practice of theologians to minimize, depreciate, and stultify the truth concerning the work that God was doing in the Acts period. This has been done both wittingly and unwittingly. The actual divine history of this time has been rewritten by commentators on the book of Acts. They are determined to see nothing in this period of time except the founding and development of what they call "the Christian church." They read this into every passage, they interpret it into every event, and they even translate so it will be found throughout this period. They actually minimize everything that belongs to this period of time, then they magnify everything in Christendom today so that both might meet on a common level and one be a continuation of the other. Thus, they insist that it was "the church" that began at Pentecost; then they make the organized religious establishments of today to be "the church" that began there — the outgrowth of what began at Penecost.

They make the *ecclesia* of God (the outcalled ones) of the Acts period to be nothing more than church members; then they make the church members of today to be the outcalled of God. The divinely commissioned and inspired heralds of that time are made to be preachers and pastors; then the preachers and pastors of today are made to be divinely called and commissioned servants of God. Thus past positions are deflated and present positions are inflated so that they will appear to be the same.

An apostle, such as Paul, is made to be a "missionary" and his travels are made to be missionary journeys. The divinely-inspired proclamations of the apostles are made to be "sermons," and the chief purpose of these men is said to have been "the founding of churches." We are further told that all the great miracles that these men performed could also be performed by us if only we had sufficient faith. Yes, we are now being told that the God-given ability to speak in a foreign language was only an ecstatic and unintelligible babble, and that the head-jerking, eye-rolling, unintelligible uttering of meaningless sounds experienced today is the Biblical gift of tongues. Thus it is that the past is deflated and the present inflated, God's highest is made to be man's lowest and man's lowest is made to be God's highest, so that everything that happened in the Acts period is made to be the same as denominational programs today.

Even Dr. C. I. Scofield fell into this trap, giving in his reference Bible such paragraph headings in the Book of Acts as "The first Church," "Peter's second Sermon," "The first missionaries," "Elders appointed in every church," "Founding of the church at Thessolonica," and "Founding of the church at Corinth." Thus a modern denominational and organized religious program is stamped upon every page of the Book of Acts when in reality it cannot be found there.

In the years that I have given to the study of the history of the Acts period I have sought to saturate myself with the life and spirit of that time. These studies have brought the conviction that certain great truths related to this period stand out like mountain peaks and these need to be recognized and emphasized by all who would deal honestly with the history recorded in the Book of Acts and with the epistles that were written during this time. These mountain peaks of truth must not be bulldozed away.

At the close of the Acts period God had accomplished everything that He set out to do. No purpose is left unfinished, no project is incomplete. The message has gone forth to the ends of the earth, all Israel has heard, the remnant has been established, a company for His name has been called from among the Gentiles. The blade stage and the ear stage of the kingdom of God have run their course (Mark 4:28). The next stage of "the full grain in the ear," the manifest kingdom of God is ready to burst upon mankind. But it did not come.

God's kingdom purposes are held in suspension while He accomplishes a purpose which had never before been revealed. He will take time to write into the history of His long dealings with mankind a complete record of the grace that is inherent in His character. This is now being done in a dispensation of absolute grace. The truths that were applicable in the Acts period may or may not be applicable today. As Paul tells us in Philippians 1:10, we must be testing the things that carry through (See Greek). We must study "rightly to divide the word of truth" (2 Tim. 2:15).

The SEED and BREAD Bible-Study leaflets are published as often as time and means permit and are sent free to all names on THE WORD OF TRUTH MINISTRY mailing list. Send us your name. There will be no obligation, solicitation, or visitation. Additional copies of any issue available on request.   ISSUE NO. 7

SEED & BREAD

FOR THE SOWER   ISA. 55:10   FOR THE EATER

BRIEF BIBLICAL MESSAGES

FROM

THE WORD OF TRUTH MINISTRY

339 South Orange Drive, Los Angeles, Cal. 90036

Otis Q. Sellers, Bible Teacher

WHAT DOES *SŌTĒRION* MEAN?

The word *sōtērion* is the Greek word that is translated "salvation" in Acts 28:28. It is of the utmost importance since it is the subject of the sentence that makes up this passage. If we do not know for sure what it means then we can never be certain as to what Paul was saying in this important announcement. If we do not arrive at a faithful translation of this word, we will be guilty of changing the subject and have Paul saying something that he is not. This word does not mean "salvation", as it is translated in the KJV and most other versions. If Paul had been speaking of salvation here he would have used the noun *sōtēria*, not the adjective *sōtērion*.

The noun *sōtēria* is found forty-five times in the New Testament and is translated "salvation" in forty of these occurrences. The adjective *sōtērion* is found five times as shown in the following concordance:

Luke 2:30   For mine eyes have seen thy *salvation*
Luke 3:6   all flesh shall see the *salvation* of God
Acts 28:28   the *salvation* of God is sent to the Gentiles
Eph. 6:17   And take the helmet of *salvation*
Tit. 2:11   the grace of God *that bringeth salvation*

From this list it will be seen that the translators have treated this divinely-inspired adjective as if it were a noun when it is not. This is not a grammatically correct translation, and it robs the reader of the exact truth that the Spirit of God intended to convey by the use of this adjective.

There is no doubt but that this word literally means *saving*, even as we would use it in speaking of "saving grace" or "the saving work of Christ", and it is also clear that in four of the five occurrences in the New Testament it is substantivized; that is, it is used as if it were a noun. Nevertheless, the fact remains that it is an adjective, and there is one fixed rule about adjectives that cannot be altered; they never stand alone. If they seem to stand alone, as they do in the five passages cited above, then the noun which they qualify must be found in the context. More on this later, but first of all we must define this word more accurately. There is no question but that it has a technical meaning and is so used in the New Testament.

The King James Version came very near to the true meaning of this word in Titus 2:11 where it was translated by using three words "that bringeth salvation," for the technical meaning of *sōtērion* is salvation-bringing. The lexicons are practically unanimous in regard to this:

> Abbott-Smith: "saving, bringing salvation."
> Cremer: "saving, bringing salvation."
> Lidell and Scott: "savings, delivering, bringing safety."
> Thayer: "saving, bringing salvation."
> Bullinger: "saving, delivering, bringing salvation."
> Arndt and Gingrich: "saving, bringing salvation."
> W. E. Vine: "saving, bringing salvation."

Moulton and Millegan say that in the papyrus this word is used in the neuter as a substantive with reference to what produces *sōtēria*, e.g., a sacrifice or a gift.

As stated before, this word is an adjective and no adjective ever stands alone in a sentence. In fact this is so true that one meaning of the word *adjective* is "something that cannot stand alone." In any sentence where it seems to stand alone we must always seek for that which it modifies. In such statements as, "It is beautiful," or "This is good," we have adjectives which appear to stand alone, yet these words say nothing about anything until we find something in the physical context that supplies the subject. If we are gazing at a sunset or eating a meal when these words are spoken they become full of meaning at once.

Adjectives can be used as substantives only when the idea that is being qualified or modified is clear from the context, either written or apparent. Even a sentence like, "The young are impatient," if spoken without context would quickly bring the terse question, "Young what?"

With these facts before us we can now take up the examination of the five passages in which this adjective is found, keeping in mind that it means salvation-bringing.

If this definition is followed out it would mean that Luke 2:30 would read, "For mine eyes have seen thy salvation-bringing." This is evidently not a complete statement and yet it is exactly what Simeon said, as literally as it can be translated. And it is bound to cause the question to be asked, "Salvation-bringing what?" However, this is good, for the question sends us at once to the context to find out what it is that is described as "salvation-bringing."

Moffitt recognizes the adjective here and renders it "thy saving power," as does also Lenski, translating it "thy saving gift." Both of these are linguistically wrong as there is nothing about "power" or "gift" in the context.

Simeon, the one who spoke these words, was an aged man who had been told that he should not see death before he had seen the Messiah, that is, Jehovah (Luke 2:26). When this man, led by the Spirit of God, came into the temple and saw the infant Jesus he declared to God, the One who before had spoken to him, "Lord now lettest Thou Thy servant depart in peace, according to Thy word, for mine eyes have seen Thy salvation-bringing." This is literally what he said, and the context leaves no doubt about the noun that should be supplied. Simeon had seen God's salvation-bringing Messiah (Christ), the world's long awaited Savior. He had seen what God had told him he would see — not power, not a gift, but the Christ.

In the second occurrence of *sōtērion* (Luke 3:6) the noun that needs to be supplied is not so readily apparent, yet there can be no mistake as to the intent of the Spirit in this place. Literally this passage would read, "And all flesh shall see the salvation-bringing of God." This is grammatically correct, and it is true to the Greek. Yet some will again respectfully inquire: "Salvation-bringing what?" and again the answer must be found in the context. This makes it plain that this statement is in complete harmony with something written in the prophecy of Isaiah, where it says "And the glory of the Lord shall be revealed, and all flesh shall see it together" (Isa. 40:5). In view of this the noun to be supplied is *glory*, making the passage under consideration to read, "And all flesh shall see the salvation-bringing glory of God." The reference here is to world salvation.

The occurrence in Eph. 6:17 belongs to a portion on which so many sermons have been preached that few are now able to distinguish between these and the actual message of God. If this is translated literally it would read, "And receive the helmet of the salvation-bringing, even the sword of the Spirit, which is a declaration of God." Here again we must seek an honest answer to the question, "Salvation-bringing what?"

In this passage "the helmet" equals "the salvation-bringing" for they are appositional — one defines the other. And then by a further apposition these are defined as "the sword of the Spirit" which in turn is described as being "a declaration from God." In view of this we should read here, "And take the helmet of the salvation-bringing declaration (the gospel)." And let it not be thought strange that the salvation-bringing declaration of God is both the believer's helmet and the Spirit's sword. There is no mixing of metaphors here, but two distinct metaphors setting forth two separate uses of the same thing. It is my firm opinion that the salvation-bringing declaration of God is the gospel according to John, the only book in the Bible that was written so that men might believe that Jesus is the Christ, the Son of God, and believing have life through His name (John 20:31). The one who is not securely grounded upon this message will not be able to stand against the wiles of the devil. We need this helmet.

In Titus 2:11 we do not need to search for the noun which the adjective qualifies as it is in the passage. This passage should read, "For the salvation-bringing grace of God has shone forth in behalf of all humanity."

We will now consider the occurrence in the main passage under consideration, Acts 28:28. If this is translated literally it will read, "Let it then be known to you that the salvation-bringing of God has been authorized (made freely available) to the nations and they will hear it." But again we must ask, "Salvation-bringing what?"

In the context this "salvation-bringing of God" is something that the nations will hear; therefore, it is a divine communication. Thus we should read here, "the salvation-bringing message of God." Some may prefer some other term such as *word, utterance, declaration* or *gospel*, and there can be no objection to these since they all describe a communication that is intended to be heard. They are somewhat synonymous terms and they can be used for emphasis and variety. Thus it is that we have the subject of Paul's great declaration in Acts 28:28. He is talking about the salvation-bringing message of God.

The words "has been authorized" declare an accomplished fact, the effect of which continues, so the tense here is the second aorist. The words "they will hear it" declare a future result so the tense is future.

The great change that took place at Acts 28:28 is declared in the words "has been authorized to the nations." It is quite evident from Acts 10:36 and Acts 13:26 that the salvation-bringing message of God was authorized and made freely available to the nation of Israel from the day of Pentecost. At Acts 10 Peter was authorized to proclaim it to one Gentile household, but his commission did not go beyond this. The Apostle Paul was authorized to proclaim it to Gentiles, but it was severely restricted. It had to be to the Jew first in every place that he visited. Thus that which had been freely available only to Israel became freely available to all other nations at Acts 28:28.

In the words "they will hear it" we have a pledge and guarantee from God made by His agent and spokesman, Paul. These words actually mean that it will get through to the nations for their benefit. God made good on this pledge when He caused the Gospel of John to be written. The salvation-bringing message is no longer in the hands of men. It is written and it stands written.

The SEED and BREAD Bible-Study leaflets are published as often as time and means permit and are sent free to all names on THE WORD OF TRUTH MINISTRY mailing list. Send us your name. There will be no obligation, solicitation, or visitation. Additional copies of any issue available on request.   ISSUE NO. 8

SEED & BREAD

FOR THE SOWER   ISA. 55:10   FOR THE EATER

BRIEF BIBLICAL MESSAGES

FROM

THE WORD OF TRUTH MINISTRY

339 South Orange Drive, Los Angeles, Cal. 90036

Otis Q. Sellers, Bible Teacher

TRUTHS CONCERNING ACTS

Truth is that which accords with the facts. Divine facts are declared in the Word of God, and what we believe must be in harmony with them. Seventeen facts representing the same number of truths will be set forth in this study. These can be accepted or rejected. What will the reader do with them? A request is made for honest consideration.

1. The 120 that assembled on the day of Pentecost (Acts 1:15) were without exception Jews who believed that Jesus of Nazareth was the Messiah and the Son of God. This fact and truth had been generated in them by the Father in heaven (Matt. 16:17). They were the result of the personal ministry of Jesus Christ, whose words and works had led them to this belief. They did not cease to be Jews because of this new-found faith. As Sir Robert Anderson has so well said: "The divine religion of Judaism in every part of it, both in the spirit and the letter, pointed to the coming of a promised Messiah; and to maintain that a man ceased to be a Jew because he cherished that hope, and accepted the Messiah when He came—this is a position absolutely grotesque in its absurdity" (*The Silence of God*, page 85).

2. Those who heard the Word on that memorable day of Pentecost were "Jews, devout men out of every nation under heaven" (Acts 2:5). They had been of the diaspora but had returned to the land of their fathers. The 3000 who became believers on that day (Acts 2:41) were without exception "Jews, devout men." They remained such after they believed (Acts 2:46).

3. The salvation-bringing message of God was authorized to everyone in Israel from the day of Pentecost onward (Acts 2:39, 10:36, 13:26). This message centered in the fact that the man Christ Jesus was the long-awaited Messiah (the Christ) and the Son of God. He was presented as an object for personal faith, offered to Israelites as a personal Savior. Forgiveness of sins was promised to all who believed in Him (Acts 2:21, 36, 38). This salvation-bringing

message could be heralded by any believing Israelite who was commissioned of God to do so. This commission consisted of the Word of God coming to a man as a message intended for another. See Luke 3:2 for an example of this. It seems that every believing Jew in the Acts period had the blessing of this experience. The message may have come to them for only one person, but there could be no proclamation apart from such a commission (Rom. 10:15).

4. In the eight years that elapsed between Pentecost and Peter's visit to the house of Cornelius the gospel was to the Jew only. Every believer during that time was a Jew, a man of Israel. No one was authorized to speak the salvation-bringing message to anyone else. Even if a Gentile overheard it as it was being proclaimed, as Cornelius certainly had (Acts 10:37), it was still not for him.

5. The thrice-repeated vision which Peter saw while on the housetop (Acts 10:9-16) was a special commission and authorization for him to go to the house of Cornelius, a God-fearing, devout Gentile. This proclamation of Jesus Christ to the household of one Roman centurion represents Peter's entire ministry to the Gentiles. He had no commission to any others outside Israel. He was not God's commissioned one to the Gentiles. This was Paul's perogative (Rom. 11:13). This one act of Peter served to prepare the believers in Israel for the ministry of Paul among the Gentiles, which began six years later.

6. Cornelius did not become a herald of the salvation-bringing message to the Gentiles. He did not abandon his military position and return to Rome to herald the Gospel. He may have wished to do this but could not do so without a divine commission. If he had such a commission it would have made him, and not Paul, God's commissioned one to the Gentiles.

7. It was God's purpose and program in the Acts period that every responsible person in Israel should hear the salvation-bringing gospel and have one clear-cut opportunity to receive the Lord Jesus as the Messiah and to believe in Him as a personal Savior (Rom. 15:21). This witness was made to every Israelite in the land and to the uttermost parts of the earth (Acts 1:8).

8. God's purpose in this period was accomplished. Every Israelite was covered (Rom. 10:18, Rom. 15:23). Those outside the land lived in tight pockets and could easily be reached by the herald going to the synagogue in that locality (Acts 17:1-3).

9. In the Acts period the proclamation of the gospel of Jesus Christ was always done by God-commissioned men (Rom.10:15), the message they heralded was always spoken by divine inspiration (1 Cor. 2:13), every word of it was the Word of God (1 Thess. 2:13), it was always absolute truth (2 Cor. 13:3), it was not written, it was not memorized and repeated over and over, and it was always fresh from God each time it was spoken. It was varied each time to

meet the exact needs of those who heard it, but these variations were inspired by God and were not made by the heralds. One man could proclaim it as well as another. Ignorant fishermen spoke it as well as the educated statesmen.

10. In order to avoid all delays, all misunderstandings, and any need for translation, the gospel of God was always spoken in the mother tongue of the one for whom it was intended. The gift of tongues was a meaningful reality in the Acts period (Acts 2:6, 8, 11). See Issue No. 6.

11. In the Acts dispensation the proclamation of the gospel was always confirmed to the hearers by evidential miracles (Mark 16:20; John 14:12; Acts 2:43; Acts 5:12; Rom. 15:18, 19; 1 Cor.1:6; Heb. 2:4). These might precede the proclamation, accompany it, or follow it, but they were always there. No one was asked to believe without seeing. Physical evidence was always a part of the proclamation (1 Thess. 1:5).

12. Under the divine administration that prevailed in the Acts period a man was given only one opportunity to hear and believe the gospel (Acts 13:46). The heralds of the gospel never spoke it twice to the same people. A herald did not go over ground that had already been covered (Rom. 15:20, 21). The message was at once either a "savor of life" or a "savor of death" to all who heard it (2 Cor. 2:16). If a man could not immediately believe the testimony of a God-commissioned man speaking a divinely-inspired message, the truth of which was confirmed by signs following, there was nothing more that God would do. All who heard were enlightened, they tasted of the heavenly gift, they were partakers of the Holy Spirit, they had tasted the good Word of God, and experienced the powers of the coming eon (Heb. 6:4, 5). If after all this they fell away it was impossible to bring them back again to the place of submission (Heb. 6:6-7).

13. In the Acts dispensation the faith of a believer was always publicly accredited and confirmed by God. "These signs shall follow them that believe," was the promise of Jesus Christ (Mark 16:17). And they did (1 Cor. 1:6, 7). A man's relationship to God was a manifest thing. There were no secret believers. The life of an Acts period believer was not "hid with Christ in God," as ours is today (Col. 3:3).

14. After Peter's visit to the house of Cornelius, Paul was the only man commissioned by God to herald His salvation-bringing message to the Gentiles. This ministry began in Pisidian Antioch (Acts 13:46, 47). Nevertheless, Paul's ministry even after Acts 13 was always to the Jew first and to the Jew primarily (Acts 13:46; Rom. 1:16; Acts 17: 1, 2). He would go straight through a city without stopping if there were no company of Jews in it (Acts 17:1). The true, Biblical picture of the Acts period is one of thousands of heralds carrying the salvation-bringing message of God to every

Israelite (Acts 11:19), but only one herald taking it to the Gentiles, and this only after he had fulfilled every obligation to his own people, Israel. This may not be the picture that people want to see, but it is the true Biblical one nevertheless.

15. In the Acts period the children of Israel are likened to being "as the sand of the sea" (Rom. 9:27). It was God's purpose in this thirty-three years to sift through and test every grain of sand that made up this company. Among these were many true gems that would shine forth the moment they heard the message and saw its confirmation. These gems would have a special place and perform a special service in the day when He makes up His jewels (Mal. 3:17). These become in truth "the Israel of God" (Gal. 6:16).

16. At the close of the Acts period God had accomplished everything He set out to do. He had finished the work, He had cut it short in righteousness. A conclusive and concise work had been done on earth (Rom. 9:28). Israel had heard the word and saw the works of God (Rom. 10:18). The Israel of God had been discovered (Gal. 6:16). The remnant had been established (Rom. 11:5). A definite company from among the Gentiles had been called for His name (Acts 15:14). Everything was ready for the full establishment of the manifest kingdom of God upon the earth (Rom. 13:11, 12). But it did not come. At the close of the Acts period all of God's kingdom purposes were suspended while He accomplishes a purpose that had never before been revealed.

17. The end of the Acts dispensation is marked by Paul's pronouncement in Acts 28:28. The Bible student must discover when he comes to this declaration what things come to an end, what things carry through, and what new circumstances and conditions prevail. That the circumstances and conditions set forth above came to an end is obvious. That a new dispensation began is evident. The words of Acts 28:28 are of the utmost importance. Understanding that the word translated "salvation" (*sōtērion*) is an adjective, and that no adjective ever stands alone in a sentence (see Issue No. 8); knowing also that the word "sent" is *apostellō*, and since it is used as an inanimate thing it means *authorized*, or, made freely available (see Issue No. 5), I would accurately translate this passage as follows: "Let it then be known unto you that the salvation-bringing message of God has been authorized to the nations, and they will hear it.

Published as often as time and means permit and sent free to all names on THE WORD OF TRUTH MINISTRY mailing list. Additional copies available on request.   ISSUE NO. 9

SEED & BREAD

FOR THE SOWER ISA. 55:10 FOR THE EATER

BRIEF BIBLICAL MESSAGES
FROM
THE WORD OF TRUTH MINISTRY
339 South Orange Drive, Los Angeles, Cal. 90036

Otis Q. Sellers, Bible Teacher

FROM CANA TO CALVARY

"This beginning of miracles did Jesus in Cana of Galilee" (John 2:11). These words point to the beginning of the public ministry of Jesus Christ. "And when they came to the place which is called Calvary, there they crucified Him" (Luke 23:33). These words denote the end of what the writer of Hebrews calls "the days of His flesh" (Heb. 5:7). Our study concerns these days, the three years of His earthly ministry.

In his brief introduction to the book of Acts the writer Luke describes his previous writing, the Gospel of Luke, as being an account of what Jesus began both to do and to teach until the day of His ascension (Acts 1:1, 2). Thus all that the Lord did and all that He said before He ascended to heaven set the stage for all that was done in the Acts period. The thirty-three years that form this period are a continuation of the three years of His earthly ministry; therefore, what He said and did upon the earth demands careful consideration. If the great truths of this short three-year period are hid in our hearts, it will provide a well-prepared piece of ground upon which the seeds of truth of the Acts period can fall and take root. Everyone knows that He "went about doing good, and healing all that were oppressed of the devil" (Acts 10:38), but beyond this they know very little.

At one point in His ministry the Lord Jesus made certain declarations of truth that caused many of His disciples to turn back and walk no more with Him (John 6:66). Their profession of submission (repentance) came to a sudden end. This defection did not cause the Lord to send someone after them with the promise of a brighter, lighter, happier message the next time He spoke to them. He simply turned to the twelve disciples and asked, "Will ye also go away?"

In answering Peter became the spokesman for the twelve and said, "Lord, to whom shall we go? Thou hast the words of eternal life. And we believe and are sure that Thou art that Christ, the Son of the living God" (John 6:68, 69).

Peter was entirely right in his statement. At the time of this incident there was only One upon the earth who could speak a message which a man by believing could get the guarantee of eternal life. If they turned away from Him there was none other to whom they could go. No one else could make the offer of eternal life. None but the Lord Jesus could utter this salvation-bringing, life-giving message.

Before this time the Lord had commissioned the twelve as heralds. These men were not preachers; they were heralds. They were given authority over "unclean spirits, to cast them out, and to heal all manner of sickness and all manner of disease" (Matt. 10:1). In commissioning them they were barred from taking any road that would lead them to Gentiles, and from entering into any Samaritan city (10:5). They were directed to go only to the lost sheep of the house of Israel (10:6), and their message was limited to a call to submission (repentance) in view of the fact that God's government was impending (10:7). Thus, under their proclamation any Israelite could take the place of submission, and these men could identify such with the submissive ones. This was only a step toward eternal life, only a start on the road to salvation.

The twelve would not have dared to add to the message the Lord gave to them, even though they probably would very much like to have done so. Certainly they would have preferred to proclaim that they had found One who gave every evidence that He was the long-awaited Messiah, to have recounted the works they had seen Him do, and to have held Him up as an object of faith in the hope of eternal life. But this was not their mission or message at that time. Note carefully His specific instructions to them:

These twelve Jesus sent forth (*apostellō*, see Issue No. 5) and commanded them, saying, Go not into the way of the Gentiles, and into any city of the Samaritans enter ye not: But go rather to the lost sheep of the house of Israel. And as ye go, preach, saying, the kingdom of the heavens is at hand. Heal the sick, cleanse the lepers, raise the dead, cast out devils: freely ye have received, freely give. Matt. 10:5-8.

This was their commission. They were heralds. They were told exactly what to say and do. Their instructions amounted to divine directives.

Sir Robert Anderson tells of an incident that happened in the French Chamber concerning trouble which was caused in a certain district through the general in command having communicated a War Office order in his own words. When the Minister of War was challenged in Parliament for punishing him, his answer was, "He committed an offense, and I removed him; he paraphrased an order which it was his duty only to read."

The Lord's directive as to what the heralds should say was explicit. They did not paraphrase the words given them in order to inflate their message and make it more spectacular. They had accepted the call to submission (repentance) with resolute sincerity. Later interpreters would enlarge their commission and have these heralds going forth with the salvation-bringing, life-giving message to all kinds of men in all places. This is a false conception. It was not at that time their privilege to speak the message that would bring forgiveness, redemption, and life to lost men.

As their consciousness grew in regard to Jesus being the Messiah (the Christ) and they confessed to Him that this was their conviction, they were charged that they should tell no man about it (Matt. 16:20). Even after Peter, James, and John saw Him transfigured they were charged to, "Tell the vision to no man until the Son of man be risen again from the dead" (Matt. 17:9). Not until after His death and resurrection, and the pouring out of the Spirit on the day of Pentecost, could they speak the words that would bring about theogenic faith in the great truth that Jesus is the Christ the Son of God. Until then the Lord Jesus alone could speak this message. This is in complete harmony with Paul's later declaration:

> How shall we escape if we neglect so great a salvation; which at the first began to be spoken by the Lord, and was confirmed unto us by them that heard Him; God also bearing them witness, both with signs and wonders, and with divers miracles, and gifts of the Holy Spirit, according to His own will. Heb. 2:3, 4.

Thus, three things need to be firmly fixed in our minds and held as divine truth: (1) Jesus Christ was the first to speak a message that men by believing could lay hold of God's promise of life through Him; (2) Before His ascension He was the only one who could speak it; (3) He spoke it only to a limited number of the lost sheep of the house of Israel.

During His earthly ministry when a Syrophonecian woman (a Gentile) made an appeal to Him for help in regard to her daughter, He, at first, made no reply at all (Matt. 15:21-23). But she was not easily discouraged, so she troubled the disciples about her need to such an extent that they came to Him with the request, "Dismiss her, for she is crying after us." His answer to the disciples (not the woman) was, "I am not commissioned (apostellō) but unto the lost sheep of the house of Israel" (Matt. 15:24).

It seems that they reported His words to the woman for she came to Him again with the almost pitiful plea, "Lord, help me." His answer to this was, "It is not meet (proper) to take the children's bread, and cast it to the dogs" (Matt. 15:26).

There are many expositors who seem to wish that these statements would go away and get lost. They do not at all fit in with the popular conception that the earthly ministry of Jesus Christ was to all men without distinction. But they are in the Word and they stand written. They are His own positive statements as to the extent of His commission and the limits set upon it. All who believe in Him should not hesitate to accept His own declarations in regard to this. In His own complete submission to the will of God, He would not be guilty of extending His own personal commission. During His earthly ministry only two Gentiles were touched by Him. The Syrophonecian woman got healing for her daughter, and a Roman centurion got healing for his slave.

On the evening after His resurrection He appeared to His disciples, demonstrating to them the reality of His own restoration to life, saying to them, "Peace be unto you: as My Father has commissioned *(apostellō)* Me, even so send *(pempo)* I you" (John 20:21).

By these words He limited their future service to the lost sheep of the house of Israel, even as His own commission was also limited. Any change in this would require additional revelations from Him. After He said this, He breathed on them, and said, "Receive ye the Holy Spirit: Whose soever sins ye remit, they are remitted unto them; and whose soever sins ye retain, they are retained" (John 20:22-23).

By this act and by these words He constituted these eleven men His specially commissioned ones *(apostolos)*. They would perform upon the earth the acts that He would decree in heaven, and He would work with them in all they were called to do. Thus it was that for a thirty-three year period these men were the most gifted, able, powerful, dynamic, spiritual, energetic and incredible men that ever operated upon this earth in behalf of God. Later Matthias was added to their number (Acts 1:26) and Paul was personally commissioned and empowered. It was the presence of such men upon the earth that did so much to make the Acts period a unique dispensation in God's dealings with men.

I have piled up adjectives in describing these men, and all of these are true of them, even though very little of their works are recorded. They covered the known world, reaching all Israel, in one generation. They were despised and ignored by the world of their day, and they are misrepresented, stultified, and belittled by the theological world of today. These men were not eleven old fuddy-duddies running around in bathrobes, the way they are represented in all religious pageantry of today. They were God's commissioned ones; they were apostles; they had the signs of apostles; they were earthly respresentatives of the One Who was seated in the heavens.

The SEED and BREAD Bible-Study leaflets are published as often as time and means permit and are sent free to all names on THE WORD OF TRUTH MINISTRY mailing list. Send us your name. There will be no obligation, solicitation, or visitation. Additional copies of any issue available on request.   ISSUE NO. 10

SEED & BREAD

FOR THE SOWER   ISA. 55:10   FOR THE EATER

BRIEF BIBLICAL MESSAGES
FROM
THE WORD OF TRUTH MINISTRY

339 South Orange Drive, Los Angeles, Cal. 90036

Otis Q. Sellers, Bible Teacher

The Importance of Acts 28:28

Great and complex truths cannot be said to be known until we have known and worked with them for a long time. It was in 1934 that I tentatively embraced the idea that Acts 28:28 marks a dispensational boundary line. Since then I have never ceased to search for a fuller and more complete understanding of the truth declared in this passage, to relate it to all that happened in the thirty-three years of the Acts period and to all that is now true since this declaration was made. Paul's words in this passage, spoken and recorded by inspiration of God, mark the close of the Acts period and the beginning of the Dispensation of Grace.

We hear much today about commitments, and no professing Christian should be without them. Some commitments are made with reservations and are subject to change. Others are made without reservations and can undergo no alteration. I believe that God will accept and watch over a true and proper commitment made by one of His own.

I will not attempt to set forth all the steps that led me to commit myself to the Lord Jesus as a perpetual and progressive student of the written word of God. It is sufficient to say that such a commitment was made long ago, that it was without reservations, and is, therefore, not subject to any change. Perpetual and progressive Bible study is my service unto and before the Lord. It has a single goal — to find for myself God's truth in the words He has given. In this I will be judged alone before my Lord and Master. I stand or fall before Him.

My conviction in regard to the Old and the New Testament is that they are the verbally inspired Word of God, that they are without error in their original writings, that they are of supreme and final authority in regard to all matters of faith. By verbal inspiration, I mean that supernatural work of the Holy Spirit by which, without setting aside the personalities and literary abilities of the human instrument, He constituted the words of the Bible in its entirety as His written word to you and to me. I believe that every word of scripture was produced under the guidance of God's Spirit, that "holy men of God spake as they were moved by the Holy Spirit" (2 Peter 1:21). This conviction has stood the test of more than a half century of personal Bible research and study.

When one is led to devote himself to some task that is related to the service of the Lord, he should never dwell upon his capabilities or his shortcomings, his knowledge or the lack of it, his educated or his uneducated state. All these things are known to God, Who does not consider them when He leads a man into the study of His word. We serve the God to Whom belongs all power, wisdom, and knowledge. All thoughts of our capabilities or incapabilities are meaningless in view of this. It is to Him we must turn if we would be successful in our studies in His Word and a help to others who may desire to know His truth. The things of men we can know because of the spirit of man which is in us, but the things of God no man can know but by the Spirit of God (1 Cor. 2:11).

A good share of my own Bible study efforts over many years have been applied to discovering the true character of the Acts dispensation and to finding the distinctive truths that apply in the present Dispensation of Grace. The difference between these two periods turns upon Paul's declaration in Acts 28:28, so to the assidous study of this passage I return again and again. My understanding of this declaration has progressed and changed somewhat over the years, but my conviction has grown that these words do mark a dispensational boundary line.

I am not able to say who was the first to suggest that Acts 28:28 marks a dispensational change. I came upon this in 1929 in the book, The Silence of God, by Sir Robert Anderson, in which he says, "The Pentecostal dispensation is brought to a close by the promulgation of the solemn decree, "The salvation of God is sent to the Gentiles." (page 56). This book was written in 1897, and it could be that this is one of the earliest references to this illuminating idea.

There is no evidence that Sir Robert Anderson ever followed this idea out to all its logical conclusions. In his writings he made no distinction between those epistles written before Acts 28:28 and those written after. He treated them as though they had all been written under one divine administration, which they were not. First and Second Thessalonians, First and Second Corinthians, Galatians, and Romans were written before the dispensational change, and in many passages set forth the distinct truths that prevailed only in the Acts period. Philippians, Colossians, Ephesians, 1 Timothy, Titus, 2 Timothy, and Philemon were written after the dispensational change and they take on the character of the time in which they were written.

Dr. E. W. Bullinger made the same mistake as Sir Robert

SEED & BREAD

FOR THE SOWER   ISA. 55:10   FOR THE EATER

BRIEF BIBLICAL MESSAGES

FROM

THE WORD OF TRUTH MINISTRY

339 South Orange Drive, Los Angeles, Cal. 90036

Otis Q. Sellers, Bible Teacher

THIS GENERATION SHALL NOT PASS
The Interpretation of Matthew 24:34, 35

The unequivocal statement made by the Lord Jesus Christ is that "this generation shall not pass, till all these things be fulfilled. Heaven and earth shall pass away, but My words shall not pass away."

These words have long been a burden to interpreters, and many and varied have been the meanings given to them. A. T. Robertson says that, "these words give a great deal of trouble to expositors," and J. C. Ryle says, "The meaning of this statement is a point on which commentators differ widely." How true these statements are, most students of Biblical literature well know.

The popular and generally accepted interpretation is that the word translated "generation" *(genea)* primarily means race, family, stock, and that the statement here concerns the nation or family of Israel which will be preserved as a people until all these things are fulfilled. This interpretation will be found in the notes of the *Scofield Reference Bible* (page 1034).

To take this passage and force it to teach that the Jews will always remain as a people is neither an adequate or satisfactory interpretation for many reasons, an important one being that *genea* does not primarily mean a race, kind, or family. It is found forty-two times in the New Testament where it is translated "generation," 37 times; "time", 2 times; "age," 2 times; and "nation," 1 time. This word primarily means *generation* and should be so translated in every occurrence. That Israel will persist as a people is a truth abundantly taught in Scripture, but it is not the truth that is being declared in this passage.

The weakest and most untenable of all interpretations is that which makes "this generation" to mean the total people that were upon the earth when these words were spoken, and that out of all these people some would still be alive when all these things were fulfilled. Those who hold this view usually make the destruction of Jerusalem in A.D. 70 to have been the second coming of Christ. This requires a most violent twisting of the words of our Lord, for the sudden coming of the Son of man with power and great glory certainly has to be a vastly different thing from a Roman general besieging and totally destroying a city. In A.D. 70, Jerusalem died by inches.

Another interpretation of this passage holds that "this generation" refers to that company of evil and wicked men that were then, and always had been, upon the earth since the entrance of sin. This view sees the Lord declaring that a company of wicked unbelievers and persecutors would persist through all time until He comes again. This interpretation is set forth by R. C. H. Lenski in his commentary on Matthew.

Those who contend for this idea are prone to cite the numerous passages of Scripture which speak of "this wicked generation," "an adulterous and sinful generation," and "an evil generation," as evidence that this occurrence of the word *generation* must also be understood this way. But the very opposite is true. The omission here does not signify that some such word as *evil* should be inserted. It indicates that it should be left out. The exquisite accuracy and completeness of inspired Scripture forbids the insertion of any such adjective in Matt. 24:34, unless it should be indicated by the context, which it certainly is not in this passage. Our Lord could easily have said, "this wicked generation shall not pass," if that had been what He meant. But He did not say this because He was not talking about the persistence of an evil generation.

This interpretation is unacceptable since "all these things" spoken of here includes the return of Jesus Christ to the earth. The company of evil men that has persisted on the earth since the days of Cain is going to be brought to an end long before the Lord returns. This end is clearly indicated in Psalm 37:9, 64:7, 46:6, Isa. 59:19, and 2 Tim. 3:9. All these passages speak of an event that takes place long before the Lord leaves His present place at the right hand of God. "Sit on My right hand, until I make thine enemies Thy footstool," is God's word to Him (Heb. 1:13).

A single continuing company cannot properly be called a generation. And if there is a continuing company of evil men, which is readily admitted, then there is also a continuing company of good men, and the words "this generation shall not pass" could just as easily be applied to the good company. The truth is that it does not refer to either.

Another interpretation that is widespread, having been adopted by the Jehovah Witness group and propagated by their literature, is that the generation that would see the beginning of these signs would also see the end of them. This is an unnatural and contrived explanation that is wholly contrary to the sense of the Greek words used here. Only by the wildest stretch of imagination can the words "this generation" be made to mean one that would appear two thousand years later.

From the various ideas set forth above it becomes quite clear that a true interpretation of the Lord's words depends entirely on what He meant by "this generation." This is the subject of His declaration. If we miss the meaning of this we will never comprehend the truth declared in His words.

In most cases where a word has a common and popular usage we are prone to forget that it may have other meanings that are seldom used or heard. The word *generation* is so often used of people that we fail to consider that it has usages and meanings where people are not at all in view.

In order to arrive at the true meaning of "this generation" certain simple facts will need to be faced and remembered. The word *generation* is one of a family of words, the parent word being the verb *generate*, which means to produce. That which produces is a *generator,* and that which is produced is a *generation*. The *-ion* suffix is used to name the result of a process. Thus, since electricity must be *generated,* to do this we need a *generator,* and the electricity it produces is a *generation*. You may never have heard electricity called a *generation,* but that is undeniably what it is.

Since each step in a lineage is produced by a forefather, these steps are properly called *generations* as we see in Matthew 1:17. This is a typical example of the use of this word in relationship to people. In 2 Tim. 2:23 we are told that foolish and unlearned questions do generate strifes; therefore, strife is a *generation* when it is produced by something else.

A more pertinent example would be that since "holy men of old spake as they were moved by the Holy Spirit" (2 Peter 1:21) it is clear that the Spirit of God was the *generator* and that the body of truth that came from these men was and is a *generation*. These are the prophecies we now call by the names of Isaiah, Jeremiah, Ezekiel, and others. Each one of these books is a generation. And since there were speaking prophets and writing prophets, the *generations* of the speaking prophets have passed away but those of the writing prophets are still with us today.

If we consider the declarations of the Lord Jesus Christ we find that both His words and His works were divine generations. See John 5:30, 5:19, 17:8, 12:49. Furthermore, His words are called this in Scripture. In Isaiah 53:8 we find a statement that has puzzled interpreters, "Who shall declare His generation?" Many have attempted to solve the problem here by changing the translation, but this is futile since there can be no doubt but that the Hebrew word *dor* means generation. And yet our Lord had no offspring, therefore, no generations, according to the common definition given to this word. However, He did produce a very important body of truth, and this can rightly be called a *generation*.

Since He was "cut off out of the land of the living" (Isa. 53:8), it is apropos that the question should be asked, "Who shall declare His generation?" There was no answer to this question in the Old Testament, but there is an answer in the New. Out of the Lord's many disciples twelve were specially chosen and commissioned, and it was to these He said, "When He, the Spirit of truth is come, He will guide you into all truth: for He shall not speak of Himself: but whatsoever He shall hear, that shall He speak, and He will show you things to come. He shall glorify Me: for He shall receive of Mine and shall show it unto you." John 16:13, 14.

Our Lord was a speaking prophet. He wrote nothing except a few words in the sand. Nevertheless, not one word which He wanted perpetuated has ever been lost. The body of truth which He generated has been preserved. It was His promise to the twelve that "the Comforter, which is the Holy Spirit, whom the Father will send in My name, He will teach you all things, and bring all things to your remembrance, whatsoever I have said unto you" (John 14:26).

When our Lord by speaking produced that body of truth that precedes the words we are considering, no stenographer took down His words and no instrument recorded His message. When He finished speaking not one of His disciples could have fully and accurately repeated what He said. It would seem that His words would soon be confused and then forgotten. Yet in the face of these possibilities our Lord boldly declared, "Verily I say unto you, This generation shall not pass till all these things be fulfilled" (Matt. 24:34).

By the words "this generation" He meant the body of truth He had produced in speaking to them. Confirmation of this is seen in His next statement which is a reiteration of what He had already said: "Heaven and earth shall pass away, but My words shall not pass away." Thus, "the generation" He was speaking of here was the words He had just spoken.

In the two statements, "this generation" and "My words" we find a figure of speech called a *pleonasm*. In the construction of this figure that which has been said is immediately after declared in another or opposite way in order to make it impossible for the meaning to be missed or misunderstood. By this method the meaning is locked in. May we not be guilty of breaking this lock and making "this generation" to mean something that the Lord never had in mind.

The SEED and BREAD Bible-Study leaflets are published as often as time and means permit and are sent free to all names on THE WORD OF TRUTH MINISTRY mailing list. Send us your name. There will be no obligation, solicitation, or visitation. Additional copies of any issue available on request.   ISSUE NO. 12

SEED & BREAD

FOR THE SOWER ISA. 55:10 FOR THE EATER

BRIEF BIBLICAL MESSAGES
FROM
THE WORD OF TRUTH MINISTRY

339 South Orange Drive, Los Angeles, Cal. 90036

Otis Q. Sellers, Bible Teacher

THE DIVINE COMMISSIONS

Three great commissions are set forth in Matthew, Mark, and Luke. These are not the same, even though they are often treated as though they were. There are those who insist that the wording of all these commissions demonstrate that it was the declared intention of Jesus Christ that His apostles, and anyone else who felt inclined to do so, should go at once and proclaim the salvation-bringing message of God to all mankind. They further insist that the ministry of the apostles in the Acts period was greatly hindered and restricted by their nationalistic feelings and their Jewish prejudices against the Gentiles. Such charges are grossly unfair to these faithful servants of God. In view of this, these commissions need to be carefully examined in order to find the exact instructions of Jesus Christ in each one of them. This we will do in this study. The first of these is recorded in Matthew.

And Jesus came and spake to them saying, All power is given unto Me in heaven and in earth. Go ye therefore, and teach all nations, baptizing them in the name of the Father, and of the Son, and of the Holy Ghost; teaching them to observe all things whatsoever I have commanded you: and, lo, I am with you alway, even to the end of the world. Matt. 28:18-20.

There is hardly any passage in the New Testament that has been subject to as much twisting and wresting, and to as many misapplications and misinterpretations as this one. And all this has been helped along by the very careless translation we find in the King James Version. A more accurate rendering of the Greek is a crying necessity here, so I submit the following resultant paraphrase. The reader will note that it is my conviction that the Greek verb *baptizō* has in it the idea of establishing a fixed relationship; that is, the idea of identification. A literal, grammatic rendering of this commision would read as follows:

And Jesus approaching them, spoke unto them saying, All authority in heaven and on the earth has been given to Me. Going, therefore, make disciples of all the nations, relating them to the name of the Father and of the Son and of the Holy Spirit, and then teach these discipled nations to observe all whatsoever I direct you. And lo, I am with you all the days even to the consummation of the eon. Matt. 28:18-20.

These words were spoken to "the eleven disciples" (Matt. 28:16), and when honestly interpreted have nothing to do with the proclamation of God's salvation-bringing message, nothing to do with proclaiming the gospel which is the power of God unto salvation. This commission did not have to do with the apostles course of action in the present evil eon. This directive belongs to that condition and state of things called the kingdom of God, the time when He governs the earth and the nations upon it (Psa. 67:4). It will be fulfilled and performed to the letter in the time after the Lord Jesus has assumed sovereignty, after He has taken to Himself His great power and is exercising it upon the earth.

The central command in these directives is to "make disciples of all the nations." This does not mean to preach to them in the hope that a few will accept. This commision does not have to do with individuals, but with nations. These are to be discipled and are to be identified with or related to the name (the character) of the Father, the Son, and the Holy Spirit. These are to be merged into all the purposes and programs of the Deity at that time (See Psalms 22:27,28; 66:3,4; 82:8; 86:9; 102:15; 138:4). The words "in the Name of the Father, the Son, and the Holy Spirit" were never intended to be some magic formula that a clergyman was supposed to repeat as he dipped a person into water or sprinkled water upon them.

This commission cannot be carried out until Jesus Christ makes request of the Father and the nations are given to Him as His portion (Psa. 2:8; 82:8); not until God is governing the nations upon the earth (Psa. 67:4). At this time the men to whom these words were spoken will be sitting "upon twelve thrones judging the twelve tribes of Israel" (Matt. 19:28), and because of their positions, powers, and past histories will be the most honored and revered statesman upon the earth. And since the nations at that time will want to be identified with the Deity (Psa. 67:4; 72:11, 17; 138:4; Isa. 55:5; Matt. 12:21; Rom. 15:12), these powerful men will go forth and relate nations to God in Christ in a formal and declared union. Furthermore, they will instruct the nations in regard to their responsibilities and conduct under God's government.

To those who insist that the commission in Matthew sends all believers to herald God's salvation-bringing message to men of every nation, there is one perfect answer. The men to whom these words were spoken did not understand them this way. We are on safe ground when we interpret these words in the same manner as they were understood by these divinely-possessed, Spirit-filled apostles of the Lord Jesus Christ, whose words were confirmed by the God they were serving. Who are we to say 1900 years later that they misunderstood and failed to obey His commission?

The Commission in Mark

The commission recorded in Mark is entirely different from the one given in Matthew, even though it was spoken to the same eleven men.

And He said unto them, Go ye into all the world, and preach the gospel to every creature. He that believeth and is baptized shall be saved; and he that believeth not shall be damned. And these signs shall follow them that believe; In My name shall they cast out devils; they shall speak with new tongues; they shall take up serpents; and if they drink any deadly thing, it shall not hurt them; they shall lay hands on the sick and they shall recover. Mark 16:15-20.

This commission was performed and fulfilled to the letter in the thirty-three years of which the book of Acts is the history, and it was the fulfillment of this commission that did so much to give the Acts period its peculiar character. The heralds went forth and proclaimed everywhere, covering every Israelite in Palestine and those who were dispersed throughout the world. They did what they were told to do, and God did what He promised He would do. The final verse of this chapter is proof of this:

And they went forth, and preached everywhere, the Lord working with them, and confirming the word with signs following. Mark 16:20.

The words *pasē tē ktisei* which are here translated "to every creature" obviously do not mean this. If it did it would include the animals, which pushes it into the ridiculous. This phrase means "in every creation." Few indeed have dared to translate this phrase literally, since there is very little understanding as to how *ktisis* (creation) is used in the New Testament.

In 1 Peter 2:13 where *pasē anthrōpinē ktisei* is translated "every ordinance of man," it should read "every human creation," and these creations are then described as being kings and governors. In Col. 1:15 where *prōtotokos pasēs ktiseōs* is translated "firstborn of every creature," it should read "firstborn of every creation." These creations are then described as being thrones, dominions, principalities, and powers. Thus empires, nations, states, cities, and all their officials would be "creations" in the Biblical use of this term.

As the heralds went forth some of these creations would take a very hostile attitude toward the proclamation of the gospel in their countries; others might be more or less friendly, such as those on the Isle of Paphos, where Sergius Paulus was the procounsul (Acts 13:6-7). But the heralds were not to choose the easy places; they were to preach the gospel "in every creation" whether the political climate was favorable or not. If there were Israelites within the borders of these creations, they were to go there.

Some may continue to insist that the words "in every creation" mean that these men were to go everywhere and preach to everyone without exception or distinction. However, again let it be noted that the men to whom these words were spoken never understood them to mean this. Their conduct in the early chapters of Acts make this plain, and we can arrive at no better understanding of these words. The apostles limited their ministry to the lost sheep of the house of Israel. In Acts 10, after a vision was repeated three times, Peter went to the devout, God-fearing, Gentile family. This was the way God wanted it, and this was the way they did it. We should honor their faithfulness.

The Commission in Luke

The commission recorded in Luke is different from those set forth in Matthew and Mark. In Luke we are told that after the Lord had opened their understanding that they might understand the Scriptures, He said unto them:

Thus it is written, and thus it behoved Christ to suffer, and to rise from the dead the third day: and that repentance and remission of sins should be preached among all nations beginning at Jerusalem. And ye are witnesses of these things. Luke 24:46-48.

There were Israelites in every nation, and it was the pledge of God that, "To whom He was not spoken of, they shall see: and they that have not heard shall understand" (Rom. 15:21; Isa. 52:15). This is why repentance and remission of sins was to be proclaimed "among all nations, beginning at Jerusalem."

This was no command or commission to proclaim God's salvation-bringing message to all men without exception or distinction. Those to whom these words were spoken did not understand them this way, and these were the very men whose understanding had been opened so that they could comprehend the truth (Luke 24:45). Peter did not understand them this way. It took a spectacular vision thrice repeated and some direct conversation with the Lord before he would go to even one Gentile household.

We lose nothing by acknowledging the unique place of Israel in the Acts period. We gain much in the way of truth when we do. From the day of Pentecost to the house of Cornelius, an eight year period, the gospel was to the Jew only. At Acts 10 one Gentile household is evangelized, but nothing more is done or can be done until the great apostle to the Gentiles, Paul, begins his ministry. We read of this in Acts 13. From that point on a company of Gentiles was called out and participated in the blessings of Israel. After Acts 28:28 the salvation bringing message of God was made freely available to all men. This produced a new and different company of believers of which we are a part.

The SEED and BREAD Bible-Study leaflets are published as often as time and means permit and are sent free to all names on THE WORD OF TRUTH MINISTRY mailing list. Send us your name. There will be no obligation, solicitation, or visitation. Additional copies of any issue available on request.   ISSUE NO. 13

SEED & BREAD

FOR THE SOWER   ISA. 55:10   FOR THE EATER

BRIEF BIBLICAL MESSAGES
FROM

THE WORD OF TRUTH MINISTRY

339 South Orange Drive, Los Angeles, Cal. 90036

Otis Q. Sellers, Bible Teacher

WHAT ARE "THE LAST DAYS"?

It is my conviction that "the last days" spoken of in 2 Timothy 3:1 is a segment of time at the end of God's present dispensation of grace. It immediately precedes the divine assumption of sovereignty which inaugurates the kingdom of God upon the earth. It is also my firm belief that this segment of time is characterized by twenty-one specific manifestations of unusual wickedness listed in 2 Tim. 3:1-8, and that the definite appearance of these things in concert and intensity will demonstrate to the believer that he is living in the last days of the present evil eon. Believing these things to be true it becomes my duty to proclaim them and also to defend them from every assault. All who know me personally will admit my veracity when I say that these convictions are the result of long and assiduous study of the Word of God.

Paul in his final epistle, which was written to his fellow-laborer Timothy, declares that "in the last days perilous times shall come" (2 Tim. 3:1). The simple obvious meaning of "the last days" is that they refer to the final days of God's long display of grace, but since the word "last" (eschatos) has in it the idea of result or outcome, we also see portrayed the result or outcome of man's long practice and tolerance of iniquity. Sin begets sin, and the cumulative effects of man's long indulgence of sin is seen in human character in the last days as detailed here. And since the result is always at the end, the word "last" here must carry the idea of finality.

On one point all believers in the Word must agree. This dispensation is not going on forever. God's present method of dealing with mankind is not a permanent one. His long display of grace is most certainly going to come to an end. This being true it will have its last days, its final days, its concluding days, and it is of these days that Paul speaks here. He tells us what the character of mankind will be when these days are upon us.

Paul's statement here about "the last days" has to do with a time

that was still future when these words were written, a fact suffi-
ciently evidenced to the unbiased mind by the use of the future
verb "shall come" (enstēnsontai). This clearly indicates that "the
last days" were not then a reality when this epistle was written, a
fact established by the accuracy of God's inspired words.

This letter was a communication from God through Paul to the
man Timothy. When he received it, he knew quite well that he was
not reading an ordinary letter. He was reading the original copy of
an epistle that was destined to be a portion of holy Scripture, a
part of the written Word of God. From the simple act of reading
it, he would know that whatever Paul said in it was to be committed in turn to believing men who also in turn were to teach
these things to others (2 Tim. 2:2). That this refers to this epistle
is demonstrated by Paul's use of the aorist ēkousas (not "that thou
hast heard of me," but "which you hear from me"). Furthermore, the
phrase "among many witnesses" would indicate that the matters
dealt with in this letter are not private.

Timothy experienced no problems in understanding this letter.
Let him do his simple part and God would do His. "Consider what
I say, and the Lord will be giving (dōsei, future) thee understanding" (2 Tim. 2:7). Thus he would read, "For men will be"
(2 Tim. 3:2), and consider the additional use of a verb in the
future tense (esontai) and would know not then to look for these
twenty-one indicators that would denote the presence of "the last
days". He would know from this future tense that the twenty-one
manifestations of resultant wickedness were not then a present reality
that would continue on and characterize the entire dispensation of
grace. He would understand that the picture of men painted here
would not be an actuality until after "evil men and seducers had
waxed worse and worse" (2 Tim. 3:13), and the world had come
into the result of man's long indulgence of sin. He would know
quite well that the time period referred to, as "the last days"
did not cover the whole of the dispensation that began with Paul's
pronouncement at Acts 28:28, as some are saying today.

There are those who insist that the instructions given in 2 Tim.
3:5 would indicate that the conditions described were already
there. Why would Timothy be told to shun such men if they were
not then in existence?

This imposes no problem, since it is readily admitted that men
like this have always been upon the earth. If not, how could it
be said that they would "wax worse and worse." Furthermore, if
we are going to make the presence of wicked men to be a demonstration of "the last days," then we should be consistent and begin
this time with Cain. What Timothy is told here is that when he
met up with men, or even one man, who showed these characteris-

tics, he should turn away from them. This is a continuing divine directive to all to whom these truths have been committed.

There have always been evil men upon the earth since the entrance of sin. The first chapter of Romans gives a description of men "who hold down the truth in unrighteousness" (Romans 1:18), and among the sins of which these are guilty are listed boasters, proud, disobedient to parents, and without natural affection. Men of this character were common in the Roman empire in Paul's day, and they were practicing their vices long before the present dispensation began. However, it is only when we see the result of this iniquity long-practiced so that it is manifested in twenty-one (3x7) characteristics that we know we are in the last days of the dispensation of grace. It should also be noted that these manifestations of wickedness are not given as signs of something to come, but as indications of a malignancy that would at some future time be present.

It is up to the individual believer to consider diligently each one of these features, to look at them in light of present world conditions and decide for himself whether or not we are now living in the last days of God's dispensation of grace.

I have done this. I have made a long and careful study of this portion in the inspired Greek in which it was first written. I believe I have used every means by which a man arrives at a true meaning of a word used in holy Scripture. Furthermore, for more than fifty years I have watched the conduct of men and observed the progress of iniquity. As a result, it is my personal conviction that we are now living in the resultant days of man's long practice of iniquity and in the last days of God's long display of grace. Believing this as I do, I shall live every day of my life anticipating and expecting that blessed hope which is the blazing forth of the glory of the great God, even our Savior Christ Jesus (Titus 2:13, Isa. 40:5). God's kingdom is coming, and my understanding of 2 Tim. 3:1-9 tells me that it may be nearer than we think.

Three of the most definite features of the last days are in the world today as they have never been before in history. These are the final three set forth in this list of twenty-one. They are (1) the multitudes today who are lovers of pleasure more than they are lovers of God, (2) the great multiplicity of the forms of godliness that deny the power of godliness, and (3) the Jannes and Jambres characteristic which substitutes the false for the true work of God. These three things are today showing a manifest and extraordinary development never before seen in history.

The interpretation I have given of "the last days" is in complete harmony with other portions of Scripture that declare a deluge of iniquity just before God assumes sovereignty and establishes His beneficent government upon the earth. The teaching of 2 Tim.

3:1-9 is that following a time of unusual wickedness, God intervenes and wicked men are stopped in their tracks. "They shall proceed no further" is the triumphant declaration of Paul. The act of God that stops all wicked men in their tracks is that "their dementia will become obvious to all men." This will be realized when God speaks from heaven once again and says, "let there be light" (Psalm 97:4).

The truth declared in 2 Tim. 3:1-9 is parallel to Psalm 64 in so many points that it is somewhat startling. In this Psalm David describes an "insurrection of the workers of iniquity," which is what Paul also set forth in 2 Tim. 3. This is not the ordinary flow of iniquity that has always characterized the human race. Both passages describe an unusual surge of the workers of iniquity, and both describe how God will deal with it. "God shall shoot at them with an arrow, suddenly shall they be wounded. So shall they make their own tongue to fall upon themselves" (Psa. 64:7-8). These are the words David uses to describe what is going to happen. "But they shall proceed no further: for their folly shall be manifest to all men" (2 Tim. 3:9). These are the words Paul uses to describe the same event. In both passages the wickedness of the wicked comes to a sudden and dramatic end.

The Word of God reveals in many places that divine intervention takes place in a time of unusual iniquity. The promise that "evildoers shall be cut off" (Psa. 37:9) is in complete harmony with the declaration in 2 Tim. 3:9 that "they shall proceed no further." It is when nations are in turmoil and governments totter on their foundations that God speaks in heaven and the people of the earth become soft like wax that is heated (Psa. 46:6). It is when the wicked spring up as the grass, and when all the workers of iniquity do flourish (Psa. 92:7) that they shall be destroyed. It is when the enemy shall come in like a flood that the Spirit of the Lord shall lift up a standard against him (Isa. 59:19).

We take our stand on His promises. Evildoers shall be cut off, they shall proceed no further, the wickedness of the wicked will come to an end, God will shoot at the wicked with His arrow of truth, they will be wounded, He will cause judgment to be heard from heaven, His lightnings will enlighten the world, His divine standard will stop the flood of wickedness. These are divine promises. They will be fulfilled to the letter.

The SEED and BREAD Bible-Study leaflets are published as often as time and means permit and are sent free to all names on THE WORD OF TRUTH MINISTRY mailing list. Send us your name. There will be no obligation, solicitation, or visitation. Additional copies of any issue available on request.   ISSUE NO. 14

SEED & BREAD

FOR THE SOWER   ISA. 55:10   FOR THE EATER

BRIEF BIBLICAL MESSAGES
FROM
THE WORD OF TRUTH MINISTRY
339 South Orange Drive, Los Angeles, Cal. 90036

Otis Q. Sellers, Bible Teacher

WHAT THE WORLD NEEDS NOW

When the man Lazarus was sick in Bethany his sisters sent a message to the Lord Jesus which said, "Lord, behold, He whom Thou lovest is sick" (John 11:3). Their appeal was based upon His personal love for one who was then in great need, and while it did not immediately work out as they had hoped, it did come to a happy conclusion for all concerned.

Today, we live in a world that is sick unto death. Its condition is obvious and its desperate needs are manifest realities. It is beset with complex maladies and malignancies that threaten its destruction, and the ministrations of those who would alleviate its sufferings seem only to add to its miseries. To "save the world" has become the purpose of many, but the attractive, simplistic remedies now being proposed by its would-be healers are nothing more than the old, quack remedies offered under new labels. Science has not saved it, education has not saved it, organized religion has not saved it. This has caused some to abandon all hope.

The world needs to be saved. Its desperate needs must soon be met or this world, this order, this system, this ecology will perish. In view of this the God-fearing man is inclined to cry out to the One who made this world and say, "Lord, that which you love is sick" (John 3:16). Yes, the world that God so loved that He was willing to give His only Son in relationship to it is desperately ill. Many of His people are now asking what He will do, or what can He do in regards to its present needs.

There is a wide disagreement among men as to what it is that the world needs or what should be done to cure its present ills. They admit it is sick but differ as to what will cure it. And since man is a part of it and the prime cause of much of its troubles, we need to ask what it is that will cure mankind of its hate, its greed, its selfishness, its fierceness, its lusts, its treachery, its pride, its envy, its murdering instincts, its thievery, its drunkenness, and the rest of the catalog of sins and crimes which so adversely affect the world today.

The Bible-taught man can answer this question without hesitation. What the world needs now is divine intervention. It needs a supreme miracle of the kind that God alone can perform. It needs divine action that will cure its ills and restore it to health and happiness once again.

The world needs no adverse action that will compound its troubles. It needs no pouring out of divine wrath. This would bring its destruction but not its salvation. It needs someone big enough and great enough to intervene in its behalf, and to intervene favorably. Yes, the world that God loves is sick unto death and it is not unreasonable for us to expect that He will intervene in its behalf.

The most unrecognized and unappreciated message in the Bible is that over and over, again and again, in the Old Testament and in the New, God has promised and declared, that He is going to intervene, perform the miracle that needs to be performed, and do whatever needs to be done in order that Jesus Christ may stand and be honored in all His glory as the Savior of the world (John 4:42). "God sent not His Son into the world to condemn the world; but that the world through Him might be saved" (John 3:17). "The Father sent the Son to be the Savior of the world" (1 John 4:14).

The reason that this great truth of divine intervention is unknown and unappreciated is because that men have been blinded by the idea that when God acts it is only in wrath, and the idea that God's next great act is the removal of all His people from earth. This is called "the rapture", a term not found in the Scripture. Of this it can be said that it would not help the world at all. It would only compound its miseries. God's people are not the cause of the world's ills, and it would not help if we were all removed.

Others, ignoring altogether the divine order and timetables, are blinded by making the second coming of Christ to be the next great event. Those who face up to all that Scripture has revealed in regard to the second advent know that this would not help the world at all, since it is emphatically declared that when Jesus Christ returns He comes "in flaming fire taking vengeance on them that know not God, and that obey not the gospel of our Lord Jesus Christ" (2 Thess. 1:8). And since these shall be punished with "everlasting destruction from the presence of the Lord and from the glory of His power" (2 Thess. 1:9), we can truthfully say that the worst thing that could happen to mankind is for Christ to return while the world is in its present condition. There are today so few who know God and fewer still who obey the gospel of Jesus Christ that the overwhelming majority of mankind would be wiped out.

Thus, if the people of God were removed by a rapture and the balance be destroyed, the earth would be swept clean of all inhabitants. I, for one, cannot believe this. Is this the best that the Savior of the world can do? No, He can intervene, He can inject Himself into the affairs of men, He can reverse the flow of history and turn it to Himself.

If we take our stand upon the promises of God, if we believe He will do what He has said He will do, then divine intervention will become a positive part of our faith and it will become our blessed hope. Let us consider a few of these promises that are found by the hundreds. They begin to appear in the Psalms, a sadly neglected book in our day.

All the ends of the world shall remember and turn unto the LORD: and all the kindreds of the nations shall worship before Thee. For the kingdom is the LORD'S: and He is the governor among the nations. Psalms 22:27,28.

This passage is both a promise and a prophecy. In its interpretation we need to recognize that "All the ends of the world" means all the people of the earth, even those living in remote places. "Shall remember" means that a communication direct from God will be imprinted on their minds. "And turn unto the Lord" means they will be turned unto the Lord. This reverses mankind's attitude toward God that began with the entrance of sin and will persist until God turns him around. "All the kindreds of the nations" means the different kinds of families or people that make up a nation. These have ever been a source of strife and conflict, but after God intervenes they are seen bowing before Jehovah. This is accomplished not by the minority triumphing over the majority nor by the majority subjecting the minority, but by all being brought to acknowledge the kingship of Jehovah.

"For the kingdom is the Lord's" means the government belongs to Jehovah. In order for this to be true, He will have to take to Himself His great power and govern. When He assumes sovereignty, then that which is true by right (de jure) will be true in fact (de facto). He will then be the governor among the nations. This entire passage speaks of divine intervention. This is what the world needs now. And just think how much better this would be than for God to take all His people out of the world and destroy those who are left.

Another great promise, entirely ignored by most expositors because it does not fit into their ideas of the second coming of Christ, is found in Psalm 64. In this remarkable Psalm there is presented a picture of great wickedness that is described as an "insurrection of the workers of iniquity," a phrase that perfectly describes what we are witnessing on earth today. This insurrection is stopped by divine intervention, and this is promised in a declaration that is as important as any promise in God's Word:

But God shall shoot at them with an arrow; suddenly shall they be wounded. Psalm 64:7.

This arrow is God's truth. It will make known who God is and what God is. It will reveal to all men His attitude toward all iniquity. The result of this divine action is declared. The workers of iniquity will lash themselves with their own tongues. A flood of self-condemnation will flow from their lips (Psa. 64:8). A universal awe and recognition of God will come upon all mankind. They will unitedly declare that this is a work of God. They will logically consider the work He has done. The righteous will be glad in the Lord. They will trust in Him, and all the upright in heart shall glory (Psa. 64:9,10). Read this Psalm. Memorize it. Bind it to your heart. This is our hope. This is our blessed hope. It will become your hope if you incorporate into your thinking God's message in this Psalm.

Promises of divine intervention at a time when iniquity is about to triumph are so numerous that it is difficult to decide which ones to present in the space of this study. However, one of the most emphatic ones is to be found in Isaiah 59:19. In this passage which begins by presenting the results of divine action we find then the promise, "When the enemy shall come in like a flood, the Spirit of the Lord shall lift up a standard against him."

It should be noted here that this is a great work of the Holy Spirit, and it is not the personal return of Christ to the earth. All who examine this passage will have to admit that the words that speak of the enemy coming in like a flood are most applicable to the present time. Every day we are witnessing the onrush of diabolical evils which preceding generations would have said were impossible for civilized men. What the world needs now is divine action that will stop this flood. Divine intervention is our present and most positive need. We need to pray:

Arise, O God, plead Thine own cause: remember how the foolish man reproacheth Thee daily. Forget not the voice of Thine enemies: the tumult of those who rise up against Thee increaseth continually. Psalm 74:22,23.

The SEED and BREAD Bible-Study leaflets are published as often as time and means permit and are sent free to all names on THE WORD OF TRUTH MINISTRY mailing list. Send us your name. There will be no obligation, solicitation, or visitation. Additional copies of any issue available on request.   ISSUE NO. 15

SEED & BREAD

FOR THE SOWER   ISA. 55:10   FOR THE EATER

BRIEF BIBLICAL MESSAGES

FROM

THE WORD OF TRUTH MINISTRY

339 South Orange Drive, Los Angeles, Cal. 90036

Otis Q. Sellers, Bible Teacher

CHARACTER OF THE LAST DAYS

In Issue No. 14 I set forth my conviction that the "last days" set forth in 2 Timothy 3:1 are the concluding days of God's present dispensation of grace. It was further stated that this segment of time is characterized by twenty-one specific manifestations of unusual wickedness and that the appearance of these evils in concert and intensity will demonstrate to the believer in God's Word that we are living in the last days of the present evil eon. In this study we will together examine these twenty-one social conditions that make up the syndrome of the last days. The reader should have his Bible open to the third chapter of 2 Timothy.

1. PERILOUS TIMES. The word translated "perilous" here is *chalepos*. It is found in the New Testament only here and in Matt. 8:28 where it is translated "fierce." It could be literally translated "dangerously violent." If one is discerning and sensitive all he needs to do is to read a summary of the news for any week and he will say, "These are dangerously violent times."

2. LOVERS OF THEIR OWN SELVES. These five words are but one in the Greek, *philautos*, which means self-lovers, and it describes those who care unduly or supremely for themselves and who feel that any desire within themselves justifies any moral action.

3. COVETOUS. The Greek word here is *philarguros*. It means lovers of money, but more specifically means a lover of silver. The love of money and especially the love of silver is a prominent characteristic of men throughout the world today. Its manifestation is especially seen in the great rash of gambling that is prevalent everywhere.

4. BOASTERS. The Greek word used here (*alazones*) has to do with those who speak and think more of themselves than the reality justifies. It speaks of the ostentatious, the empty pretenders, those given to pretentious parades. This characteristic is seen in most religions today. A whole book has been written on this characteristic by Vance Packard under title of *The Status Seekers*.

5. PROUD. The word here is *huperphanoi*. It means haughty, arrogant, a disposition to take to oneself more honor than is warranted or justly due. This type of person abounds in society today. Many world leaders are afflicted with this malady.

6. BLASPHEMERS. The Greek word *blasphemoi* means a calumniator, one who accuses falsely and maliciously, one who seeks by aspersion and villification to destroy the name or reputation of another. This is now normal practice in political warfare. It is the chief tool of fanatical extremists.

7. DISOBEDIENT TO PARENTS. The Greek word translated "disobedient" here is *apeithēs*. It means to be stubborn or unpersuadable, or, to be more specific, to be in obstinate opposition. There is no social condition that is quite as prominent and conspicuous in the world today as is the obstinate opposition of children toward parents. Books and articles by the thousands have been written on this phenomenon. Even the titles of these are quite revealing. *The Revolt of Youth, The Teen-Age Tyranny, The Rebellious Young, The Overthrow of Parental Authority*, and *Parents on the Run* are a sample. The stubborn rebellion of children is one of the frightful characteristics of our times.

8. UNTHANKFUL. The word here is *acharistoi*, which is the word for *grace* with the negating prefix *"a" (alpha)* before it. It means ungrateful, and it speaks of those who have no proper sense of feeling for favors received and no willingness to acknowledge or repay a benefit. However, this word may also mean without grace, and can be used to describe anything that lacks attractiveness or charm, so much of which is seen in the unkempt looks and crude manners of today.

9. UNHOLY. This is a very poor translation of the Greek word *anosios*, which means unbenign or malignant. Anyone is malignant who is actuated or characterized by virulent ill will or extreme malevolence. This word describes those who are disposed to do harm, to inflict suffering, or ot cause distress. There are so many of this kind today that it is a cause of anxiety to legislators, educators, peace officers, and parents. The cry of "Hate, Hate," is rampant in many lands.

10. WITHOUT NATURAL AFFECTION. These three words are one *(astrogos)* in the Greek. It means calloused, hardened in sensibility and feeling. Every case of child abuse and every abortion gives testimony to the prevalence of this condition.

11. TRUCEBREAKERS. This is a very poor translation of *aspondos*, which means implacable, and is so translated in its only other occurrence in Rom. 1:31. It has reference to those who are not satisfied until they have done their worst. Such people are devoid of any pity or feeling that would cause them to relent and restrain through compassion the fury or violence of their rage, hatred, or hostility. In the commission of crimes, more people are being beaten, stomped, or kicked to death than has ever been

known in the recorded history of mankind.

12. FALSE ACCUSERS. The word here is _diabolos_, which is probably familiar even to those who know no Greek. It is translated "devil" in thirty-five out of thirty-eight occurrences in the New Testament. It means a slanderer, one who speaks evil for the purpose of injuring and without regard for the truth. However the word _devil_ seems to properly characterize many men today when their acts are considered.

13. INCONTINENT. A continent person is one who exercises restraint in the indulgences of desires. The incontinent are those who constrain no desire, particularly the sexual desire. The Greek word _akrates_ means without self control or uncontrollable. This is seen everywhere today in alcoholism, compulsive gambling, impulsive killings, and especially in the great wave of unrestrained sexual indulgence that is now sweeping the world.

14. FIERCE. The word _anēmēros_ means brutal, inhuman, cruel. Civilization boasts of its long and gradual rise from a savage state, but at present it is faced with a truly savage spirit among men. The violence that is reported daily in the news is proof of this.

15. DESPISERS OF THOSE THAT ARE GOOD. These six words are only one in the Greek, _aphilagathos_. It means averse to the good or despisers of goodness. This describes perfectly all who would destroy every moral landmark and principle simply because they have no relish for that which is good. They "call evil good, and good evil; they put darkness for light, and light for darkness; they put bitter for sweet, and sweet for bitter," as the prophet Isaiah (5:20) so graphically declares it. On every hand today we find those who heartily approve wicked practices. Those who despise good are never neutral. They love wickedness.

16. TRAITORS. The Greek word _prodotēs_ used here can best be understood when we consider that it is used to describe Judas Iscariot in Luke 6:16. It has reference to all who today betray the Lord, His word, and His work.

17. HEADY. Rash or headstrong is the meaning of the word _propetēs_ which is used here. It means imprudent hastiness in word or action. It describes those who rush imprudently in pursuit of their own will. It is seen in the rush of the young to get married, and the rush of the married for divorce; in the sudden changes of belief, and precipitate disavowals of God and Christ. We see it in mobs, in riots, and in revolts. We see it in nations that are seized with a sudden passion for war that none can explain.

18. HIGHMINDED. The Greek word here is _tuphoomai_. It means conceited, but it has also the meaning of beclouded or besotted, as when something has made one blindly or stupidly foolish. This may have reference to those whose minds are deranged by the use of drugs. But it may have to do with the multitudes whose minds have become so beclouded and besotted by sin that they cannot think clearly in regard to any matter.

19. LOVERS OF PLEASURE. The Greek word for this characteristic is *philēdonos,* and the full description is that they are "lovers of pleasure more than lovers of God." Who could be so blind as to deny this manifest and extraordinary development seen everywhere today, pleasure-loving more than God-loving? A more accurate description of man's present attitude could hardly be given. The love of pleasure is a social characteristic of the present time.

20. HAVING THE FORM OF GODLINESS, BUT DENYING THE POWER THEREOF. The greatest religion on earth today is unbiblical and unspiritual Christianity, in which the forms of godliness predominate while the power of godliness is denied. Among professing Christians there is a total ignorance of everything that is Biblical. The prevailing view today is that it is important to have faith but that it does not matter much in what or in whom.

21. THE JANNES AND JAMBRES DECEPTION. These two appear in a lengthy statement (2 Tim. 3:6-8) and they have reference to the two magicians who stood before Pharaoh and reproduced the same miracles that Moses produced in confirmation of his divine mission and credentials. Everywhere today we find miracle workers who claim that they are acting in behalf of God in the works they are doing. They loudly proclaim their belief in miracles but will never be heard to proclaim their belief in the divine statement that there is one mediator between God and men, the man Christ Jesus.

The twenty-one characteristics that have been set forth are in no way intended to be signs of the second coming of Jesus Christ. They are the signs of the last days of God's long display of grace. They do not tell us that Christ is coming soon, but they do tell us that we are in the closing days of the present dispensation. The second coming of Christ is not next. The next act of God is to intervene and inject Himself into the affairs of men and of nations. In this passage this act of intervention is set forth in the words, "But they shall proceed no further." Evil men are going to be stopped. May God speed the day.

The SEED and BREAD Bible-Study leaflets are published as often as time and means permit and are sent free to all names on THE WORD OF TRUTH MINISTRY mailing list. Send us your name. There will be no obligation, solicitation, or visitation. Additional copies of any issue available on request.   ISSUE NO. 16

SEED & BREAD

FOR THE SOWER   ISA. 55:10   FOR THE EATER

BRIEF BIBLICAL MESSAGES
FROM

THE WORD OF TRUTH MINISTRY

339 South Orange Drive, Los Angeles, Cal. 90036

Otis Q. Sellers, Bible Teacher

THE ONE MEDIATOR

Some truths declared in the Bible are dispensational. They apply only to certain periods of time. Other truths are everlasting. They have been true from the moment they were revealed and always will be true. They are not subject to dispensational changes. The present-day believer in the Lord Jesus Christ should always be seeking out God's distinctive truths for today. His goal should ever be "to be established in the present truth" (2 Pet. 1:12).

Of all the truths in God's Word that must be classified as present truth, there is none more important than that declared by Paul when he proclaimed "one mediator between God and men, the man Christ Jesus" (1 Tim. 2:5). This is a distinct truth that is true only in the dispensation of the grace of God. It was not true before Paul's great declaration in Acts 28:28 (See Issue No. 11), it is true now, and it will not be true in the coming dispensation of God's government.

The great truth of one mediator between God and men has never been emphasized as it should be. It has not been followed out to all its conclusions. The writings of men will be searched in vain for even one interpretation which allows this great declaration to mean what it specifically says. This is probably due to the fact that the majority who seek to serve God in some capacity would like to believe that they are mediators in some respect. They strike the pose and give out the idea that they enjoy some mediatorial position. Thus with so many thinking that they are mediators and multitudes desiring them to so be, the result is indescribable confusion. God's emphatic declaration that there is now only one mediator denies the proud claims and wishes of so many that it will be believed and received by very few.

Honesty in interpretation demands that we define the word *mediator* and that we do this by means of its usage in the Word of God. There are many who stultify the truth here by making a mediator to be a god or a savior. This is not true. A mediator is always between two parties, but a savior need not be. This truth is expressly declared in Gal. 3:20 where we are told that "a mediator is not a mediator of one." A passerby rescuing a child who has fallen into deep water becomes a savior, but not a mediator. He did not act between two parties.

The Greek word for "mediator" is *mesites*. It is found six times in the New Testament and means one in the middle between two parties who acts as a transmitter. In fact transmission is the most important idea in this word. Most lexicons say that its means "one in the middle between two parties that are at variance," but this idea of "variance" is an unwarranted addition that is refuted by its usage in the New Testament.

In Gal. 3:19 we are told that the law which was given to Israel at Mount Sinai was "ordained by angels in the hands of a mediator." This mediator was Moses. He transmitted God's commandments to Israel at a time when there was no variance between God and this people. He said to them when He proposed the covenant: "Ye have seen what I did unto the Egyptians, and how I bare you on eagles wings and brought you unto Myself" (Exo. 19:4). These words reveal the closeness of their relationship at that time. Furthermore, if *mediator* means one who operates between two parties at variance, then Jesus Christ is not the mediator of those who have been reconciled to God.

Beyond all question, the Word of God declares that Moses was a mediator between God and Israel. He transmitted the law from God to Israel and afterward acted as an arbiter between the two. Later when Aaron became the high priest and was the only man who could perform certain services in relationship with God, he too became a mediator. These things being true, it would have been a falsehood to have proclaimed at that time "one mediator between God and men." This was not truth at that time.

In the days of the Lord Jesus upon the earth we find the mediatorial position of the twelve Apostles emphasized when He said to them, "He that receiveth you receiveth Me" (Matt. 10:40). Later He said to them, "I will give you the keys to the kingdom of heaven: and whatsoever thou shalt bind on earth shall be bound in heaven: and whatsoever thou shalt loose on earth will be loosed in heaven" (Matt. 16:19). When this promise became a reality He breathed on them and said, "Receive ye the Holy Spirit: whose soever sins ye remit, they are remitted unto them; and whose soever sins ye retain, they are retained" (John 20:22,23). If words mean anything, these words established them as mediators between God and men. They were in the middle as transmitters of both good and ill from God. The great truth of "one mediator" was evidently not truth for that time.

We see this mediatorial power at work in Acts 3:1-8 when Peter said to the lame man who had never walked, "I have no silver or gold to give to you, but that which I do have I transmit to you. In the name of Jesus Christ the Nazarene, Walk!" His words and his acts were those of a mediator. The blessing of healing and health flowed out of God in Christ and down through Peter to this lame man.

Another clear example of men acting as mediators is seen in Acts 8: 12-17. After Philip's successful ministry in Samaria, the Apostles at Jerusalem sent Peter and John to these new converts. After praying for these men, we are told "they laid their hands on them and they received the Holy Spirit." These Apostles were not originators. They were the transmitters of this gift of God.

The chief characteristic of the thirty-three year period of which the Books of Acts is the history was the presence of many mediators between God and men. Every apostle, prophet, evangelist, herald, healer, miracle worker, and governor was a mediator. They received from God and transmitted it to men. To have proclaimed the truth of "one mediator between God and men" in that thirty-three year period would have been to proclaim a lie and deny the very work that God was doing.

The greatest of all human mediators in the Acts period was the Apostle Paul, the very one who later proclaimed the great truth of "one mediator between God and men." This paradox in his life cannot be explained unless the Acts 28:28 dispensational change is recognized. After Paul's conversion God declared of him, "He is a chosen vessel unto Me, to bear My name before both the nations and their kings, also the sons of Israel" (Acts 9:15). If ever any man was placed in the middle to transmit the inspired message from God to men, it was this man Paul. Later he insists that his mediatorial position be recognized when he says, "Inasmuch as I am the apostle (commissioned one) to the nations, I magnify my office" (Rom. 11:13). Again Paul puts the Roman Christians in mind of his mediatorial position when he says: "That I should be the minister of Jesus Christ to the nations, ministering (acting as a priest of) the gospel of God, that the offering up of the nations might be acceptable, being sanctified by the Holy Spirit" (Rom. 15:16).

The truth of "one mediator between God and men, the man Christ Jesus" provides us with a positive key to the right division of the word of truth. In the Acts period every believing Israelite became a mediator in some manner. Paul's entire ministry in that time was one of receiving the message and transmitting it to men (1 Thess. 2:13). He spoke the inspired word as it was given by God. All of this ceased at Acts 28:28, and its cessation was confirmed when he announced the present truth of one mediator.

The truth of "one mediator" also provides a criterion, a most positive touchstone, in judging the claims of men today. Any man who in any manner assumes the mediatorial position, no matter how small, is out of the will of God. His assumption is a positive denial of this great truth, and in turn this truth is a denial of his assumption. "Let God be true, but every man a liar," certainly applies here (Rom. 3:4).

The mediatorial position is assumed today by all who claim the gift of healing. "I cannot heal you, it is God that heals you through me," is the proud claim made by these self-appointed mediators. Oral Roberts says that God revealed to him that the power to heal would be in his right hand. By this claim he makes his hand to be the mediator, the transmitter of God's gift of health. His claim is false when judged in the light of the great truth of "one mediator between God and men."

Some may point out that there is no word for "between" in the original, and that it should read "one mediator of God and men." This is true, but it changes it not at all. The idea of "between" is inherent in the Greek word *mesites* and we can best say it in English by the words "mediator between."

Others will point out the fact that Paul continued to receive the inspired word after Acts 28:28. This is also true, but it was not a direct transmission from God through Paul to men as it so often was in the Acts period. It was God transmitting His words through Paul to a written oracle.

The great truth of "one mediator between God and men" tells us why there is no angelic ministry today. The services of angels in behalf of mankind were quite prominent in the Acts period (Acts 1:10; 5:19; 10:3, 12:7, 27:23). Angelic ministry came to an end at Acts 28:28. At present the believer is shut up to Jesus Christ and to Him alone. We must find Him to be all-sufficient and find our completeness in Him (Col. 2:10).

Why turn to the spirits that peep and mutter and try to find in them the transmission of Gods light and truth? Why turn to the sun, moon, planets, and stars and place them in the mediatorial position as the astrologers are doing today? Why turn to the dead who know not anything (Ecc. 9:5) and seek to place them as transmitters of God's truth to you? All these practices are shown to be false by the truth of one mediator between God and men, the man Christ Jesus. Let us do nothing which by word or deed denies this great truth.

The SEED and BREAD Bible-Study leaflets are published as often as time and means permit and are sent free to all names on THE WORD OF TRUTH MINISTRY mailing list. Send us your name. There will be no obligation, solicitation, or visitation. Additional copies of any issue available on request.   ISSUE NO. 17

SEED & BREAD

FOR THE SOWER   ISA. 55:10   FOR THE EATER

BRIEF BIBLICAL MESSAGES
FROM
THE WORD OF TRUTH MINISTRY

339 South Orange Drive, Los Angeles, Cal. 90036

Otis Q. Sellers, Bible Teacher

JESUS ONLY

On the Mount of Transfiguration when Peter saw the Lord Jesus standing with Moses and Elijah, he suggested that a tabernacle be built for each, probably hoping that the scene would become a permanent one. By so doing he foolishly placed Moses and Elijah in the same exalted company as the Lord Jesus. These two men were probably venerated by Peter, and rightly so, for Moses had been Israel's great mediator and law giver, and Elijah was the principal and best-known prophet. But when Peter tried to give them a place of importance alongside of the Lord Jesus, they disappeared from view and he saw no man save JESUS ONLY. The recording of this event in the Word of God provides a lesson that teaches every man that no matter how great or important a thing may be by itself, there is nothing that is important when placed with or alongside the Lord Jesus Christ. Thus we are taught the all-sufficiency of the Lord of glory.

Has the reader ever come to that place in his Christian experience where all else disappeared from the scene and he saw no man or no thing save JESUS ONLY? I do not speak of an actual vision such as Peter saw. I speak of a truth, an actual realization of the mind and heart, an experience which is the need of all who seek to know the Christ revealed in the Word of God.

Blessed indeed is the believer whom God has led into the experience and reality of seeing no man or no thing save JESUS ONLY. Few there are who have entered into this great truth. The overwhelming majority of those who profess faith in Christ have no conception of Christ alone. They cannot think of Him except in connection with something else or someone else. They justify their attitudes by arguments concerning the importance of these things or the veneration in which they are held. However, in spite of all such arguments, these people need to learn that nothing is of any importance when man tries to essentially link it up with Christ. They need to be brought in truth to that place that God brought Peter, James, and John in reality, where all else vanishes from sight and they see no man save JESUS ONLY.

On every hand we find those who profess faith in Jesus Christ and who avow their love for Him but who have no conception of anyone being related to Christ apart from being related to a church of some kind. In fact, to them, to be related to a church is to be related to Christ, and not to be related to a church is not to be related to Him. They accept a man's relationship to a church, just any church, as conclusive evidence of his connection with Christ, never even considering that he may have joined the church for business reasons. They reject any man's avowal of faith in Christ if he does not have his name on some church roll. The simple, honest confession, "I am a believer in and follower of the Lord Jesus Christ," is always met with the question, "What denomination?" If one tries to tell them of a relationship with Jesus Christ that has no connection whatsoever with any church, they regard him as an ignorant heathen who has never been told how men receive Christ.

These deluded people believe that one is joined to Christ when he joins a church. They make the church to be the mediator between man and Christ. To them, to quit the church is to give up Christ and to return to the church is to return to Christ.

All such ideas are delusions created in the mind of men by Satan so that Jesus Christ will never have the preeminence in their lives. He will never be the all-sufficient One, but must always be associated with something else in His person and work. Satan would make men think that God has placed something between the sinner and the Savior — an institution or organization that must also be accepted in order to receive Christ.

Upon the basis of the truth that is set forth in the Word of God, I do not hesitate to emphatically declare that the believer in and follower of the Lord Jesus Christ can bear the closest possible relationship to Him, he can enjoy the fullest possible fellowship with Him, he can feast upon His word and witness to His truth wholly apart from ever passing through the doors of anything called a church, chapel, or mission. Furthermore, he can maintain a true and acceptable worship of God apart from the services of any church. God did not say that He was to be worshipped "in Spirit and in truth and in a church." He still seeks for those who will worship Him in Spirit and in truth, and He will never reject such worship even if the worshipper is doing it wholly apart from the institutions that call themselves churches.

There are those who insist that a church is positively essential if one is to make spiritual growth and progress. This is the judgment of those who recognize nothing as growth unless it be in the service of the church and nothing as spiritual unless it be in connection with some denomination. "Can one maintain a life, worship, and service that is acceptable to God apart from a church?" is the question often asked.

In answer to this, let us look at the facts. All will readily admit that CHRIST is essential to spiritual growth and progress, also to a life, worship and service that is acceptable to God. If a church is also essential to these things then it must be given a place of essentiality alongside the Lord Jesus. This would force us to admit that without a church, He is insufficient, thus ending once and for all the truth of the all-sufficiency of Jesus Christ.

Those who see something which they call a "church" as being essential to a God-honoring life, service, and worship have never stopped to consider just what a "church" is. I can get a dozen men, more or less, to join with me and quickly set up an organization that has just as much right to call itself a "church" as anything that convenes on this earth. I and those who join with me have just as much right to found a church as Wesley, Luther, or Campbell had. Furthermore, we can call our church by some grandiose title such as *Church of God, Church of Christ, True Church* or *Bible Church,* but it is nothing more than an organization that men brought into existence. And what is true of the whole church must also be true of the individuals that make it up. If no man is essential to the believer's life, worship, and service, then they do not become essential if they join together and call themselves a church.

I reject in its entirety this mystical deification of church as being something greater than the sum of their individual components. At their very best organizations called "churches" are nothing more than groups of men. Therefore, when anyone insists that acceptable life, service, and worship before God is dependent upon being identified with some group of men traveling under the name of a church, I repudiate his claim. Those who hold such ideas are destitute of any true vision of the person and work of the all-sufficient Christ. And this lack of true vision must be attributed to the fact that they have not come to that place in their knowledge and experience where no man or no thing is seen save JESUS ONLY. They have no conception of Christ apart from the churches of men. They have no vision of Christ apart from the churches of men. They have no vision of Christ apart from rituals, sacraments, and ordinances. They need to come to that place where nothing is any longer of importance when placed alongside of Christ. All things need to be eclipsed by the radiance of Christ preeminent.

Has the reader ever considered that most people when coming to Christ bring with themselves a collection of things which they are determined to attach to His holy person and work? A course of action is determined upon in advance of receiving Him; therefore, there can be no honest asking of the question, "Lord, what will You have me to do?" They have determined in advance what they are going to do. "I will receive Christ, then I will be baptized, become a member of the church, and observe the communion according to the rules of my denomination," is usually their predetermined course. Then they will declare that Christ gave them these things to be done. But the truth is that they came dragging these things along when they came to Him. And, worst of all, these things have become so important that without them

Christ would not be complete. Thus their attitude bars them from ever realizing and confessing the great truth declared by Paul, "And ye are complete in Him" (Col. 2:10).

As one who has given His life to the proclamation and presentation of Jesus Christ as the sinners' Savior and the believers' Lord, I have found again and again that the assertion of many that they trust in Christ is a false claim. Their real confidence is in the things that they have given a place of importance in connection with Him, such as their church, their baptism, and that ceremony they call "the Lord's supper." When a faith in Christ and a relationship to God is presented that is entirely separated from churches and ordinances, they show at once that they feel the great foundation stones upon which their faith rests are being removed. "You are taking away everything," they exclaim in fright. In answer I ask, "Have I taken Christ from you?" And often the look upon their faces declares that in their mind there is no relationship to Christ apart from these things. If these things were removed they feel they would be without hope. To them, Christ alone is not sufficient. They reject the position of any man who finds his completeness in Christ. The true follower of Jesus Christ must learn that neither the approval or disapproval of men has any meaning in the sight of God.

"Examine yourselves, whether ye be in the faith: prove your own selves" (2 Cor. 13:5) is a scriptural admonition that few seem willing to act upon. May I urge that this be done by the reader of these lines? Is your faith in Jesus Christ a simple and implicit belief in the record God has given of His Son? "He that has the Son has life" (1 John 5:12), is the monosyllabic testimony of Scripture. Do you have Him, or do you have only some things that are supposed to be related to Him? If in some way you should be stripped of all the externalities of religion, would you then have complete confidence that you are related to God through Jesus Christ? Could you truthfully say, "I have that which perfectly satisfies my heart — I have Christ?"

The SEED and BREAD Bible-Study leaflets are published as often as time and means permit and are sent free to all names on THE WORD OF TRUTH MINISTRY mailing list. Send us your name. There will be no obligation, solicitation, or visitation. Additional copies of any issue available on request.   ISSUE NO. 18

SEED & BREAD

FOR THE SOWER ISA. 55:10 FOR THE EATER

BRIEF BIBLICAL MESSAGES

FROM

THE WORD OF TRUTH MINISTRY

339 South Orange Drive, Los Angeles, Cal. 90036

Otis Q. Sellers, Bible Teacher

THE CHARISMATIC DISPENSATION

The failure of those who handle God's Word to distinguish between the charismatic dispensation and the present dispensation of the grace of God has resulted in great confusion. The Greek word *charisma* has to do with divine favor that is manifested as a special gift, and there is one period of time in sacred history that was so completely characterized by these gifts that it can well be called the charismatic dispensation. This period of time began with the resurrection of Jesus Christ and continued until Paul's great pronouncement recorded in Acts 28:28. It is the thirty-three years of which the Book of Acts is the history, and the foundation was laid for it in the words of the Lord Jesus to His eleven disciples (Mark 16:14).

And He said unto them, Go ye into all the world, and preach the gospel to every creature. He that believeth and is baptized shall be saved; and he that believeth not shall be damned. And these signs shall follow them that believe; In My name shall they cast out devils; they shall speak with new tongues; they shall take up serpents; and if they drink any deadly thing, it shall not hurt them; they shall lay hands on the sick, and they shall recover. Mark 16:15-18.

A statement by statement examination of this passage will show that it was in full force and operative during the Acts period. It declares God's method of dealing with His people at that time. It produced the charismatic dispensation.

"Go ye into all the world and preach the gospel to every creature." This commission was performed and fulfilled to the letter in the thirty-three years that followed the resurrection of Jesus Christ. Some will quibble about this, but we who make a practice of taking God at His Word and thinking accordingly will take our stand upon its statements. "And they went forth and preached every where" (Mark 16:20). "Therefore they that were scattered abroad went every where preaching the word" (Acts 8:4). These statements settle the matter for all who settle things by the Word of God. See Issue No. 13 for a fuller study of this commission.

"He that believeth and is baptized shall be saved." This is a divine declaration made with all the precision that characterizes divine things. And all this is ruined when men read the water ritual into the word *baptize*. There is a ritual called "baptism" and there is a reality called "baptism," and the ritual is not in view in these words. Very few know anything about the reality which is the most important meaning of the word *baptism*.

"And these signs shall follow them that believe." These words were spoken to the eleven disciples concerning all who believe. Not the apostles only but all who believed. The Greek word translated "follow" here is a forceful word that means to fully follow or to follow so as to be parallel with. These signs were the divine accreditation of the faith of all who believed during the charismatic dispensation. There were no secret believers in that day. No believer's life was "hid with Christ in God" as ours is today. Faith was a manifest thing that was evident to all.

"In My name shall they cast out devils." The divine activity at that time, the purpose that was being fulfilled, and the short time in which it was to be fully accomplished (Rom. 9:28) brought forth intense demonic activity in opposition to all that God was doing. The Lord said they would cast them out, and they did. When Philip, who was not one of the twelve, proclaimed Christ in Samaria, his word was confirmed by such miracles. "For unclean spirits, crying with a loud voice, came out of many that were possessed with them; and many taken with palsies, and that were lame, were healed" (Acts 8:7).

"They shall speak with new tongues." This gift was one of the great features of the charismatic dispensation. It was the God-given ability to speak another language as if it were one's native tongue. This happened first on the day of Pentecost when men out of fifteen or more countries bewilderedly confessed that they were hearing "every man in our own tongue wherein we were born" (Acts 2:8). These words tell us that the 120 believers on the day of Pentecost were able to freely and fluently speak seventeen languages and dialects. "We do hear them speak in our tongues the wonderful works of God" (Acts 2:11).

"They shall take up serpents." Poisonous snakes abounded in Palestine, Syria, and Sinai. As men walked about bare-legged and in sandals, their feet and legs were the common targets of these vipers. Even before this they had been promised power to tread on serpents and scorpions (Luke 10:19). Here they were told that they could pick up serpents. This was a most valuable and relevant power to those whose lives would be given to continuous travel, always walking, most the time sleeping in the open in snake-infested areas, wrapped only in their own garments or any other covering they carried along. The warmth of their bodies was a constant invitation to vipers to crawl in. If this happened they were in no danger. All they needed to do was pick it up and cast it aside.

A record concerning this is found in Acts 28:3-6. There we read that Paul and his traveling companions, shipwrecked on the Isle of

Melita, were warming themselves at a fire that had been kindled. When he had gathered a bundle of sticks and laid them on the fire, a viper came out of the heat and fastened on his hand. The inhabitants of the island knew the poisonous nature of this serpent and expected that the venom would cause swelling at once and that in a short time he would be dead. But Paul shook off the serpent into the fire and felt no harm. This was a normal experience in the charismatic dispensation, and this incident, happening when it did is proof that the dispensation under which such things were normal extended to and was in full force until the close of the Acts period.

"**And if they drink any deadly thing it shall not hurt them.**" Poisoning was the favorite method of assassination at the time these words were spoken. It is quite probable that when the Pharisees held a council against Jesus as to "how they might destroy Him" (Matt. 12:14) assassination by means of poisoning was probably suggested. In that time if poison could be secretly administered it resulted in a crime that could not be detected, there being no such thing as autopsies or chemical analysis of the contents of the stomach. The believers of the Acts period were the objects of the most malignant, Satan-generated hatred that men have ever known. Many would have gladly murdered them, thinking they were serving God by so doing (John 16:2).

It should be noted here that all other items in this declaration are prefaced by the positive words "they shall," while this one begins with the hypothetical words "if they shall." There is no record that they did drink any deadly poisons, and if they did no one would have known it save those who had secretly administered it. The disciples in the charismatic dispensation were free from any danger of death by this common form of assassination.

"**They shall lay hands on the sick, and they shall recover.**" Note it does not say "pray for the sick" as that is another matter. They laid hands on the sick, for they were performing a mediatorial service, and the sick recovered. Faith on the part of those who were healed was not a prerequisite. See Acts 28:7-9. There were no gimmicks, false claims, or deceitful practices. They did not pitch tents, organize choirs, or work up the people into frenzied emotional states. They never failed. They simply laid hands on the sick and the sick recovered

The commission recorded in Mark 16:15-18 is the divine constitution of the charismatic dispensation. It is not applicable to the present dispensation of the grace of God. It was the principles embodied in this declaration that gave the Acts period its peculiar character, one that is unique in all sacred history. The charismatic dispensation fulfilled its purpose, ran its glorious course and came to an end by Paul's pronouncement in Acts 28:28 (See Issue No. 11). This pronouncement brought an end to Paul's peculiar apostolic ministry, even though under new and special commissions he wrote seven epistles after that time.

Among all the gifted men of the Acts period there was none who exceeded the Apostle Paul. He was "not a whit behind the very chiefest apostles" (2 Cor. 11:5). His ability to heal the sick was demonstrated over and over. God even wrought special miracles by the hand of Paul (Acts 19:11) so that "from his body were brought unto the sick handkerchiefs or aprons, and the diseases departed from them, and the evil spirits went out of them" (Acts 19:12). These miracles were the credentials of his apostleship and it is evident that they did not continue after Acts 28:28. There is no reference to such things in the epistles written after this time. These are Ephesians, Philippians, Colossians, First Timothy, Second Timothy, and Philemon. It is in the epistles that we find positive evidence of the great change.

In Philippians 2:25-30 Paul speaks of Epaphroditus and describes him in such glowing and affectionate terms as "my brother, and companion in labor, and fellow soldier." The believers in Philippi had sent him with money for Paul, also to remain with him and look after his needs. However, after his arrival in Rome he became ill with a sickness that Paul describes as being "nigh unto death," and if anyone should ever have been healed by Paul it was this man Epaphroditus. But there was no miraculous healing. His illness followed about the same course as ours do today. It took prayer, time, rest, and good care before he was able to return to Philippi.

Another clear evidence of a dispensational change is found in Paul's advice to Timothy set forth in 1 Tim. 5:23. "Drink no longer water, but use a little wine for thy stomach's sake and thine often infirmities." This passage has long been the security blanket of the so-called "social drinker," but he fails to see the real lesson it teaches. Epaphroditus was with Paul when he took sick, but there was no attempt made to heal him by laying on hands. Timothy was at a distance, but Paul did not send him a handkerchief. In the charismatic dispensation, poison could not hurt Timothy, but here the bad water is a definite threat. Paul's advice that he use a little wine for his "often infirmities" (Gk. *asthenia*) needs to be compared with his healing of "diseases" (Gk. *asthenia*) on the Isle of Melita. Paul's advice is a lesson in dispensational truth, and it was never intended to be encouragement to incipient alcoholics.

In just about the last word he ever wrote by divine inspiration, Paul confesses that he had left Trophimus at Miletum sick (2 Tim. 4:20). This would have been unthinkable during the charismatic dispensation. Not so under the dispensation of the grace of God.

The SEED and BREAD Bible-Study leaflets are published as often as time and means permit and are sent free to all names on THE WORD OF TRUTH MINISTRY mailing list. Send us your name. There will be no obligation, solicitation, or visitation. Additional copies of any issue available on request.   ISSUE NO. 19

SEED & BREAD

FOR THE SOWER   ISA. 55:10   FOR THE EATER

BRIEF BIBLICAL MESSAGES
FROM
THE WORD OF TRUTH MINISTRY
339 South Orange Drive, Los Angeles, Cal. 90036

Otis Q. Sellers, Bible Teacher

THE JIGSAW PUZZLE OF PROPHECY

The title for this study comes from an article that appeared in *Christianity Today* which asks the question, "Is Prophecy a Jigsaw Puzzle?" The article is a review of seven recently published books that deal with the future. The reviewer's conclusion is that prophecy is indeed a jigsaw puzzle and that we cannot put it together in a well developed eschatological scheme because some of the pieces are missing. He feels that the variations in Matthew, Mark, and Luke "warn us that none of them have it all, and that, perhaps all of them put together may have omitted extremely vital pieces of information."

I certainly agree that prophecy is a jigsaw puzzle that God expects us to put together, and I also agree that so far as men are concerned many pieces are still missing, but I believe with all my heart that these pieces are in the Word of God waiting to be brought forth. As Bishop Butler has said, "It is not at all incredible, that a book, which has been so long in possession of mankind, should contain many truths as yet undiscovered."

Throughout my Christian experience I have believed this to be true and have given myself for more than a half century to the task of finding the missing truths that would make the prophetic puzzle fit together and that would serve as a key to prophetic interpretation. As a result of my studies I believe that I have found the missing piece that is the key that brings it all together. This is the truth that God is going to invade this earth by His Spirit and assume sovereignty over the earth and all men upon it, that Jesus Christ will govern this earth from His present place in heaven, and that all this will be before the second advent of Jesus Christ for the thousand years of His personal presence. This long period of time and all that takes place in it is the piece that is missing in all attempts to piece together the jigsaw of prophecy. Permit me to tell a little of how I arrived at this conviction.

During the first thirty years of my Christian life I was a diligent reader, student, and teacher of the Word of God. In all this I always proceeded from the conviction that God had spoken in His

Word and it was my supreme duty to know for myself what He had said. What He meant by what He said (the interpretation) would, I believed, come more easily and truly if I had a good degree of familiarity with the entire Word. At the same time I was an avid reader of the books on prophetic subjects that were produced by men who believed that the Bible is the inspired Word of God, especially men of that persuasion which can best be designated as the dispensational premillennial school of interpretation

At one time I became especially interested in the study of the seventieth week of Israel's Seventy Weeks as set forth in Daniel, chapter nine. This is that amazing period of seven years, the last half of which covers the period of the great tribulation. After much consideration I became convinced that this great drama could not be played out until the principal actor was in her proper place. This principal actor is the nation of Israel, restored to her land, with a rebuilt temple that would qualify as the temple of God, and a restored priesthood with the stamp of divine acceptance upon it. Furthermore, I became convinced that "the great tribulation" was to be a time of divine testing which would try every man that dwells upon the earth (Rev. 3:10). Then when I considered the state of men upon the earth today, their abject failure in all matters related to God, it seemed to me to be the height of folly to try that which is such an obvious failure.

Further study along these lines brought to me the conviction that there would have to be a great divine work in behalf of Israel before the great tribulation and before the second advent of Jesus Christ. If the man of sin seats himself in the temple of God (2 Thess. 2:4) and if he is destroyed by the blazing forth (*epiphaneia*) of the Lord's personal presence (*parousia*), then all this has to be true and in place before Jesus Christ returns to the earth.

At first the conviction that there would be a period of divine activity and blessing for Israel before the second advent of Jesus Christ was one that came out of necessity based upon what was required if many prophecies were ever fulfilled. I determined not to declare this conviction publicly until I could find ample Scripture for its support. Once I came upon the first passage that declared it, fifty more were found quickly and easily.

I was at this time trying to teach the minor prophets and had come to the second chapter of Hosea. There I found all the support that one who believes the Word could ask. The pertinent passage is Hosea 2:14-23 and the reader will now need to open his own Bible to this portion. It is preceded by a divine indictment of Israel because of her sins and a threat of severe punishment. Then the Lord tells what He will do after she has been punished. The picture is one of courtship and betrothal.

Jehovah declares that He will allure Israel. By this He means that He will make Himself alluring and desirable unto her, something any wise young man should do who seeks to win the maiden he desires. He will bring her into the wilderness, that is, into the place of separation, an ideal state if a man would win the heart of the one he loves. He will speak comfortably unto her, which means He will speak to her heart words of love in great tenderness. The results of such speaking to Israel on the part of Jehovah will be miraculous to say the least. This will produce "the Israel of God," a nation born in a day.

Jehovah declares that He will give her vineyards from thence. These "vineyards" signify material blessings, and the words "from thence" speak of both time and place. As to time it will be after God has spoken to her and won her back to Himself, after she has said, "I will go and return to my first husband; for then it was better with me than now" (Hos. 2:7). As to place it will be while she is in the wilderness, the place of separation from the nations, and wholly dependent upon God. The spiritual blessings come first and the material blessings follow.

These words declare the future of Israel, and all this is in advance of the great tribulation as is seen in the promise that Jehovah will give her "the valley of Achor for a door of hope." The name "Achor" means trouble (Josh. 7:24-26). When Irsael is in the place of blessing described in Hosea 2:15, she will look ahead and see the greatest pressure that the nation has ever known, a time of testing that will put to the test all who dwell upon the earth. This is a valley through which she must pass as she travels upon her foreordained way from the pre-advent kingdom to the thousand years of the personal presence of Christ. However, as she looks at it through eyes enlightened by the Spirit of God, this "valley of Achor" will be to her "a door of hope", and she shall sing there, as in the days of her youth, as in the day when she came up out of the land of Egypt (Hos. 2:15). "Happy is that people whose God is Jehovah" (Psa. 144:15).

It is the policy of many interpreters to take what they want of Scriptural statements concerning the second advent of Christ while ignoring plain and direct statements that would upset their prophetic theories. They make much of the second coming of Christ in 1 Thess. 4:16, and rightly so, but ignore altogether the plain statement made in 2 Thess. 1:7-10 that when Jesus Christ does return that He comes "in flaming fire taking vengeance on them that know not God and that obey not the gospel of our Lord Jesus Christ." It is further declared that these "shall be punished with everlasting destruction from the presence of the Lord and from the glory of His power." From this it can be seen that if the Lord should return as of today, the overwhelming majority of men upon the earth would be liable to the extreme penalty described in these words, and it would make impossible the fulfillment of many prophetic passages in the Old and New Testament, especially those that concern the nations.

In Psalm 67:4 we find one of the truly great prophetic promises that God has made.

O let the nations be glad and sing for joy; for thou shalt judge the peoples righteously, and govern the nations upon earth.

Here we have the positive promise that God will govern the nations upon earth, not just Israel, but all nations. Thus the question arises and demands an answer: Does He govern these nations after He has destroyed their people or before? And there can be only one answer. There is nothing left to govern after the people have been destroyed. Passages like this indicate a time of divine government before the return of Christ, and this government will be so successful that few indeed will need to be destroyed when He comes.

Yes, prophecy is indeed a jigsaw puzzle that we are expected to put together, but we cannot put it together unless we have all the pieces. The most important piece that is missing from present pictures of the future is a definite period of divine government that embraces the whole earth, every nation, and every man upon it. This government will become a reality when God speaks the word in heaven. All He needs to do is speak and every man on earth will know that from that moment forth he is under the government of God.

There are those who will insist that divine government of the earth does not begin until Jesus Christ returns and is personally present upon it. "You cannot have a kingdom without a king," is the oft repeated battle cry of those who hold this view.

What they are saying is that there can be no divine government over the earth as long as the Lord is in heaven. This is both false and foolish. In both the Old and New Testament God has emphatically declared that heaven is His throne and the earth is His footstool (Isa. 66:1, Acts 7:49). We can rest assured that when God governs this earth it will be from His throne and not from His footstool. There is the mistaken idea that Jesus Christ returns to the earth in order to govern it. This is not true. He comes back in order to be personally present in order to make a full revelation and disclosure of God.

The present dispensation of the grace of God is not going to continue forever God will fulfill His purpose in it and bring it to an end. It will be followed by a dispensation of divine government.

This is not ushered in by the second coming of Jesus Christ. It will begin when He decrees it in heaven. Psalm 46:6, Psalm 107:42.

(Note: A chart illustrating the truth declared above will be sent free to all who request it.)

The SEED and BREAD Bible-Study leaflets are published as often as time and means permit and are sent free to all names on THE WORD OF TRUTH MINISTRY mailing list. Send us your name. There will be no obligation, solicitation, or visitation. Additional copies of any issue available on request. ISSUE NO. 20

SEED & BREAD

FOR THE SOWER ISA. 55:10 FOR THE EATER

BRIEF BIBLICAL MESSAGES
FROM
THE WORD OF TRUTH MINISTRY
339 South Orange Drive, Los Angeles, Cal. 90036

Otis Q. Sellers, Bible Teacher

GOD OUR SAVIOR

"Christ Jesus came into the world to save sinners" (1 Tim. 1:15). "The Father sent the Son to be the Savior of the world" (1 John 4:14). These statements are true; they are from the inspired Word of God. However, the question is now whether this joint effort of the Father and the Son has fulfilled its purpose and become effective in my life, in your life. Can we honestly say in the language of Scripture, "God my Savior"?

There are no words that are more precious that can come from the lips of an individual than these words spoken in truth. They were spoken by Mary the mother of our Lord when she said in her beautiful magnificat: "My soul doth magnify the Lord, and my spirit hath rejoiced in God my Savior" (Luke 1:46,47). If one can in truth say, "God my Savior," he can rest assured that he has the ultimate Savior. There can be none that is better, none more perfect, none that can give better assurance of salvation. If God is our Savior then we are saved, and we can assert this as a fact that is founded upon the solid rock of God's Word. One can only feel sorry for those unstable souls who glory in His power as the Creator, but doubt His ability as a Savior.

The words "God our Savior" can well be said to be the most precious and most important in the Bible. The unsettled state of so many professing Christians is the result of never having fully entered into the meaning of these words. The lack of settled peace and confidence, so common among God's people, is the outcome of not appreciating and not believing the truth declared in them. We need to know Who the Savior is and what the Savior is before we can fully trust Him.

To fully appreciate the meaning of the words "God our Savior", we must approach them through the Old Testament. The prophet Isaiah is the one who most fully develops this theme. It was through him that Jehovah declared:

Ye are My witness, saith the LORD, and My servant whom I have chosen: that ye may know and believe Me, and understand that I am He: before Me there was no God formed, neither shall there be after Me. I, even I am the LORD (Jehovah); and beside Me there is no Savior. Isa. 43:10, 11.

In response to this declaration that there is no God but Jehovah and no Savior but Jehovah, let all who read these lines say, "It is truth" (Isa. 43:9). Let us remember that one becomes a believer by believing the truth that is at hand, even if it is the first truth that one has heard. There is no profit in disputing, in doubting, in arguing. There is no value in demanding that all truth be in hand before any is believed. God has spoken, and here we have a truth before us to be believed. There is no Savior but Jehovah, the God who is seen throughout the Old Testament. This great truth is repeated in the words of Jehovah in Isa. 45:21,22:

Tell ye, and bring them near; yea, let them take counsel together: who hath declared this from ancient time? who hath told it from that time? have not I the LORD (Jehovah)? and there is no God else beside Me; a just God and a Savior; there is none beside Me. Look unto Me, and be ye saved, all the ends of the earth: for I am God, and there is none else.

In these words we see God presenting Himself as the Savior, the one and only Savior, calling upon men to look to Him and be saved, even those living in the most remote places, which is what the idiomatic phrase "all the ends of the earth" really means. Thus this call is to all mankind, and if mankind as a whole does not respond, then let the individual look to Him and He will not be sent away empty handed.

If the majority rejects and if the minority is slow to believe, then let us break with both of them and believe as individuals in the Savior, in the salvation He provides, and in the declared way of obtaining both the Savior and salvation. Let us not follow a multitude to do evil (Ex. 23:2). For while this great offering of Jehovah Himself as the Savior was primarily to Israel and then to all mankind, it was also to the individual as will be seen in the passage that follows this offer:

Surely, shall *one* say, in the LORD have I righteousness and strength: even to Him shall *men* come; and all that are incensed against Him shall be ashamed. Isa. 45:24.

In the italicized word *one* in the above passage we have an attempt of the translators to express the singular in number which is what it is in the Hebrew text. But they did not follow through when they supplied the word *men* in the following clause. This is also singular and should read "shall *one* come".

The great truth that Jehovah was the only God and the only Savior was well known in Israel at that point of time when the New Testament begins. While there is evidence that they neglected most of the Old Testament, having made it void through their traditions, this was not so concerning the prophecy of Isaiah. This was the one scroll that would be found in the synagogue if they could afford only one portion.

When the Messiah was born in Bethlehem it was the specific instructions of the angel of the Lord that His parents should "call His name Jesus, for He shall save His people from their sins"

(Matt. 1:21). The name "Jesus" is the Greek form of the Hebrew name "Jehoshua" which means "Jehovah the Savior". From this His supposed father Joseph must have known that He was an unusual person, for this name was not given to Him to proclaim the fact that Jehovah saves, as in the case of others who bore it, but to emphasize the fact that One who bore it was Himself to do the saving. This is seen in the reason declared for giving it to Him. "For He shall save His people from their sins."

This is in harmony with the message proclaimed by the angels to the shepherds:

For unto you is born this day in the city of David a Savior, which is Christ the Lord. Luke 2:11.

This announcement must have created a dilemma for all who heard it since it announced a Savior which is Christ the Lord, but it is apparent it did not. The shepherds who first heard it said at once, "Let us now go even unto Bethlehem, and see this thing which is come to pass, which the Lord hath made known to us" (Luke 2:15). They faced no predicament of two Saviors for these humble men had light and faith which few have today. They knew that Jehovah of old had declared that He alone was the Savior and that there is no Savior but Him. Yet they faced no problem in receiving this babe born in Bethlehem as the Savior, something they could not have done if the one named Jesus was not Jehovah. However, this was the very truth announced by the angel, that this one born in Bethlehem was "Messiah Jehovah", which is what the Greek *Christos Kurios* actually means.

The people of Israel never had to face the dilemma of two Saviors, one the Jehovah of the Old Testament who declared that He was the only Savior, and Jesus Christ of the New Testament who is presented by the angels as the Savior and in turn presented Himself as such. Thus the faithful believed, just as we need to believe, that this One born in Bethlehem was in reality the Jehovah of the Old Testament. If not, then there are two who claim to be the Savior and one of them must be branded as an imposter. In fact Jesus should be rejected as such if He is not Jehovah. See Issue No. 2 for a fuller treatment of this important truth.

As we trace out further the theme of "God our Savior" through the New Testament we come to the testimony of the Apostle Paul who sets forth beyond all question that the God who is our Savior is the Lord Jesus Christ. In his epistle to Titus he speaks of "the commandment of God our Savior" (Titus 1:3) and in the same sentence speaks of "the Lord Jesus Christ our Savior" (Titus 1:4). Can it be that he is presenting two Saviors here? Certainly not. He would not be guilty of such a thought. God our Savior and the Lord Jesus Christ are one and the same. Any conception of God that does not recognize this is false and contrary to divine revelation.

It is quite evident that the Spirit of God desired to emphasize this truth since it is brought out again in the next chapter of this epistle. In Titus 2:10 he speaks of "God our Savior" and in the same sentence speaks of "the great God and our Savior Jesus Christ" (2:13). And as if to establish the truth by three witnesses, in Titus 3:4 he speaks of "the kindness and love of God our Savior" and in the same sentence speaks of "Jesus Christ our Savior". Truly our God is our Savior.

There is solid encouragement for every child of God in the realization of this great truth. The joy of salvation comes from knowing the One who is our Savior. Think what it means to be able to say that the Great Creator became our Savior. And if the Creator is not God, then who is God?

In Isaiah 44:24 the great Jehovah declares that He alone is the Creator, that He did it Himself, and no agents were involved. This truth is repeated in Isa. 45:12. Thus it is clear that the One called Jehovah (LORD) in Isaiah is the One called Elohim in Genesis 1:1, where we read, "In the beginning God (Elohim) created the heaven and the earth." Continuing in the Word we come to John 1:1 where one called the Word (Logos) is set before us, and we are told that "the Word (Logos) was God". And as a further means of identification we are told that, "All things were made by Him, and without Him was not anything made that was made" (John 1:3). Therefore, whether it is Elohim who is presented as the Creator in Genesis 1:1, or Jehovah who is declared to be the only Creator in Isaiah 45:12 or the Logos who is presented as the Creator in John 1:3, it is the same One. Then when we come to John 1:14 we are told that the Word (Logos) was made flesh and became a man upon this earth beheld by others. This is our Lord Christ Jesus, and this is our Savior. This is the One who fills the pages of God's book.

"Look unto Me and be ye saved, for I am God and there is none else" (Isa. 45:22) is the divine invitation. It was Jehovah who issued this bid, and by it He proclaimed that He alone is the Savior and that He wants men to be saved. "I am the way, the truth, and the life; no man cometh unto the Father, but by Me," is the declaration of the Lord Jesus. All who ever came to Jesus Christ came to God the Father, and no one has ever come to the Father save by the Son of God. "I and My Father are one", is His word concerning this. "Whosoever denieth the Son, the same has not the Father; but he that acknowledgeth the Son hath the Father also" (1 John 2:23).

I have already said that a man becomes a believer by believing the truth that is at hand. Let every reader of these lines go over the preceding paragraph once again and then ask himself if this is his belief. If so, he may have the right to say, "God my Savior".

The SEED and BREAD Bible-Study leaflets are published as often as time and means permit and are sent free to all names on THE WORD OF TRUTH MINISTRY mailing list. Send us your name. There will be no obligation, solicitation, or visitation. Additional copies of any issue available on request.   ISSUE NO. 21

SEED & BREAD

FOR THE SOWER   ISA. 55:10   FOR THE EATER

BRIEF BIBLICAL MESSAGES
FROM

THE WORD OF TRUTH MINISTRY

339 South Orange Drive, Los Angeles, Cal. 90036

Otis Q. Sellers, Bible Teacher

LET US GO ALSO

The mind of God was made known by the Apostle John when he said by divine inspiration, "I have no greater joy than to hear that my children walk in truth" (3 John 1:4). It should therefore be the earnest desire of every Christian to bring this joy to the heart of God. Truth, of course, is that which accords with the facts, and if facts are ignored we will never be found walking in the truth.

There are no records of the birth of Jesus Christ save that one which is found in the Word of God. Secular history knows nothing of this important event. All facts concerning it are to be found in the opening chapters of Matthew and Luke. Anything that is presented concerning the birth and childhood of Jesus Christ that is not found in these records is without foundation.

Those who read carefully the inspired history of the birth of the Savior will soon discover that the record of this event is somewhat different from that which is generally believed. The popular concept has been taken from the paintings of the old masters. They tried to assemble in one scene events and personages widely separated in time and place, treating them as if they were simultaneous.

The picture is familiar one: a stable, a manger, Mary and Joseph, domestic animals, a bright star shining over the building, shepherds with their staffs, three gaudily attired persons on their knees, with glittering crowns upon their heads, and in their extended hands a casket containing jewels upon which the eye of a babe, very precocious for one new born, is resting.

Scenes like this falsify the Word of God. Every creche (representation of the nativity scene) which I have ever seen proclaimed a falsehood. These have usurped the Biblical revelation, denying the record that God has given of His Son. If it were possible to turn back the hands of time for two thousand years so that we could be in Bethlehem as witnessses and observers of all that happened when Christ was born we would see a somewhat different scene. And if we were lovers of truth we would return to the twentieth century as earnest warriors against all worldly traditions concerning His birth that have made the truth of God void. However, we cannot turn back the hands of time and be in Bethlehem that night, but we can turn to that which is better yet than fallible human observation. We can go to the inspired record of all that happened then and there.

The shepherds when they learned of His birth said one to another, "Let us now go even unto Bethlehem, and see this thing which has come to pass" (Luke 2:15). And, led by the Spirit of God LET US GO ALSO, and by means of the sacred scriptures be in Bethlehem on the day when Christ was born. Let us learn anew the record God has given of the birth of His Son.

THE WITNESS OF LUKE

And it came to pass in those days that there went out a decree from Caesar Augustus, that all the world should be taxed. (And this taxing was first done when Cyrenius was governor of Syria.) And all went to be taxed every one into his own city. And Joseph also went up from Galilee, out of the city of Nazareth, into Judea, unto the city of David, which is called Bethlehem; (because he was of the house and lineage of David:) to be taxed with Mary his espoused wife, being great with child. And so it was, that, while they were there, the days were accomplished that she should be delivered. And she brought forth her firstborn son, and wrapped him in swaddling clothes, and laid Him in a manger; because there was no room for them in the Inn.

And there were in the same country shepherds abiding in the field, keeping watch over their flock by night. And lo, the angel of the Lord came upon them, and the glory of the Lord shone round about them; and they were sore afraid. And the angel said unto them, Fear not: for, behold, I bring you good tidings of great joy, which will be to all people. For unto you is born this day in the city of David a Savior, which is Christ the Lord. And this shall be a sign unto you; Ye shall find the babe wrapped in swaddling clothes, lying in a manger.

And suddenly there was with the angel a multitude of the heavenly host praising God, and saying, Glory to God in the highest, and on earth peace, good will toward men. And it came to pass, as the angels were gone away from them into heaven, the shepherds said one to another, LET US NOW GO EVEN UNTO BETHELEHEM, and see this thing which has come to pass, which the Lord hath made known unto us. And they came with haste, and found Mary and Joseph, and the babe lying in the manger. And when they had seen him, they made known abroad the saying which was told them concerning this child. And all they that heard it wondered at those things which were told them by the shepherds. But Mary kept all these things, and pondered them in her heart. Luke 2:1-19 *King James Version.*

This is the record as we have it from the inspired pen of Luke. When stripped of all the tinsel and sentimentalites that men have attached to it the report is plain and simple. It tells us what happened in Bethlehem the day Christ was born.

An edict had been issued by Ceasar Augustus for the registration of everyone in the Roman Empire, and all went to the city which was his ancestral home. Joseph, being of the house and kindred of David, went from his home in Nazareth to Bethlehem, taking with him his betrothed wife Mary who was with child. While they were in Bethlehem the child was born, and since there was no room in the inn she laid him in a manger. There is nothing about a stable in this inspired record.

To the people in Bethlehem, His birth was not unusual. The populace and visitors paid little attention to it. However, at that same time and in that same locality certain shepherds were keeping watch over their flock at night in the open fields. To them alone was given a positive witness that this was not the commonplace birth of a commonplace babe. Suddenly an angel of the Lord appeared among them and the glory of the Lord shone round about them, filling them with terror. But the angel bade them not to be afraid, declaring that he brought them joyful news—a Savior had been born in the city of David who is Christ the Lord. The identifying sign of the babe was that He would be found wrapped in swaddling clothes lying in a manger.

The shepherds departed immediately for Bethlehem where they found Joseph, and Mary and the babe. They told all that had happened and what the angel had said about this child. All who heard them were astonished, but Mary treasured these things in her heart and often pondered about them.

Certain facts stand out here and need to be noted. No one saw or heard the angel except the sheperds. No star appeared in the sky or over the manger. The shepherds went to Bethlehem because they were told by the angel that the Savior would be found there. No wise men were present that day, either in Jerusalem or in Bethlehem. There is positive proof in other scripture that the wise men did not arrive until the Lord was about two years of age. The record of this is found in Matthew 2:1-16.

There we learn that an extraordinary star had made its appearance, not in Jerusalem or in Bethlehem, but in a locality designated only as "the East." We do not know that it appeared on the night that He was born, but it may have. However, it was seen by certain wise men who evidently were men who sought the true God they knew existed (Acts 17:27). The star spoke to them of some exceptional event, and by some additional revelation their steps were directed toward Jerusalem to look for one who had been born king of the Jews. We are not told how many came. That there were three or that they were oriental kings are traditions without foundation in the Word of God. In all probability it was a larger number accompanied by many attendants. They did not follow a star to Jerusalem. They saw it in the East, and after due time for necessary preparation they made the slow and difficult journey to the city of the great King (Matt. 5:25).

When they arrived in Jerusalem they asked, "Where is He that is born King of the Jews?" They explained that they had seen His star in the East and had come to worship Him. If they had been following the star they would not have asked this question. There is no truth in the idea that they followed a shining star day and night over "moor and mountain" until it brought them to Bethlehem.

The appearance of these visitors startled the inhabitants of Jerusalem and troubled the wicked king. While the wise men waited for an answer, he assembled the priests and the scribes, demanding to know of them where the Messiah should be born. From the Scripture they told him it would be in Bethlehem of Judea.

With this information in hand, Herod called in the wise men secretly and enquired of them diligently as to what time the star appeared. The answer appears to have been that it was not more than two years before. The King sent them to Bethlehem to search for the child, making request that when they located Him to send him word that he also might worship Him. When they departed from the king's presence, to their great surprise and joy, the star which they had seen in the East went before them until it stood over the house (not a stable) where the young child (not a babe) was. Even though Christ was born in Bethlehem and Herod mistakenly directed the wise men there, there is no evidence that the star led them there. All the evidence points to a house in Nazareth (Luke 2:39).

When they arrived where the young child was they went into the house where in the presence of Mary (no shepherds) they worshipped Him and presented their gifts of gold, frankincense, and myrrh. Then the same God that had spoken to them in the East spoke to them again warning them not to return to Herod, so they went home another way. Herod was furious when he found that the wise men had ignored his request and he ordered the killing of all children that were in Bethlehem, and in all its boundaries, "from two years and under, according to the time which he had dilligently enquired of the wise men" (Matt. 2:16).

This is the true story. This is the record God has given of His Son. Those who believe this record can trace their belief to a safe and sure foundation. Those who believe not God have made Him a liar, because they believe not the record God has given of His Son (1 John 5:10). And to all men let it be known that I believe.

The SEED and BREAD Bible-Study leaflets are published as often as time and means permit and are sent free to all names on THE WORD OF TRUTH MINISTRY mailing list. Send us your name. There will be no obligation, solicitation, or visitation. Additional copies of any issue available on request.   ISSUE NO. 22

SEED & BREAD

FOR THE SOWER   ISA. 55:10   FOR THE EATER

BRIEF BIBLICAL MESSAGES

FROM

THE WORD OF TRUTH MINISTRY

339 South Orange Drive, Los Angeles, Cal. 90036

Otis Q. Sellers, Bible Teacher

NEW TESTAMENT TIME PERIODS

Disordered and confused thinking in regard to the New Testament is a characteristic of those who handle the Bible today. Details of truth are picked up and placed anywhere with no consideration being given to the divinely revealed order. This compares with the error of Hymenaeus and Philetus, spoken of in 2 Tim. 2:17, 18, who laid hold of the fact of resurrection and then declared that it was past already.

If we would be orderly in our thinking about the New Testament, eight clearly marked and definite time periods need to be recognized. This will give us a place for everything and each detail can be put into its proper place. These time periods form the true basis for fulfilling the directive of "rightly dividing the word of truth" (2 Tim. 2:15).

These time periods are in order:

1. The Earthly Ministry. This began with the birth of Jesus Christ in Bethlehem and ended with His resurrection from the dead. It was thirty-three years in length and is called in Scripture, "the days of His flesh" (Heb. 5:7). This is a definite time period but it is not a dispensation. The birth of Christ made no change in God's dealings with His people Israel or with other nations. While Jesus Christ was indeed the Messiah, He was never presented to Israel as such. When certain favored men discovered this truth by divine revelation, they were forbidden to tell any man that He was Jesus the Christ (Matt. 16:16-20).

2. The Acts Period. This period began with the resurrection of Jesus Christ and continued for a little more than thirty-three years. It ended definitely and absolutely with Paul's great pronouncement in Acts 28:28 (see issue no. 11). This time period is a definite dispensation in which God's purposes, methods, and administrations were different from what they had ever been before or ever have been since. Theologians have willfully ignored the peculiar character of the Acts period and have always depreciated its unique dispensational character. It should be plain even to the simplest reader that the presence of divinely commissioned men (heralds and apostles),

Rm 13.1

who spoke a divinely given and inspired message, and which message was always confirmed to the hearers by signs that followed, is bound to result in a different condition than that which prevails today.

3. The Dispensation of Grace. The pronouncement (Acts 28:28) that closed the Acts period began the dispensation of grace, the time in which we are now living. This time period is also a unique dispensation in which God's method of dealing with the world is one of pure grace, in which every act of God is one of love and favor to the undeserving. In fact, at the present time, if God cannot act in grace, He will not act at all. His purpose in this dispensation is to write into the history of His long dealings with mankind an absolute record of the grace that is inherent in His character. Thus, every act of His is one of love, kindness, favor, compassion, pity, good will, sympathy and tenderness.

God's present administration (dispensation) is not only gracious, it is also in secret (Eph. 3:8) so that the wealth of goodness He pours out daily upon mankind is untraceable. There is no manifestation of what God is now doing, but the believer is able by faith to say, "Blessed be the Lord, Who daily loadeth us with benefits, even the God of our salvation." Psalm 68:19.

The dispensation of grace is not going on forever, but we can rest assured that God will not spoil the record He has been writing for over 1900 years by a great display of wrath and anger. It will end in the greatest display of grace that He has ever shown. God will speak from heaven and enlighten the world (Psa. 85:8, 11, 97:4). He will remove the veil from Christ (1 Cor. 1:7). He will pour out of His Spirit upon all flesh (Acts 2:17). He will govern the nations upon the earth (Psa. 67:4). All this together will certainly amount to a divine inbreaking into the flow of human history. God will invade the earth by His Spirit, conquer the earth by His Spirit, set up His own order upon the earth, and the result will be a dispensation of absolute, divine government. The Bible calls this the kingdom (government) of God.

4. The Kingdom (Government) of God. Our God has established His throne (seat of government) in the heavens (Psa. 103:19), and it is from there that Jesus Christ will govern the earth. He has declared that heaven is His throne and the earth is His footstool (Isa. 66:1). We can rest in the fact that when He governs, it will be from the throne and not from the footstool. This can properly be called the pre-advent kingdom since it precedes the second coming of Christ and prepares mankind for the thousand years of His glorious presence. The kingdom of God is in reality the subject of the Bible and it is the true hope of mankind. It begins with divine intervention and it is entirely the work of God. There is nothing that man can do toward it. The zeal of the Lord of hosts will perform it (Isa. 9:7). It comes upon men bringing great blessings, but its advent is followed immediately by a judgment of all who are living and this will determine who are to continue to live upon this glorious earth when it is governed by God. There will also be a judgment of all who are dead to determine who should be raised to enjoy life under God's government (2 Tim. 4:1). Every promise and prophecy in the Old Testament has to do with this glorious time. There is no truth to be gained by assigning these prophecies to the thousand years of His personal presence.

5. The Great Testing (Tribulation). Many wild and incoherent prophets of doom have created great fear concerning this seven year period of time, but those who have knowledge of Scripture concerning it will neither be afraid of it nor disturbed by it. Vivid descriptions of the great tribulation have become the stock in trade of many so-called evangelists. It is described as being "the hour of trial which is coming upon the inhabited earth to try those that dwell upon the earth" (Rev. 3:10). Common sense will tell us that there would be no value in such a test being made today. The present failure of mankind is an evident fact and testing would reveal nothing that is not manifest. The great testing will come only after men have lived long under God's benevolent government. Those who learn well the lessons taught by the day-to-day experiences of the kingdom of God will have nothing to fear from this time of testing. Yet if they do not learn, then the punishment threatened in 2 Thessalonians 1:7-10, will be fully justified.

6. The Parousia of Jesus Christ (1,000 years). The great truth expressed by the word *parousia* was lost when it was erroneously translated "coming." It is the coming of Christ that will result in His parousia. He will be personally present upon this earth because of Who He is and what He does in view of His many offices. This is a term in God's school for which we are not ready. This time is usually called "the **millennium**" by the world and "the millennial kingdom" by the theologians. The Bible calls it "the parousia of the Lord" and it has to do with the great work of revealing God to mankind. Those who are in it are people who have learned their previous lessons under government and have no need of the disciplines and restraints that government imposes. However "rule and authority" (1 Cor. 15:24) are not nullified until the end of the thousand years of His personal presence. Thomas Jefferson said, "That government is best which governs least." The true purpose of all government should be to produce a people who need none at all. The kingdom (government) of God will do this.

During the parousia of Christ, Satan is bound (Rev. 20:2) in order that he should deceive the nations no more, and after that he must be loosed for a little season. This brings us to the seventh time period.

7. The Little Season. We know very little about this as the entire Biblical revelation concerning it is found in Revelation 20:1-3, 7-9. In these verses we learn of an uprising caused by Satanic deception after he has been loosed from being bound during the thousand years. We are told that Satan *must* be loosed for a little season and that he shall be loosed out of his prison. Once he is loosed he goes forth to deceive the nations which are in the four corners of the earth, Gog and Magog, to gather them together to battle, the number of whom is as the sand of the sea. Of course, it pains us to read of this, and it seems to be utterly impossible after two great periods of divine light and activity. Nevertheless, we accept the divine record without question.

The true picture set forth in Revelation 20:7-9 is one in which we see Satan, one of the cherubim, the greatest deceiver of all times, probably posing as an angel of light, going forth to the nations that are in the four corners of the earth to practice again his wiles upon men who have had no recent experience, if any at all, with this master of deception. The Word reveals that he has some success, but it must be remembered that those who act upon his advice are deceived by him. We do not know what devices he will use, what lies he will tell, what representations he will make, or what rewards he will offer. But we do know that those who succumb to his wiles will think they are following God's messenger, and that when they march toward Jerusalem they will think they are performing God a service.

Their great mistake will be that they fail to put this professed "messenger of light" to the tests that certainly were readily available to them, and this leads to their deception. The outcome of this deception is that they travel toward Jerusalem, unopposed by God or man, and they circle this "beloved city." Up to this point they have harmed no one and they have not been harmed. But the moment they circle the camp of the saints fire comes down from God out of heaven and devours them. One flash, and nothing remains but a handful of ashes where each man stood. Thus, again men have been tested and the divine realm is purged.

8. The New Heaven and the New Earth. The words "heaven(s) and earth" when used together in Scripture represent an order, system, world *(kosmos)*. The words are used interchangeably in 2 Peter 3:5-7, 13. There we learn of the heavens and earth that were of old, the heavens and earth which are now, and the heavens and earth which shall be. We know very little of this and we are told very little about it, there being nothing in our knowledge or experience whereby we could comprehend it. But as we advance through the kingdom of God and through the parousia of Christ we will gain the basis which will make understanding possible. This time period is as far as the Bible takes us.

The SEED and BREAD Bible-Study leaflets are published as often as time and means permit and are sent free to all names on THE WORD OF TRUTH MINISTRY mailing list. Send us your name. There will be no obligation, solicitation, or visitation. Additional copies of any issue available on request.   ISSUE NO. 23

SEED & BREAD

FOR THE SOWER   ISA. 55:10   FOR THE EATER

BRIEF BIBLICAL MESSAGES

FROM

THE WORD OF TRUTH MINISTRY

339 South Orange Drive, Los Angeles, Cal. 90036

Otis Q. Sellers, Bible Teacher

WHAT DOES *PAROUSIA* MEAN?

In the study of things to come there is no word that encompasses any greater truth than the word *parousia*. This is a Greek word that has been brought over into English without any change in its spelling, and it will be found in most dictionaries, even though the definition given is far from accurate. It is a word that should be found in the vocabulary of every diligent Bible student. There is no English word that will accurately express the Greek word *parousia;* therefore, it should be transliterated and a maximum effort should be made to fix in our minds its meaning as used by the Spirit of God in the New Testament.

This word is found twenty-four times in the Greek New Testament and is used in numerous contexts making it possible for us to discover its true meaning from its usage, the only way that any word in any language should ever be defined.

In the *King James Version* it is translated "coming" twenty-two times and "presence" twice. Other translations as a rule have used the words *coming, presence, arrival,* and *personal presence* to represent the word *parousia.* And at this point it needs to be stated unequivocally that it does not mean coming in any occurrence in the New Testament. To so translate it was an egregious error that is constantly perpetuated by lexicographers and theologians. I do not believe that the definition of "coming" would be given in any lexicon, there being not one shred of evidence to support it, if it had not been for the fact that the *King James Version* translators arbitrarily rendered it this way so that it would not flatly contradict their creedal position.

The translators of the *King James Version* were men who held firmly to the theology that arose out of the reformation, and especially to the later ideas developed by John Calvin, a man who studiously avoided ever coming to grips with the great eschatological problems of Scripture. A very simple doctrine of future events was worked out which was a slight refinement of Roman Catholic doctrine. According to this, there was to come what was called "the day of judgment," and this was equated with the second coming of Christ, even though it was not held that He returned in person. On this day of judgment all mankind, living and dead, were to be summoned before God to be judged. A great separation was to be made, with all the righteous finding a place forever in heaven, and all the wicked being consigned to live forever in a place of torment called hell. The earth was then to be destroyed by fire, an event that was supported by mistranslating *sunteleias tou aiōnos* by "the end of the world."

In view of beliefs such as these there was no place in the thinking of these men for a time to come when Jesus Christ would be personally present upon the earth. So they eliminated the *parousia* by translating it "coming" and making it to be a coming universal judgment.

There is no truth to be gained by pointing to 1 Cor. 16:17 (as many do) as proof that *parousia* means coming, where Paul declares that he was glad for the *parousia* of Stephanas and Fortunatus.. The fact that the word "coming" seems to fit well in this sentence is no proof that this is what it means. The word *health* or *prosperity* would fit just as well, but the fact is that *parousia* does not mean health or prosperity and neither does it mean coming. These men were a deputation from the Corinthian ecclesia to the Apostle Paul. Thus they were there because of who they were and the help they could be to Paul. He was rejoicing in their personal presence, a presence which he exalts and honors by calling it a *parousia*. The importance of this designation will be seen when we get to the actual technical meaning of this word.

The word *parousia* does not mean "arrival" as the occurrence in 2 Cor. 10:10 will clearly show. The weakness of Paul's "bodily presence" was not limited to his arrival. It continued through his entire *parousia* in Corinth. And this word does not mean "presence" or "bodily presence" even though it does contain these two ideas. It means more than "presence" and more than "bodily presence" and to so translate it is to weaken this strong word. It is actually a simple word and should present no problem to the translator as long as he can rise fully above the confusion that was imposed upon it when it was made to mean "coming." It is made up of the word *para* which means "beside," and the participial form of the word "to be," *ousia*, which means "being." The compound word *parousia* means being beside, being with, or being present. However when all occurrences of this word in the New Testament, in Classical Greek, in the Septuagint, and in the papyrus manuscripts are examined it will be found that this word means more than presence and more even than personal presence. It is used of a certain kind of personal presence, and only such a presence can be properly called a *parousia*.

Adolf Deissmann's pertinent comment that *parousia* is "a technical expression" has been repeated by many commentators, but invariably they leave us without any explanation of the technical (exact) meaning of this word. This is a fault of which I do not wish to be guilty so I will give at once the technical definition of this important term.

The Greek word *parousia* means a personal presence when one is present because of who he is and what he does. Thus, a personal presence may not be a parousia if the one present is not there in relationship to his position or office and the service he performs as such.

The word for "personal presence" in the New Testament is *pareimi,* not *parousia,* a fact that is easily established by its many occurrences. (See list on page 594 of the *Englishman's Greek Concordance.*) These occurrences show that *pareimi* always means a personal presence when it is used of men, and an actual presence when it is used of things.

At first glance these two words may seem to be only different inflections of the same word, but usage has established them as two words with distinct meanings. We must not stultify *parousia* by giving it the same meaning as *pareimi.* The distinction between the two is of the utmost importance, so I will give several illustrations of these two words.

If I should go to the courthouse and sit in on a trial, my presence there would most certainly be a personal one, and it could be described by the Greek word *pareimi,* but not by *parousia.* I am not there because of who I am, any position I hold or service I will perform. However, the judge, the prosecutor, the attorneys, and the witnesses are all there because of who they are and the service they will render in view of this. Thus, their personal presence there can be called a *parousia.*

Consider another illustration. A teacher of a class in New Testament Greek begins by calling the roll to which each member responds, "Pareimi" (present), a word they had learned in the previous lesson. The teacher then says, "Your personal presence, that is, your *pareimi* having been established, I now trust that your *pareimi* will at once become a *parousia,* that you will be here because you are students and, therefore, are here to learn."

The definition of a word can be determined only by an analysis of its usage. This is the method by which dictionaries are compiled. In getting the definition of New Testament words we are primarily interested in the usage made by the Holy Spirit in its pages. Nevertheless, consideration needs to be given to occurrences outside of the Bible.

CLASSICAL GREEK USAGE

Of special interest is a quotation by Sophocles, cited by Liddell and Scott, where one said, "that we have no friends present (*parousia*) to assist us." This man desired the presence of friends who would be there because they were friends and who would undertake to do what a friend would do under such circumstances.

Adolf Deissmann cites many of these occurrences, prefacing them by saying, "From the Ptolemaic period down to the second century A.D. (about 500 years) we are able to trace the word in the East as a technical expressional for the arrival or visit of the king or the emperor." (Light from the Ancient East, Pages 368 to 373.) However, all the examples cited by Deissmann are indicative of an official visit rather than a mere arrival. On the occasion of such visits *parousia* coins were struck and *parousia* taxes were levied. And it will also be seen in every occurrence that these visits were described as *parousias* because they were present because of who they were and were there to perform the duties of their position.

The occurrences in the papyrus are most interesting. These are pointed out by Moulton and Milligan (*Vocabulary of the Greek New Testament*, page 497). In one a man says, "The repair of what has been swept away by the river requires my *parousia*." The owner would need to be there because of who he was and what he would direct to be done.

In another occurrence someone says, "It is no use if a person comes too late for what required his *parousia*." The correctness of the definition that has already been given is evident in this sentence.

Another occurrence is quite intriguing, causing us to wonder about the incident that generated it. A woman declares that her husband, "swore in the *parousia* of the overseers (*episkopōn*) and of his own brothers, 'Henceforward I will not hide all my keys from her.'" One can only surmise from this that there was serious trouble between a man and his wife and that the overseers and his brothers were called in to arbitrate the matter. Thus they were there because of their positions and relationship, also the services they were to perform.

In the pre-recorded history (prophecies) of the benevolent services which the Lord Jesus Christ will yet perform on behalf of mankind the most important service will be accomplished in His *parousia*. He is to be personally present upon the earth for a thousand years and He will be present because of all that He is and the services to be performed in view of each glory given to Him. The good that will come out of this is beyond comprehension and volumes would not suffice to tell about it. For now, it is enough to say that this thousand year term in God's school of life, when the master teacher is personally present, will produce a people who know God to the fullest extent that He can be known by man.

Since the Lord Jesus Christ is not now upon the earth, a coming will be required in order for Him to be personally present. I believe in the second coming of Christ (Acts 1:11). His coming will result in His *parousia*, and we should not confuse the two.

The SEED and BREAD Bible-Study leaflets are published as often as time and means permit and are sent free to all names on THE WORD OF TRUTH MINISTRY mailing list. Send us your name. There will be no obligation, solicitation, or visitation. Additional copies of any issue available on request.   ISSUE NO. 24

```
┌─────────────────────────────────────────────────┐
│                                                 │
│  SEED & BREAD                                    │
│  FOR THE SOWER    ISA. 55:10    FOR THE EATER    │
│        BRIEF BIBLICAL MESSAGES                   │
│                 FROM                             │
│      THE WORD OF TRUTH MINISTRY                  │
│  339 South Orange Drive, Los Angeles, Cal. 90036 │
│        Otis Q. Sellers, Bible Teacher            │
│                                                 │
└─────────────────────────────────────────────────┘
```

THE PAROUSIA OF THE LORD JESUS

In the prerecorded history (prophecies) of the future benevolent services which the Lord Jesus Christ will yet perform for mankind, one of the most important is that which will be accomplished in His thousand year parousia. Having established in Issue No. 23 the meaning of the Greek word *parousia*, I shall henceforth use it as an English word in the confidence that my readers will understand that by it I mean a personal presence when one is present because of who or what he is and what he does in view of this.

The great truth of the parousia of the Lord Jesus is unknown and unrecognized by most readers of the English Bible since the word is not found there. It is wrongly translated "coming" in twenty-two of its twenty-four occurrences. It is the parousia of Jesus Christ that will prepare and qualify mankind for the place he will have and the services he will perform in the new heaven and new earth. Under that new order the tabernacle of God will be with men and He will dwell with them and they will be His people and He will be their God (Rev. 21:3). Not even that long term of school in the kingdom of God will fully prepare men for this position and service. We will yet need the learning and discipline that comes from Christ being personally present because of Who He is and what He will do.

When we consider that the event which is commonly called "the rapture" is one that is related to the parousia, and which so many are saying is the next event in God's prophetic program, it causes us to realize the need for an objective study of the parousia of the Lord Jesus.

It is in Matthew 24:3 that we find the first mention of this great event. The Lord's twelve apostles came to Him privately upon the Mount of Olives and asked the question, "What will be the sign of your parousia, even the consummation of the eon?"

The eon here is the kingdom eon, that pre-advent time of divine government that prepares mankind for the parousia of Jesus Christ. The eon consummates in the parousia, and it is the consummation of that eon. In justification of the above translation I would cite the following: There is a rule of Greek grammar which is as follows. When two nouns in the same case are connected by the word *kai* (and), and the second noun lacks the definite article, then the second noun refers to the same person or thing as the first noun and is a definition of it. An example of this will be found in 1 Cor. 15:24 where Paul speaks of "God, even the Father" (*Theo kai patri*).

This rule applies to the two nouns found in the question asked by the apostles (*parousia* and *sunteleia*). They are asking about one thing, not two things. The parousia of the Lord Jesus Christ is the consummation of the eon — not this present evil eon, but the glorious eon of the day of Christ, that eon of divine government which is next to come upon the earth.

I am fully convinced that the word *sunteleia* means a coming together of all that is necessary to produce a desired goal or end, so I have used the word consummation to translate it. The word here is not *telos* (the actual end) but *sunteleia*, the act of completing to produce a desired result.

It will help us to fix the meaning of *sunteleia* in our minds if we will remember that the consummation of a woman's pregnancy is the birth of a living child. A child born dead would be the end of her pregnancy but it would not be the consummation of it. The goal would not have been reached.

There is nothing in this passage about the coming of Christ. How could there be when He was then present with them? The disciples' question concerns His parousia, which they further describe as being "the consummation of the eon." As said before, the eon spoken of here is the eon of the kingdom of God. The consummation of the kingdom eon is the parousia of the Lord Jesus Christ. However, His parousia will not be ushered in without a great struggle of opposition on the part of Satan. The developments and the outcome of this struggle are set forth in the ensuing portion of Matthew 24.

In answer to their question the Lord sets forth certain significant events that will precede His parousia. They asked for the signs of it and this is what He gives to them. These are: 1. Men coming in His character claiming they are the Anointed One, 2. Battles and reports of battles, 3. Nation rising up against nation and government against government, 4. Famines, 5. Pestilences, and 6. Earthquakes. And since these things have always been prominent in the earth from the time of the entrance of sin (they were prominent when the Lord spoke these words and have been prominent ever since) the logical mind will wonder how they can possibly be signs of the nearness of His parousia.

The answer is that they cannot be and it is illogical to cry "signs of the times" every time a famine or earthquake or pestilence occurs. However, when we understand the flow of events set forth in the time periods of the New Testament we realize that these things have ceased under God's government which precedes these events and the parousia. The rigid restraints (Isa. 30:31) and the swift punishments that will characterize the government of God will keep all such things from happening. But when these restraints are lifted and the restrainer Himself (the Holy Spirit) is removed, evil men and evil conditions will again appear and be highly significant. It should also be apparent that the great drama that is written out in detail in Matthew 24 can never be acted out until the twelve apostles have been raised from the dead and are in their positions as judges of the twelve tribes of Israel. These words and warnings were spoken to them, and not to us. Nevertheless, all readers are cautioned, "Whoso readeth, let him understand" (Matt. 24:15).

The actual period of time being dealt with here is the seventieth week, a seven year period, of Israels seventy 'weeks as revealed in Daniel 9. This seven year period is divided into two parts and it is the last three and one-half years that makes up "the great tribulation." This begins the great struggle for it in the middle of the week that Satan is cast down to earth, raging with great wrath because he knows his time is short (Rev. 12:12).

It is then that all the governing people in Israel ("them which be in Judea," Matt. 24:16) must flee to the mountains. This will be an orderly migration, a work of faith, and the apostles will be in absolute charge. They are to take nothing, since the same Lord who fed and clothed their murmuring fathers in these same mountains for forty years can certainly supply the needs of this righteous band for forty-two months.

It is the presence of Satan, the great deceiver, upon the earth, that makes this to be a time of affliction such as has never been before. But they are safe in their divinely appointed place in the mountains and the forces of antichrist do not dare to go in and bring them out, so they spend their time marching up and down the streets of Jerusalem. This is the time when "Jerusalem shall be trodden of the Gentiles until the times of the Gentiles be fulfilled." See Eze. 30:2, Luke 21:24, Rev. 11:2. But it seems they begin to look foolish marching up and down the streets of Jerusalem when the ones they seek to capture and destroy are in the mountains. And it is when they assemble at Megiddo in preparation for turning into the mountains that the Lord comes and fights against them. This is the battle of Armageddon, in which not one life is lost except those who are in revolt against Israel and against God's government. Remember that the "man of sin" is destroyed by the blazing forth (*epiphaneia*) of His parousia (2 Thess. 2:8).

In answering their question concerning the signs of His parousia He warns them to disregard all declarations that He has returned to the earth and is in the desert or hidden away in some secret chamber in the city, thus to avoid all stratagems that would lure them out of their divinely appointed place of safety. He then states with absolute finality:

"For as the lightning cometh out of the east, and shineth even unto the west; so shall the parousia of the Son of Man be." (Matt. 24:27.)

From this we know that His parousia will be sudden, dramatic, and public. The idea of a secret parousia is unknown in the Word of God.

As the Lord continues His message He declares that it is "immediately after the tribulation of those days" that they shall see the Son of Man coming in the clouds of heaven with power and great glory (Matt. 24:29, 30). This is the coming that results in His parousia.

One evident fact that will be apparent to all who examine the four occurrences of the word *parousia* in Matthew 24, is that it is an event that comes after the great tribulation and not before. It cannot be moved around to suit the whims of faulty prophetic schemes. It is also seen to be one definite event. Any attempt to make two *parousias* will not stand the test of Scripture.

One of the most important references to the parousia of the Lord is found in 1 Thess. 4:15-17 where Paul prefaces his declaration by saying, "This we say unto you by the word of the Lord," which indicates a new revelation not made by anyone before. He continues by saying that those who are alive and remain unto the parousia of the Lord shall in no wise be a step ahead of those who are asleep. He declares that the Lord himself shall descend from heaven with a shout, with the voice of the chief messenger, and with the trump of God. This is His coming, His coming in order to be personally present. As He descends those who are then "dead in Christ," a martyred group who gave up their lives in the great tribulation, will be raised and these with the living shall be caught up with them in clouds to meet the Lord in the air. It is wrong to twist this into the idea that He is coming to take these people to heaven. He is coming to be personally present upon the earth and here to accomplish all the great works that His many offices indicate. He is not coming to govern. After the kingdom experience those who still need government have not acquired the maturity that is necessary for a place on earth when He is personally present in view of all that He is and all that He will do.

The words of the scoffers who ask, "Where is the promise of His parousia?" (2 Pet. 3:4) are tantamount to saying, "There is no promise of a parousia in the Bible." The amillennial school of interpretation is doing this today. They are a sign that we are in the closing days of this dispensation. Don't listen to them.

The SEED and BREAD Bible-Study leaflets are published as often as time and means permit and are sent free to all names on THE WORD OF TRUTH MINISTRY mailing list. Send us your name. There will be no obligation, solicitation, or visitation. Additional copies of any issue available on request.   ISSUE NO. 25

SEED & BREAD

FOR THE SOWER   ISA. 55:10   FOR THE EATER

BRIEF BIBLICAL MESSAGES

FROM

THE WORD OF TRUTH MINISTRY

339 South Orange Drive, Los Angeles, Cal. 90036

Otis Q. Sellers, Bible Teacher

THE DIVINE PURPOSE

In all the work that God has done for mankind, is now doing for mankind, and will yet do for mankind, there is a definite goal, a fixed purpose. To state it as simply as possible, His object in all His work is to produce a people who know Him, who understand Him, who love and appreciate Him, a people with whom He can joyfully dwell, and among whom He can center Himself in view of a greater program for the universe.

If the Bible is read carefully from Genesis to Revelation it will be found that this end is reached and becomes a reality in Revelation 21. There under a new order of things described as "a new heaven and new earth" the tabernacle of God is seen as being with men, He is dwelling (tabernacling) with them, they are His people, and He is their God. This is as far as Revelation takes us, yet we can rightfully go a step beyond this and envision a great divine program in which mankind will be vitally involved as those who are working and not those upon whom God is working. A tabernacle *(skēnos)* in scripture when used figuratively always denotes a center of activity, and it could not be that God would bring about such a center and then not use it.

God will yet use this earth and mankind that He has developed upon it as a center of divine activity to fulfill His program for the universe. This earth with mankind upon it will yet be the mediatorial planet and the mediatorial people. When this blessed state is realized no man will ever again say, "Our Father which art in heaven," for that will no longer be true. He will have changed the center of His activities from angels in heaven to mankind upon the earth. And, of course, this earth is where you and I will want to be when the divine goal is realized. "The earth is the Lord's." It has a most wonderful future; first, under God's government; then, under the parousia of Christ; and finally, as the tabernacle of God. Its future blessedness, even under God's government, defies understanding at the present time. We may not be able to comprehend it, but taking the long-range view we say, "Nevertheless we, according to His promise look for a new heaven and new earth, wherein dwelleth righteousness." (2 Pet. 3:13).

However, it must be remembered that this experimental and transcendent knowledge of God is not reached in a short time or by any one experience. This earth and those who remain upon it must pass through two long periods of manifest divine activity. These two periods can well be called two terms in the school of God. During these times mankind will be made ready for his place in the new earth by a long process of learning, experience and development.

The first of these two great periods of manifest divine activity is described in Scripture by many terms, but its great overall designation is the kingdom of God. The word *kingdom* means government, as the Encyclopedia Britannica says, "KINGDOM — not a geographical area, nor the people inhabiting the realm, but the activity of the king himself, his exercise of his sovereign power." The kingdom of God is the government of God and it should be applied to that period of time when a dispensation of divine government is a reality upon the earth, even though this is not the totality of its use in Scripture. However, this term is applied to a definite time in the future when the character of divine rule will be of such nature that this period of time above all others is worthy of the transcendent title, "the kingdom of God."

No matter how much or in what ways God has governed (exercised His sovereignty) in times past, no matter what events in the past may be pointed out as divine government in action (such as the destruction of Sodom), a time is coming when God is going to govern the earth in such completeness and totality that it is called in the Bible, and should be called by us, the kingdom of God. This is the time of which the Psalmist prophetically speaks when he says, "For the kingdom is the LORD'S: and He is the governor among the nations," (Psalm 22:28). "O let the nations be glad and sing for joy: for thou shalt judge the peoples righteously, and govern the nations upon earth," (Psalm 67:4).

The kingdom of God begins with the divine assumption of sovereignty over the earth and all upon it, living men and also the dead. This can happen at any moment. There are no events that precede it and no signs indicate its coming. All God needs to do is to speak and all men will be under His government. However, He will do more than speak. He will enlighten the world (Psa. 97:4). He will pour out of His Spirit upon all flesh (Joel 2:28). The glory of the Lord shall be revealed and all flesh will see it in the same amount and at the same time (Isa. 40:5). He will cause judgment to be heard from heaven; the earth will fear and become quiet (Psalm 76:8).

God's government comes bringing great blessings of light, knowl-

Anderson, not correcting it until five years before his death, a fact that does not show in most of his writings. Others have declared for Acts 28:28 and then withdrew from the field of battle. A. E. Knoch declared, "It was not until the end of the Acts era that the salvation of God is sent directly to the nations (Acts 28:28)." (*Concordant Version* notes on Matt. 15:21).

In regards to Acts 28:28 one cardinal fact needs to be faced and admitted. If Paul's words in this passage mark the dispensational boundary line, if they mark a new method of divine dealing with mankind, then the change that took place, or at least the most important feature of that change, must be epitomized in these words. In this passage there has to be a declaration of something that was not true before, but became true from that moment on. In Paul's words we must find summed up the answer to the question, What was the change that took place at Acts 28:28?

All through secular history there have been great declarations that brought about great changes. In all these pronouncements the change has always been clearly stated. Lincoln's Emancipation Proclamation was one of these. The force of and the change declared in his powerful words cannot be missed. "All persons held as slaves within any State . . . shall be then, thenceforward, and forever free." These words proclaimed a great administrational change in the United States government, setting free those who were slaves and settling the question of human slavery in this country.

Even so it is with the divine decree announced by Paul in Acts 28:28. The major feature of the change it brought about must be declared by its words. It is a succint statement, compressing a great truth into the fewest possible words. In studying it we must discover exactly what it says and then what is meant by what is said. The first of these has to do with translation and the second with interpretation. The translation must be correct from the literary and grammatical standpoint. The interpretation must be correct from the historical aspect.

At the close of that all-day meeting with the chief of the Jews in Rome, Paul declared in his final words to them, as we find it in the *King James Version*: "Be it known therefore unto you, that the salvation of God is sent to the Gentiles, and that they will hear it."

This statement is either important or unimportant. It either declares something that had long been true, as many say, or it declares something that became true from this point onward. My own position is that these words are of the utmost importance, that they say much in one brief statement, and that they declare a new overarching truth.

There are four important words in this statement that must be examined. These are *salvation, sent, Gentiles,* and *hear*. It is obvious that these words need to be considered in their Greek originals.

I have exhaustively studied the word *sōtērion* which here is translated "salvation", and have come to the conclusion that this adjective means *salvation-bringing*. See Issue No. 8 for all details. Supplying the noun from the context I would render this "the salvation-bringing message."

The word translated "sent" is *apostellō*, which since it is used here of an inanimate thing should be translated "authorized", in the sense of being made freely available. See Issue No. 5 for all details.

The word translated "Gentiles" in Acts 28:28 is *ethnos*. It is preceded by the definite article. All scholars, lexicographers, and commentators agree that *ethnos* means "nation", even though they think that at times it signifies those who are not of Israel and should in such places be translated "Gentile." However, all such renderings are interpretations and not translations. There are passages where the term "the nations" includes the nation of Israel, and to translate it "the Gentiles" would exclude that nation. See Matt. 12:18, 21 and Eph. 3:6 for example of this. In Acts 28:28 the words *tois ethnesin*, being dative, plural, neuter, should be translated "to the nations." But since it is evident from Acts 10:36 and 13:26 that God's salvation-bringing word had been authorized to Israel from the day of Pentecost, this nation is not particularly in view in this pronouncement.

The word translated "hear" in Acts 28:28 is *akouō*. That this word means "to hear" cannot be questioned. But if each one of the 437 occurrences of this word is considered we soon get the feeling that this word often means getting through to a person. An example of this is seen in Matt. 18:15, "if he shall hear thee, thou hast gained thy brother." While, as a rule, hearing is related to the ear, yet one can be said to have heard that which he has read. In this passage "they will hear it" means it will get through to them for their benefit. This is God's guarantee made by His spokesman Paul.

Thus an honest, grammatical, and literal translation of Acts 28:28 should read:

Let it then be known unto you, that the salvation-bringing message of God has been authorized to the nations, and they will hear it.

The words "has been authorized" declare an accomplished fact. The words "they will hear it" declare a future result. In the first statement the tense is the second aorist, and in the second it is future. This is the way it should be.

The SEED and BREAD Bible-Study leaflets are published as often as time and means permit and are sent free to all names on THE WORD OF TRUTH MINISTRY mailing list. Send us your name. There will be no obligation, solicitation, or visitation. Additional copies of any issue available on request.   ISSUE NO. 11

edge, truth, yes, and even a gift of perfect health for every man upon the earth. However, there is no proclamation of amnesty for such as idolaters, thieves, drunkards, revilers, or extortioners. These will have no place nor portion in the kingdom of God (1 Cor. 6:9-11). God will make a personal judgment of every member of the human race who has lived since Adam; first of all the living to determine who shall be allowed to continue to live on this earth under His benevolent government; then of all the dead to determine who shall be raised from among the dead to live upon the earth in that glorious day (2 Tim. 4:1).

All who continue to live and all who are raised from the dead will then be in the school of God. This term of school lasts for centuries, and it ends with an examination that will try every man that dwells upon the earth (Rev. 3:10). This period of testing is commonly called "the great tribulation," for that is what it is, for the nation of Israel, and it will try every man that dwells upon the earth. It is a very much maligned, misplaced, and misunderstood period of time. It comes at the end of the long kingdom period and it weeds out all who then know not God and who do not obey the gospel of the Lord Jesus Christ, (2 Thess. 1:8-9). By then these should be few in number, and they are eliminated because they do not qualify for the next great term of school, the thousand years of parousia (personal presence) of the Lord Jesus Christ.

In previous studies (Issue No. 24) it has been shown that the word *parousia* is a technical term that designates, when used of beings, a personal presence when one is present because of who he is and what he does in fulfillment of his position or office. Let us think on this.

Jesus Christ is the Expression (Logos) of God (John 1:1). When He is personally present as the Expression, then God will be fully expressed to mankind for a thousand years.

Jesus Christ is the Truth and the words He speaks are truth. When He is personally present as the Truth, no error or lie can find a place (John 14:6).

Jesus Christ is the Life (John 14:6) and death can find no room when He is present as the Life. He never came into contact with a dead person who He did not raise.

Jesus Christ is the Interpreter (Declarer) of God (John 1:18). Therefore, God is going to be truly interpreted and declared to mankind for a thousand years. No misinterpretation of God by anyone will be possible.

Jesus Christ is the Son of God (John 1:34). The most prominent idea in the word *son (huios)* is representation. As Son of God, He represents God to man and as Son of man, He represents man to God. This arrangement will reach the zenith of perfection during His parousia and will result in an understanding of the Deity such as has never been known by man before.

Jesus Christ is the Image of God. An image makes visible and real that which is invisible and incomprehensible. The Son of God is the visible, tangible embodiment of the Deity. In Him the entire fullness of the Deity dwells in essence (Col. 1:15; 2:9). Only in Him will God be seen. And this One is to be personally present for a thousand years to accomplish all that would be expected of the One who holds this position.

It would be easy to go on and remark upon each one of the offices that God has given unto Him. Each one would add to the glory of His personal presence. For it is the thousand years of His parousia that brings mankind to as much knowledge and understanding as finite beings are able to contain concerning God.

From what has been said it is easy to see that mankind is not ready for the parousia of Jesus Christ. At the best we are only in the primary grades of our knowledge and appreciation of God, and are certainly far from ready for that postgraduate course in the presence of the Master Teacher.

In every time and under all conditions God has ever held out to men the hope that they could live upon this earth in the day when God governs. "For evildoers shall be cut off: but they that wait upon the Lord shall inherit the earth," (Psa. 37:9) is His promise. To "inherit" means to have a place and enjoy a portion. "For such as be blessed of Him shall have a place and enjoy a portion in the earth," (37:22), He tells us in the same Psalm. For many who are among the dead it will require resurrection in order for them to matriculate in the first term of God's great school.

The kingdom of God comes with great blessings for the earth and all who are alive upon it, but, as said before, some who are then living will not be allowed to continue to live to enjoy them. Each individual should do what is necessary to insure that He will be allowed to live if among the living and have the guarantee of resurrection if he is among the dead. God caused a book to be written to this end. Of John's Gospel He declares: "But these are written, that ye might believe that Jesus is the Christ, the Son of God; and that believing ye might have life through His name." John 20:30,31.

The SEED and BREAD Bible-Study leaflets are published as often as time and means permit and are sent free to all names on THE WORD OF TRUTH MINISTRY mailing list. Send us your name. There will be no obligation, solicitation, or visitation. Additional copies of any issue available on request.   ISSUE NO. 26

SEED & BREAD

FOR THE SOWER   ISA. 55:10   FOR THE EATER

BRIEF BIBLICAL MESSAGES FROM

THE WORD OF TRUTH MINISTRY

228 N. El Molino Ave., Pasadena, CA 91101-1675

Otis Q. Sellers, Bible Teacher

27

THE KINGDOM OF GOD

The theme of the Bible is the kingdom of God. This statement is made in full recognition of the fact that Christ fills its pages, that He is the crown of its revelation, and that all Scripture points to Him. He is the personality set forth as the principal actor. He is the Jehovah of the Old Testament and the Lord Jesus Christ of the New. Nevertheless, its main subject from beginning to end is the kingdom of God. This is its central idea and the concept that embraces its total message. This is the truth that is found in one form or another throughout the length and breadth of God's Holy Word. To understand what is meant by the kingdom of God is to hold the key that will unlock its treasures.

Any book that makes sense, that conveys a message, must have a central idea, a theme, a plot. When men make the claim, as many do, that the Bible is a confusing book, and that it has no relevancy to the present time, it may be that they have failed altogether to find its central theme. As long as men regard it as being nothing more than a book of moral instruction, a compendium of religious rituals and observances, or as a handbook of church customs and practices, it is bound to be a confusing book.

On the title page of my own Bible I have written, "The Book of the Coming Kingdom of God." This is what I believe it to be, and while the actual term "the kingdom of God" is not found in the Old Testament, this does not mean that the truth concerning it is not found there. In fact, it is in the Old Testament that the thousand and one prophetic declarations are found which are later subsumed in the New Testament under the great designation, "the kingdom of God."

When the Lord Jesus came into Galilee, preaching the gospel of the kingdom of God, and saying, "The time is fulfilled, and the kingdom of God is at hand" (Mark 1:14, 15), He did not need to define this term. He was proclaiming something which every

Israelite understood and for which the faithful in Israel had hoped. He was announcing the imminency of that condition of things upon the earth that the Hebrew prophets had already set forth, a period of time when this earth and all nations upon it would be governed by God (Psalm 67:4). This was not a new concept. It was an ancient body of truth summed up in the neat descriptive term, "the kingdom of God."

The disciples of the Lord Jesus were exhorted to give the kingdom of God first place in their lives (Matt. 6:33). It was the kingdom of God that Christ proclaimed when He began His public ministry (Mark 1:14). Its proclamation was the work that God had commissioned (apostellō) Him to do (Luke 4:43). It was the kingdom of God that He proclaimed and demonstrated in every city (Luke 8:1). It was the message the twelve were sent forth to herald (Luke 9:2), and it was the truth the seventy were told to proclaim (Luke 10:9). His disciples were taught to pray for its coming (Luke 11:2). It was the hope and the destiny of Abraham, Isaac, Jacob, and all the prophets (Luke 13:28). It was the hope awaited by Joseph, that good man who arranged for the entombment of the Lord Jesus after His crucifixion (Luke 23:50, 51).

In the ministry of the Lord Jesus the kingdom of God was the subject of the parable of the sower (Matt. 13:19), of the tares among the wheat (Matt. 13:24), of the mustard seed (Matt. 13:31), of the leaven (Matt. 13:33), of the hid treasure (Matt. 13:44), of the pearl of great price (Matt. 13:45, 46), of the net cast into the sea (Matt. 13:47), of the laborers in the vineyard (Matt. 20:1), of the marriage of the king's son (Matt. 22:2), of the wise and foolish virgins (Matt. 25:1), of the seed growing secretly (Mark 4:26).

The kingdom of God was the subject of the ministry of Jesus Christ in the forty days that elapsed between His resurrection and ascension. It was the subject of some of the most important declarations He made while upon the earth (Matt. 12:28, Luke 17:20, Luke 17:21, John 3:3).

When all the facts are gathered, there can be no doubt but that the kingdom of God was the subject of Paul's ministry from beginning to end. It was the hope he held out to those whom he had brought into relationship with Jesus Christ (Acts 14:22). It was the subject of his ministry in the synagogue in Ephesus (Acts 19:8), and the entire three years of his ministry there is described as being one of "proclaiming the kingdom of God" (Acts 20:25). And it was because he had proclaimed the kingdom of God to them that he was able to say he had not "shunned to declare unto them all the counsel of God" (Acts 20:27). It also made it possible for him to say that he was pure from the blood of all men (Acts 20:26, 27).

The kingdom of God was Paul's message during the full day (from morning till evening) that he met with the chief of the Jews in Rome (Acts 28:23). It was at the close of this day that God declared by the lips of Paul the momentous words recorded in Acts 28:28. These words brought an end to the Acts dispensation and signaled the beginning of God's administration of absolute grace. Nevertheless, the kingdom of God continued to be Paul's message in the two years of his life of which we have a record after Acts 28:28 (Acts 28:31). And it should be noted here that the proclamation of the kingdom of God is vitally linked up with the teaching of those things which concern the Lord Jesus Christ, even as in Acts 28:23 and in Acts 8:12. In Acts 20:24, 25, proclaiming the kingdom of God is equivalent to and is used interchangeably with testifying to the gospel of the grace of God.

Paul's words in 1 Cor. 6:9, 10, 1 Thess. 2:12 and 2 Thess. 1:5, make it plain that the kingdom of God in its full manifestation was both the hope and destiny of those addressed in these epistles. Ephesians 5:5, Colossians 4:11, 2 Tim. 4:1 and 18 give witness to the truth that the kingdom of God remained the hope proclaimed by Paul until the close of his ministry.

Indeed, the kingdom of God is the grand central theme of all Scripture. So much so, that the man who has little knowledge of the kingdom of God has no real knowledge of the Bible, no matter how many bits and pieces of the Word he may have collected. In order to make sense, these bits and pieces must sooner or later be related to a central theme. If they are related to Christ, this is still not the end. If His glories revealed in the Word are considered, we will always come to the kingdom of God of which He is the divine King.

The one who is not instructed in the kingdom of God will never understand the parables, for this is what most of the parables are about. He can never be like the Christ-commended householder who brings forth out of his treasure things both new and old (Matt. 13:52). Furthermore, the one who does not study the kingdom of God is not studying the Bible, and he who is not proclaiming the kingdom of God is not proclaiming the Bible. Those who fail to declare the truth concerning it are not declaring the whole counsel of God. They cannot honestly claim to be "pure from the blood of all men."

In view of the important place that the kingdom of God has in the Bible, one would think that this term would often be upon the lips of all whose lives have been shaped by God's Book, and that it would have a very large place in the writings of those who claim to be expounding the Word of God. But, alas, it is not. One can only be amazed at the small place that is given to this theme among believers, and the writings of many Bible teachers will be searched in vain for any mention of it. The indexes of their writings will show that the treatment of it is very meager indeed. This is especially true of those classed as dispensationalists.

Before me is the index of one Bible study magazine that covers twenty volumes representing twenty years of writing. In this index the references to the kingdom of God can be counted on the fingers of one hand; and when these are traced out, the material is so insignificant that one can only conclude that the neglect of this subject was intentional. And the indexes to another Bible study publication covering a period of fifty years, show an almost total neglect of this subject. I have leaved through four years 24 (issues) of another publication, but I cannot find any treatment whatsoever of the kingdom of God. It seems to be the policy of these editors to keep the subject out of their written ministry.

In regard to this I would appropriate the words of James and say, "My brethern, these things ought not so to be." Furthermore, there should be no such thing as a book or a sermon that professes to deal with the parables while consistently ignoring that the subject of these parables is the kingdom of God.

In the words of the translators of the *King James Version*, they have the Lord saying that the kingdom has suffered violence (Matt. 11:12). And while this translation is open to question and the passage in which it is found is an obscure one, the meaning of which is not yet fully understood, yet the phrase is an apt one and we can say beyond question that the truth concerning the kingdom of God has suffered great violence at the hands of men all through the Christian era. It has been incorrectly defined, erroneously interpreted, and hopelessly confused.

To define the kingdom of God as being the church establishment is a disgrace. To define it as being the universal sovereignty of God which has always been and always will be, as so many do, and then to apply this concept to the occurrences of this phrase found in the New Testament is to do violence to the truth declared in the many usages of this term by the Lord Jesus Christ. To say that the kingdom of God is something within all Christians, and then to prove this by citing words that He spoke to His malignant enemies, can only be described as a wicked usage of the word of our Lord.

There is one debt that all Christians owe to God. This is to get into His Book and find the real truth concerning the kingdom of God.

The SEED & BREAD Bible-Study leaflets are published as often as time and means permit and are sent free to all names on THE WORD OF TRUTH MINISTRY mailing list. Send us your name. There will be no obligation, solicitation or visitation. Additional copies of any issue available on request.

ISSUE NO. 27

Reprinted Oct. 17, 2001

SEED & BREAD

FOR THE SOWER   ISA. 55:10   FOR THE EATER

BRIEF BIBLICAL MESSAGES
FROM
THE WORD OF TRUTH MINISTRY

339 South Orange Drive, Los Angeles, Cal. 90036

Otis Q. Sellers, Bible Teacher

THE KINGDOM: WHY TWO NAMES?

The Biblical doctrine of the kingdom of God has suffered greatly from the puerile and erroneous interpretation of many passages in which important truth concerning it is found. As examples I would cite Matt. 12:28; Luke 17:20, 21; Rom. 14:17 and 1 Cor. 15:50. It has also suffered violence by lines of teaching that are contrary to the truth revealed concerning it. This is especially true among those who are partial dispensationalists, who have created great confusion by insisting on a sharp distinction between the kingdom of Heaven and the kingdom of God.

This position was made popular by Dr. C. I. Scofield and is capably set forth by Lewis Sperry Chafer in his *Systematic Theology* (Vol. 4, page 26).

That form of interpretation which rides on occasional similarities and passes over vital differences is displayed by those who argue that the kingdom of heaven, as referred to in Matthew, must be the same as the kingdom of God since some parables regarding the kingdom of heaven are reported in Mark and Luke under the designation, *the kingdom of God.* No attempt is made by these expositors to explain why the term kingdom of heaven is used by Matthew only, nor do they seem to recognize the fact that the real difference between that which these designations represent is to be discovered in connection with the instances where they are not and cannot be used interchangeably rather than in the instances where they are used interchangeably. Certain features are common to both the kingdom of heaven and the kingdom of God, and in such instances the interchange of the terms is justified. Closer attention will reveal that the kingdom of heaven is always earthly while the kingdom of God is as wide as the universe and includes as much of earthly things as are germane to it. Likewise the kingdom of heaven is entered by a righteousness exceeding the righteousness of the scribes and the Pharisees (Matt. 5:20), while the kingdom of God is entered by a new birth (John 3:1-16).

I, for one, do not want to be guilty of riding on "occasional similarities" while ignoring "vital differences." Neverthless, after prolonged study which forced a change of opinion, I have the firm conviction that the terms "kingdom of heaven" and "kingdom of God" are two names for the same thing and that they are identical in every respect. Furthermore, I believe there are sound explanations as to why the term "kingdom of heaven" is used only by Matthew. And I also know that there is no explanation as to why he is the only writer who uses it if we make this term to be something unique and different from the kingdom of God. Can it be that this term represents a distinct truth of great importance of which no other Biblical writer has anything to say save Matthew? Not in the least. Mark and Luke present this same truth under the title of the kingdom of God.

Since the only proper approach to the New Testament is through the Old, it is illogical to interpret Matthew without giving due consideration to revelations in the Hebrew scriptures that have a direct bearing upon the subject.

In Daniel 4, in connection with God's dealing with Nebuchadnezzar, we read, "that the living may know that the Most High ruleth in the kingdom of men, and giveth it to whomsoever He will, and setteth up over it the basest of men" (Dan. 4:17). The only kingdom on earth at that time was that of Nebuchadnezzar, and the Most High determined to let him know that no matter how much liberty He permitted him, He still held the sovereignty (the right to govern) in His own hands. So the Most High took him off the throne, caused him to be insane for seven years, then restored him to it with greater majesty than ever before.

When Daniel interpreted the king's vision, he reiterated the divine declaration, "till you know that the Most High ruleth in the kingdom of men," but as he continues, he declares that the king's discipline would be until, "after thou shalt have known that the Heavens do rule" (Dan. 4. 26). Later the declaration concerning the Most High ruling is repeated. Thus we see in this one chapter the following declarations:

> "that the Most High ruleth" Dan. 4:17
> "that the Most High ruleth" Dan. 4:25
> "that the heavens do rule" Dan. 4:26
> "that the Most High ruleth" Dan. 4:32

These four statements express identical truth. In them there is an easy change from "the Most High" to "the heavens." This is because these two terms are synonymous. They can be used interchangeably. No matter what other meanings it may have, the term "the Heavens" in the Old Testament is used as a descriptive title of the Deity. It is also used this way in many places in the New Testament. There is no differnce in meaning between the terms "The kingdom of God" and "the kingdom of the heavens" (as it always reads in the Greek).

In Matt. 4:12, 17 we are told that after John was cast into prison, "from that time Jesus began to preach, and to say, 'Repent for the kingdom of heaven is at hand." Mark, in reporting the same incident, declares that He preached, "the kingdom of God is at hand" (Mark 1:15). If these two terms are identical there is no problem. But if they describe two different concepts, it becomes necessary for us to decide which writer is giving the more accurate report.

This is usually explained by saying that the kingdom of God is a universal sphere of which the kingdom of heaven is a part, and that the name of a part can also be called by the name of the whole, such as calling Colorado the United States. However, this explanation is fraught with serious difficulties. Let us consider two statements as an illustration: (1) He lectured on the mountains of the United States; (2) he lectured on the mountains of Colorado. Either one of these statements can be true, since Colorado is a part of the United States, but it still leaves the question, just what mountains did he speak about? Which report is the most accurate?

In Matt. 5:3 the Lord Jesus said, "Blessed are the poor in spirit: for theirs is the kingdom of heaven"; but in Luke 6:20 we read that He said, "Blessed be ye poor: for your's is the kingdom of God."

In Matt. 8:11 the Lord Jesus places Abraham, Isaac, and Jacob in the kingdom of heaven. Luke, in reporting the same incident, says that He placed them in the kingdom of God (Luke 13:28). There is no difficulty here if these two terms are identical, which they are.

Matthew reports that when the Lord Jesus sent forth the twelve, He told them to "go, preach, saying the kingdom of heaven is at hand" (10:7). But Luke says He sent them to preach the kingdom of God (9:2). If these terms set forth two different concepts, one limited and the other unlimited, then which concept were they supposed to proclaim?

Again Matthew reports that the Lord Jesus spoke of those who were "least in the kingdom of heaven" (Matt. 11:11), while Luke reports that He said, "least in the kingdom of God" (Luke 7:28).

Matthew quotes the Lord as saying that the parables have to do with "the mysteries of the kingdom of heaven" (Matt. 13:11), while both Mark (4:11) and Luke (8:10) say they have to do with "the mysteries of the kingdom of God."

Matthew reports that the Lord said, "the kingdom of heaven is like a grain of mustard seed" (13:31), while Mark says He declared it to be a likeness of "the kingdom of God" (4:30-32). Matthew quotes the Lord as saying, "the kingdom of heaven is like unto leaven" (13:33), but Luke reports the Lord as saying it is a likeness of the kingdom of God (Luke 13:20-21).

In all these passages if these two terms mean the same thing, then there are no problems; but if they present two different concepts, then they present problems that cannot be solved. I believe they are synonymous. In one place our Lord used these two terms interchangeably. After His conversation with the rich young ruler, He said to His disciples:

Verily I say unto you, that a rich man shall hardly enter into the KINGDOM OF HEAVEN. And again I say unto you, it is easier for a camel to go through the eye of a needle, than for a rich man to enter into the KINGDOM OF GOD (Matt. 19:23, 24).

In this passage the two terms are identical and synonymous. We will do well to follow the example of our Lord and use them this way. However, the question posed in the subject of this article has not yet been answered—"Why Two Terms?"

It is well known that the reverence of the Hebrew people for the name of God led them to avoid the use of the divine name as much as possible and to substitute other expressions. A very common substitute was "Heaven," which should not seem strange at all since we do this in English. Note such sayings as, "an appeal to Heaven," "Heaven help us," and "Heaven only knows." The prodigal son said, "Father, I have sinned against heaven" (Luke 15:21). The Lord Jesus asked the Jews, "The baptism of John, whence was it? from heaven or of men?" (Matt 21:25). Again He said, "He that shall swear by heaven, sweareth by the throne of God, and by Him that sitteth thereon" (Matt. 23:22). G. Dalman points out rabbinic usage in such phrases as, "by the hand of heaven," "the name of heaven," "the word of heaven," "the mercy of heaven," and "the decrees of heaven," all of which are references to God.

Matthew, writing his gospel with the Hebrew people primarily in mind, as evidenced by his introductory words, made use of this substitution as much as possible in order to give no offense and to make his language as appealing to them as possible.

Thus, after the most careful consideration in which no stone has been left unturned in the search for the truth in regard to this matter, it is my conviction and teaching that the terms "kingdom of heaven" and "kingdom of God" are identical in meaning and can be used interchangeably by the teacher of God's Word without harming in the least His revelation of truth. However, since in my ministry I feel no need of using a term that will not give offense to the feelings of the Jewish people, I habitually use the term, "the kingdom of God," except in places where I am quoting Scripture verbatim.

The SEED and BREAD Bible-Study leaflets are published as often as time and means permit and are sent free to all names on THE WORD OF TRUTH MINISTRY mailing list. Send us your name. There will be no obligation, solicitation, or visitation. Additional copies of any issue available on request.   ISSUE NO. 28

SEED & BREAD

FOR THE SOWER   ISA. 55:10   FOR THE EATER

BRIEF BIBLICAL MESSAGES

FROM

THE WORD OF TRUTH MINISTRY

339 South Orange Drive, Los Angeles, Cal. 90036

Otis Q. Sellers, Bible Teacher

'KINGDOM' MEANS 'GOVERNMENT'

The truth that is boldly declared in the title of the study is a most important one that will prove to be a key to many treasures that are waiting to be discovered in the Word of God. Arbitrary and erroneous definitions have been given to the word *kingdom* in order to make it fit certain creedal views and theological schemes. To say that *kingdom* means "government" is a simple and honest statement that some will reject the moment they hear it. Simple truths are not looked upon favorably by many theologians. They prefer to keep everything exceedingly complex so that it can be understood only by the few they recognize as scholars. Since this word appears over and over, in the Old as well as the New Testament, to understand it is to comprehend the message of much of the Bible that has been obscure heretofore.

Today, the common definition of the word *kingdom* is that it means a country, governed by one who is called a king; but this is a modern adaptation and it was not the basic meaning of this word when the *King James Version* was translated. The elements of the word reveal this. A king was a monarch, one who ruled alone. He made the laws, interpreted the laws, and enforced the laws. The *dom* portion of this word is a shortened form of *doom,* which meant judgment. Thus the monarch's judgments were his government. All this is demonstrated by Scripture usage. In Ecclesiastes 8:4 we read: "Where the word of a king is, there is power: and who may say unto him, What doest thou?" This alone is sufficient to show the strength of the word *king (melek)* in the Bible. I am sure that most of my readers have heard of "judgment day" being called "doomsday."

In Psalm 103:19 it is declared that, "The Lord hath prepared His throne in the heavens; and His kingdom rules over all." From this we can see that His kingdom is that which rules; therefore, it is His government, and it is not the realm that is governed.

The Greek word translated "kingdom" is *basileia.* This being

EWB —the power or form of government, its territory the development of God's purpose

true, the problem to be solved is not what the word kingdom means, but what the Greek word *basileia* means. The word *kingdom* is a word in a living language that has undergone quite a few changes since it was enshrined in the *King James Version* over 350 years ago. The word *basileia* belongs to first century Greek which has now become a fixed or dead language, and its meaning must be settled by its usage at that time.

That the basic, fundamental idea in the word *basileia* is government is a fact that becomes increasingly obvious the more its usages are examined. That it is an abstract word, not concrete, is another fact that must be accepted. If it is ever used in the concrete as denoting a realm governed, (and I question if it ever is) it is a figurative use. Such occurrences should not be used to determine its primary meaning.

Thus, that which is called "the kingdom of God" in the *King James Version* is actually the government of God or God's government. This being true, there are many things recorded in Scripture that can be called "the kingdom of God" when we understand this term to mean God's government. For example, in the fact that God set two great lights in the firmament of the heaven to give light upon the earth, and to rule over the day and over the night (Gen. 1:17, 18), we have a clear case of God's government in action. This was an exercise of sovereignty, for the sovereignty of the universe belongs to God, and He reserves to Himself the right to govern in any or all matters, even setting someone or something to govern or rule under Himself.

Later, after the creation of man, we find Him declaring a certain prohibition in regard to eating the fruit of the tree of the knowledge of good and evil. This is also God acting in government, exercising His sovereignty, and this act can properly be described as the government of God. And we could go on through the Old Testament and point out a thousand things such as these, all of which can be called the government of God in action.

Such things as these are what men are referring to when they speak of "the kingdom in the Old Testament." However, they should not carry this simple concept of God's government into the New Testament and declare that this is what the Lord Jesus was speaking about when He came into Galilee heralding the gospel of the kingdom (government) of God. This is not what He meant when He said, "The time is fulfilled, and the kingdom of God is at hand" (Mark 1:14, 15).

The careful Bible student will quickly come to know that the term "the kingdom (government) of God," which can have many applications, is in the New Testament applied to a definite time that is still future when certain conditions will prevail upon the earth and the character of divine rule will be so complete and of such nature that this time above all other times is worthy of being called the kingdom of God. No matter how much or in what ways God has governed (exercised His sovereignty) in the past, no matter what events may be pointed out as evidence of divine government in action, a time is coming when God is going to govern this earth and men upon it in such manner that it will be unlike anything He has ever done before. Even as it is written:

"For since the beginning of the world men have not heard, nor perceived by the ear, neither hath the eye seen, O God, beside Thee, what He hath prepared for him that waiteth for Him" (Isa. 64:4).

This is what Joseph was waiting for when he waited for the kingdom of God (Luke 23:51). This is what David meant when he said, "Thou shalt judge the peoples righteously and govern the nations upon earth" (Psa. 67:4). This is what Isaiah prophesied when He said, "And the government shall be upon His shoulder" (Isa. 9:6).

From this we can see that to enter into the kingdom of God is not simply to come under His sovereignty, for we are always under His sovereignty and there is no place that man can flee to get away from it. However, even though we are under God's sovereignty, we will err grievously if we adopt the idea that God is always exercising it to the fullest extent over all things at all times. This is the view of many, and they are usually ready with a proof text from Ephesians which says that God "worketh all things after the counsel of His own will" (Eph 1:11). They insist that "all things" means everything, the evil as well as the good, but they steadfastly refuse to recognize the true meaning of the Greek idiom *ta panta*, which Paul himself established in Colossians 3:8, where it obviously means "all these" and has reference to things set forth in the context.

The idea that everything is fully controlled by God now, that He is now governing every detail of the lives of all mankind is the great mental stumbling block that stands in the road of men seeing, understanding, and believing the truth that the world will yet be fully governed by God in a dispensation of divine government and this time of divine rule is called the kingdom of God.

We need to distinguish between such things as sovereignty and the exercise of sovereignty, as authority and the exercise of authority, as power and the exercise of power. We have clear evidence of this in the words of Paul spoken in Lystra, that in times past God suffered (permitted or allowed) all nations to walk in their own ways (Acts 14:16). He did not exercise His sovereignty over them once He gave them this freedom.

In Revelation 11:17 we read of the twenty-four elders saying: "We give Thee thanks, O Lord God Almighty, which art, and wast, and art to come; because Thou has taken to Thee Thy great power and hast reigned." The *King James Version* here is somewhat inexact. The tenses are very important. A more accurate rendering of the Greek would be: "For You have taken to Yourself Your great power and You do govern" *(ebasileusas)*.

To His disciples the Lord Jesus declared that all authority *(exousia)* in heaven and in earth had been given unto Him (Matt. 28:18). Power *(dunamis)* is that which comes from authority that has been given. Thus we see in these passages from Matthew and Revelation, the authority given, the power taken and both being exercised which resulted in government. However, this is still future. The time will come when Jesus Christ will take to Himself His great power and will govern the earth and all men upon it. When He does, this will be the kingdom of God. And it is quite evident from the position of this act in the book of Revelation that it precedes the return of Jesus Christ to the earth. This is one more reason why I believe in and teach the pre-advent kingdom of God, that long period of divine government which will be a reality before the return of Jesus Christ to be personally present for a thousand years and present because of Who He is and what He does in fulfillment of all His offices.

The old rabbis had ⌐NOT SECRET a term for this aspect of divine government. They called this "the manifest kingdom of God," and linked it up with the fulfillment of all the glorious promises found in the Hebrew scriptures. We will do well to adopt this term and use it in our attempts to make plain the truth of the kingdom of God.

Another term which we need if we would speak clearly on the kingdom of God is the phrase "the divine assumption of sovereignty," for this is the act of God that will bring His kingdom to the earth.

I take my stand with that small but ever increasing number of careful students of the Word who have come to the fixed conclusion that the kingdom of God as proclaimed by Jesus Christ is a future condition of things, a future reality that will exist upon this earth only after a miraculous intervention by God.

The word *government* says everything that is found in the Greek word *basileia*. It is a more solid word since it has not gone through the changes that have happened to the word *kingdom*, a word that has ended up not meaning much more than a country whose ceremonial chief of state is designated by the title of *King*.

The SEED and BREAD Bible-Study leaflets are published as often as time and means permit and are sent free to all names on THE WORD OF TRUTH MINISTRY mailing list. Send us your name. There will be no obligation, solicitation, or visitation. Additional copies of any issue available on request.　　　ISSUE NO. 29

1-3745M

SEED & BREAD

FOR THE SOWER   ISA. 55:10   FOR THE EATER

BRIEF BIBLICAL MESSAGES
FROM

THE WORD OF TRUTH MINISTRY

339 South Orange Drive, Los Angeles, Cal. 90036

Otis Q. Sellers, Bible Teacher

KINGDOM TRUTH

The descriptive phrase, "the kingdom of God," has suffered many things at the hands of its interpreters. Today, it is grossly misunderstood throughout Christendom. It has been taken and applied to many things and used in ways that are contrary to all that the Bible teaches. It is so commonly used in religious circles that there is a widespread illusion that its meaning is well understood. This is contrary to the facts in the case, for it is quite evident that the average Christian does not know what it means when he hears it or what idea it conveys when he uses it. This Biblical phrase has become part of the ritualistic language of Christendom. Men talk of "building the kingdom of God," ignoring altogether that God alone can build His kingdom. Certain dispensationalists say, "the kingdom of God is Jewish," in woeful ignorance of the fact that if this were true it would be "the kingdom of the Jews," or "the kingdom of Israel," not the kingdom of God. There are built-in safeguards in this phrase against all such errors; but, alas, they go unheeded.

Furthermore, there is in this phrase a definite safeguard against the common error of defining the word *kingdom* as signifying "a realm ruled over by a king." This definition will not fit into this phrase, and if it is accepted it will draw a veil over every occurrence of this phrase in the New Testament. It is a usage based on accommodation, and fastened onto the Greek word *basileia*. This is the same as taking the modern meaning of the word *libertine* and fastening it onto the occurrence in Acts 6:9. Everyone who seeks to understand the Word of God should pause and ask himself the question, "How do *I* define the kingdom of God?"

My own definition of the kingdom of God is that I understand the Greek word *basileia* to mean government, although such synonymous terms as rule, sovereignty, jurisdiction, and reign may also be used to indicate certain shades of meaning when the context so indicates. Therefore, in its basic, fundamental meaning "the kingdom of God" is the government of God. However, in the New Testament this term is repeatedly used to designate a certain future time period, that is, absolute divine government in a definite period of time. In that day the words "government of the people, by the people, and for the people" will be used only to refer to a condition that existed in the past. In the kingdom of God the government will be of God, by God, and for His glory. As Dr. George E. Ladd rightly says: "The day is surely coming when God will take the reins of government into His hands and the kingdom of God will come on earth and His will be done even as it is in heaven" (The Blessed Hope, page 6).

In medieval times it was customary to look upon organized religion, the visible ecclesiastical system, as being "the church," and then insist that the church was the kingdom of God. This is a concept still held by many, but it is one that cannot be equated with the truth revealed in the New Testament.

In the nineteenth century many Christians became deeply disturbed about the kind of a world in which they lived and were anxious to make it a better one. In their desires they saw an ideal state of affairs among men toward which they felt "the church" should strive. They appropriated the Biblical term "the kingdom of God" to describe this ideal state of affairs and proclaimed that it was the sacred duty of "the church" to bring the kingdom of God upon the earth. Thus, they misappropriated this phrase to give credence to and dignify their programs for social progress, employing it constantly in a manner that was foreign to the New Testament.

This error spread like a brush fire. The use of this term in this manner was taken up and widely developed by leading theologians in Europe and America until the idea of the church bringing in the kingdom of God became the popular religious idea of the day.

Thus, at the turn of the century many Christian leaders were turning their attention to the social ills that plagued mankind. They were convinced that the principal task of organized religion was to rectify all that was wrong in the social order. "To create a civilization that is Christian in spirit and passion throughout the earth," were the glowing words used to describe this goal by one interchurch movement. A new gospel called "the social gospel" became the vogue of the day. This "gospel" was concerned with the betterment of mankind. In almost every theological seminary in the U.S.A. it displaced that gospel which had always been concerned with the salvation of the individual.

In the social gospel the idea of a "united church" bringing justice, righteousness, equity and peace upon the earth was given the paramount place. And the phrase commonly used to describe this goal was "bringing the kingdom of God upon the earth." "Building the kingdom of God," "extending the kingdom of God," and "advancing the kingdom of God" were the popular phrases used to describe every effort and program of this time. They were used when a new church was organized, a church building was dedicated, a mission field opened, a church school was founded or enlarged, a minister was ordained, or even when a baby was baptized. All these accomplishments were looked upon as being facets of building, extending, advancing, or increasing the kingdom of God. And the drive was always to get more men and get more money, for these were the two main things needed to build the kingdom of God on earth.

There is a demonstrable law related to the use of words which is parallel to Gresham's law in regard to money. (Gresham's law is simply that bad money drives out the good.) This law in regard to words is that the improper and false usage of a term will drive the proper and true use out of circulation. This is exactly what happened to the true meaning of the term "the kingdom of God." A meaning established by 74 occurrences of this phrase in the New Testament was debased by a false meaning and a deliberate misappropriation. The true Scriptural meaning and usage was almost driven from the minds of men and the term itself came into disrepute. In the great revival of Bible study and preaching that came in the last quarter of the nineteenth century, those who participated hesitated to use this term.

Reactions to this mass of error were bound to come, and they took place in the great resurgence of Bible study in the last quarter of the nineteenth and first quarter of the twentieth century. In this resurgence the "social gospel" was assailed and contradicted with many infallible proofs from the Word of God. It was demonstrated to be a perversion of the gospel of Christ and its programs foreign to the facts of God's revealed truth. And the great dispensational-premillennial movement came to the forefront to lead and to challenge in respect to a new and honest approach to the prophetic (eschatological) portions of God's Word.

History demonstrates that most reactions go too far. This was true of the reaction against the great mass of erroneous teaching which had usurped and falsely used the Biblical term "the kingdom of God." The idea of the dispensational premillennialists seemed to be—stay away from the kingdom of God, let it alone. No real attempt was made to rescue it from the clutches of those who had misappropriated it to characterize their programs. The real truth concerning it was sorely neglected. It was made to be "the millennium," which it certainly is not. All attention was centered on "the signs of the times," "the rapture," "the tribulation," and "the second coming." And since the great prominence of the kingdom of God in

Scripture could not be ignored, they gave it in insipid and generalized definition which robbed it of all value so far as being an expression of truth is concerned. It was defined as being the sovereignty of God, which is moral and universal, including all moral intelligences willingly subject to the will of God, whether angels or the saints of past and future dispensations. It was said to have existed from the beginning and will know no end, that it is over all and embraces all. This, in essence, is the definition given in both the *Scofield Reference Bible* and *The Companion Bible*.

This is what is known as a "Mother Hubbard definition," named after the dress of yesteryears. It covers everything and reveals nothing. The real weakness of it is that it will not fit into, neither will it shed any light upon any of the 74 occurrences of the term "the kingdom of God," in the New Testament. Is this what the Lord Jesus was proclaiming when He came into Galilee, preaching the gospel of the kingdom of God, and saying, "the time is fulfilled, and the kingdom of God is at hand"? Not in the least! I hesitate to be critical of both Dr. Scofield and Dr. Bullinger. However, if all their published writings are examined, it becomes plain that the assiduous study of the kingdom of God was simply not their cup of tea.

In my opinion the greatest weakness of the dispensational premillennialists has been their failure to include in their system of interpretation any sound and worthwhile teaching in regard to the kingdom of God. Their reaction in regard to all "kingdom now" and "kingdom is here" teaching, also against the false idea of men bringing in the kingdom by education, democratization, and culturization of the peoples of the earth, has been so strong that it has lead to an almost complete failure to lay hold of the Biblical truth of the kingdom of God. All truth concerning the kingdom is under suspicion in dispensational circles. This should not be, and as a dispensationalist for fifty-five years I intend to do my part to correct this situation.

The SEED and BREAD Bible-Study leaflets are published as often as time and means permit and are sent free to all names on THE WORD OF TRUTH MINISTRY mailing list. Send us your name. There will be no obligation, solicitation, or visitation. Additional copies of any issue available on request.   ISSUE NO. 30

SEED & BREAD

FOR THE SOWER   ISA. 55:10   FOR THE EATER

BRIEF BIBLICAL MESSAGES
FROM
THE WORD OF TRUTH MINISTRY
339 South Orange Drive, Los Angeles, Cal. 90036

Otis Q. Sellers, Bible Teacher

THE KINGDOM-PRESENT OR FUTURE?

It comes as a shock to many people to find that some things in the Bible are exceedingly simple. Some do not want this to be so. To them the divine Word must never be plain; it must always be mysterious. Therefore, when it is said that "kingdom" means "government," the statement is rejected with the curt dismissal, "Too simple!" They are somewhat like Naaman, whom Elisha told to go and wash in Jordan seven times if he desired to be cleansed from his leprosy. The great commander in chief thought this was far too simple a solution of his complex problem. It was good that his servants straightened him out on this or he would have been a leper till the day of his death.

The word *government* says everything that is contained in the Greek word *basileia*. There is no occurrence of this word in the New Testament where the word government will not fit; even though there are places where the synonymous terms *rule, sovereignty, jurisdiction* and *reign* might be more apropos due to the context.

In theological writings two main interpretations of the kingdom of God will be found, the eschatological and the non-eschatological. These interpretations are in respect to the question: Is the kingdom of God present or future? Is it the present reign of God in the hearts of submissive men, or is it the future reign of Jesus Christ over the earth? The eschatological position is that it is future. The non-eschatological position is that it is a present spiritual reality.

I take my position with that great number of careful and believing students of the Word who have come to the fixed conclusion that the kingdom of God is a future condition of things, a future reality of divine government that will exist upon the earth after a miraculous intervention by God. Many have written eloquently to this end, and what they have said is worthy of careful consideration. Samuel J. Andrews has said:

All prophecy, as we have abundantly seen, pointed forward to the universal kingdom of Jehovah, administered by the promised Son of David. For this the world is to wait, in it all nature will be blessed: it is the consummation of prophetic hope. All His prior actings in redemption are to prepare the way for this, its last stage.... Thus there is during the Kingdom period a well-ordered system of government, embracing the whole earth, administered by Christ through those whom He appoints; a system adapted to meet the needs of all its inhabitants in all their varied conditions and degrees of intellectual and spiritual development. Now is first seen the full power of the Divine institutions of the family and state, when filled by His Spirit, to produce the purest and noblest fruits in individual life. Now is, also, seen the full development of national life, the solution of all social and political questions, and the true unity of nations. All that men have ever imagined of human progress in science and art will fall far short of those who will study God's works, not from personal ambition or vanity, but out of love for Him, delighting in every new discovery of His wisdom and goodness, and using all knowledge for the blessing of their fellow-men. (*God's Revelations of Himself to Men,* pages 318, 323, 324).

This is a profound statement in respect to the eschatological position, the belief that the kingdom of God is a future divine condition of things upon this earth. I utter a fervent "Amen" to every word quoted above, and declare that when this is a reality I want to be a part of it; and I would be perpetually happy if it should be the will of God and my portion to be among those "who will study God's works, not from personal ambition or vanity, but out of love for Him." Along these same lines Alva J. McClain has said in his book *The Greatness of the Kingdom* (Zondervan, 1959):

There is a current and popular idea that the coming of the kingdom of God to earth is a process, long and gradual; at times so imperceptible that skeptics may be able to dispute seriously whether there be such a thing as the reign of God. Such a notion has no foundation in the writings of the Old Testament prophets (page 174). In the day of the coming Kingdom, it will not be necessary to write endless volumes on Christian "evidences" and "apologetics." Debates on the existence of God will become absurd and obsolete, suited only to be classed with arguments over the existence of sunlight. Eschatological systems which define the Kingdom of God wholly in terms of the invisible will need to be revised. For the supernatural evidences of the existence of God, and of His Christ, and of His Kingdom, will be open to all men (page 176). These great moral principles of the mediatorial government will be enforced by *sanctions of supernatural power.* The answer of God to all people and kings who venture to set themselves against the beneficent rule of the coming Kingdom is a solemn commission to His anointed King: "Thou art my son.... Ask of me, and I shall give Thee the heathen (nations) for thine inheritance.... Thou shalt break them with a rod of iron; Thou shalt dash them in pieces like a potters vessel" (Ps. 2:7-9). No longer will the wicked oppressor of the poor be able to utter his cynical judgment: "God hath forgotten; He hideth His face; He will never see it" (Psa. 10:9-11). No longer will the righteous be troubled about the ways of God in a world where things seem to be upside down (Ps. 73:2-16). The question as to whether or not we live in a "moral universe" will no longer be a subject for philosophic debate. For in the coming Kingdom the judgments of God will be immediate and tangible to all men (Zech. 14:17-19;

Isa. 66:24). The long period of God's judicial silence, which men have perversely construed as an evidence of moral indifference instead of long-suffering mercy on the part of God, will come to an end (Psa. 50:21). And with the judgments of a Holy God once more manifest in the earth, "the inhabitants of the world will learn righteousness" (Isa. 26:9). (Pages 208, 209).

A paragraph from the writings of George E. Ladd is also pertinent here:

> The kingdom of God is therefore primarily a soteriological concept. It is God acting in power and exercising His sovereignty for the defeat of Satan and the restoration of human society to its rightful place of willing subservience to the will of God. It is not the sovereignty of God as such; God is always and everywhere the sovereign God. It is the sovereignty of God in action to frustrate every enemy which would oppose God's will (I Cor. 15:25). It is not the reign of God as such; for God is ultimately reigning as the eternal King. It is the action of the sovereign God of heaven by which His reign is restored in power to those areas of His creation which He has permitted to move outside the actual acknowledgment of His rule. The kingdom of God then is God's reign, the activity of God's sovereign and kingly authority. German has a better word for it than English: *Gottesherrschaft.* The central meaning is not realm, but authority. (*Crucial Questions About the Kingdom of God,* page 83).

Quotations such as these could be multiplied, since many writers have declared themselves along these same lines. Great indeed is the number of Bible students who see the kingdom of God as being the future reign of God over this earth and its inhabitants. They hold that the manifest kingdom of God upon the earth will be the result of a "cataclysmic irruption of God into history," as Ladd so aptly states it. They reject the idea that the kingdom of God will come through the efforts of men, and hold that it will be inaugurated by a supernatural act or acts of God. Among that "mighty army" past and present who have held and taught the "future kingdom" view, can be listed such names as Darby, Kelly, Andrews, Anderson, Seiss, Bullinger, Gray, Gabelein, Torrey, Pierson, Tregelles, Scofield, Haldeman, Chafer, Riley, Ironside, McClain, Walvoord, Culbertson, Pentecost, and many more. I follow in their train.

However, in the writings of all those mentioned above there are two errors constantly found which I am convinced vitiate and stultify the Bible revelation of the kingdom of God. Present space limits will permit me to deal with only one of these.

This one, seen especially in the writings of George E. Ladd, is that the kingdom of God is both present and future; that there is some action of God now among men that can be called the kingdom of God, and a future glorious reign of Christ over the earth that is also called the kingdom of God. As Ladd puts the question: "Can it involve both a millennial reign of Christ on earth in the future and a present spiritual reign of Christ in the hearts of His people?" His answer is that it involves both.

It is apparent that this position would require the sorting out of every statement concerning the kingdom of God in the New Testament into two groups — those that apply to the kingdom which is now and those that apply to the kingdom which is future. If this is attempted, it will be found that there are only about four out of seventy-four which might be applied to the "kingdom now" idea; but when these are properly interpreted, they will be seen to belong to the future kingdom.

I do not believe that anyone can point to anything on this earth today and say, "That is God's government; that is the kingdom of God." That which is called "the present spiritual reign of Christ in the hearts of His people," whatever this may be, is not what the Bible is talking about when it speaks of the kingdom of God.

It is certainly true that in the 33 years of the Acts period there were definite events that one could point to and, calling a part by the name of the whole, say, "That is a manifestation of divine sovereignty; there is a sample of God's government in action." There are innumerable things today of which we can say, "This is God's providence," and many more of which we can say, "This is God's grace;" but there is nothing we can point to and say, "That is God's government."

The SEED and BREAD Bible-Study leaflets are published as often as time and means permit and are sent free to all names on THE WORD OF TRUTH MINISTRY mailing list. Send us your name. There will be no obligation, solicitation, or visitation. Additional copies of any issue available on request.   ISSUE NO. 31

SEED & BREAD

FOR THE SOWER   ISA. 55:10   FOR THE EATER

BRIEF BIBLICAL MESSAGES

FROM

THE WORD OF TRUTH MINISTRY

339 South Orange Drive, Los Angeles, Cal. 90036

Otis Q. Sellers, Bible Teacher

KINGDOM BLUNDERS

There are those who teach that the kingdom of God is entirely now, and others who teach that only certain aspects are present now with the greatest aspect to be in the future. I believe that both of these are kingdom blunders, and in the realm of theology once a blunder has been put into print it is never corrected. However, the error of saying that certain aspects of the kingdom are present now is not the most serious one. The error which has led to more confusion of thought than any other is the great blunder which has been repeated and perpetuated by almost every teacher who has dealt with the future kingdom of God. It is the idea that the future kingdom is inaugurated by the personal return of Jesus Christ to the earth. This position, of course, equates the future kingdom of God with the millennium of Revelation 20. This is the great error that is behind almost every problem of prophetic interpretation.

I want it to be known here that I take second place to no man in believing in the actual, personal return of Jesus Christ to the earth and in His personal presence (parousia) for a thousand years. This has been an article of faith with me for 54 years and an equal number of years of Bible study have served to deepen this conviction. "This same Jesus, which is taken up from you into heaven, shall so come in like manner as ye have seen Him go into heaven." (Acts 1:11) These words epitomize my faith in the return of the Lord Jesus to the earth.

A bit of personal history will be apropos here. Soon after I came to know the Lord Jesus as my Savior, I found myself a member of a church that was going through the exercise of much controversy concerning the doctrine of the second coming of Christ. The argument concerned whether it would be premillennial or postmillennial, and I was an observer of the debate which raged between the pastor and the congregation. I decided I would need a vast amount of knowledge before I could settle the question for myself, and refrained from taking sides; even though my sympathies were with the young minister, a premillennialist.

Looking for books to help me in my Bible study, I saw on the bargain table of one bookstore a small volume called *The Second-Coming New Testament.* This was simply a *King James Version* with every verse in it that the editors thought referred to the second coming, printed in boldface type and all other passages, more or less related, printed in italics. I went over these passages again and again and, having a retentive memory, soon found that I could quote verbatim all the passages in boldface and had a good familiarity with all those in italics. Thus, from the very beginning of my Bible study I have been well acquainted with all passages that have to do with the second coming. And I also learned that there is a divine timetable for this event with many things that must precede it, such as the coming of Elijah, the restoration of Israel, and the rebuilding of the temple of God. I also learned that when Jesus Christ does come back, He will take vengeance on them that know not God, and that obey not the gospel of our Lord Jesus Christ. These shall be punished with everlasting destruction from the presence of the Lord and from the glory of His power (2 Thess. 1:7-10). Thus, if the Lord came back today the earth would be wiped clean of its inhabitants; (all who know God having previously been removed) and there would be no nations or peoples left to whom God could fulfill all the glorious promises of the Old Testament, especially those that concern the future of Israel. (See Ezekiel 20:33-44.) All the talk of Israel's finding Christ as a result of the wrath poured out in the great tribulation is sheer nonsense. (See Isa. 1:5.)

Therefore, while I firmly believe in the return of Jesus Christ to this earth, I do not believe that this is imminent or that it is next in order on the divine calendar of future events. Neither do I believe that the personal presence of Jesus Christ on the earth is essential to God's governing it or the men upon it. I believe in a coming dispensation of divine government, brought about by Jesus Christ acting from His place of power at the right hand of God.

This coming dispensation of divine government is called in the Bible "the kingdom of God." It is pre-advent; that is, it is before the second coming of Christ. It is pre-parousia; it precedes the thousand years of His personal presence. One of my chief reasons for believing as I do is because of the truth I have learned concerning the presence of Jesus Christ at God's right hand in heaven. The reader of the Bible will come upon this truth seven times, once in the Old and six times in the New Testament. This fact alone makes it to be a revelation of supreme importance. The Old Testament passage declares, "The LORD said unto my Lord, Sit Thou on My right hand, until I make Thine enemies Thy footstool"

(Psalm 110:1). This identical truth is repeated in Matt. 22:44; Mark 12:36; Luke 20:42, 43; Acts 2:34, 35; and Heb. 1:13. The same truth stated in a slightly different manner is found in 1 Cor. 15:23 and Hebrews 10:12, 13.

Even though the truth stated in these passages is repeated many times it is constantly glossed over by those who begin the coming kingdom with the return of Jesus Christ to the earth. We could not be told more emphatically that Jesus Christ is now seated at the right hand of God and will remain there until His enemies are made His footstool. All this is in accord with one of the great promises of God in Psalm 66:3, 4: "Say unto God, How terrible art Thou in all Thy works! Through the greatness of Thy power shall Thine enemies submit themselves unto Thee. All the earth shall worship Thee, and shall sing unto Thee; they shall sing to Thy name."

There is nothing in past history that fulfills these words. They stand as an unfulfilled prophecy until, as Delitzsch says: "To this it will come when absolute omnipotence for and through the exalted Christ shows its effectiveness."

In the passages cited above we find two terms which have the same meaning. These are "Thy footstool," and "under His feet." Both of these are figures of speech and they mean, to be in subjection; that is, under the power, control and government of another, being in a state of obedience or submissiveness.

In Isaiah 66:1 we find the word *footstool* in close proximity with the word *throne* and this helps us to understand both of these terms: "Thus saith the LORD, The heaven is My throne, and the earth is My footstool." In Scripture the word *throne*, almost always means a seat of government, and we belittle most occurrences when we think of it as some ornate chair intended to be occupied by kings for ceremonial purposes. Thus David declares: "The LORD hath prepared His throne in the heavens; and His kingdom ruleth over all." (Psalm 103:19) We can rest assured that when Jesus Christ governs this earth it will be from the throne and not from the footstool.

From the Psalms we learn the location of His seat of government and the extent of His sovereignty. This seat of government is not going to move from heaven and relocate in Jerusalem when God establishes His government in the earth. When God in Christ takes to Himself His great power and reigns over the earth, the seat of His government will be in heaven. Jesus Christ will remain centered in this seat of government until all His enemies are subject to Him.

Death is the first enemy to become absolutely subject to Him, and it is the last enemy to be abolished (1 Cor. 15:26). When God governs, death will no longer run rampant through the earth but will be under God's control. If anyone dies it will be because God allowed it to be. There will be swift and sure capital punishment under God's government. (See Jer. 31:29, 30.)

In 1 Cor. 15:25 we learn the process by which all enemies are put under His feet. It is one of government. "For He must reign, till He hath put all enemies under His feet." To "reign" (Greek *basileuō*) means to exercise sovereign power or authority. Thus it is by divine government that all enemies are put under His feet and become subject to Him. There is no such process going on today. God is showing grace; He is not governing.

In view of the facts presented, logic demands that we accept the following conclusions:

1. Jesus Christ is now seated at God's right hand in the heavens. (Mark 16:19, Heb. 10:12)

2. It is from this advantageous location that He expects His enemies to be made His footstool. (Heb. 10:13)

3. He has been directed to remain there until this is a reality. (Psalm 110:1) Once this is realized we can expect there will be many visits by Him to this earth before His personal coming for His thousand year parousia.

4. He must reign (or, govern) until He hath put all enemies under His feet, that is, until they become His footstool. (1 Cor. 15:25)

5. There is at present no exercise of divine authority that is working toward the subjection of all enemies. Today we are impelled to cry out in prayer with the Psalmist: "Arise, O God, plead Thine own cause: remember how the foolish man reproacheth Thee daily. Forget not the voice of Thine enemies: the tumult of those that rise up against Thee increaseth continually"(Psalm 74:22, 23).

6. Since Jesus Christ remains at the right hand of God until His enemies are made His footstool, and since He must reign until they are under His feet, the exercise of divine power that overcomes and conquers all enemies cannot begin with His leaving the throne of God to return to the earth.

7. Therefore, Biblical truth demands that there must be a period of divine government over this earth and all men and nations upon it before the second advent, before the parousia, before the millennium.

The SEED and BREAD Bible-Study leaflets are published as often as time and means permit and are sent free to all names on THE WORD OF TRUTH MINISTRY mailing list. Send us your name. There will be no obligation, solicitation, or visitation. Additional copies of any issue available on request. ISSUE NO. 32

SEED & BREAD

FOR THE SOWER   ISA. 55:10   FOR THE EATER

BRIEF BIBLICAL MESSAGES

FROM

THE WORD OF TRUTH MINISTRY

339 South Orange Drive, Los Angeles, Cal. 90036

Otis Q. Sellers, Bible Teacher

THE WORD "JUDGMENT"

The Lord Jesus rebuked the Pharisees because they made "the Word of God of none effect" through their traditions. In man's handling of God's Word at the present time, we find a parallel to this in the way the word *judgment* is treated. In all theology, almost without exception, the word *judgment* is taken to mean punishment; so much so, that this has fixed upon it one definition given in the dictionary that makes it to mean "a calamity sent by God by way of recompence for wrongs committed." It has come to mean this in English because men have persisted in using it this way, but it is a very serious error when this definition is carried into the Word of God. Promises of infinitely great blessings are turned into dire threats of terrible calamities when this false meaning is read into the word *judgment*. Thus, the truth of God is turned into a lie.

Many who handle God's Word are prone to use such adjectives as "fearful," "frightful," and "terrible" when speaking of the judgments of God. This is sheer misrepresentation and such descriptions do not come from the sacred Scriptures. In Scripture we are told that God's judgments are more to be desired than gold, yea, than much fine gold, that they are sweeter also than honey and the honeycomb, that by them God's servants are warned, and in the keeping of them there is great reward. (See Psalm 19:10, 11). How can these things be true if God's judgments have to do with punishments, calamities, curses, and woes? This passage alone should settle it — that judgment does not mean wrath or punishment. And it will settle it for all who allow God's Word to settle things. But there is more to be said.

The English word *judgment* is found 294 times in the Old Testament as the translation of the Hebrew word *mishpat*, and it never means punishment in a single one of these occurrences. At times it may signify an adverse judgment, and this, of course, could result in the punishment of the one who has been so judged; but we should never confuse the two. In 118 other occurrences *mishpat* is translated twenty-eight different ways. In view of this wealth of occurrences it is possible for the diligent student to discover what the Spirit of God meant by this word from the use that is made of it.

I often wonder if there are very many who realize the great wealth of truth that God has provided for us in the fact that most major words are found in numerous sentences where the meaning of them becomes unmistakably clear from the use made of them and where variations and shades of meaning can be detected and established.

In the making of dictionaries, this is the way that words are defined. Vast amounts of literature are constantly read by researchers; and as they read they copy every new, interesting or rare word, also new and different uses of common words along with the sentences in which they occur. They may collect as many as five hundred sentences in which a word has appeared as it is used by speakers of ability and importance. To give a word a definition, an editor will take the group of cards that illustrate its usages, and after careful consideration he writes its definition. He is guided solely by what the sentences reveal as to the usage made of it.

In defining new words, especially those that come to us from other languages, the editors of dictionaries will often find that their definitions are challenged. In reply or defense their only appeal can be to the way in which the word is generally used. They cannot, of course, appeal to the dictionary. All they can do is show that the meaning given is in harmony with the general use of the word being made by the best speakers and writers.

It is my conviction and practice that God's words can best be defined by the usage made of them by the Holy Spirit in the sacred Scriptures. And since the meaning of a word is determined by the use made of it, there is indeed a wealth of truth to be found in a word that occurs in 412 sentences in the Old Testament, as does the word *mishpat*. The *Englishman's Hebrew and Chaldee Concordance* gives a full list of these occurrences on page 776. It is a formidable task to examine each one of these and it cannot be done in this brief study. However, the meaning of this word can be established in its first ten occurrences; and, once this is done, when we come upon the word *judgment*, we can check and see if it is *mishpat* (other words are also translated "judgment") and if it is we can read this meaning into it.

I do not believe that anyone who makes an honest study of these first ten occurrences will ever again be guilty of perverting it to mean punishment. Here is the list. The italicized word or words in each segment represent the Hebrew word *mishpat*.

Gen. 18:19 — to do justice and *judgment*
Gen. 18:25 — shall not the Judge of all the earth do *right?*
Gen. 40:13 — after the former *manner*
Exo. 15:25 — made for them a statute and *ordinance*

Exo. 21:1 — these are the *judgments*
Exo. 21:9 — after the *manner* of daughters
Exo. 21:31 — according to this *judgment* shall it be done
Exo. 23:6 — shalt not wrest *the judgment* of thy poor
Exo. 24:3 — and all the *judgments*
Exo. 26:30 — according to *the fashion* thereof

These ten passages are sufficient to show us that the word *mishpat* does not mean punishment and they give us some indication as to what it does mean. It has to do with an established order, system, or arrangement; and when it is used of God's judgments, it has to do with an established order, system, or arrangement that has its source in Him. This is quite clear in those passages where *mishpat* is translated "order," such as Judges 13:12, 1 Chron. 6:32, 15:13, 23:31, 2 Chron. 8:14, or in any of the thirty-nine places where it is translated "manner." Any single aspect of God's order may be designated by the word *mishpat,* so our definition must not be too narrow or limited. We are now awaiting that day when we can say among the nations that, "the LORD reigneth: the world (order or system) also shall be established that it shall not be moved: He shall judge the peoples righteously" (Psalm 96:10). Consider the following illustration.

In the State of California there is a body of laws, directives, regulations, and interpretations which are properly called the judgments of the people of this State regarding the operation of motor vehicles within its boundries. Each detail can be called a "judgment." When one comes upon a stop sign on the highway, it is the judgment of a traffic engineer that such a sign is needed there for the safety of those who travel. The driver of an automobile will find an abundance of signs, lines, warnings, instructions, etc., posted along the highway which inform him of these judgments. All who drive are expected to study and know these judgments. Ignorance of them is no excuse if they are violated.

To state the obvious, it can be said that there are judgments in this State which set the order, determine the manner, and regulate the operation of motor vehicles. The driver who knows the laws knows the judgments, those who keep them keep the judgments; and the one who violates them can be charged with failure to observe the judgments of this State. However, these judgments cover only one aspect of life in California. Other judgments cover other aspects of life. Personally, I do not find it difficult to live and work in harmony with these judgments. And if all these should suddenly be superseded by the judgments of God (Psa. 76:8), I am sure I would have no difficulty living, working, and serving in harmony with His judgments.

There are many who believe that God's judgments are in the earth today, that we live in a moral universe, and His judgments regulate, control, and set the order for all life upon it. In proof of this they usually cite Eph. 1:11, which seems to say that God is now working all things after the counsel of His own will. They tear this text from its context and ignore the meaning of *ta panta* (all things) which Paul himself defines for us by usage in Colossians 3:8 (all these), which is limited to things in the context. However, if God's judgments are in the earth, then the inhabitants of the earth should be learning righteousness (Isa. 26:9), which they are not. Furthermore, it would be God's responsibility to make His judgments unmistakably clear and known to all men. He would need to make the facts known concerning sin, righteousness, and judgment. And He would need to maintain His judgments by punishing all who violate them. All this awaits the coming of the kingdom (government) of God. Then we can say, "His judgments are in all the earth" Psa. 105:7. And how do they get here? He caused judgment to be heard from heaven (Psa. 76:8). The people of the earth will stand in awe and become quiet.

In the New Testament the Spirit speaks of the coming of the kingdom of God upon the earth while in the Old Testament the prophets speak of the same thing and call it the coming of the judgments of God. Some of the most glorious prophecies of the Old Testament are those that promise the coming of God's judgments upon the earth. We will consider some of these in which the writers speak prophetically of the day when God's judgments will control and regulate all life upon this planet.

One of the most important prophecies has already been mentioned. Isaiah declares: "When Thy JUDGMENTS are in the earth, the inhabitants of the world will learn righteousness" (26:9). This will be accomplished. He will not fail, neither will He be discouraged till He has set JUDGMENT in the earth (Isa. 42:4). "The zeal of the LORD of hosts will perform this" (Isa. 9:7), is the divine decree concerning this. And when the context is examined, it will be found that this statement has to do with the order of His government, to establish it with judgment and with justice.

God's judgments will be in the earth from the moment He speaks and causes judgment to be heard from heaven (Psa. 76:8). He will send forth judgment and thus gain the victory. He will show judgment to the nations (Matt. 12:18, 20).

The promises of judgment to come are some of the most precious in the Bible. Let us not be guilty of twisting these into threats of destruction.

The SEED and BREAD Bible-Study leaflets are published as often as time and means permit and are sent free to all names on THE WORD OF TRUTH MINISTRY mailing list. Send us your name. There will be no obligation, solicitation, or visitation. Additional copies of any issue available on request.   ISSUE NO. 33

SEED & BREAD

FOR THE SOWER   ISA. 55:10   FOR THE EATER

BRIEF BIBLICAL MESSAGES

FROM

THE WORD OF TRUTH MINISTRY

339 South Orange Drive, Los Angeles, Cal. 90036

Otis Q. Sellers, Bible Teacher

THE WORD "HEAVEN"

The study of the Word of God is very much a study of the words that God has used. The way a word is used is a positive indication of all its meanings. Certain comments which I made concerning the word *heaven* in Issue No. 28 (*The Kingdom—Why Two Names?*) has generated requests for more information concerning this term. I trust the following will be of help.

The word *heaven* is one that can be applied to anything or anyone that is over and above, whether used of space or position. We do not use it too much this way in English since it has settled down and become somewhat fixed as signifying that place in space where the omnipresent God is more manifest than any other, the place where Jesus Christ is now seated at God's right hand (Mark 16:19). This is the place that because of its glory and inhabitants is over and above all other places in the universe. It is the place where God has established His throne, the seat of His government (Psa. 103:19), and is, therefore, rightly called *heaven*. However, this is not its sole meaning and usage, either in the Bible or in common English.

Consider the following illustration. The word *motor* is one that can be applied to anything that imparts motion, to any source of mechanical power. This meaning is inherent in the word *motor*. A squirrel inside a wheel causing it to spin could properly be called a motor. If in the future someone comes up with a new device for imparting motion, he will not need to search far and wide for a word to describe it. There is a word available that fits all such things, the word *motor*. Even so, the word *heaven* can be properly applied to anything or anyone that is over and above, even to the One Who is over and above all, God.

In the Hebrew word *shamayim,* the Greek word *ouranos,* and the English word *heaven* we have three words that are as equal as four quarters are to one dollar in American currency. Our word *heaven* will always properly translate either of the other two. But in order to understand these three words, their basic value must be clearly understood.

In the first eight verses of Genesis we find that *shamayim* is used of two different things. It is used first of that which God created in the beginning (1:1), and then of that which He made on the second day (1:8). Thus, it is clear that there is some basic meaning in this word that allows it to be used in two different ways, and the things of which it is used must have certain definite characteristics or this word will not properly represent them.

In considering all the uses of *shamayim* in the Old Testament and the uses of *ouranos* in the New Testament, along with many usages in profane Greek literature, and our own usage of the word *heaven,* the conviction is inescapable that the basic idea in all these words is *height,* in the sense of being *over and above.* These words, therefore, can be properly applied to any being, place, or thing that is over and above, whether in space or position. In other words, if it is elevated, if it is over and above, the Holy Spirit may see fit to use the word *shamayim* or *ouranos* to designate it. And we who speak English may use the word *heaven* to describe such things if we see fit to do so.

In the occurrence of *shamayim* in Genesis 1:1 it is not possible for anyone to say dogmatically what was created; but since the word is plural and we know its basic meaning, we can say that it has to do with things that are over and above the earth. In Psalm 19 we learn that in the heavens, God has set a tabernacle for the sun. A tabernacle, in Scripture, being a center of activity, we have good reason to think that "the heavens" of Gen. 1:1 refers to the planets in our solar system with one planet, the earth being singled out for special attention. In relationship to the earth, all other planets are over and above us and, thus, could be called *shamayim* (the heavens). Could it be that when God speaks of "planting the heavens" (Isa. 51:16), He refers to a time when these planets will be inhabited? I do not believe that they are fit for any life as we know it today, but I do not think they will be forever in this condition. Remember that the planet earth was once "waste and empty" (Gen. 1:2).

In the second occurrence of *shamayim* (Gen. 1:8), we learn that God made the firmament (or expanse) and that this firmament or expanse being over and above the earth is properly called *heaven.*

A reading of the portion that includes Daniel 4:17, 25, 26 and 32 will show that the words "the Most High" and "the heavens" are used interchangeably in reference to the same exalted Being. Both of these terms are descriptive titles of God, He being the One Who is higher than all and, thus, is over and above all. That the word *heaven* in numerous places in the Old Testament means God is a fact that must be acknowledged by all who have honestly considered the matter.

At this point it may be well to note that it is a mistake to think that a word can mean only one thing, that it has only one application and can have no other. In fact there is scarcely a leading word in any language, especially descriptive words, that can be held to a single meaning. The English word *give* has more than twenty applications or meanings. A man would make himself ridiculous if he argues that *give* cannot mean "to bestow without receiving a return," since it cannot mean this in the sentence, "I will give you ten dollars for a day's work."

In view of this it is just as foolish to say that *shamayim* (heaven) cannot mean "God" in Dan. 4:26 since it cannot possibly mean "God" in Gen. 1:1. Yet this was the fallacious argument used against me when I set forth the fact that *ouranos* in the plural meant "the celestials," (that is, heavenly beings) in certain occurrences. It was argued that it could not mean this since this meaning will not fit in 2 Peter 3:12 which speaks of "the heavens being on fire."

The Greek word *ouranos* follows the same pattern as the Hebrew word. It is derived from the verb *orō* which means *to raise,* and *anō* which means *above* or *up.* In it we have the idea of raised up, with the meaning of *over and above* being basic in it. This is seen in its use in Classical as well as New Testament Greek.

In the New Testament *ouranos* is used as a designation for God in Luke 15:18. This is to be expected since God is the One Who is over and above all. This, I believe, is also its meaning in Luke 10:18. Satan fell from God, not from the place called *heaven;* and the Lord Jesus was a witness to his fall. And if this truth is realized in John 3:13, it clears up a difficulty that has long bothered students of the Word.

In the plural the word *ouranos* is used of celestial beings in Eph. 4:10 where the Greek reads, "He ascends up over all the heavens." If this refers to places, it would put Christ beyond and out of these places altogether. But this cannot be as Eph. 6:9 and Col. 4:1 clearly show. However, if it speaks of those beings who are over and above in their exalted position, it makes sense and speaks a great truth.

The word *ouranos* is used of the place to which the Lord Jesus ascended and where He is now located. (See Mark 16:19). It is also used of supreme monarchs such as the Caesars, of whom there was none higher in the Roman Empire. Note this in Acts 2:5 and Col. 1:23. These passages leave us with insoluble problems unless this is recognized. It is expected that this will be denied by some who have no solutions for any problems, but who have many problems for every solution. The use of the word *heaven* (*shamayim*) of earthly rulers should also be noted in Jeremiah 14:22, where the parallelism indicates that "the heavens" spoken of there were the rulers of the nations.

From ancient sources outside of the New Testament we find that *ouraniskos* (diminutive of *ouranos,* meaning a little heaven) is used of the vaulted ceiling of a room, the top of a tent, and a canopy, all of which are over and above. An interesting use of *ouranos* is seen in the fact that it is used of the hard palate, what we commonly call the roof of the mouth. This is certainly a proper use since the hard palate is over and above in the mouth. The same usage is found also in the Dutch and German language, which all who are familiar with these will know.

While in English the word *heaven* has become quite restricted by usage to indicate the special place where the good are supposed to go at death, this is not entirely so. The meaning of "God" is found in such common sayings as "Heaven help us," and "Heaven only knows." A reference to the dictionary will show that one meaning of *heaven* is "the sovereign of heaven, God."

In the figurative use of the word *heaven* it often has reference to that which is exalted, and the idea of exaltation is found in the word. Remember that the chief element in this word is *heave* which means to lift up. We should keep in mind the words of Solomon: "The heavens for height, and the earth for depth." Prov. 25:3.

In English the word *heaven* is turned into an adjective by the addition of the suffix -ly. This gives us the word *heavenly.* This is also done in Greek where *ouranos* becomes *ouranios.* This adjective is then intensified by adding an accelerative prefix which gives us *epouranios.* Like all adjectives this one gets its nuances or shades of meaning from the word or words which it qualifies, even as in the words "dark day" and "dark night," we find different ideas in the word *dark.*

After much consideration I am convinced that the idea of exaltation is the one the Spirit of God intended in this adjective, and the intensified character can best be expressed by the words "most exalted." Thus, the Lord said to Nicodemus: "If I have told you the most basic things and you are not believing, how shall you be believing if I should be telling you the most exalted things." John 3:12.

There is much more that could be said about this word but space does not permit, so take what I have said, go to your Bible with it and have yourself a good time.

The SEED and BREAD Bible-Study leaflets are published as often as time and means permit and are sent free to all names on THE WORD OF TRUTH MINISTRY mailing list. Send us your name. There will be no obligation, solicitation, or visitation. Additional copies of any issue available on request.   ISSUE NO. 34

SEED & BREAD

FOR THE SOWER   ISA. 55:10   FOR THE EATER

BRIEF BIBLICAL MESSAGES

FROM

THE WORD OF TRUTH MINISTRY

339 South Orange Drive, Los Angeles, Cal. 90036

Otis Q. Sellers, Bible Teacher

THE KINGDOM IN REALITY

The coming of God's kingdom, that is, the coming of divine government in and over the earth and within the lives of men upon it, is definitely prophesied in Scripture. This fact cannot be honestly questioned. If any think so, then let them explain Psalm 67:4; Isa. 9:6,7; and Rom. 15:12. The day will yet come when divine government will be a reality. This is a fact so positive that God often speaks of it as if it were here now. "Say among the nations that the Lord reigneth" (Psalm 96:10). Or, as Rotherham more accurately translates it, "Say among the nations that Jehovah has become King."

I wish very much that we could say this now, that this were true today, that we could proclaim among the nations that Jehovah has become King, that He has assumed sovereignty, that He has taken to Himself His great power and is governing. However, this is not true today, for this Psalm is a prophecy that has not been fulfilled. In this declaration God is heard speaking of "those things which be not as though they were" (Rom. 4:17), something which He often does and for which we must ever be alert as we read and study His Word.

God is not reigning (governing) today. He is not judging (setting the order for) the world in righteousness by that Man Whom He has ordained (Acts 17:31). The present era is a part of that long period of time when He suffers all nations and the individuals within them to walk in their own ways (Acts 14:16).

As we look upon the earth today and consider all nations, we see nothing anywhere but fallible human government. There is no evidence anywhere of that infallible divine rule which God has clearly promised that the nations will someday experience and enjoy. This was the expectation held out to mankind when Christ proclaimed the kingdom of God. "Kingdom" means "government," but there is nothing upon this earth today that can be called "the government of God." His government is nowhere to be seen.

It is God's own government, it is divine rule that is more sorely needed today than anything else. Man has reached the end of his rope. He cannot govern. Any honest facing up to the facts forces the admission that human governments are not equal to the problems they face. Man's technical and material progress has advanced so fast that all men stand now in fear of the discoveries that have been made.

All the evidence of history shows that human governments do not bring peace to the people. Of many governments it must be said, "Destruction and misery are in their ways, and the way of peace have they not known" (Rom. 3:16,17). Divine government is now man's greatest need. God must intervene and impose His moral law upon all men. There needs to be a manifest assumption of sovereignty by God over all men and all nations, the institution of the kingdom of God upon the earth. The only hope of mankind is the advent of divine government which will be of such power that it will bring swift retribution to all who rise up or even stiffen themselves against it. We should hail the coming of this, and we should anticipate it as the great hope of this misgoverned world.

In the past twenty-five years I have given much thought and study to the conditions that will prevail when God's government is a reality. Many truths concerning these conditions can be based upon direct statements of Scripture, such as, "they shall beat their swords into plowshares, and their spears into pruning hooks: nation shall not lift up sword against nation, neither shall they learn war any more" (Isa. 2:4). From this direct statement we can go on to logically deduce further results, such as the closing and clearing away of every college of war such as West Point, Annapolis, Sandhurst and Saint-Cyr. The mind is staggered by the changes this one new condition will bring about. I am glad that it will be in the hands of God.

The advent of God's government upon the earth will result in the immediate lifting of the curse that came both upon the earth and mankind when Adam sinned. One act of Adam brought sin and death into the world, and one act of Jesus Christ has made possible the entrance of righteousness and life. Remember, He is the Lamb of God that takes away the sin of the world (John 1:29). His work upon the cross of Calvary is now an accomplished fact of history, and there is not one thing more that needs to be done before the curse of sin and death is lifted. All that is needed now is for God to speak the word and the reign of sin and death will be ended and a reign of righteousness and life will begin.

When this word is spoken, never again will Adamic death with all its ills be working in mankind. Adamic death and all the death processes that precede it will be abolished. "The inhabitant shall not say, I am sick" (Isa. 33:24). His saving health will be known among all nations (Psa. 67:2). Even the sickest will be astonished and marvel as his illness is suddenly arrested. And as the physician listens with his stethoscope to the last wavering heartbeats of one who is at death's door, he will get the surprise of his life if death is conquered and life takes over to begin its healing processes.

This conquering of death and the gift of health, I firmly believe, will come upon all living men alike, whether good or bad. "Yea, for the rebellious also" (Psalm 68:18). And since everyone will be touched in some manner by this stupendous miracle, all will be under responsibility to recognize the One Who did it and give Him the glory. If it seems strange that such blessing should come upon all living men without distinction, let it be remembered that Jesus Christ and His apostles, when proclaiming the kingdom, healed all who had need of healing. See Luke 4:40, Matt. 12:15, Luke 9:11. Thus, it will be that God's long display of grace comes to an end in the greatest and widest display of grace He has ever shown. Truly, "He is kind unto the unthankful and to the evil" (Luke 6:35).

It must never be forgotten that when God's government makes its advent upon the earth, it will come with a gift of light, healing, and health for every man upon it. It will not make demands before it gives. It will give first and then make its demands. In that day if anyone is sick, it will be because he had sinned against God; and if anyone dies, it will be for the same reason. There will be "a sin unto death" (1 John 5:16,17), but never again will death be working in men because of the sin of Adam; never again will anyone die because Adam sinned.

When one considers the tremendous revolution in human affairs this will bring about, the mind cannot conceive its magnitude. We would be appalled at the very thought of it if we did not know that God is in complete charge and directing every detail. Consider all the disease, degradation, sickness, sorrow, and misery that is upon the earth that works in each of us all because of the entrance and fact of sin being in the world. Then try to grasp what it would be like if the reign of sin and death should be replaced by the reign of God under which Adamic death and all its attendant ills would be abolished. Under such conditions sin, sickness, and death would be rarities; and if any were sick, the cause of the illness and the way of relief would be perfectly manifest. In that day if any sin, and it is not a sin unto death, they will know that there is an Advocate ready to act in their behalf with the Father. If they will confess their sins, God will be faithful and just to forgive and cleanse them from all unrighteousness (1 John 1:9). It is a sad thing to see people trying to obtain forgiveness today by means of confession in a time when we have the forgiveness of our sins in accord with the riches of His grace (Eph. 1:7).

It can readily be seen that the end of the reign of sin and death will bring about a tremendous revolution in our economy, much of which is based upon the presence of sin and death in the world. It is difficult indeed for us to conceive of a world in which there are no hospitals, no doctors, no nurses, no drugs, and no remedies; in which there are no prisons, no jails, and no policemen; in which there are no military establishments, no arms, and no conflicts; in which there are no insurance companies, since there will be nothing against which to insure. And if this should trouble any who may now be engaged in such pursuits, let them rest assured that God's government will be benevolent and beneficent; and no man engaged in any honest pursuit will ever be harmed by any change God brings about. It is ridiculous, however, to imagine that when God governs the earth, He will allow some sickness and crime to continue just so doctors, policemen, and lawyers will not be thrown out of work.

I trust the reader will ever keep in mind that the glorious picture I have tried to set forth is one that is to come upon this earth, and not some other planet. It is to come upon the human race, not some other order of beings. This is to happen to mankind. The earth is not to be wiped clean before God imposes His government upon it. He will speak from heaven, and men will begin to know from that moment on what it is to live upon this earth where everything is under God's complete control. The kingdom comes upon the earth as it is and upon men as they are. All judgments to be made, all punishments to be meted out, and any changes that are to be made will come after God has assumed sovereignty.

This glorious prospect is one that fills the pages of God's Word. It is there that we learn of all the benevolent changes that will alter the climate, the habitability, and the fruitfulness of the earth. "Then shall the earth yield her increase" (Psalm 67:6).

However, when this picture of the future is presented, the inevitable question that arises concerns what will happen to wicked men who are living upon the earth when this blessed condition comes with all its glorious benefits. And, what will be our lot and what will be our hope if we should die before God assumes sovereignty? I will try to answer these in our next study.

The SEED and BREAD Bible-Study leaflets are published as often as time and means permit and are sent free to all names on THE WORD OF TRUTH MINISTRY mailing list. Send us your name. There will be no obligation, solicitation, or visitation. Additional copies of any issue available on request.   ISSUE NO. 35

SEED & BREAD

FOR THE SOWER   ISA. 55:10   FOR THE EATER

BRIEF BIBLICAL MESSAGES

FROM

THE WORD OF TRUTH MINISTRY

339 South Orange Drive, Los Angeles, Cal. 90036

Otis Q. Sellers, Bible Teacher

THE KINGDOM JUDGMENT

In religious literature the term "general judgment" is quite common, but no such thing is to be found in Scripture. Men may speak of "the great consummating judgment to come," and of "the great assize," which is supposed to be the gathering together at the bar of justice all who have ever lived upon the earth, but this idea is the product of human imagination and has no foundation in the Word of God. It is a flagrant error to think of future judgment as being one great assize, taking place at the end of the world, when all human beings, saints and sinners, Jews and Gentiles, the living and the dead, shall stand before "the great white throne," and there have their destiny settled as to whether it will be "heaven forever" or "hell forever." Those who put forth the idea of one so-called "final and universal judgment" simply reveal that they have not been firsthand students of divine revelation.

It has to be recognized by the careful student of Scripture that there are various future judgments which are separated as to time, subjects, and circumstances. Many attempts have been made to distinguish between these as will be seen in the *Scofield Reference Bible,* notes on Rev. 20:12; but it seems that Scofield's teaching was developed out of certain passages and made to fit in with his dispensational ideas. This is far from being satisfactory, as can be seen in the fact that one of the most important passages concerning future judgment is ignored. This passage is 2 Timothy 4:1, which in the *King James Version* reads:

I charge thee therefore before God, and the Lord Jesus Christ, who shall judge the quick and the dead at His appearing and His kingdom.

The strange thing about this passage is that it does not fit in with and is even contradictory to all present ideas concerning things to come. Those who make "His appearing" (*epiphaneia*) to be "His coming" or "the rapture" are very much embarrassed by this verse because of the universal judgment of mankind that is to take place in accord with this event. In view of this there has been an enormous amount of trifling with the Greek text of this passage, and this questioning of the text is usually set forth in comments on this verse when interpreters are forced to deal with it. Most commentators ignore it altogether. This can be seen in *Chafer's Systematic Theology*, which claims to be exhaustive, where there is no reference to it in the index, even though much space is given to the consideration of judgment. If the reader will check other commentators, he will see how weak they become in dealing with this passage.

This is truly a most important kingdom passage, and one with which the student should be completely familiar. It must be given a prominent place in all our thinking concerning the kingdom of God. In considering it we should note that the terms "God, and the Lord Jesus Christ" refer to the same person. No man can serve two masters. The construction here is such that it should read, "God, even Christ Jesus," the word "Lord" not appearing in most Greek texts. "Who shall" in the Greek is "the One about to be" (*mellō*) and is used in Scripture of those things which will come to pass by fixed necessity or divine appointment. The word *judge* in this passage does not have to do with settling the final destiny of either the living or the dead. Many of the dead who are judged at this time will have to wait until the end of the thousand years of His parousia before they are raised and their final destiny is settled (Rev. 20:5). To judge is to review and consider a matter and come to a conclusion concerning it.

The "quick" is an old English word that means the living. The word "at" is *kata* which means "according to" or "in harmony with." "Appearing" is *epiphaneia*, which means a blazing forth but always is indicative of a favorable intervention. "Kingdom" (*basileia*) means "government." The words *epiphaneia* and *basileia* are so related here that one defines the other. Even as the coronation is the beginning of the reign of a king, so the *epiphaneia* is the beginning of God's government, the one great difference being that the *epiphaneia* of the Lord Jesus will have a lasting effect upon and influence the course of the kingdom of God from beginning to end. In view of all these facts I will furnish my own carefully studied paraphrase of the Greek text:

I am solemnly charging you in the sight of God, even Christ Jesus, who will be judging the living and the dead in accord with His favorable intervention, even His kingdom.

The plainest message in the Bible is that when God assumes sovereignty and the manifest kingdom of God becomes a reality, He does not begin with some ferocious attack on mankind, not even the wicked portion of it. In order to gain the victory He desires, He sends forth judgment (Matt. 12:20), which means enlightenment and understanding for every man. Apart from these there can be no judgment. Furthermore, the long reign of death comes to an end and a gift of health and healing becomes the portion of every living man. However, a gift of light, understanding, and health does not mean that all will be allowed to live to enjoy these blessings and the magnificent glory of an earth that is being governed and continually blessed by God. (Read here, 1 Cor. 6:9-11). There must be a judgment of all who are living, and this judgment will determine if they are to be allowed to continue on earth.

I trust that the reader recognizes and believes in the ability of God to bring the entire life of any man in review before Him, and to make an instantaneous judgment concerning him. If not, then your God is too small. There being no past or future with God, He can at any time He desires, see our entire lives as a present fact. This He will do when the kingdom comes with all its attendant blessings. He will judge all who are living. The purpose of this judgment will be to determine continuance in or exclusion from the kingdom of God. However, it will also determine the place, the privileges, the honors, and the glory of all who are to continue to live under God's government.

Permit me to say personally, and I trust all my readers can say it, that if I should be among the living (and I very much would like to be) when God assumes sovereignty and my life comes in complete review before Him, one fact will stand out, like Mt. Everest, above everything else. This fact is that I have done the work of God which is demanded of all such in my state and condition, I believed in the Lord Jesus Christ. I believed in Him in a day of unbelief, believed in Him without seeing, believed in Him wholly on the basis of His written word, completely apart from any sign or miracle save those which are recorded in Scripture. I have believed, and I do now believe that Jesus is the Christ, the Son of God. And I will permit no man or demon to diminish aught from the promise and hope that He gave to me, that believing I shall have life through His name.

Following the judgment of the living there is to be a review of the dead. The total life of every man that has ever lived and died will be looked upon by God and a determination will be made as to who should be raised from the dead to begin life anew and enjoy it when this earth is governed by God. Note carefully that they are not raised and then judged, otherwise this too would be a judgment of the living. They are judged to determine if they deserve to be raised, to live as citizens under God's government. If so they will be raised in accord with the order and arrangement that God will establish. The Bible does not teach a general resurrection of the righteous at the beginning of the kingdom. It will be, "Every man in His own order" (I Cor. 15:23).

All of this is in harmony with His favorable intervention, even His kingdom. The order is (1) His blazing forth in a favorable intervention, (2) His government in reality, (3) a judgment of all living, (4) a judgment of all who are dead, (5) the resurrection of those who are granted entrance into His kingdom.

A place in the kingdom of God is the hope of mankind. There is no other hope held out to anyone in the Word of God. Our positions may differ, our rewards may differ, our services may differ, but it will be upon this earth when God governs. The Bible teaches that the destiny of men is in a redeemed society living on a transformed earth. The Biblical hope is always an earthly hope. The Psalmist declares that such as be blessed of Him shall be given a place and enjoy a portion upon the earth; and they that be cursed of Him shall be cut off (Psalm 37:22). The judgment that takes place at the inauguration of God's government will determine all of this.

The SEED and BREAD Bible-Study leaflets are published as often as time and means permit and are sent free to all names on THE WORD OF TRUTH MINISTRY mailing list. Send us your name. There will be no obligation, solicitation, or visitation. Additional copies of any issue available on request.   ISSUE NO. 36

SEED & BREAD

FOR THE SOWER   ISA. 55:10   FOR THE EATER

BRIEF BIBLICAL MESSAGES
FROM

THE WORD OF TRUTH MINISTRY

339 South Orange Drive, Los Angeles, Cal. 90036

Otis Q. Sellers, Bible Teacher

WHAT DOES *EPIPHANEIA* MEAN?

There is a passage in Scripture which, when honestly translated and faithfully interpreted, tells us that we should live anticipating that happy expectation; and this event is then defined as being the favorable intervention (*epiphaneia*) of the glory of the great God, even our Savior Jesus Christ. See Titus 2:13. Thus, we are brought face-to-face with a vital matter that is an important part of the lives of all who are believers in the Lord Jesus Christ in this the dispensation of the grace of God.

The weak translation of this passage found in the *King James Version* has made it easy for superficial interpreters of the Word of God to say that this means the second coming of Christ; although about as many say that this is "the rapture," or the sudden removal of all living believers from the earth, an event they say is to occur seven years before His return. I believe that these are arbitrary opinions, not based upon any real facts of Scripture. To actually live looking for our sudden removal from this earth would result in a life so disordered and unreal that we would disgrace the great God Whom we claim to follow. We need to discover and know what this event is which we are to live anticipating.

It will be evident at once to the careful student that this matter can be settled only by a true understanding of the Greek word translated "appearing" in Titus 2:13. As already noted this is the word *epiphaneia* (pronounced, *epi-FAN-ee-ah*), a word in regard to which there are many opinions. In order to free ourselves of this confusion, we will need to take this word in its unforced, natural meaning as used by the New Testament writers, then allow this basic meaning to guide us in dealing with every occurrence.

This word has an interesting history which is not difficult to trace. Its origin is found in the verb *phainō* (pronounced *FAH-ee-no*), which originally had to do with the action of throwing or shining light upon, and in course of time came to mean "to shine forth." By an easy transition this word was applied to the appearing of men and things; so, as a rule, when this word is found in the New

Testament, it usually means "to appear." This will be seen in Matt. 1:20; 2:7; and 13:26. However, it should be noted that this is a later meaning of *phainō*, and when it began to be used this way, it did not lose its earlier meaning. This will be found in numerous occurrences where *phainō* means "to shine." See Matt. 24:27; John 1:5; 5:35; Phil. 2:15 and Rev. 1:16.

From the word *phainō* another word developed by the addition of the accelerative prefix *epi*. This is the verb *epiphainō* which is certainly a much stronger word. And in order to express this strength, it would be much better to use the words "blaze forth" in certain occurrences. This verb appears four times in the New Testament where it is very weakly translated and treated as if it meant the same as *phainō*. A concordance is given.

Luke 1:79—*to give light* to them that sit in darkness
Acts 27:20—sun nor stars in many days *appeared*
Titus 2:11—bringeth salvation *hath appeared*
Titus 3:4—love of God our Savior toward man *appeared*

From the above references it can be seen that some form of the idea, "to blaze forth," is in all these occurrences.

It is from the verb *epiphainō* that the noun *epiphaneia* developed. This is found six times in Scripture as follows:

2 Thess. 2:8—with the *brightness* of His coming
1 Tim. 6:14—the *appearing* of our Lord Jesus Christ
2 Tim. 1:10—the *appearing* of our Savior Jesus Christ
2 Tim. 4:1—at His *appearing* and His kingdom
2 Tim. 4:8—them also that love His *appearing*
Titus 2:13—the glorious *appearing of the great God*

The inadequacy of the translations displayed above is apparent. They also treat *epiphaneia* as if it were derived from the verb *phainō*. It could be better translated "blazing forth" in each occurrence. However, it is evident from both New Testament and Classical Greek usage that this word was developed to express a very special idea, so much so, that it can be said that, while *epiphaneia* means a "blazing forth," it always carries in it the idea of a favorable intervention.

This definition is not a private translation. The celebrated Herman Cremer (*Biblico-Theological Lexicon*) defines this word by using such phrases as, "the help-bringing appearing of the gods," "the manifestation of divine power and providence in extraordinary events," and "a miraculous interposition of God in behalf of His people." It is as Archbishop Trench says, "This grand word was constantly employed to set forth these gracious appearances of the higher Powers in aid of men."

A great body of evidence shows that this word was used to indicate a blazing forth or a breaking through in order to help, that is, a favorable intervention. In this definition we have a truth that will illuminate every passage in which this word occurs. If we use "blazing forth" to translate it, we must always think of a favorable intervention.

In the first occurrence of *epiphaneia* (2 Thess. 2:8), it is used with the word *parousia;* but we should not conclude that the *epiphaneia* of this passage and that of Titus 2:13 are the same. This tells us that the man of sin, that wicked one, will be destroyed by the blazing forth (favorable intervention) of His parousia. It is illogical to think that these two words are identical in meaning simply because they are found in the same sentence. The parousia of Christ is an *epiphaneia,* a breaking through, a blazing forth, a favorable intervention. Thus, there is nothing secret about His parousia. It is a blazing forth even as described in Matt. 24:27.

The most important occurrence of *epiphaneia* to the present day believer is the one found in Titus 2:13, where in the *King James Version* it reads: "Looking for that blessed hope and the glorious appearing of the great God and our Savior Jesus Christ." In this the translators have treated the word *doxa* (glory) as if it were an adjective, which it is not. This alone changes the force and meaning of this declaration altogether, and since *epiphaneia* is weakly translated "appearing," we are left with very little of the great truth of the original. As already suggested this passage tells us that we are to live "anticipating that blessed expectation, even the blazing forth (favorable intervention) of the glory of our great God and Savior, Christ Jesus." Thus, we see that the "blessed expectation" is the blazing forth of His glory. All the emphasis here is on His "glory."

The word *glory* is a common one, especially in religious circles, where it is used as an utterance in moments of emotional ecstasy. Very few have any understanding of its actual meaning, or could define it if challenged to do so. John declares that the apostles beheld the glory of the Lord Jesus Christ (John 1:14). They could not give Him this glory or add to it, but they did behold it. The knowledge of it was made clear to them. There were many who beheld Him in person, but they saw nothing more than a carpenter's son who worked miracles (Matt. 13:55). His own apostles saw Him as "the Christ, the Son of the living God," and this was because the Father had revealed this unto them (Matt. 16:17). The true glory of Jesus Christ is all that He is in the sight of God. It is what God thinks of Him, what He esteems and declares Him to be, not what man esteems Him to be.

We live in a time when Christ is veiled. There is yet to be an unveiling. The time may come at any moment when it will suddenly, dramatically, and divinely be made plain to every human being upon the earth, to the aborigines in the jungle and the professors and students in the great universities, exactly Who Christ is and What Christ is in the sight of God. The esteem in which God holds Him will be revealed. This is the knowledge that God will force upon every man, so much so, that it becomes the common knowledge (conscience) of the human race. This is what Paul is talking about when he speaks of "the blazing forth of the glory of our great God and Savior, Jesus Christ." This will be the *epiphaneia* of His glory. This is our blessed hope.

This is not His second coming. This is not the *epiphaneia* of His parousia. This is that great work which God is going to do when He again speaks from heaven and says of mankind, "Let there be light." This will fulfill His great promise made in Hab. 2:14; "For the earth shall be filled with the knowledge of the glory of the LORD, as the waters cover the sea."

Titus 2:13 is not the revelation of a secret, a truth that had never been declared before. It is identical with Isaiah 40:5:"And the glory of the LORD shall be revealed, and all flesh shall see it together: for the mouth of the LORD hath spoken it."

The *epiphaneia* (blazing forth) of His glory is the great foundation stone upon which God's government in the earth will be established. It is God's first act when He makes His move. May we live anticipating this. It could be at any moment.

The SEED and BREAD Bible-Study leaflets are published as often as time and means permit and are sent free to all names on THE WORD OF TRUTH MINISTRY mailing list. Send us your name. There will be no obligation, solicitation, or visitation. Additional copies of any issue available on request.   ISSUE NO. 37

SEED & BREAD

FOR THE SOWER   ISA. 55:10   FOR THE EATER

BRIEF BIBLICAL MESSAGES

FROM

THE WORD OF TRUTH MINISTRY

339 South Orange Drive, Los Angeles, Cal. 90036

Otis Q. Sellers, Bible Teacher

A NEGLECTED PROPHECY

One of the greatest prophecies of the Old Testament, the importance of which is emphasized by its restatement in the New Testament, is, I believe, one of the most neglected and ignored of all prophetic declarations in the Bible. I refer to that declared by Matthew 12:18-21 which in the *King James Version* reads as follows:

"Behold My Servant, Whom I have chosen; My Beloved, in Whom My soul is well pleased: I will put My Spirit upon Him, and He shall shew judgment to the Gentiles (nations). He shall not strive, nor cry; neither shall any man hear His voice in the streets. A bruised reed shall He not break, and smoking flax shall He not quench, till He send forth judgment unto victory. And in His name shall the Gentiles (nations) trust."

In the past twenty-five years I have examined scores of commentaries on Matthew to see what has been said on this passage, those on my own shelves, those in libraries, and those offered for sale in the many bookstores which I regularly visit. This has been an exercise in futility; for I am amazed at how completely this passage is ignored, how sadly it is neglected, and how many explain it away by inferring that it was fulfilled during the earthly ministry of Jesus Christ. Some infer that it will be fulfilled at His second advent, but they make no attempt to reconcile the statements, "He shall not cry, neither shall any man hear His voice in the streets," with "The Lord Himself shall descend from heaven with a shout" (1 Thess. 4:16). Both of these statements cannot refer to the same event.

Three positive statements are made in this prophecy: (1) He shall show judgment to the nations; (2) He will send forth judgment unto victory; (3) In His name shall the nations trust. These three things were not done at His first coming, and there is nothing in history to show they have been accomplished since. This remains an unfulfilled prophecy.

I am convinced that the neglect of this beautiful prediction is based upon the fact that it cannot be fitted into and that it even contradicts all present schemes of prophetic fulfillment. However, there is one prophetic plan that it fits perfectly. This is the truth that the next great event in God's prophetic calendar is the divine assumption of sovereignty which brings God's beneficent government, even the kingdom of God, upon the earth.

We need to examine the entire portion in which this passage is found, become familiar with it, incorporate it into our thinking about the future, and make it our expectation concerning what God is going to do for the nations of the earth.

This portion began with an omnipotent miracle which I challenge any healer to duplicate. A man with a withered hand stood before the Lord and the Pharisees assembled in the synagogue. Instantaneously, and in the sight of every one of them, the withered hand was healed. He did not touch the hand; He did not command it to be healed; He only asked the man to stretch forth his hand. When he did, it was restored whole, like the other.

The rage of the Pharisees was immediate. They left at once and "held a council," an official meeting, to consider ways and means whereby they might destroy Him. These were powerful men and the machinery of government was in their hands. They had the capability of doing what they set out to do, bring His life and ministry to an end. Our Lord did not treat their plans with contempt, as He certainly could have done. He was equal to any attempt they could have made against Him, but He did not want to be forced into the position of kill or be killed. Yet, He would not yield to death one step short of His appointed time at Calvary.

So when Jesus knew of their plans, in order to avoid conflict, He withdrew Himself from that locality. Still great multitudes followed Him, and He healed them all, but gave them the strict charge that they should not make Him known. If they reported these miracles, it would excite still greater opposition from the Pharisees, and they would come after Him bent upon His assassination. Of course, if they did, all He needed to do was speak the word and bring about their incineration. But He had not come to destroy any man's life, so He did not want this conflict. What He wanted was, "that it might be fulfilled which was spoken by Isaiah the prophet" (Matt. 12:17), a prophecy that gives us much information as to how divine government, the kingdom of God comes upon the earth. The idea that His withdrawal and the charge that they would not make Him known fulfilled Isaiah's prophecy is sheer foolishness. God's prophecies are not fulfilled by something being done of which the prophet has not even spoken.

"Behold My Servant." These words call upon the hearer to attend to what is said, to give due heed, observe, and consider the person of the One Whom God calls "My Servant" and "My Beloved," Who was chosen to be God's man, Who would bring into complete fulfillment every Old Testament promise and prophecy. There was nothing in this Servant that could in any way be displeasing to the Absolute of Whom He was the projection.

"I will put My Spirit upon Him." This is His complete equipment for the task He will perform. He will invade the earth by His Spirit, conquer the earth by His Spirit, and set up His own order upon it by His Spirit. Indeed it is, "Not by might, nor by power, but by My Spirit, saith the Lord." He will pour out of His Spirit upon all flesh as the initial step of bringing His government upon the earth. In fact, divine government in this earth is brought about by the second coming of the Holy Spirit, not by the second coming of Jesus Christ. He will never leave His position at the right hand of God until His enemies have become His footstool.

"He will shew judgment to the nations." The Greek word for "shew" (*apangellō*) means to proclaim, to make known openly, to declare. The Psalmist spoke of a time when God's judgments would be in all the earth (105:7), when He would cause judgment to be heard from heaven (76:8). Amos spoke of the day when judgment would run down as waters and righteousness as a mighty stream. (Amos 5:24). All these promises will be fulfilled when He proclaims judgment to the nations. Judgment is a commodity that all nations lack today. There is a world scarcity of this valuable asset. There is no nation on earth that knows what to do. All this will be changed when He makes known judgment to the nations.

"He shall not strive." All governments have had their beginning in strife and conflict. Not so God's government. When God invades the earth by His Spirit, there will be no conflict, no wrangling.

"Nor cry." This is definite proof that this passage has no reference to His first advent, for then, "Jesus stood and cried, saying, If any man thirst, let Him come unto Me and drink" (John 7:37). Neither can this prophecy have to do with His second coming, for then "the Lord Himself shall descend from heaven with a shout" (1 Thess. 4:16).

"Neither shall any man hear His voice in the streets." This cannot be said of His first advent, nor can it be said of His second. This passage deals with Jesus Christ coming in His government, not in person.

"A bruised reed shall He not break, and smoking flax shall He not quench." No one is hurt or injured by the divine assumption of sovereignty, which is something that cannot be said of His second coming. Then He will be revealed from heaven with His mighty angels, in flaming fire, taking vengeance on them that know not God, and that obey not the gospel of Jesus Christ. These shall be punished with everlasting punishment from the presence of the Lord, and from the glory of His power (2 Thess. 1:7-10). However, let no one make the mistake of thinking that none will be punished when God assumes sovereignty. The next phrase makes this clear.

"Till He send forth judgment unto victory." This sets forth the process by which He overcomes all opposition. He sends forth judgment. All judgment is based upon light, knowledge, truth, and understanding. Wave upon wave of these will flow forth from God so that the victory will be His. Then, and not until then, He will deal with the rebellious and those who are unfit for a place upon this earth under His righteous government. The outcome of His victory is declared in the next sentence.

"And in His name shall the nations trust." This is a beautiful picture — the nations trusting in Jesus Christ. The word "nations" here means exactly the same as when we say, "Canada and the United States are nations with a written constitution," or when we speak of the 130 nations that form the United Nations. This is a truth that is hard to believe, yet it is going to be even as God said, "In His Name shall the nations trust." This truth is repeated in Romans 15:12, and it explains why the nations will then be willing to beat their swords into plowshares and their spears into pruning hooks — in other words to turn all their instruments of war to peaceful uses. May God speed the day.

We have considered one of the most important prophecies in the Bible, yet it is one that is ignored and neglected. Do you have any room for its fulfillment in your thinking?

The SEED and BREAD Bible-Study leaflets are published as often as time and means permit and are sent free to all names on THE WORD OF TRUTH MINISTRY mailing list. Send us your name. There will be no obligation, solicitation, or visitation. Additional copies of any issue available on request.   ISSUE NO. 38

SEED & BREAD

FOR THE SOWER   ISA. 55:10   FOR THE EATER

BRIEF BIBLICAL MESSAGES

FROM

THE WORD OF TRUTH MINISTRY

339 South Orange Drive, Los Angeles, Cal. 90036

Otis Q. Sellers, Bible Teacher

THE GREAT TRIBULATION

In the study of NEW TESTAMENT TIME PERIODS (SEED AND BREAD, Issue No. 23) "the great tribulation" was set forth as being a time period that follows the kingdom of God and which precedes the thousand years of His parousia (personal presence). More accurately this time period should be called "Israel's Seventieth Week," since it is the final seven-year period of that long span of time concerning which God said through Daniel, "Seventy weeks are determined upon thy people and upon thy holy city" (Dan. 9:24). And to be yet more exact, the great tribulation covers only the last three-and-one-half years of this seven-year period. The fact that this occurs after the kingdom of God comes as a shock to many who have been taught that this introduces it. They cannot comprehend why "this terrible time of wrath" should come at the close of the serene and glorious days of God's government.

That God will intervene and establish His government over the earth and its inhabitants is a truth that is held by most men who know and believe the Bible. However, almost without exception, it is also believed that this blessed condition will never come to pass until there has been a divine outpouring of wrath that will eclipse anything that mankind has ever experienced before. This is declared to be "a time of God's fierce anger." In it He is set forth as displaying a fiendish and foolish cruelty which will far exceed all the cruel and unusual punishments that men have ever created in the long and sorrowful record of man's inhumanity to man.

This time of wrath is usually called "the great tribulation," a term that has been lifted from the Word of God (Matt. 24:21), embellished with every possible crude idea of sadistic torture, then used in a mystical manner to support every wild statement made by present-day prophets of doom. This concoction of wrath is then directed toward Israel as being God's punishment of them for their long rejection of Jesus as the Messiah, and as a means to bring them to their senses and to an acceptance of Him.

The teaching that a great display of fierce anger is the first work of God, when He resumes His prophetic program, is illogical, unreasonable and unscriptural. An honest consideration of the prophecies concerning the future of Israel will show this.

If a study is made of every prophecy related to the future of Israel (a task I have undertaken numerous times), it will be seen that the future of the seed of Abraham is one of great blessing, not one of cruel punishment. And while it is true that certain individuals will need to be purged from among them (Ezek. 20:38), this is far different from indiscriminate wrath being poured out on all of them. The divine prophecies concerning Israel tell of a long dispersion (an accomplished fact) followed by a regathering; of punishment followed by a blessing. Today, we can review the history of Israel and say: Israel has been dispersed, the next thing is for Israel to be regathered; Israel has been punished, the next thing is for Israel to be blessed; Israel has been long out of her land, the next thing is for Israel to be restored to her land. These facts are made clear by many prophecies. One in Ezekiel 34 is an example of this.

For thus saith the Lord God; Behold, I, even I, will both search My sheep, and seek them out. As a shepherd seeketh out his flock in the day that he is among his sheep that are scattered; so will I seek out My sheep, and will deliver them out of all places where they have been scattered in the cloudy and dark day. And I will bring them out from the peoples; and gather them from the countries, and will bring them to their own land, and feed them upon the mountains of Israel by the rivers, and in all the inhabited places of the country. I will feed them in a good pasture, and upon the high mountains of Israel shall their fold be: there shall they lie in a good fold, and in a fat pasture shall they feed upon the mountains of Israel. I will feed My flock, and I will cause them to lie down, saith the Lord God. Ezek. 34:11-15.

From this passage it can be seen that Israel is in a state of dispersion and disorder when this work of God in their behalf begins. And He does not begin by tearing them to pieces as a wolf would do when it is among the sheep. A divine order is established by this prophecy. Note the words: searching, seeking, delivering, bringing, feeding, binding, resting, and strengthening. This passage is sufficient to demonstrate that the next thing in view for the seed of Abraham is regathering, restoration, and blessing.

Today, the average teacher and preacher of prophecy will hear to none of this. They see no immediate future for the seed of Abraham. According to the present popular and somewhat anti-semitic interpretation of prophecy, Israel's present expectation from the hand of God is a frightful and fiendish torture, more cruel and unusual than Satan or man has ever yet devised. As said before, this time of torture is usually described as "the great tribulation."

This time is described by one teacher as being, "a time of unprecedented suffering that is to come upon the world in general and

Israel in particular." Another calls it, "the hour of earth's matchless agony"; and still another describes it by saying, "In character it is absolutely without parallel as to its destructive and terrifying effects, and it is world wide."

The Book of Revelation, chapter 16 to 18, is held by these men to describe this time of divine torture in exquisite detail, and it is to this portion that they go for proof of its frightful character. From these chapters they gather such terms as famine, earthquakes, blood, fire, locusts, and scorpions; and this horrific potpourri is screamed out at audiences in the hope that someone will be frightened into rushing to Christ for deliverance from it. In fact vivid and lurid descriptions of the great tribulation have become a stock in trade of many so-called evangelists.

These men never stop to consider that a divine idiom is used throughout these chapters of Revelation which is mostly incomprehensible to us now, but which will be clearly understood when mankind stands on the threshold of the day of the Lord. And if any disagree with this, then let them explain what is meant in Rev. 14:20 by, "and blood came out of the winepress, even unto the horse bridles, by the space of a thousand and six hundred furlongs" (about 180 miles). Sixteen hundred furlongs is the length of Palestine.

It is a well-known fact of life that once men are committed to a certain position they are not inclined to give consideration to any facts that may militate against it. This seems to be especially true of those who through public declarations, both spoken and written have committed themselves to the idea that the next great work of God will be to remove all believers from the earth, then pour out upon those who remain all the pent-up wrath that He is supposed to have been accumulating over more than nineteen centuries. And yet, if men would carefully think upon this, they would realize that such a display of wrath does not make sense. It would accomplish no good purpose, neither would it be just, inasmuch as most sinners have passed on and thus have escaped it.

The idea that God is going to accomplish His declared purposes for Israel and the world by plunging all mankind into a time of unprecedented torture, torment, and suffering is an idea that God Himself has declared to be senseless. "Why should ye be stricken more? Ye will revolt more and more: the whole head is sick, and the whole heart is faint." These are His words in Isa. 1:5. Thus, God Himself has declared that any further punishment of Israel would accomplish nothing so far as bringing them back to Himself is concerned. And it would go beyond the demands of divine justice since she has already received of the Lord's hand double for all her sins (Isa. 40:1). Whatever God may be doing now, whatever Israel may be experiencing now, they are not being punished for sins either past or present. In this the dispensation of God's grace, every act of His toward Israel is one of love and favor to the undeserving.

Since Israel's condition was then, and still is, a condition of the head and heart (Isa. 1:5), further punishment would result in their "revolting more and more." To punish them more would be the same as flogging a sick man because of his illness. Therefore, God must do more than exact a penalty for sins committed if they are ever to be brought into harmonious relationship with Him. In the declaration that follows, He tells what He is going to do.

And I will turn My hand upon thee, and purely purge away thy dross, and take away all thy tin (alloy): And I will restore thy judges as at the first, and thy counsellors as at the beginning: afterward thou shalt be called, the city of righteousness, the faithful city. Isa. 1:25,26.

In view of these facts, I insist that we need to restudy, to rethink, and to reevaluate the entire subject of "the great tribulation." I would suggest the following truths as a help in so doing.

Whatever "the great tribulation" may be, it is "the time of Jacob's trouble" (Jer. 30:7). Because of this divine description, and because of the locale of the events described in Matt. 24, we have reason to believe that this will be limited to the land of Israel and to the nation there at that time. And since it is declared in advance that "he shall be saved out of it" (not decimated in it), we have no doubt as to its outcome.

It should also be noted that even though it is limited as to locale it is also described as, "the hour of temptation, which shall come upon all the world, to try them that dwell upon the earth" (Rev. 3:10). This description provides a definite clue to the meaning, nature, and purpose of the great tribulation. This will be considered in another study on this subject under title of THE GREAT TESTING.

The SEED and BREAD Bible-Study leaflets are published as often as time and means permit and are sent free to all names on THE WORD OF TRUTH MINISTRY mailing list. Send us your name. There will be no obligation, solicitation, or visitation. Additional copies of any issue available on request.   ISSUE NO. 39

SEED & BREAD

FOR THE SOWER   ISA. 55:10   FOR THE EATER

BRIEF BIBLICAL MESSAGES
FROM
THE WORD OF TRUTH MINISTRY
339 South Orange Drive, Los Angeles, Cal. 90036

Otis Q. Sellers, Bible Teacher

THE GREAT TESTING

The national crisis, a part of the prophesied future of Israel, which is called in Matthew "great tribulation" (there being no definite article in the Greek), is called in the Old Testament "the time of Jacob's trouble," (Jer. 30:7), and in Hosea 2:15, "the valley of Achor." Achor is a Hebrew word that means "trouble." In Revelation 3:10 this short period of time is called "the hour of temptation (trial), which shall come upon the world to try them that dwell upon the earth." However, in all these descriptions of this juncture in Israel's history, concurrent blessings are promised which give a different character to this period of time which is far different from the one being set forth by many prophets of doom and despair today.

In Jeremiah 30:7 the promise concerning "Jacob" is that "he shall be saved out of it," and in Hosea the valley of Achor is declared to be a "door of hope" wherein Israel in passing through shall sing, "as in the days of her youth, and as in the day when she came up out of the land of Egypt." Again, in Rev. 3:10 there is the promise to those who have "kept the word of His endurance," that He will be keeping them out of "the hour of trial which shall come upon all the world."

Thus, it is quite clear from Scripture that there will be saints innumerable in the great tribulation, and that it will be a glorious experience for them because of the manifest divine help and safekeeping which will surely be their portion. It will be even as He has promised: "When thou passest through the waters, I will be with thee; and through the rivers, they shall not overflow thee; when thou walkest through the fire, thou shalt not be burned; neither shall the flame kindle upon thee." Isa. 43:2. These facts alone greatly change the character of the great tribulation for all the people of God who will pass through it.

Consider this illustration. Let us suppose that a man without family, friends, money, and all that goes to make up a comfortable life is suddenly stricken with a serious illness. Then another man with a devoted family, a host of friends, and plentiful means is stricken with an identical illness. Would not the first man suffer far more then the second? Even so, in the great tribulation the fact God is going to show openly His love and care for His own, causes all the dire experiences of this time to take on a different character.

In view of this, I for one will boldly say that if God will be with me, I will gladly enter into this time with a song of His goodness and mercies upon my lips, and walk happily through every day of it, saying, "The Lord is my helper, and I will not fear what man shall do unto me" (Heb. 13:6). I have no sympathy for those who are so cravenly afraid of the great tribulation that they joyfully receive the idea of a pre-tribulation rapture that will deliver them out of it. This is a doctrine that can only be supported by ruthlessly severing the words "caught up" of 1 Thess. 4:17 from "we who are alive and remain unto the parousia of the Lord" of 1 Thess. 4:15. God has joined the rapture and the parousia together, and what God has joined together, man should not put asunder.

The declaration concerning "the hour of testing, which shall come upon all the world, to try them that dwell upon the earth," the "great tribulation," tells us that the experience of Israel is in reality a means of testing all men upon the earth.

If we give it any honest consideration, it can be seen at once that there would be no value in God testing Israel, the nations, or the men upon the earth as long as they are in their present state. Israel and the nations have failed, and any further testing would be about the same as testing a plane that has crashed and is a wreck. Furthermore, the idea of God bringing about a time of testing after His removal of all from the earth who might have passed such a test, is completely without logic. Why test those whose failure is already manifested by their rejection? The failure of mankind is not only obvious, it is admitted by the majority of men. However, if a divine testing of mankind should follow a long period of enlightenment, instruction, discipline, and blessing, it would be proper, reasonable, and of great value.

This is the way it will be. Blessing will come first and testing will follow. The benign and blessed conditions that will exist in the kingdom of God will be the portion of Israel and all other nations before the great tribulation takes place. This is why I believe not only in a post-tribulation rapture but also in a post-kingdom tribulation. See my study on *New Testament Time Periods* (Issue No. 23).

If we insist on making the words *trouble* and *tribulation* to mean torture, torment, punishment, and persecution, as almost everyone seems to be doing, then there is little hope of ever coming to a true understanding of what the Lord Jesus meant when He spoke of "great tribulation." True, He describes it as being a tribulation "such as was not since the beginning of the world to this time, no, nor ever shall be" (Matt. 24:21). Using this statement as a springboard, many have jumped to the conclusion that this will be a time of torture, torment, pain, anguish, and suffering such as has never been before or will ever occur again. From this conclusion, they have described God as acting in such manner that they actually dishonor the One Who is full of love and compassion and set Him forth as a sadistic monster.

An interesting fact here is that our word *tribulation* is derived from the Latin *tribulum*, which meant a threshing sled. This was a heavy, wooden platform, and various means were used to make its underside rough. Oxen were yoked to this to drag it back and forth over the wheat breaking the kernels from the straw and husk. Then with large forks or shovels this mixture of wheat, straw, and chaff was flung high into the air. The wind would then carry straw and chaff to one side, while the grain fell by itself into a golden pile. It can be readily seen that the purpose in all this was not to hurt the wheat, but to separate it from the chaff. This is also the purpose of the great tribulation. And while it is true that in it, Israel will be afflicted, yet in all their afflictions God will be with them.

The declaration that this will be a time of great tribulation that cannot be compared with any other time does not have to do with excessive torment or torture. This will be because the devil has come down to earth, having great wrath, because he knows that he has but a short time (Rev. 12:12). This will be the first time this happens and it will be the last, and this accounts for the exceedingly strange character of this time.

The Greek words that have to do with this time are *thlibō* and *thlipsis*. The first of these is usually translated "trouble," but it means to press or to constrict. The second is usually translated "tribulation," but it means pressure or constriction. An interesting occurrence of *thlibō* is found in Matt. 7:14 where it is translated "narrow" in the Lord's declaration, "narrow is the way."

When God's government of this earth and mankind upon it is spoken into existence, it will embrace all living men. Men come under it because God has assumed sovereignty, and not by any choice of their own. Jehovah will become King and He will govern. He will deal severely with anyone who violates its judgments or resists His will in any manner. The Holy Spirit will then act as the restrainer and He will not fail in His task. Prevention will be His purpose. Then after centuries of blessing and learning under God's government, the world will draw nigh to the time of the personal presence of Christ, even His 1000 year parousia. At this point everything begins to narrow; for none, who are unworthy of it, are going to pass from God's pre-advent kingdom into the personal presence of Christ. So a divine testing of all who dwell upon the earth is arranged by God.

Under this test all the divine restraints are lifted, and even the Holy Spirit is removed as a restrainer. Men are now completely free, and their true character, whether good or bad, will show forth. At this time there is a revolt against the kingdom, but God's government is well able to take care of it. However, Israel must go under the *tribulum,* and so must all men, that the chaff may be separated from the wheat. At this time all the faithful in Israel stand in the place of Christ toward all men and the actions and attitudes men take toward them will be judged as their attitude toward Christ. "Inasmuch as ye have done it unto one of the least of these My brethren, ye have done it unto Me" (Matt. 25:40). These are the words of Christ that will be applicable to these times.

Never in all history will men have faced a time of testing such as this. The pressure from Satan and his followers will be enormous. Some will fail, but those who have learned well the lessons taught by day-to-day experience under God's government will have nothing to fear from this time of testing. Furthermore, it has nothing to do with those who are described as being "holy and without blame before Him" (Eph. 1:4). We have met the supreme test of God by believing now. There will be no further testing of those whose faith has conquered in this the dispensation of the grace of God.

Let us keep the divine order straight. There must be the kingdom of God first and this will be followed by a short period of "great tribulation."

The SEED and BREAD Bible-Study leaflets are published as often as time and means permit and are sent free to all names on THE WORD OF TRUTH MINISTRY mailing list. Send us your name. There will be no obligation, solicitation, or visitation. Additional copies of any issue available on request.   ISSUE NO. 40

SEED & BREAD

FOR THE SOWER   ISA. 55:10   FOR THE EATER

BRIEF BIBLICAL MESSAGES

FROM

THE WORD OF TRUTH MINISTRY

339 South Orange Drive, Los Angeles, Cal. 90036

Otis Q. Sellers, Bible Teacher

GOD'S NEXT MOVE

At the time this is being written, I have been a reader, student, interpreter, and teacher of the Bible for fifty-five years. This is not said in any spirit of boasting. It is simply the fact in the case, and I cite it as my right to speak concerning the subject of this study. I started out fully accepting and following the *Darby-Scofield* system of Biblical interpretation and came up through the dispensational-premillennial school of thought, but in time I became convinced that this method of interpretation failed to answer a multitude of questions which an ever increasing familiarity with God's Word imposed upon me. I also became convinced that this school of thought was somewhat arbitrary in its interpretation of many passages of Scripture in order to make them fit what had become a fixed and unchangeable creedal position. Furthermore, those who made up this group were quite intolerant toward those who raised any doubts or questions concerning its favorite and widely proclaimed doctrines such as the restoration of the old Roman Empire, and especially that teaching commonly called "the rapture of the church," which was then, and still is, being set forth as God's next move.

The term "the rapture" is nowhere found in Scripture, and it is not the proper translation of any Greek word found in it. Therefore, it cannot be considered as a word "which the Holy Spirit teacheth" (1 Cor. 2:13), but as a word which man's wisdom has produced. The idea of "the rapture" is based upon a passage found in 1 Thess. 4:16, 17, where we read:

For the Lord Himself shall descend from heaven with a shout, with the voice of the archangel, and with the trump of God: and the dead in Christ shall rise first: then we which are alive and remain shall be caught up together with them in the clouds, to meet the Lord in the air: and so shall we ever be with the Lord.

It is my conviction that this passage describes that future moment in time when the Lord Jesus shall leave His present position at the right hand of God in heaven and descend to the earth in order to be personally present here for a thousand years (His parousia). See SEED AND BREAD, Nos. 24 and 25. I feel it is the wildest form of human imagination and false interpretation to make this event to be a partial descent from heaven in order to catch away all believers and take them back to heaven, as so many today are declaring and still more are blindly believing. This is His personal coming to earth, not an approach to it in order to remove His own from it. As a high honor and privilege a vast multitude of those who are then living upon the earth and many who have been raised from the dead will ascend into the air to meet Him and to return with Him. Let us not be afraid to think about this event.

The planet earth is a sphere, as the beautiful and impressive pictures taken by the astronauts have clearly revealed. Thus, the direction which is "up" at one point on its surface would in contrast be "down" at the opposite point. At the time of the Lord's descent to the earth all of the outcalled of God will be "caught up" wherever they are, and this will be a glorious spherical grid or canopy that will enclose the earth. Through this grid the Lord will enter; and as He settles toward His appointed place upon the earth, probably the Mount of Olives, all who have gone forth to meet Him in the air will settle back to the place from whence they were caught up. And while it is true that this is only my conception of what will take place, I think all friendly readers will admit that it is a much more beautiful picture than that of all of God's people coming together at the same point in one big ball of confusion. The God I worship is a God of order.

This conception is in complete harmony with Rev. 1:7 where it is declared that "He cometh with clouds." These are clouds of people, not clouds of moisture. See also Jude 1:14. The added declaration, "and every eye shall see Him," does not have to do with the physical eye or physical sight, but with the discernment that will be granted to every human being upon the earth. This will bring to them the full realization that the Lord Jesus has returned, that He is upon the earth — not as the emptied One in abject humiliation, but as the exalted One in all the glory of His Father with the holy angels (Mark 8:38).

If any dispensational-premillenialist who holds that the removal from earth of all believers will be God's next public move will trace out the word *parousia,* even in its first four occurrences (Matt. 24:3, 27, 37, 39), he will find that it is an event that takes place after the three-and-one-half years that are called "the great tribulation." Every event listed in Matt. 24:1-32 must be fulfilled to the letter before the parousia can be a reality. Even as our Lord declared, "when ye shall see all these things, know that it is near, even at the doors" (Matt. 24:33). Among these things that must be realized is the appearance of "the abomination of desolation, spoken of by Daniel the prophet, standing in the holy place" (Matt. 24:15). This detail alone is an event that can never take place until Israel has been restored to her land by God, until the priesthood is restored and duly consecrated by Elijah, and the temple is rebuilt with its "holy place" as the center.

The "catching up" of living ones and the resurrection of dead ones set forth in 1 Thess. 4:16, 17 are events that introduce and are part and parcel of the parousia of Jesus Christ. If they are separated from it by seven years, as so many are teaching, the events become meaningless. They might well be likened to a home run in a baseball game. A batter could knock fifty balls over the fence and they would count for nothing if the game were not in orderly progress.

Those prophets of doom who try to frighten people into taking some action (so they can be displayed and counted) make much of the great tribulation, magnifying every detail into a sadistic tale of torture and horror. They also make much of "the rapture," holding it forth as a means of escape for those who will "come forward and receive Christ." Their conception of God's next move is the removal of all believers from the earth, followed by the pouring out of indiscriminate wrath upon all who remain. However, at times seeming to recoil from their own descriptions of this terrible visitation, they attempt to alleviate it by making it one of the greatest times of salvation the world has ever known. C. I. Scofield declared "that between the coming of the Lord for His church, and His return to the earth with His saints, the overwhelming majority of living humanity will be saved." He held that this would be the outcome of "the simultaneous appearance of 144,000 Pauls," an idea which Hal Lindsey has fawningly changed to "144,000 Billy Grahams."

If the fulfillment of 1 Thess. 4:17 is God's next move, then let all who hold this be honest with the Word of God and declare that the parousia (personal presence) is next. Note carefully that Paul said, "we which are alive and remain unto the parousia of the Lord." God has joined the "catching up" and "the parousia" together, and what God has joined together, no man should separate by a period of seven years.

It will always be a source of amazement to me that most students of prophecy can find nothing but predictions of divine wrath when they consider God's next move. Why is it that they do not see that present conditions upon the earth, both moral and spiritual, are very much the result of God's present silence, the lack of positive light direct from Him, and the absence of any public manifestations or evidential miracles on His part? God, being a God of justice accepts full responsibility for this. This lack of action and restraint upon His part are necessary while He works out His present purpose in grace; but the time will come when His present purpose will be accomplished and then He will act openly and manifestly as He should act in relationship to the needs of mankind upon the earth. God will arise; He will go into action; He will plead His own cause; He will enlighten and rebuke the foolish men who now reproach Him every day; He will no longer ignore the challenge of His enemies; He will bring an end to the ever-increasing tumult that now grows continually. See Psalm 74:22, 23.

It is my firm belief and my constant proclamation that God's next move is to assume sovereignty over this earth, all men upon it (the living), and all men in it (the dead). This will be accomplished by God speaking in heaven, by a revelation of His glory to all flesh, and by causing His judgments to be heard from heaven. Jesus Christ will blaze forth (His *epiphaneia*) in all His glory, and this will result in the manifest kingdom (government) of God becoming a reality upon the earth. This is what we are asking for when we pray, "Thy kingdom come."

The present-day preachers of wrath-to-come do not seem to know or care that God has declared, "When the enemy shall come in like a flood, the Spirit of the Lord shall lift up a standard against him" (Isa. 59:19), and that this shall result in men fearing "the name of the LORD from the west, and His glory from the rising of the sun." They neither know nor care that at a time when darkness covers the earth and gross darkness the peoples, the LORD shall arise upon Israel, and His glory shall be seen in them (Isa. 60:2). They are ignorant of the fact that whenever God begins His great work of restoring and repatriating Israel, He will seek them out as a shepherd seeks out His flock when they are scattered (Eze. 34:11-15). Why then do they present Him as a wolf who will first tear the flock into pieces?

If there ever were a time in human history when the enemy has come in like a flood (Isa. 59:19), when there is an insurrection of the workers of iniquity (Psa. 64:2), when there are recurring periods of fierceness (2 Tim. 3:1), when evil men and seducers have waxed worse and worse (to the worst) (2 Tim. 3:13), it is this time in which we now live. The world needs divine intervention. God must assume sovereignty. He must take to Himself His great power and govern. Sin and death have reigned long enough. We need His kingdom. We want it to come. Tomorrow will not be too soon. May God speed the day.

The SEED and BREAD Bible-Study leaflets are published as often as time and means permit and are sent free to all names on THE WORD OF TRUTH MINISTRY mailing list. Send us your name. There will be no obligation, solicitation, or visitation. Additional copies of any issue available on request.   ISSUE NO. 41

SEED & BREAD

FOR THE SOWER   ISA. 55:10   FOR THE EATER

BRIEF BIBLICAL MESSAGES
FROM
THE WORD OF TRUTH MINISTRY
339 South Orange Drive, Los Angeles, Cal. 90036

Otis Q. Sellers, Bible Teacher

THE INHERITED LIE

The prophet Jeremiah received from the Lord God a revelation of the punishment that He would send upon the kingdom of Judah. The southern kingdom was to suffer the same experience that the ten-tribe northern kingdom had gone through a century before. They too would be cast out of their land and go into exile and captivity. The prospect was a bleak one indeed. However, at the same time Jeremiah received a revelation of their repatriation and restoration by means of a divine miracle that would outshine in glory their miraculous deliverance from the land of Egypt.

Therefore, behold, the days come, saith the LORD, that it shall no more be said, the LORD liveth, that brought up the children of Israel out of the land of Egypt; but, the LORD liveth, that brought up the children of Israel from the land of the north, and from all lands whither He had driven them: and I will bring them again into their own land that I gave unto their fathers. (Jer. 16:14, 15.)

This revelation of their miraculous restoration to God and to their land caused Jeremiah to burst forth in a declaration of adoration and majestic truth that is unsurpassed in the Old Testament:

O LORD, my strength, and my fortress, and my refuge in the day of affliction, the Gentiles (the nations) shall come unto Thee from the ends of the earth, and shall say, Surely our fathers have inherited lies, vanity, and things wherein there is no profit. (Jer. 16:19.)

All who believe the Bible to be the Word of God, and who make their faith in it to be active and working by making a constant study of it, if honest, will have to make the confession that we too have inherited many lies. And it will be my purpose in this study to deal with one of these which I feel is the worst, the emptiest, and the most unprofitable lie of all.

This is the lie that the two and one-half million Israelites who lived in the land of Palestine between A.D. 1 and 33 rejected and repudiated the man Christ Jesus, refused to listen to His teachings, rejected Him as their Messiah, and finally crucified Him. Growing out of this lie is the further falsehood that for this they were severed from God as a people, that for almost 2,000 years they have constantly suffered at His hand for this sin, and that after the crucifixion Israel has no place in God's plan.

This monumental falsehood needs to be recognized, confessed, and repudiated by all who now profess to be believers in and followers of the Lord Jesus Christ. It also needs to be exposed by having the white light of God's Word turned upon it; and this I intend to do by means of plain, easily-understood facts from the New Testament. It will be shown from Scripture that the overwhelming majority of the Jews who then lived in Palestine became followers of Him, going as far in faith and obedience as they could possibly go at that time. Furthermore, this will be my declaration to all concerned of my complete break with the commonly-accepted, anti-Semitic interpretations of the four Gospels, the Acts, and the Pauline epistles.

When John the Baptist began his ministry as the forerunner of the Lord Jesus, he was freely accepted by the people of Israel who then lived in Palestine. Even though he made his stand in the uninhabited places of Judea, nevertheless, there "went out to him Jerusalem, and all Judea, and all the region round about Jordan, and were baptized of him in Jordan, confessing their sins" (Matt. 3:5, 6; Mark 1:5). Even the Pharisees and the Sadducees did not reject him. However, he rejected them, castigating them in the strongest possible terms. These two groups made up the core of a small but influential, wealthy, and ruling class in Israel, and John's rejection of them at this time probably started much of the malignant hatred they afterward showed toward the Lord. In spite of this, we can truly say that through the ministry of John the Baptist, a people were made ready for the Lord (Luke 1:17). And many of the sons of Israel he turned to the Lord their God (Luke 1:16). His ministry could not fail; it did not fail.

We must note that when the Lord began His earthly ministry, the Palestinian Israelites knew little about Him at that time. In all Israel only two people, Mary and Joseph, knew about His miraculous birth. Certain shepherds knew that the babe born in Bethlehem was destined to be a Savior, and that this Savior was Christ, the Lord. These men probably found personal salvation by believing the message of the angels, but they were not commissioned as heralds to lead others to the acceptance of the babe born in the city of David. However, they did make known that which was told them concerning this child and all who heard marveled at these things (Luke 2:11-20). Even their message was not rejected. The short ministry of John had produced a state of mind where God's truth was credible to those who heard it. The people did not know much about the man Jesus; but what little they knew, they believed.

The early ministry of the Lord Jesus consisted of an announcement that the kingdom of heaven was at hand and a call to repentance (submission). There was no declaration concerning Himself (Matt. 4:17). When He called certain men (Israelites) to follow Him, not one of them hesitated or refused (Matt. 4:18-23). As He went about all Galilee teaching in their synagogues, heralding the gospel of the kingdom, and performing many miracles, His fame went throughout all Syria; and there followed Him great multitudes of people from Galilee, Decapolis, Jerusalem, Judea, and from beyond Jordan (Matt. 4:23-25). The term "great multitudes" should be noted here as it appears again and again in Matthew, Mark, and Luke in regard to the response to His ministry. If ever any man on earth enjoyed a successful ministry, so far as public response is concerned, it was the Lord Jesus.

After He gave the long discourse commonly called the sermon on the mount, we are told that the people were astonished at His teaching (Matt. 7:28); but when He came down from the mountain, great multitudes followed Him (Matt. 8:1). At times the number was so great that He had to move away from them (Matt. 8:18). We know from this that there was no rejection.

In Matt. 8:28-34 we find what seems to be a rejection of Him on the part of the Gergesenes (Gadarines); but this was due to ignorance and a misunderstanding which He did nothing to clear away. Following this a miracle was performed causing the multitudes to marvel and glorify "God, which had given such power unto men."

Through all of this, their acceptance is obvious; however, we need to note the increasing hostility of the Pharisees in Matt. 9:11 and 9:34. They now slandered the source of His power. But His ministry continued; and He went about all the cities and villages, teaching in their synagogues, heralding the gospel of the kingdom, and healing every sickness and every disease among the people (Matt. 9:35). At this time He made a statement to His disciples that does much to set forth a true picture of the conditions that existed in Palestine. When He saw the multitudes, He was moved with compassion on them, because they fainted and were scattered abroad, as sheep having no shepherd. These people were totally without leadership or true guidance. The Pharisees, Sadducees, scribes, lawyers, and priests were in positions of influence and power; but they disdained offering any help to the common people. They fleeced the flock, but never fed them. This situation caused the Lord to declare, "The harvest truly is plenteous, but the laborers are few; pray ye therefore the Lord of the harvest, that He will send forth laborers into His harvest" (Matt. 9:37, 38).

This was done; and if we follow each step of Scripture carefully, it will be found that when we come to the end of the Acts period, the overwhelming majority of the eight million Israelites who lived in the Roman Empire were believers in the Lord Jesus as being their Savior and Messiah.

In Matt. 11:20-24 we find that Jesus upbraided the cities where most of His mighty works had been done. Common sense will tell us that this could not have been an indictment of all the people of these cities, but of its rulers and leaders. His works in them should have produced a Nineveh like repentance (Jonah 3:4-9), but it did not. However, let it be noted that there were probably very few people in these cities who knew that He was the Christ, the Son of God. This had not yet been proclaimed. But in spite of the failure of "the wise and the prudent" in these places (Matt. 11:25-26), the multitudes still followed Him. See Matt. 12:15; 13:2; 14:14; 15-29-31.

In Matt. 16:13, 14 we find that there was great confusion among men as to just Who and What He was. They can hardly be blamed for this, due to the lack of a positive declaration on His part. However, His disciples had learned with certainty and by means of a divine revelation that He was the Christ (Messiah), the Son of the living God. But they were charged that they should tell no man that He was the Christ (Matt. 16:20). And when Peter, James and John learned from the vision given on the Mount of Transfiguration that He was in reality a projection of God Himself, they were charged to tell the vision to no man until the Son of Man be risen again from the dead (Matt. 17:9). In view of all this secrecy as to Who He was and What He was, how could the mass of people be charged with repudiating and rejecting Him since they knew so very little about Him? The complete proclamation of Him had to await until after His death and resurrection.

The multitudes continued to follow Him and receive His blessings (Matt. 19:2; 20:29), even up to His entrance into Jerusalem. Upon His arrival there, all the city was stirred and asked, "Who is this?" Their question shows their scanty knowledge of Him. His followers answered, "This is Jesus the prophet of Nazareth of Galilee" (Matt. 21:10, 11); and the multitudes accepted and acted upon what little they knew.

It was this complete acceptance of Him by the common people that raised the ire of the oligarchy that ruled in Jerusalem. Throughout the Gospels, they are identified as the Pharisees, Sadducees, priests, scribes, and elders of the people. They were the objects of some of the most scathing denunciations ever spoken by the Lord Jesus (Matt. 23). They determined to kill the Lord Jesus; but when they sought to lay hands on Him, they feared the multitude who took Him for a prophet (Matt. 21:46).

It was this corrupt political machine that finally brought about the crucifixion of the Lord Jesus, an exceedingly wicked act with which the great majority of Israelites had nothing to do.

In view of these Biblical facts, how could a just God reject and punish the people of Israel for an act with which very few of them had anything to do? And yet, the idea that God rejected and divorced Himself from Israel because of the crucifixion of Jesus is a cardinal doctrine in the creeds of many denominations. And, while it is an idea held by most Gentiles, it is an inherited lie. I want no part of it.

The SEED and BREAD Bible-Study leaflets are published as often as time and means permit and are sent free to all names on THE WORD OF TRUTH MINISTRY mailing list. Send us your name. There will be no obligation, solicitation, or visitation. Additional copies of any issue available on request.   ISSUE NO. 42

SEED & BREAD

FOR THE SOWER   ISA. 55:10   FOR THE EATER

BRIEF BIBLICAL MESSAGES
FROM
THE WORD OF TRUTH MINISTRY
339 South Orange Drive, Los Angeles, Cal. 90036

Otis Q. Sellers, Bible Teacher

WHO CRUCIFIED JESUS?

If the answer to the question raised in the subject of this study is, "The Jews — not only those who lived then, but all their descendants who have lived since then," the answer is wrong, it is libelous, and it is slanderous. Furthermore, it flatly contradicts the plain statements made in the four Gospels, all of which can be summed up by the epigrammatic statements: "And the common people heard Him gladly" (Mark 12:37); and, "All the people were very attentive to hear Him" (Luke 19:48). Inasmuch as "the common people" made up the great bulk of the Jews who then lived in Palestine, it is nothing more than anti-Semitic prejudice to say that the Jews crucified Jesus.

Yet, the average Christian believes that this is what the Bible teaches. In fact, this indictment is so sweeping that the five and one-half million Israelites who lived outside of Palestine are included along with the two and one-half million Israelites who lived in the land. And by some figment of Satanically-inspired imagination, this guilt is also charged to all their descendants, so much so that the epithet "Christ-killer" as a synonym for "Jew" has been in common use for almost nineteen hundred years.

Since, as a Christian, I believe that all guilt is personal, that it is never inherited, and that it cannot be collective beyond those actually involved, I repudiate altogether the idea that any Jew living today had anything to do, even remotely, with the crucifixion of Jesus Christ. And I often wonder if some professing Christians have any knowledge whatsoever of Peter's great declaration recorded in Acts 4:27, 28: "For of a truth against Thy holy Servant Jesus, Whom Thou hast anointed, both Herod and Pontius Pilate, with the Gentiles, and the people of Israel, were gathered together, for to do whatsoever Thy hand and Thy counsel determined before to be done."

In order to honestly answer the question which is before us, we need to have some degree of familiarity with the political and economic situation that existed in Palestine in A.D. 33. To keep it as simple as possible, we need only to understand and consider the great gulf that existed between the two classes of people who lived then in the land of Israel — the rich and the poor, or to state it in other terms, the aristocracy and the common people. A rich and powerful aristocracy had created a veritable caste system. These two classes stand out distinctly in the four Gospels, and it seems that none ever passed from one class to another. Since it was not a money economy or system, to be among the rich in Israel was not based upon the possession of money, but on power, influence, social position, education, and learning. The poor had none of these, and it was impossible for them to obtain them.

The three main groups that made up the aristocracy in Palestine were the Pharisees, Sadducees, and Herodians. These were all Jews. They are further classified according to their positions as elders, lawyers, Levites, scribes, priests, and rulers. These formed an oligarchy (the rule of a few) that controlled all political, religious, and economic life in Israel. Their power was much greater than their number. They were not all bad men. The finest men in Israel could be found among them, but they were too few to have the balance of power.

The Lord Jesus castigated and rejected this powerful oligarchy very early in His ministry by saying: "Woe unto you that are rich! for ye have received your consolation" (Luke 6:24). These were the men who had the favored place in the *status quo* in Palestine, and they had trampled under foot the majority of their brethren in order to get such a place. When they came to John's baptism, he rejected them on the spot (Matt. 3:7). And, very early in the ministry of our Lord, their malignant opposition to Him came to the surface (Matt. 9:34).

At about the end of the second year of His ministry, we find that "from that time forth began Jesus to show unto His disciples, how that He must go unto Jerusalem, and suffer many things of the elders, the chief priests, and scribes, and be killed and and be raised again the third day" (Matt. 16:21). This was something with which the outspoken Peter did not agree, and he so declared it in few words. Again the Lord said, "The Son of Man is delivered into the hands of men, and they shall kill Him; and after He is killed, He shall rise the third day" (Mark 9:31). At this point He did not positively identify the men into whose hands He would be delivered, but later He does. In Luke 18:31 He declared: "Behold, we go up to Jerusalem, and all things that are written by the prophets concerning the Son of Man shall be accomplished. For He shall be delivered to the Gentiles, and shall be mocked, and spitefully entreated, and spitted on: And they shall scourge Him, and put Him to death: and the third day He shall rise again."

From these statements we can conclude that if Jesus was "delivered to the Gentiles," then Pontius Pilate, the Roman prefect of Judea, had complete juridical and administrative responsibility for the trial and crucifixion of Jesus Christ.

The death of Jesus Christ was a predetermined matter in the counsels of God. "Yet it pleased the LORD to bruise Him; He hath put Him to grief" (Isa. 53:10). His death could happen only at God's appointed time; and when this time came, a virtual army guided by Judas Iscariot came, and with him a great multitude with swords and staves, from the chief priests and elders of the people (Matt. 26:47). Arrested, He was led away to Caiaphas, the high priest, where the scribes and elders were assembled. These sought false witnesses against Jesus to put Him to death. At last, after much searching, they found two, who gave the flimsy testimony that He had said He was able to destroy the temple of God and to build it in three days (Matt. 26:57-61).

Our Lord refused to answer these ridiculous charges, which caused the high priest to angrily demand of Him, "I adjure Thee by the living God, that Thou tell us whether Thou be the Christ, the Son of God" (Matt. 26:63). Jesus answered him by saying, "Thou hast said." Many take this to be a positive affirmation, but it could mean that He is saying to Caiaphas, "You have made the charge, now prove it or disprove it." Whatever it may mean, it caused the high priest to foam with rage.

The Lord Jesus had been arrested at night, and when morning came, all the chief priests and elders of the people took counsel against Jesus to put Him to death; so they bound Him and delivered Him to Pontius Pilate, the governor (Matt. 27:1, 2). From this moment on He is in the hands of a Gentile who can either release Him or condemn Him, and who after some dramatic moments, ordered Him to be scourged and delivered Him to be crucified. One of these dramatic moments came when the chief priests and elders persuaded the multitude that they should ask for the robber, Barabbas, and demand the destruction of Jesus (Matt. 27:15-22). Thus, a multitude becomes guiltily involved in the conspiracy against Him.

We wonder about the number and character of those involved. It was early in the morning, so it was not a "great multitude"; and quite a few in it may have been pro-Barabbas partisans who had assembled early in the morning hoping for his release. However, in answer to the question, "Who crucified Jesus?" we can say that in view of the Biblical facts, the guilty parties were the Pharisees, Sadducees, scribes, rulers of the people, and also a multitude, who at the urging of the chief priests and elders demanded His death. But it must also be noted that the ultimate juridical decision and the order for His execution was made by Pontius Pilate, a Gentile.

It was the soldiers of the governor, Gentiles all, who took Jesus into the common hall, stripped Him of His clothes, and put upon Him an old scarlet robe. It was these Gentiles who platted the crown of thorns and sadistically crushed it down upon His brow. All of this was gratuitous on their part, as it was no part of the chief priest's and elder's demands, nor any part of the governor's orders. However, after He was crucified, the chief priests, elders, and scribes joined in the mockery. Thus, if there is any such thing as collective guilt or inherited guilt, all the descendants of the Romans would be equally guilty with the Jews.

Of course, there will be many who will raise the familiar fact that after Pilate declared his personal freedom from guilt in the death of Jesus, all the people there assembled declared, "His blood be upon us, and on our children" (Matt. 27:25). This declaration, many seem to think, made all Jews guilty along with all their descendants.

In considering this we must ask two questions: "Who said this?" and, "Were they the official spokesmen for the eight million Jews who then lived upon the earth?" The answers to these questions are obvious. It was not a representative body, and no one had appointed them to speak for all Israel.

The logical thinker will recognize at once that their statement, "His blood be upon us," did not make them any more guilty than they already were; and the additional words, "and on our children," are utterly meaningless so far as being effective is concerned. They could no more bring guilt upon their children than Pilate, the Gentile, could cleanse himself of guilt by publicly washing his hands before them (Matt. 27:24).

And yet, no matter who or how many can be charged with guilty complicity in the death of Jesus Christ, it must be remembered that while He hung upon the cross, He looked down upon His tormentors and prayed: "Father, forgive them; for they know not what they do" (Luke 23:34).

I have often said that if this prayer were not answered, I would have no reason to believe that any of mine or yours would ever be answered. It was this prayer that led Peter to say in his second great message, "And now, brethern, I am aware that through ignorance ye did it, as did also your rulers" (Acts 3:17).

Thus, the answer is clear. A small number of powerful Jews along with a weak-kneed Gentile governor brought about the crucifixion of Jesus. According to our Lord and to Peter, they did it in ignorance. If they had only known the hidden wisdom which was later revealed by Paul, "they would not have crucified the Lord of glory" (I Cor. 2:8).

The SEED and BREAD Bible-Study leaflets are published as often as time and means permit and are sent free to all names on THE WORD OF TRUTH MINISTRY mailing list. Send us your name. There will be no obligation, solicitation, or visitation. Additional copies of any issue available on request.   ISSUE NO. 43

SEED & BREAD

FOR THE SOWER   ISA. 55:10   FOR THE EATER

BRIEF BIBLICAL MESSAGES

FROM

THE WORD OF TRUTH MINISTRY

339 South Orange Drive, Los Angeles, Cal. 90036

Otis Q. Sellers, Bible Teacher

ISRAEL IN THE ACTS PERIOD

The ACTS PERIOD referred to in the subject of this study has to do with that thirty-three year period of which the Book of Acts is the history. This began with the resurrection of Jesus Christ. It ended with Paul's two years of ministry in his own rented house in Rome. In this study I will seek to provide the Biblical answer to the question—What did the people of Israel, those in Palestine as well as the dispersed ones, do in regard to the presentation of the crucified and risen Savior?

We have already seen in previous studies the limited knowledge that existed concerning the man Jesus before His resurrection. The full presentation of Him could not be made until He had been crucified and risen. However, one becomes a believer by believing the truth that is at hand, and the Gospel evidence shows that the overwhelming majority of the two and one-half million Jews who then lived in Palestine believed whatever truth concerning Him was available to them. Thus, they were dealt with according to the word of Christ that "unto whomsoever much is given, of him shall much be required" (Luke 12:48).

There were those who knew by divine revelation that He was the Christ (the Messiah), the Son of God (Matt. 16:16, 17). These were told not to depart from Jerusalem, but to wait there for the promise of the Father, of which they had already been told. After this they would be witnesses unto Him in Jerusalem, in all Judea, in Samaria, and unto the uttermost part of the earth (Acts 1.4, 8). On that memorable day of Pentecost, 120 of these believers were assembled together. Every one of those was a Jew who had found in the man Jesus the fulfillment of God's promise of the Messiah.

At this time there were dwelling at Jerusalem Jews, devout men, out of every nation under heaven (Acts 2:5). This description of their character would certainly indicate that these were a part of the flock of the great Shepherd, of whom He had already said, "My sheep hear My voice, and I know them, and they follow Me" (John 10.27). After Peter's message and the witnessing of the 120 was completed, 3,000 souls were added; so the number that believed in the crucified and risen Messiah was 3,120. And this was in Jerusalem, the very city in which the Lord Jesus had been condemned to death, and where acknowledgment of Him could bring the same penalty.

As the witnessing continued and many miracles were performed, those who believed had favor with all the people; and the Lord continued to add to the 3,120 those who were being saved in that place (Acts 2:41-47). The words "to the church" do not belong to the text here, and their insertion is evidence of the concerted drive of church theologians to get Israel out and get the church in.

The second message of Peter brought further astonishing results and even though the apostles were placed under arrest, "many of them which heard the Word believed; and the number of the men was about five thousand" (Acts 4:4). Peter's success was phenomenal. Luke's accurate account speaks only of five thousand men and does not include the women and children, of whom there must have been a due proportion. A very conservative estimate would be that there were 15,000 believers in Jerusalem, every one of whom was a Jew, not a single Gentile among them. These now stand as "the Israel of God" in contrast with "Israel after the flesh" (Gal 6:16, 1 Cor. 10:18). They were Israelites by birth; they became the Israel of God by faith in Jesus Christ. They never ceased to be Israelites.

The Sadducees who had caused the arrest of the apostles could find nothing for which they might be punished; so they let them go "because of the people, for all men glorified God for that which was done" (Acts 4.21), a declaration which reveals the general attitude of the people in Jerusalem toward the Lord Jesus.

Free for the time being, the apostles continued to proclaim that Jesus was the Christ, with the result that "believers were the more added to the Lord, multitudes both of men and women" (Acts 5:14). Miracles abounded, so that out of the cities round about Jerusalem there came a multitude bringing the sick and those vexed by unclean spirits, and they were healed every one (Acts 5:16). This glorious ministry filled the high priest and the sect of the Sadducees with jealousy, so the apostles were again arrested and placed in the common prison. From this the Lord miraculously delivered them and their ministry was resumed with the result that the number of disciples multiplied in Jerusalem greatly and a great company of the priests became obedient unto the faith (Acts 6:7). We lose all track of numbers here, but in regard to this, R. C. H. Lenski, the Lutheran commentator, says: "Luke's figures and further notes about the growth make the estimate of 25,000 believers in and near Jerusalem at the time of Stephen's martyrdom seem conservative."

Twenty-five years later in Jerusalem, James said to Paul, "Thou seest brother how many thousands of Jews there are which believe, and they are all zealous of the law" (Acts 21:20). The word "thousands" here can only be considered as an attempt by translators to minimize the truth. The Greek word *murias* means ten thousand; here it is plural (*muriades*), and its means tens of thousands. And when we remember that the resident population of Jerusalem was only 30,000, we can come to no other conclusion than that the overwhelming majority of Jews in Jerusalem and Palestine became believers in and followers of the crucified and risen Jesus.

Up to the time of Stephen's martyrdom, all witnessing centered in Jerusalem. After his execution a great persecution arose and the believers were forced to scatter abroad, going everywhere heralding the Word. And many readers, of course, will wonder why, if there were so many of them, they did not fight back. The answer is obvious. They could not resist, since they had been warned "all they that take the sword shall perish with the sword" (Matt. 26:52). Furthermore, they had been told that when persecuted in one city to flee to another (Matt. 10:23). However, we know that when they were scattered abroad and went everywhere proclaiming the Word, it was proclaimed "to none but unto Jews only" (Acts 11:19). Their success continued to be phenomenal. In Samaria, the people with one accord gave heed to the message of Philip (Acts 8:6). Another witness of great power was provided by the conversion of Saul (Paul), a Jew, one of the aristocracy, who could speak to all Jews of whatever level. He would later use the fact of his conversion as positive proof that God had not severed Himself from or cast away His people (Rom. 11:1).

The healing of Aeneas by Peter resulted in all who lived at Lydda and Saron turning to the Lord (Acts 9:35); and the resurrection of Dorcas caused many in Joppa to believe in the Lord (Acts 9:42). These were Jews that believed.

At this point in the Acts period, eight years after the resurrection, a new element entered the scene. Peter was commissioned to proclaim the Word to one Gentile family, the house of Cornelius, which he did with complete success; and this was both the beginning and the end of his ministry to the Gentiles. After Acts 12, Peter was no longer prominent, and Paul began to fill the scene.

From Acts 13 to Acts 28, we follow the independent ministry of the Apostle Paul. The outcalled ones of God in Antioch were directed by the Holy Spirit to release all controls and direction of Barnabas and Paul so that they might do the work to which the Lord had called them. What this work was can be determined the moment it begins (Acts 14:1, 2).

Together they traveled to Seleucia, a seaport, and landed at Salamis on the Isle of Cyprus. There "they preached the Word in the synagogue of the Jews" (Acts 13:5). Thus, "to the Jew first" dominates every act of ministry in the Acts period (Acts 3:26; 10:36; 13:46; Rom. 1:16). To the Jew first is stamped on every page of the Acts of the Apostles. This obligation having been fulfilled on the Isle of Cyprus, they were able to accept the invitation of Sergius Paulus, a Gentile, who desired to hear the Word of God (Acts 13:7). He heard, he saw, and he believed.

Their next stop was in Antioch in Pisidia, where they went into the synagogue, and by invitation of the rulers they heralded the Word and proclaimed Jesus as the Messiah. The effect was good and the results were excellent even though much opposition arose during the week that followed which led them to break off their ministry to the Jews and turn to the Gentiles (Acts 13:42-49). Thus, the Word of the Lord was published throughout all that region.

Some interpreters try to make this to be the end of Paul's ministry to the Jews, but at their next stop in Iconium, Paul went with Barnabas into the synagogue and spake in such manner that a great multitude of the Jews and also of the Gentiles believed (Acts 14:1). The words "and so spake" indicate that they followed the divine order, "to the Jew first, and also to the Greek." Paul did not violate the truth which he later declared in his Roman epistle (Rom. 1:16). Their success created a sharp division in the city, and when persecution arose, they fled to Lystra and Derbe and there preached the gospel.

In Philippi, Thessalonica, Berea, Corinth, and Ephesus, Paul continued his ministry in the synagogues. The results were good everywhere in spite of increasing opposition on the part of some Jews and some Gentiles (Acts 16, 17, 18, 19). In Ephesus there was extreme opposition, but the results were such that we are told, "mightily grew the Word of God and prevailed." At this point Paul's ministry took a different track as he headed toward Jerusalem. There he was arrested and in time was brought as a prisoner to Rome. There, after three days, he called the chief of the Jews together, who declared they were glad to hear him, stating that all they knew about this sect was that everywhere it was spoken against (Acts 28-17-22). Gladly they appointed him a day during which he expounded and testified the kingdom of God, besides persuading them concerning Jesus, both from the law of Moses and the prophets from morning to evening. The result was that some believed the things that were spoken and some believed not. Concerning this, let us consider the words of another.

"We feel safe in saying that in all Paul's career he scored no greater success in a single day's work than on the day which Luke describes in v. 23, etc. He converted half of the rabbis and leaders of the eleven synagogues in the capital of the world! *Oi men oi de* (v. 24) equals 50—50 according to our way of speaking . . . Converting the rabbis and the leaders could mean only one thing, namely that these rabbis took the gospel of Paul into their synagogues with the result that whole synagogues were converted, and the members who refused withdrew to other synagogues." *R. C. H. Lenski.*

The conclusion is inescapable. The Word of God shows that the overwhelming majority of Jews in Palestine and in the exile became believers in the Lord Jesus Christ during the Acts period. This is the truth. Where it may lead us and what changes it makes in our thinking is up to each one of us to find out.

The SEED and BREAD Bible-Study leaflets are published as often as time and means permit and are sent free to all names on THE WORD OF TRUTH MINISTRY mailing list. Send us your name. There will be no obligation, solicitation, or visitation. Additional copies of any issue available on request.   ISSUE NO.44

SEED & BREAD

FOR THE SOWER   ISA. 55:10   FOR THE EATER

BRIEF BIBLICAL MESSAGES

FROM

THE WORD OF TRUTH MINISTRY

339 South Orange Drive, Los Angeles, Cal. 90036

Otis Q. Sellers, Bible Teacher

THE THEOLOGICAL CONSPIRACY

It was a full-blown conspiracy when it first came to the surface in history. It is not known how it started or who instigated it, but all at once it was in full operation. Its chief purpose can be set forth in few and simple words. Its goal was to get the Jew out of all God's plans and purposes and to get the Gentile in; to take every precious promise that God had made to Israel and apply each of them to organized religion called "the church," and this a Gentile church, of course; to take the glorious Old Testament concept of the kingdom of God upon the earth and make it to be a promise of "the church" in heaven.

In order to comprehend this great conspiracy, we need to know something about the early history of that which today is called "Christianity." It is also important to have certain approximate dates in mind as points of reference. Taking the commonly received date of A.D. 1 for the birth of Jesus Christ, we come to A.D. 33, the date of His death. From His resurrection to the great dispensational change marked by Paul's pronouncement in Acts 28:28, we have another 33 years. This brings us to A.D. 66. A few years later, Jerusalem was destroyed by the Roman General Titus (A.D. 70). During the years between A.D. 1 and A.D. 66, there were millions upon the earth whom we can now designate as believers in and followers of the Lord Jesus Christ; and the overwhelming majority of these were "Jews that believed." Although a certain number of Gentiles became believers, these were a minuscule minority who became partakers of Israel's spiritual things (Rom. 15:27). In fact, their salvation was primarily in view of Israel's need, "to provoke them to jealousy" (emulation) (Rom. 11:11). And while many today are prone to point to those in Israel who did not believe, let them remember that their unbelief could not make the faithfulness of God without effect (Rom. 3:3).

Between A.D. 70 and A.D. 150 there is no recorded history so far as the people of God are concerned; and this is that period of time in which the transition was made from the age of the apostles, all of whom were Jews that believed, to the age of the so-called "church fathers," none of whom were Jews. At this point we will do well to consider the scholarly words of Dean Stanley in his *History of the Eastern Church.*

"The first period is that which contains the great question, almost the greatest which Ecclesiastical History has to answer, — How was the transition effected from the age of the Apostles to the age of the Fathers, from Christianity as we see it in the New Testament, to Christianity as we see it in the next century, and as, to a certain extent, we have seen it ever since?

"No other change equally momentous has ever since affected its fortunes, yet none has ever been so silent and secret. The stream, in that most critical moment of its passage from the everlasting hills to the plain below, is lost to our view at the very point where we are most anxious to watch it; we may hear its struggles under the overarching rocks; we may catch its spray on the boughs that overlap its course; but the torrent itself we see not, or see only by imperfect glimpses. It is not so much a period for Ecclesiastical History as for ecclesiastical controversey and conjecture. A fragment here, an allegory there; romances of unknown authorship; a handful of letters of which the genuineness of every portion is contested inch by inch; the summary examination of a Roman magistrate; the pleadings of two or three Christian apologists; customs and opinions in the very act of change; last but not least, the faded paintings, the broken sculptures, the rude epitaphs in the darkness of the catacombs, — these are the scanty, though attractive, materials out of which the likeness of the early Church must be reproduced, as it was working its way, in the literal sense of the word, 'under ground,' under camp and palace, under senate and forum, —'as unknown, yet well known; as dying, and behold it lives.'

"This chasm once cleared, we find ourselves approaching the point where the story of the Church once more becomes history — becomes once more history, not of an isolated community, or of isolated individuals, but of an organized society incorporated with the political systems of the world."

This was the lament of Dean Stanley in 1861; and if we consider all the research and discovery that has taken place in the more than 100 years that have passed since he wrote, we find no facts of any kind that shed any light upon that strange, silent, and secret period between A.D. 70 and A.D. 150. Thus, today we still stand amazed at how a great company of isolated individuals who believed that Jesus was the Christ, and these predominately Jews that believed, became in 80 years an organized society, incorporated with the political systems of this world, holding beliefs and practicing rituals which were unknown in New Testament times. Furthermore, how was it possible that the great company of "Jews that believed" should in such short time become a company of Gentiles of great power in the Roman Empire, and also become anti-Semitic and the leading persecutors of Israel?

There can be only one answer to this. That stream which disappeared from view when the last word of the New Testament was written is not the same stream that emerged into view eighty years later. Christianity as we see it in the New Testament is not the Christianity that we see 100 years later; the ecclesia (out-called ones) of the New Testament is not the church of the Latin fathers. To use the words of Dean Stanley — "when this chasm is once cleared, and we find ourselves approaching the point where the story of the New Testament once more becomes history," we find a great theological conspiracy in operation whose evident purpose is to get the Jew out and get the Gentile church in, even going to the extreme of insisting that all Jews must desert their heritage and become Gentiles if they want to be any part of that which is called "Christianity."

This conspiracy led to the most terrible persecution of a people, a persecution that has no parallel in history. The anti-Semitism of that which called itself Christian does not need to be detailed in this brief study. The facts of history cannot be denied. There is no record more sickening in the annals of man's inhumanity to his fellow-man. However, the persecution of Jews by those who call themselves Christian is not our main interest at present. We are chiefly interested in that theological conspiracy and its one goal of getting the Jew out and putting "the church" in his place. This conspiracy carried on its work before the reformation under Luther, and it was in no way touched by the reformation. In fact, the theology that came out of the reformation was just as anti-Semitic as that which preceded it.

This conspiracy can be seen in the idea, almost universally accepted in Christendom, that Israel was rejected and set aside at the Cross and has no further place in God's program or purposes. All promises that God ever made to Israel are thrown up for grabs; and then the theft is justified by claiming that "the church" is "spiritual Israel" and, therefore, is the real owner of Israel's place and blessings. Thus, a sharp distinction is made between "the church" and Israel, so that any Jew who would become a part of the church must sever himself from Israel.

Out of this comes the idea that the book of Acts is the history of the beginning and growth of "the church." The truth that Israel is still the center of all God's activities throughout the Acts period is ignored or denied. "Get the Jew out and get the Gentile in" is the theological battle cry when men handle this book. Church theologians simply will not face up to the truth that in the eight year period after the resurrection when thousands were flocking to the Savior, and doing so at the risk of their lives, there was not so much as even one Gentile among them. If any think otherwise, then let that Gentile be pointed out or named.

Traditional theology would prefer that we believe that out of the 3000 who came to know Christ on the day of Pentecost, there were many Gentiles, and that these fanned out over the Roman Empire to preach the gospel to the Gentiles, and to found Gentiles churches even in such faraway places as Rome. The truth is ignored that this would make these men God's commissioned ones to the Gentiles and set aside Paul's claim that this was a prerogative in which he alone could boast.

Church theologians refuse to give any place to what God said to Israel through Peter when he declared, "Unto you first God, having raised up His Son Jesus, sent (*apostellō*, commissioned, see Issue No. 5) Him to bless you, in turning away every one of you from his iniquities" (Acts 3:26). They ignore Paul's inspired statement made thirteen years after the resurrection to the people of Israel in Pisidian Antioch, "Men and brethren, children of the stock of Abraham, and whosoever among you feareth God (the proselytes), to you is the word of this salvation sent" (*apostellō*, authorized); and also his following words, "It was necessary that the Word of God should first have been spoken to you" (Acts 13: 26, 46).

There are those who hold that since some Jews in Pisidian Antioch refused to believe, this determined the fate of all Israel. In fact, they insist that "the church" started here, a new development marking the end of God's dealing with Israel. They ignore the fact that this turning to the Gentiles which took place here was strictly a local matter, that it concerned only those Gentiles who were at hand begging to be included in the gospel message (13:42), and that at Paul's next stop in Iconium, he went at once to "the synagogue of the Jews."

Church theologians look upon Paul as a synagogue splitter and a church founder. The facts are that Paul never split a synagogue or founded a church. His actions in Ephesus, recorded in Acts 19:8, 9, did not split the synagogue and they did not start a church. True, those who believed became the outcalled (*ekklesia*) of God; but they stoutly maintained and confessed their place in Israel, even as did Paul. Note his plain words in Rom. 11:1, "For I also am an Israelite, of the seed of Abraham, of the tribe of Benjamin," words spoken as proof that God had not cast away His people. Why ignore his declaration to the multitude, "I am verily a man which am a Jew" (Acts 22:3)?

If we would know the truth and if the truth would make us free, we must abandon once and for all the anti-Semitic interpretations of the Bible which today permeate the theology of Christendom from the circumference to the core.

The SEED and BREAD Bible-Study leaflets are published as often as time and means permit and are sent free to all names on THE WORD OF TRUTH MINISTRY mailing list. Send us your name. There will be no obligation, solicitation, or visitation. Additional copies of any issue available on request.   ISSUE NO. 45

SEED & BREAD

FOR THE SOWER   ISA. 55:10   FOR THE EATER

BRIEF BIBLICAL MESSAGES
FROM
THE WORD OF TRUTH MINISTRY
339 South Orange Drive, Los Angeles, Cal. 90036

Otis Q. Sellers, Bible Teacher

"THE JEWS" IN JOHN'S GOSPEL

It is the feeling of many Christians that the Apostle John, in the Gospel that bears his name, places the blame for the crucifixion of Jesus squarely upon "the Jews" as a people. Thus, an exact definition of the term "the Jews" as used by John becomes one of extreme importance.

The declarations in John 5:16, "And therefore did the Jews persecute Jesus, and sought to slay Him"; and in 5:18, "Therefore the Jews sought the more to kill Him, because He had not only broken the sabbath, but said also that God was His Father, making Himself equal with God," are pointed to as being direct statements from God's Word concerning the involvement of all Palestinian Jews in the rejection of Jesus. And by some feat of illogical deduction, the term "the Jews" is made to mean all who lived then as well as all who have lived since, which is preposterous and absurd to say the least.

This matter arose recently and was threshed out in a civil court of law in France, in a case that came to be popularly known as "the Jesus trial." In 1967, Monsieur Jacques Isorni, a lawyer, legal historian, and author, wrote a book called *The True Trial of Jesus.* In it he blamed Pilate for the crucifixion. The Rev. George de Nantes, a Catholic priest, became so vehemently bitter in his accusations and denunciations of Isorni, that it led him to sue for libel. De Nantes charged that Isorni had falsified the New Testament, pointing to John 5:18 as proof of Jewish guilt. The trial went on for two months (Nov. and Dec. 1974) and the three justices had to decide whether the Jews or the Romans were ultimately responsible for the crucifixion of Jesus. The verdict was that the Romans killed Jesus, and De Nantes was found guilty of libel. Isorni was awarded exactly what he had asked for: symbolic damages of one franc.

Of course, such a trial settles nothing; but it again raises the question that has long needed to be answered: Who are "the Jews" in John's Gospel? What does he mean by this term?

In 1968, Rosemary Ruether, writing in *The Christian Century*, called upon all professing Christians to admit that anti-Semitism "is deeply rooted in the gospel itself," and claimed that it is fairly well established that the New Testament account of the death of Jesus is "an apologetic reworking of history to shift the blame from the Roman to the Jewish authorities."

Mrs. Ruether is one of a rather large company of liberal writers who challenge the accuracy and authority of the New Testament records. Their arguments come in many variations: The Gospels are not consistent in reporting the trial and death of Jesus Christ; the later evangelists play down the Roman involvement and magnify that of the Jews; and the latest gospel (?), John, is the most anti-Semitic of the four, it having been written to provide ammunition in the great struggle that arose between "church" and "synagogue." Thus, as these liberals rightly seek to fully renounce anti-Semitism, they fall into a more complete and wrong rejection of the fourth gospel.

The so-called anti-Semitism of John's Gospel is based upon superficial interpretations of certain passages; and such interpretations are a part of that anti-Semitic theology, the purpose of which is to get the Jew out and get the church in, to clear all Gentiles of any complicity in the crucifixion and place all blame upon the people of Israel, those living then as well as those living now. As a duty to God and out of love for the truth, we owe it to Him to find with accuracy what John meant by the term "the Jews" when he used it in his gospel. A precise understanding is all important.

The meaning of any term or word in Scripture must be determined by its usage. Attempts have been made to fix an exact meaning upon the term "the Jews," but these definitions have always fallen apart when applied to all occurrences in Scripture. One occurrence will often fully support the definition, but another will deny it. This can result in no other conclusion than that the term "the Jews" means whatever is indicated by the immediate context in which it is found. This is also true of all national designations given to any company of people, such as the Americans, the French, the Japanese, or the Jews.

For example, consider the following statements: "The Americans dropped the atomic bomb on Hiroshima"; and, "The Americans did not know that an atomic bomb existed." Both of these statements are entirely true, even though they seem to be contradictory. The moment the reader saw them, his mind went to work on them and straightened them out. How good it would be if we would do this on each occurrence of "the Jews" in John's Gospel.

In the first occurrence, John 1:19, we read that "the Jews sent *(apostellō)* priests and Levites from Jerusalem" to ask John the Baptist, "Who art thou?" Here the term "the Jews" must be limited to a very small ruling oligarchy that controlled all life in and around Jerusalem. This group had the power to commission with authority as investigators certain priests and Levites to question the Lord's forerunner. Later we are told that they which were sent *(apostellō)* were of the Pharisees, which indicates that it was the Sanhedrin that dispatched them on this official mission.

The second occurrence speaks of the six waterpots which were set after the manner of the purifying of "the Jews" (John 2:6). This purification process was a Pharasaic custom and was in no way any part of the divine ritual laid down in the Old Testament. Very few in Israel observed it, and in this occurrence the term "the Jews" would need to be severely limited, probably to the aristocracy in Jerusalem.

The third occurrence speaks of "the Jews' passover" (John 2:13), which at first glance would seem to enlarge the scope of this term, but after more careful examination we find that the rulers in Israel had so altered and encumbered "the Lord's Passover" that it had become "the Jews' passover." They had made the Word of God of none effect by their traditions (Matt. 15:6).

"The Jews" who questioned Jesus in John 2:18 and 2:20 were the rulers who were in the temple at the time He cast out the money changers in the temple. Their questions were formal and serious, and we infer from this that these were members of the Sanhedrin who were accompanied by some of the temple police.

In John 3:1 the fact that Nicodemus was "a ruler of the Jews" must here, in Jerusalem, mean that he was a member of the Sanhedrin. The rule of the Sanhedrin at this time did not extend beyond Judea. They had the authority but could not exercise it.

The next occurrence is interesting. It says that Jesus and His disciples came into the land of the Jews (not Judea, as the K.J.V. has it). He moved from the Judean capital into the Judean country (John 3:22) where the common people were, and away from the priests, Levites, and Pharisees who dominated Jerusalem.

In John 3:25 when the question arose between some of John's disciples and "the Jews" about purifying, it is quite evident that this term covered a very small number.

The declaration that "the Jews have no dealings with the Samaritans" (John 4:9) was a generalization made by a woman whose knowledge of the Jews was limited. True, certain Jews had no dealings with the Samaritans, but this was limited to those living in Judea.

Our Lord's statement that "salvation is of the Jews" (John 4:22) has reference to the fact that "the Salvation," which is the Messiah, was to be born in Bethlehem of Judea, and would therefore Himself be a Jew.

The "feast of the Jews" spoken of in John 5:1 is not identifiable. The Jews had many festivals that had no basis in Scripture. And the company referred to four times as "the Jews," on this occasion has to be limited to a very small number of the rulers (5:10, 15, 16, 18). In John 6:4 the passover is again referred to as a feast of the Jews. Compare this with Exodus 12:11, 27, and 48.

The term "the Jews" in John 6:41 and 52 must be limited to a very small number who made up part of the crowds that surrounded Him when He spoke. This is also true in John 7:1, 11, 13, 15, 35; 8:22, 48, 52, 57. There is no way that any of these occurrences can be made to mean the 2,500,000 Israelites who then lived in Palestine. "The Jews' feast of Tabernacles" spoken of in 7:2 shows that this simple celebration had degenerated due to the many symbolic features added in postexilic times.

The student can examine for himself the occurrences of "the Jews" in John 9:18, 22; 10:19, 24, 31, 33; 11:8, 19, 31, 33, 36, 45, 54, 55; 12:9, 11, and 13:33 and in every instance he will see that this term is limited to a very small number of people.

When we come to the record of the arrest, the trial, and the crucifixion of Jesus Christ, we find the term "the Jews" twenty-one times in John 18 and 19. In every occurrence it has to be limited to the rulers, scribes, and priests who were the persecutors of Jesus. There is no way it can be spread out and made to mean the 2,500,000 Israelites who lived in Palestine. The overwhelming majority of these cannot in any way be charged with the crucifixion of the Lord Jesus.

In the final occurrence in John's Gospel we find the disciples assembled behind closed doors "for fear of the Jews" (John 20:19). We are prone to ask, "Of whom were these men afraid?" Were they afraid of the common people who had heard the Lord gladly? Were they afraid of themselves? Everyone of them was a Jew. The answer is clear. They feared that small aristocracy and hierarchy that controlled all life in Jerusalem and Judea at that time.

If the reader will put his brain to work on any occurrence of the term "the Jews" in John's Gospel, he will find that it almost always refers to the enemies of Christ, a small but powerful oligarchy that brought about His crucifixion.

The SEED and BREAD Bible-Study leaflets are published as often as time and means permit and are sent free to all names on THE WORD OF TRUTH MINISTRY mailing list. Send us your name. There will be no obligation, solicitation, or visitation. Additional copies of any issue available on request.   ISSUE NO. 46

SEED & BREAD

FOR THE SOWER   ISA. 55:10   FOR THE EATER

BRIEF BIBLICAL MESSAGES
FROM
THE WORD OF TRUTH MINISTRY
339 South Orange Drive, Los Angeles, Cal. 90036

Otis Q. Sellers, Bible Teacher

QUESTIONS AND OBJECTIONS

The title of this leaflet has reference to studies set forth in Issues No. 42, 43, and 44 of SEED AND BREAD, in which it was demonstrated by the Word of God that the overwhelming majority of the 2,500,000 Israelites that lived in the land of Palestine during the earthly ministry of Jesus Christ were entirely sympathetic to His message, and that by them He was not rejected. It was also shown that after His crucifixion and resurrection, the overwhelming majority of all Israelites upon earth, those in the land as well as the 5,500,000 in exile, became believers in and followers of Him.

The results that came from the apostles and others being endued with power from on high, and their subsequent proclamation of the crucified and risen Savior in Jerusalem and its environs alone, are sufficient to demonstrate the truth of this. James declared to Paul, "Thou seest brother, how many thousands (myriads) of Jews there are which believe" (Acts 21:20). A myriad in Greek is ten thousand; and since it is in the plural here and is used in an indefinite manner, it could hardly be less than three myriads or 30,000 believers in and around this city which had a normal population of 25,000 people.

Careful and capable students of the facts of the Acts period (for example, R. C. H. Lenski, the Lutheran commentator) estimate that there were 25,000 believers in and around Jerusalem at the time of Stephen's martyrdom (Acts 7); but on Acts 21:20 Lenski says, "We saw that at the time of Stephen's death the estimate of 25,000 converts was low, and years had passed since that time."

In the case of many readers, the effect of this truth will probably be that of shining a bright light into unprepared eyes. In this state if they understand at all what is being presented, it is often in exaggerated and distorted forms. They behold "men as trees walking," which was the experience of the blind man when the Lord first opened his eyes (Mark 8:24). It takes time and thought to see things as they actually are, and very few will give the time or do the thinking that is required to lay hold of great and far-reaching truths.

Many questions and objections to this truth are based upon the statement found in John's Gospel (1:11), "He came unto His own, and His own received Him not." This statement is given the popular anti-Semitic interpretation that He came to Israel and the people of Israel refused to receive Him. By this they demonstrate that He was rejected by Israel. They fail to consider that these words tell us of the actions of Jehovah, and mankind's attitude toward Him from the fall of man until the first advent of Christ.

It has been pointed out by many expositors that the first occurrence of "own" in John 1:11 is neuter and must be understood as "His own things." Never forget that before He became a babe in Bethlehem, "He was in the world, and the world was made by Him, and the world knew Him not" (John 1:10). He declared, "For every beast of the forest is mine, and the cattle upon a thousand hills. I know all the fowls of the mountains: and the wild beasts of the field are mine. If I were hungry, I would not tell thee: for the world is mine and the fulness thereof"(Psa. 50:10-12). All through the centuries before Bethlehem, the Expression *(Logos)* of God came again and again to His own things.

The second occurrence of "own" is masculine and should read, "His own men received Him not," the term "men" to be understood generically. Here we must remember His words, "All souls are mine; as the soul of the father, so also the soul of the son is mine" (Eze. 18:4). However, the non-acceptance of the divine Expression before His incarnation was not a universal rejection. Some received Him; for we go on to read that, "As many as received Him, to them gave He authority to become the children of God, even to them that believe on His name." Thus, I reject the anti-Semitic interpretation of John 1:11. That the Word became flesh is not recorded until John 1:14.

Another question asked by quite a few concerns our Lord's reproach of the cities in which most of His mighty works were done, because they repented not (Matt. 11:20). These were Chorazin, Bethsaida, and Capernaum. It is to be noted that these words of reproach are spoken against cities, and all actions by cities must be done by those who control these cities. The guilt was that of the cities' rulers, who failed to respond to His mighty works and to desist from their acts of wickedness. What the ordinary people in these cities did is not revealed here, but the Lord's declaration that followed these words of reproach indicates that the common people in these places received Him. "At that time Jesus answered and said, "I thank Thee, O Father, Lord of heaven and earth, because Thou hast hid these things from the wise and the prudent (intelligent), and hast revealed them unto babes"

(Matt. 11:25). I reject Scofield's heading of this paragraph: "Jesus, rejected, predicts judgment."

Another pertinent question is based upon the statement made by our Lord concerning Himself in Luke 17:25: "But first must He suffer many things, and be rejected of this generation."

The word "generation" here is interpreted to mean all the Jews then living in Palestine, but it is not clear by what logic those who lived outside the land are also included. The word *generation* is a most flexible word, and no fixed meaning can ever be attached to it apart from the context in which it is found. What it means here is clearly established by three passages which any consistent reader of the New Testament will already have come upon (and it is hoped, will have assimilated) before he comes to this declaration.

In Matt. 16:21 we read that the Lord showed His disciples how He must go to Jerusalem, "and suffer many things of the elders and chief priests and scribes, and be killed, and be raised again the third day." As we read on and come to Mark 8:31, we find the same truth, His enemies being listed as "elders, chief priests, and scribes;" and the same groups are listed as His persecutors in Luke 9:22.

From these passages we learn that the phrase "this generation" in Luke 17:25 means that generation of scribes, chief priests, and elders who were controlling all life and thought in Judea at that time. These were the guilty ones in Israel who engineered the crucifixion of Jesus by the Romans.

Questions have been asked concerning the prophecy in Isaiah 53:3 which declares that He would be "despised and rejected of men." This prophecy was fulfilled to the letter. However, it does not say what men would despise and reject Him. Since we know that "the common people heard Him gladly," there is no way that "men" here can be made to mean all men in Israel.

The declaration of our Lord in Matt. 21:19 is pointed to as proof of God's total rejection of Israel. He said of the fig tree, "Let no fruit grow on thee henceforward forever." However, this object lesson had nothing to do with Israel or with the rulers of Israel at that time. It concerned those who failed to produce fruit ahead of season. If any who heard His words and saw His works failed to produce fruit, then they would produce no fruit from that day forward in respect to the eon. ("The eon" is another name for the kingdom of God.) And since many in Israel did bear much fruit after this, this could not be true of all of them. Remember, those who did all the heralding in the Acts period were believing Israelites.

The parable of the householder demanding fruit from his vineyard (Matt. 21:33-46) is also brought forth as proof of God's withdrawal and rejection of Israel. But even a cursory reading of this portion will show that these words were spoken to the chief priests and the elders of the people, the ruling aristocracy in Israel (Matt. 21:23). In verse 43 we read: "Therefore, say I unto you, The kingdom of God shall be taken from you, and given to a nation bringing forth the fruits thereof." This is the new Israel of which we read in Isa. 66:7-14 and Gal. 6:16. At the end of this parable we read that, "When the chief priests and Pharisees had heard His parables, they perceived that He spake of them. But when they sought to lay hands on Him, they feared the multitude, because they took Him for a prophet" (Matt. 21:46). This is probably as far as they could go in their knowledge of Him, inasmuch as all witnessing concerning Him had been silenced (Matt. 16:20; 17:9).

The declaration, "Behold, your house is left unto you desolate" (Matt. 23:38), is found in a long arraignment of the scribes and Pharisees, and has reference to the temple in Jerusalem, not only the building, but the whole system that centered there.

In my own studies of the attitude of the people of Israel toward the Lord Jesus, I believe I have faced every honest question and objection that anyone might raise in opposition. They cannot all be covered in the space available in this study. I established this truth in my own mind and heart by reading carefully through Matthew, Mark, Luke, John, Acts, and the Epistles, noting carefully every declaration of Israel's attitude toward the man Christ Jesus. The evidence was overwhelming that the majority of Israelites, those in the land and those in exile, became believers in and followers of Him. I also noted all statements of unfavorable attitudes and rejection; and these were always upon the part of Pharisees, Sadducees, scribes, priests, elders, rulers, and Romans. If the reader will do the same, this truth will be established in his mind. And remember, as Bishop Butler said, "A truth being established, objections are nothing; the one is founded upon our knowledge, the other upon our ignorance."

The SEED and BREAD Bible-Study leaflets are published as often as time and means permit and are sent free to all names on THE WORD OF TRUTH MINISTRY mailing list. Send us your name. There will be no obligation, solicitation, or visitation. Additional copies of any issue available on request.   ISSUE NO. 47

SEED & BREAD
FOR THE SOWER   ISA. 55:10   FOR THE EATER
BRIEF BIBLICAL MESSAGES
FROM
THE WORD OF TRUTH MINISTRY
339 South Orange Drive, Los Angeles, Cal. 90036
Otis Q. Sellers, Bible Teacher

THE MOST IMPORTANT PARABLE
The Interpretation of Mark 4:26-29

The subject of this study declares a personal opinion which is the result of long and careful consideration of all the parables. This parable is found only in the Gospel of Mark, and its importance can be seen in the fact that it tells us certain vital truths about the kingdom of God, His own government, which may at any moment become a complete reality in and upon the earth. The parable reads as follows:

> And He said, So is the kingdom of God, as if a man should cast seed into the ground; and should sleep, and rise night and day, and the seed should spring and grow up, he knoweth not how. For the earth bringeth forth fruit of herself; first the blade, then the ear, after that the full corn in the ear. But when the fruit is brought forth, immediately he putteth in the sickle, because the harvest is come.

As a rule it is a simple matter to give a descriptive title to most parables, such as "the parable of the mustard seed," or "the parable of the leaven," but not so this one. Such titles as "the unconscious growth," and "the seed growing secretly" simply indicate that those who use them do not know what this parable is about, and its force and message is misrepresented by them. The difficulty in finding an expressive title arises because there is no central or dominant figure in it — neither the sower, the seed, the ground, the sickle, or the harvest. However, when considered in the light of its declared subject, the kingdom of God, and the fact that it clearly sets forth five stages in the development and consummation of the kingdom, it probably should be called "the parable of the stages of the kingdom." And while it is a parable of superlative importance, it is one of the most neglected, misrepresented, and misinterpreted of all the thirty parables in the New Testament.[1]

Commentaries which I have consulted say that this parable deals with "the progress of the gospel in the world," "the progressive course of the spiritual life," "the course of the grace of God in our salvation," "the growth of the church," and "what happens when we preach the gospel." None seems willing to face the

---

[1] Alva J. McClain in his book on *The Greatness of the Kingdom* makes no reference whatsoever to this passage.

simple fact that it deals with progressive stages of the kingdom of God from seedtime to harvest. We will consider each word of it.

And He said. These words identify and call attention to the speaker, and they should remind us anew that we are dealing with words spoken by the Lord Christ Jesus. In view of this we need to remember three other declarations made by Him: "Take heed what ye hear" (Mark 4:24); "Let these sayings sink down in your ears" (Luke 9:44); and "Blessed are they that hear the Word of God, and keep it" (Luke 11:28).

So is the kingdom of God. The word "so" here could be better translated "thus," meaning "in this manner." It is the Greek word *houtos* which is usually translated "so," but is also translated "thus," "on this wise," or "after this manner" which are different ways of saying the same thing. Both in the Greek and in the K.J.V. this word is placed emphatically forward which would make it to mean, "After this manner is the kingdom of God and not otherwise." Thus, in certain respects, the development of the kingdom of God is like that which is here pictured in five stages: (1) the blade, (2) the ear, (3) the full grain in the ear, (4) the ripened grain, (5) the harvest.

It should be carefully noted that it is "the kingdom of God" that is the subject here. It is not the gospel, the church, the Word, or the believer. This parable has to do with God's government. Ignore the subject here and you may as well throw out the parable.

As if a man should cast seed into the ground. Since this parable has little to do with the sower, we do not need to identify the one who planted the seed. This does not refer to Christ. Of course, the fact that the Lord did plant the seed of divine government in the earth seems to make Him in some respects parallel with the sower; however, because the sleeping during the night is not applicable to Him, and neither is the expression "he knoweth not how," we will simply run into difficulty if we make the sower to be Christ. Thus, it is apparent that these opening words simply set the stage in order to lead us into the real message of the parable that comes later.

And should sleep, and rise night and day. This phrase is idiomatic; and it means that this sower went about his ordinary affairs, maintaining his habitual mode of life, doing nothing more about the seed that was sown. These words are not applicable to the Lord Jesus, since, "He that keepeth Israel shall neither slumber nor sleep" (Psa. 121:4).

And the seed should spring and grow up, he knoweth not how. As has already been pointed out, we cannot apply these words to the Lord Jesus, since He knows perfectly how seeds grow into plants and produce after their kind, how God gives to each seed a body as it pleases Him, and to every seed his own body (I Cor. 15:38). We now come to the very heart of the parable.

For the earth bringeth forth fruit of herself. In regard to the kingdom of God these words tell us that it is wholly supernatural, the work of God, and not the product of human actions. The kingdom is coming whether men want it or not and whether they receive it or not. The Lord Jesus Christ becomes King by an act of God, and His government becomes a reality by a divine assumption of sovereignty. The seed of divine government was planted when God predicted it in the Old Testament by such declarations as, "Thou shalt judge the peoples righteously, and govern the nations upon earth" (Psa. 67:4). Just as the earth automatically brings forth fruit because of the seed that is placed in it, so will divine government appear and develop because of what God has already done. All this is in harmony with God's great promise in Isaiah 61:11, "For as the earth bringeth forth her bud, and as the garden causeth the things that are in it to spring forth; so the LORD GOD will cause righteousness and praise to spring forth before all nations."

First the blade, then the ear. If words mean anything, then the words we have here tell us something about the first two stages of the kingdom of God. The blade stage of the kingdom of God began when God raised Jesus from among the dead. Men had done their worst, but God intervened and reversed what they had done. Divine sovereignty asserted itself in His resurrection. The blade stage of the kingdom of God is seen in the early days of the Acts period when even devout men had to say, "What meaneth this?" (Acts 2:12).

When we consider the character of growing grains, especially the grasses which are certainly in view here, such as wheat, oats, rye, or barley, we see that these appear first as a grass-blade, a time when all grains look alike. The farmer knows what these blades are because he planted the seed; but anyone else would need to ask, "What is it?" However, grains quickly pass from the blade stage to the ear stage. At this point the various grains have certain characteristics and those familiar with these can easily identify them.

Even so it was with the kingdom of God in the Acts period. Very quickly it passed into the ear stage and its prophesied characteristics began to show forth. "This is that which was spoken by the prophet Joel" (Acts 2:16), were the sure words of Peter. From this time forth it was evident that the long promised kingdom of God was a reality upon the earth, even though only in part, as declared later by Paul in I Cor. 13:9-10. The Acts period as a whole made up the blade and ear stage of the kingdom of God. These are now complete, and God's purpose was finished in them. We need not speculate as to just when one stage ended and the other began as there is no event to mark it, no more than when a field of grain advances from one stage to another.

After that the full corn (grain) in the ear. When growing grain reaches this stage, the farmer has every grain of wheat he is going to get. No more grains will come forth, yet each grain must develop. The "full grain in the ear" is the next stage of the kingdom of God, a stage which has long been suspended, and for which a troubled world now waits, and for which godly men now hope and pray. All of God's kingdom purposes were suspended and have been in abeyance since Paul made his momentous declaration in Acts 28:28. They are suspended while God accomplishes a purpose that was not the subject of any prophecy or previous revelation. This purpose was a secret hid in God. For more than 1900 years God has been writing into the history of His long dealings with mankind a perfect and complete record of the grace that is inherent in His character. The "God of every grace" is demonstrating that He is this. He is doing this in a dispensation of grace in which every act of His is one of love and favor to the undeserving. When His present purpose is complete, He will again speak from heaven, assume sovereignty, and the kingdom of God will be a reality that compares to "the full grain in the ear" of growing grain.

This will be the manifest kingdom of God. When it comes, it will be complete and universal. Jesus shall reign where ere the sun, doth his successive journeys run. There will never be any more divine government than there is on the day when God assumes sovereignty. Human governments always grow, reaching out to take in more and more. They must enlarge to survive. This is their greatest fault. As government accomplishes its purpose, it should be ever decreasing. As Jefferson said, "That government is best which governs least."

But when the fruit is brought forth. This is the ripened grain, the desired end of the farmer's labors. It speaks of the results of God's long period of government. These will be the mature sons of God who will be His in the personal presence of Jesus Christ. This is when the righteous shall shine forth in the kingdom of their Father (Matt. 13:43).

Immediately he putteth in the sickle. "Putteth in" is the Greek word *apostellō*, which when used of an inanimate thing means to authorize (see Issue No. 5). God's harvest from His government of mankind will be mature and ripened subjects for the thousand years of His personal presence.

Because the harvest is come. This is a blessed harvest indeed, one Paul anticipated in I Thess. 2:19 and 3:13, and which our Lord anticipated in Matt. 13:43.

The SEED and BREAD Bible-Study leaflets are published as often as time and means permit and are sent free to all names on THE WORD OF TRUTH MINISTRY mailing list. Send us your name. There will be no obligation, solicitation, or visitation. Additional copies of any issue available on request.   ISSUE NO. 48

SEED & BREAD

FOR THE SOWER   ISA. 55:10   FOR THE EATER

BRIEF BIBLICAL MESSAGES

FROM

THE WORD OF TRUTH MINISTRY

339 South Orange Drive, Los Angeles, Cal. 90036

Otis Q. Sellers, Bible Teacher

A PSALM OF DIVINE GOVERNMENT

The foundation for all that is said in the New Testament concerning the kingdom of God was laid down in the Old Testament. When John the Baptist, the Lord Jesus, and the twelve apostles went forth to herald that the kingdom of God was at hand, they did not need to explain what was meant by this term. If any did not understand, it was because they did not know the Scriptures that God had entrusted to Israel. This is also true of men today; for since the New Testament truth follows the pattern of the Old, it is important that we become completely familiar with those Old Testament passages that declare the coming of divine government upon the earth. One of these passages is a short Psalm, which, if I were forced to make a choice, I would memorize rather than Psalm 23. We need to know and believe Psalm 67.

God be merciful unto us. This is, I believe, a Psalm of David, the shepherd king of Israel. This Psalm is a prayer; almost every statement in it is a petition; and I interpret it on the basis of this principle: Every prayer in the Bible is a prophecy, and every prayer will be answered just as every prophecy will be fulfilled. David's own nation is upon his heart here, laid there by the Spirit of God Who inspired this prayer; and Israel is the subject of this expression of his desire. The Hebrew for "be merciful" here means "be gracious"; that is, show us a love and favor that we do not deserve.

And bless us. The desire for God to "be gracious" means to be passively gracious. David knows of the sins of which his nation was guilty and realizes that if the Lord should mark iniquities, none would be able to stand before Him (Psalm 130:3). However, "bless us" is positive and is a plea for active grace. The blessing he desires for his nation is not wealth, grandeur, or territorial expansion. He seeks something far better that will be more enduring.

And cause His face to shine upon us. This blessing that David asked for his nation must not be lightly regarded as if it indicates some transitory moment of happiness, uplift, or blessing. When this prayer is answered, as it certainly will be, it will be the ful-fillment of the great promise and prophecy of Isaiah that "the glory of the LORD shall be revealed, and all flesh shall see it together" (Isa. 40:5). Since the "glory of the LORD" is related to "the face of Jesus Christ" (2 Cor. 4:6), the event that David requests in his prayer is the *epiphaneia* (a blazing forth in a favorable interven-tion, see Issue No. 37); and this is the same event that we are told to live looking for and expecting, "the blazing forth of the glory of the great God, even our Savior Jesus Christ" (Titus 2:13). This is the event that marks the advent of God's government upon the earth.

Some will ask how this could be; how could David have known about the *epiphaneia* of the Lord Jesus, since Isaiah had not written his prophecy and Paul had not added his enlightening material? The difficulty is not a real one. David probably knew nothing about the *epiphaneia*, but the Holy Spirit did and He is the real author of this Psalm. If any believe that the Psalms are limited to the meager knowledge of David, he may as well excise them from his Bible.

That Thy way may be known upon the earth. Today, the knowledge of God's way, especially in regard to peoples and nations, is more sorely needed than anything else. Men have lost their way and nations have lost all sense of direction. Men do not know why they are living and nations do not know why they are existing. All the combined aspects of the work of God which are subsumed in the word *epiphaneia* will result in all men and all nations knowing God's way. When this is known, it will be possible for His will to be done on earth even as it is in heaven.

Thy saving health among all nations. It is to be noted that in this petition and the previous one, the blessing desired is widened from David's nation, Israel, to the whole earth and to all nations. The request here is for all mankind to know by experience God's saving health. Humanity's greatest physical need is complete de-liverance from all the many illnesses, diseases, infirmities, and deformities that now flow out of the fact that sin and death are ever at work in this world in which we live. And while the word *yeshuah* here, which is translated "saving health," does mean salva-tion," the idea of health is positively embodied in it. As I have stated before, the kingdom of God comes with a gift of perfect health for all who are living upon the earth on that day when God speaks from heaven and assumes sovereignty (see Issue No. 35). "Yea, for the rebellious also, that the LORD God might dwell among them" (Psa. 68:18).

Thus, in these two verses we have the divine process by which

God's government is established in the earth. (1) It is the grace of God that will be back of this greatest of all acts of grace. (2) The glory of God is revealed to all flesh at the same time and to the same extent. (3) Mankind is enlightened. (4) The sin of the world is taken away. (5) Health and soundness become. the portion of all.

If, following the kingdom judgment (see Issue No. 36), some are not allowed to live to enjoy all this, it will be because of their own sins. There is no universal forgiveness or amnesty accompanying the advent of God's government.

Let the peoples praise Thee, O God; let all the peoples praise Thee. The word *people* here is plural in the Hebrew. Old English had no plural form for this word, and this explains why it never so appears in the Old Testament. Expositors of the Psalms differ as to the meaning of the Hebrew words in this passage, and most of them translate it, "Then shall the peoples praise Thee, O God; then shall all the peoples praise Thee." However, this makes it seem as though David were telling God what the happy outcome will be if He grants the requests he has made. It is my understanding that David continues to make requests here and says: "Give the peoples cause for praising Thee, O God; give all the peoples cause for praising Thee." This is further evidence of the universality of the work of God when He blazes forth as King of all the earth (see Zech. 14:9).

O let the nations be glad and sing for joy. In harmony with the previous passage this should be rendered as, "Give the nations cause for being glad and singing for joy." Think upon this and compare it with the present state of nations today. There is no nation as such that can be described as glad or happy. They are all in turmoil. They are faced with external and internal problems that defy solution. Their songs are dirges, for they have no reasons for being glad and singing with joy. However, these words deal with nations and may not include the individual citizen. He may have, even as I have, many reasons for being glad and singing with joy; but with our nations it is another matter.

For Thou shalt judge the peoples righteously. Today, most conflicts of mankind are between different kinds of people. There are Arab and Israelite, black and white, and others too numerous to mention. When God assumes sovereignty, He will make righteous determinations that will satisfy and be acceptable to all peoples.

And govern the nations upon the earth. Note that the Psalmist has changed from petitions to direct statements as to what God is going to do. He will govern the nations upon the earth. This is a declaration of divine government to come, and it emphatically states that it is to be nations upon the earth. This was the hope of every Israelite. He knew that when God governed all nations, his nation would have a favored place; and it was his expectation that he would be called from among the dead to have a place in it. God's Word being true and faithful, we can rest assured that He will yet govern the nations upon the earth.

Let the peoples praise Thee, O God; let all the peoples praise Thee. The Psalmist repeats his request. "Give the peoples cause for praising Thee, O God; give all the peoples cause for praising Thee." This is his Spirit-inspired prayer, and, thus, becomes a prophecy. We know it will be answered, that the prophecy will be fulfilled. God will so act that universal praise of Him will be the result.

Then shall the earth yield her increase. This brings to mind a promise God made concerning the land of Israel in Lev. 26:4. Here it is the whole earth. Every square foot of it will be arable; no part of it will be unproductive. This is the divine answer to all who ask how the earth can support as many people as will certainly be upon it in the kingdom of God. No man can estimate what or how much the soil will produce when the curse of Gen. 3:18 is lifted and the beneficent climatic conditions of the kingdom prevail.

And God, even our own God, shall bless us. David recognizes the exalted position of the nation of Israel under God's government, a truth that cannot be denied by anyone who accepts God's testimony on this matter.

God shall bless us; and all the ends of the earth shall fear Him. He repeats the declaration of God's blessing of Israel, and states that "all the ends of the earth" shall fear Him. This is a Hebraism that is found often in the Old Testament. It means all mankind, even those living in the most remote places. Today, we think of these as being the Eskimos within the Artic Circle or the aboriginal people living in South America, Africa, or the New Hebrides. All these shall stand in fear before Him.

The word *fear* here does not mean to be afraid or terrified. It means to reverence, to stand in awe, to show due respect. This will be the result of God blazing forth in revealing the glory of His Son. And since "the fear of the Lord is the beginning of wisdom," we can see mankind as a whole becoming students in the school of God. Better make sure that you will be in that number.

The SEED and BREAD Bible-Study leaflets are published as often as time and means permit and are sent free to all names on THE WORD OF TRUTH MINISTRY mailing list. Send us your name. There will be no obligation, solicitation, or visitation. Additional copies of any issue available on request.   ISSUE NO. 49

SEED & BREAD

FOR THE SOWER   ISA. 55:10   FOR THE EATER

BRIEF BIBLICAL MESSAGES

FROM

THE WORD OF TRUTH MINISTRY

339 South Orange Drive, Los Angeles, Cal. 90036

Otis Q. Sellers, Bible Teacher

THE POWERS THAT BE

"Let every soul be subject unto the higher powers." This is Paul's positive declaration recorded in Romans 13:1, and there is no verse in Scripture that has been misapplied more than this one. In all church theology "the higher powers" are made to be the civil authorities, whoever they may be in any country and at any time. And it needs to be said that of all the absurd interpretations ever made by theologians, this one takes first prize. It is unworkable and unbelievable, and it cannot be followed out through the additional statements that follow this declaration.

The initial declaration of Paul seems to present no great difficulty, since most law-abiding men are quite willing to be subject to those who rule over them, so far as the submission required does not conflict with duties toward God. However, the next statement, which is actually a part of the sentence, creates impossible difficulties. If "the higher powers" means the civil authorities, I cannot believe this statement; and I doubt if any of my readers can believe it unless they are given to simple-minded credulity.

Paul enforces his first statement by declaring that "there is no power (authority) but of God." If this is applied to civil authorities, then we must believe that their authority comes from God; but the idea that those who govern derive their just powers from the consent of those governed, as our *Declaration of Independence* so majestically declares, must be rejected. That their authority comes from God, I do not believe and this I reject.

It would be interesting to know who first applied these words to civil authorities. One suspicions that this happened in the days when men believed in the divine right of kings, when the civil powers and organized religion (the church) worked hand in glove to maintain absolute domination of the lives and thoughts of the people. Whoever it was began a chain of errors that have been millstones upon the necks of many whose sole desire is to believe and practice whatever is written in the Word of God. This passage they cannot believe unless they close their eyes to the most obvious facts and divorce it from all that follows. The assiduous Bible student knows that Paul did not intend to convey any such ideas since he had already told the Corinthians to ignore the civil authorities when one believer had a matter against another (1 Cor. 6:1-3).

After his initial declaration in Romans 13:1, Paul goes on to say that "the powers that be are ordained of God." The phrase "the powers that be" has become by popular usage a familiar synonym for the civil authorities, but this cannot be what Paul meant when he first wrote these words. If this is what it means, then we must believe that all civil authorities are God ordained men, that anyone who resists them is resisting the ordinance of God, and that all who do resist shall receive to themselves condemnation. This I do not believe, and this I cannot believe.

If I believed this, I would have to believe in the divine right of all who govern. And if these words speak of civil authorities, then we must admit that some of the heroes of the faith, whom we now honor, are honored because they did the very thing condemned here. History is filled with the deeds of faithful and heroic men who defied the civil powers in order to worship and serve God according to the light they had received. With them it was even as Peter said to those who ruled in Jerusalem, "Whether it be right in the sight of God to hearken unto you more than unto God, judge ye. For we cannot but speak the things which we have seen and heard" (Acts 4:19, 20).

It would seem that the first two verses of Romans 13 present enough problems for those who insist that this passage sets forth the Christian's duty toward civil authorities, but every declaration that follows creates another major problem. "For rulers are not a terror to good works, but to the evil," Paul continues. These words, if applied to civil authorities, are in direct contradiction to those spoken by Christ when He warned the apostles to, "Beware of men: for they shall deliver you up to the councils, and they will scourge you in their synagogues; and ye shall be brought before governors and kings for My sake"(Matt. 10:17 18).

These words applied to civil authorities would make perfect saints out of all who govern, but we know from experience that this is not the case. Too numerous to mention are the rulers who have persecuted those who have done good and have favored those who have done evil. God's Word does not teach ridiculous things; therefore, it cannot be that the "higher powers" or "the powers that be" in Romans 13 has any reference to civil authorities.

This becomes still more evident when the balance of Paul's words are considered. We will go over this in a more accurate and literal translation.

You desire, do you not, to have no reason to be afraid of

the authority? Well, do the thing that is right, and you will have praise from the same. For the authority is God's servant for your good. But if you do what is wrong, be afraid, for the authority does not bear the sword for no purpose: it is God's servant, an avenger to inflict punishment on evildoers. Wherefore, it is necessary to be in subjection; not only because of wrath, but also because of conscience. For because of this you are paying taxes also; for they are God's servants, constantly attending to this very thing. Rom. 13:3-6.

After reading these words, the reader should ask himself if he believes that tax collectors are God's servants who are doing His work in imposing and collecting the taxes laid upon us.

Through the years I have consulted many commentaries on this passage, commentaries from my own library, in other libraries, and from the shelves of bookstores. All of these have agreed that Paul speaks here of civil authorities, but all problems are ignored and all difficulties are glossed over. One expositor sums up his comments by saying: "Since there are no spiritual authorities among men today to whom these words refer, then, in spite of the great difficulties created, we must apply them to civil authorities."

This commentator stumbled upon the solution when he said, "no spiritual authorities today." This is the key to the whole matter. But what about the day when these words were written, the time period to which they should be applied? Will anyone dare to say that there were no such authorities in the thirty-three years of which the book of Acts is the history? There were men of God on earth then of whom every word spoken here was true, and to whom every statement could be applied without modification or alteration. These words belong to that New Testament time period, "The Acts Period" (see Issue No. 23).

The chief characteristic of this time was the presence upon earth of God-commissioned, God-empowered, and God-authorized men called Apostles. We first read of this great authority in Matthew 10:1 where we are told that Jesus Christ gave them power (*exousia*—authority) over unclean spirits and over all manner of sickness and disease. This authority was in no way based upon their faith, devotion, or holiness. It was given even to Judas Iscariot (Matt. 10:4). This authority was renewed and extended in Matt. 16:19; John 20:22, 23; and Luke 24:49. These words made these men the "higher powers" (Gk., superior authorities) of the Acts period.

We see this authority exercised in Acts 3:6 when Peter used it to bring complete healing to a man over forty years of age who had never walked. We see it from another standpoint in Acts 5 when he pronounced a sentence of death upon Ananias and Sapphira. He spoke and their death followed. He did not wear the sword as an empty symbol. We see it in the life of Paul in Acts

13 when he spoke the words that brought total blindness on Elymas the sorcerer. We see it again in Acts 14 when Paul commanded the impotent cripple to "Stand upright on thy feet."

The superior authority that was given to men in the Acts period was not limited to the twelve apostles. In Rom. 12:8 Paul exhorts those who rule to do it with diligence. He instructed the Thessalonians to recognize those who "are over you in the Lord" (1 Thess. 5:12). There were gifts of government (1 Cor. 12:28), and some were set among the out-called ones for this specific purpose. All who possessed this gift qualified as "higher powers," or superior authorities to whom all believers were to be subject.

When we read Romans 13:1-7 in the light of these positive truths, all questions are answered and all difficulties disappear. The apostles and other divinely appointed rulers of the Acts period were the "higher powers" to whom every soul was to be subject. They had their authority from God and they were ordained of God. If anyone resisted their authority, he resisted God's arrangement; and such actions were sure to result in divine punishment. These authorities were never a terror to good works, only to the evil.

If any complained of the power of these men (the words of Rom. 13:3 would indicate that some did), they were told to do good and they would have no cause for fear, and would be sure to receive praise. But if they did evil, they would have every cause to fear; for these men did not bear in vain the power to exact the most severe penalties. They were God's servants, His avengers to execute wrath upon those who did evil.

Thus, we find in Romans 13:1-7 a most powerful argument for rightly dividing the Word of Truth (2 Tim. 2:15), and the necessity for recognizing to the fullest extent the unique position of some men in the Acts period and the unique character of God's dealings with men at that time.

In regard to the believer's present relationship and responsibility toward human government, I have said nothing. This is not the subject of this study, and with this Romans 13:1-7 has nothing to do.

The SEED and BREAD Bible-Study leaflets are published as often as time and means permit and are sent free to all names on THE WORD OF TRUTH MINISTRY mailing list. Send us your name. There will be no obligation, solicitation, or visitation. Additional copies of any issue available on request.   ISSUE NO. 50

SEED & BREAD

FOR THE SOWER   ISA. 55:10   FOR THE EATER

BRIEF BIBLICAL MESSAGES

FROM

THE WORD OF TRUTH MINISTRY

339 South Orange Drive, Los Angeles, Cal. 90036

Otis Q. Sellers, Bible Teacher

BIBLICAL CONCEPT OF GOD

The Bible declares that the wicked through the pride of his countenance will not seek after God, that God is not in all his thoughts (Psa. 10:4). Could this be a description of the attitude of the reader? Do you stand with the ungodly in this? Even the weakest believer in Him should be able to say that his desire is to understand God, that he does seek after Him, that God is ever in his thoughts. If we profess faith in Jesus Christ, our attitude toward God should be in harmony with the words of the Lord spoken by Jeremiah:

> Thus saith the LORD, Let not the wise man glory in his wisdom, neither let the mighty man glory in his might, let not the rich man glory in his riches: But let him that glorieth glory in this, that he understandeth and knoweth Me, that I am the LORD which exercise lovingkindness, judgment, and righteousness, in the earth: for in these things I delight, saith the LORD. (Jer. 9:23, 24)

The ancient creed was right when its promulgators stated that the chief purpose of man is to know God and glorify Him. And while every man does instinctively know that above his own being and all other beings there is one Being Who is Supreme (he may by custom give this one the title of God or whatever may be in his language the title of the Absolute), yet, very few indeed have any true knowledge of Him. There is an almost total absence of a Biblical concept of God in the popular religions of today; and in Christendom this vacuum is filled with concepts that are so small, so low, and so ignoble that they are unworthy of thinking and worshiping men. The sentimental and emotional concepts of God that are so prominent in the religious world today are inadequate and erroneous. Foolish conceptions that are unworthy of Him are constantly being enlarged until they have reached the point of being ridiculous.

The popular idea of God being an old man with a long beard is utterly foolish, inasmuch as He has declared in His Word that He is not a man at all. We must break ourselves of the deeply in-grained habit of thinking of the Creator as if He were a creature, a habit that will not be easy to break. God the Father will never be understood by likening Him to a human father. All human fathers are men, but God is not a man and Jesus Christ must not be thought of as God's boy.

A true concept of God is of the utmost importance, and if true, then it must be Biblical; for in order to form correct ideas con-cerning Him, we must turn to the revelation He has given of Him-self. To the question "What is God like?" there is no answer, if by that question we mean "What is God like in Himself?" The ques-tion is wrong since He in His essential nature is incomprehensible. The right question is "What has God revealed concerning Himself that we by the help of His Spirit can comprehend and believe?" If our concept of God is not Biblical, then we will be found wor-shiping a concept which is the product of our own fancy and imagi-nation. We must not substitute for the true God, a god made according to our own desires. An idol worked out by the mind is just as offensive to God as one made by hands.

At this point, taking it for granted that the reader is not among the wicked who has excluded God from all his thoughts, it seems proper to ask the question, "What is it that comes to your mind when you think about God?" In answer many will have to admit that the first thing that comes to their mind is "the church" or "the clergy"; and, thus, they reveal that to them God is represented and expressed by organizations, buildings, or church-ordained men. This is not strange since most men have been steeped in such ideas since childhood. Parents and ministers are often guilty of fostering the idea that God lives in the building, the one that has the steeple, "where we go on Sunday." Instead of allowing this erroneous con-cept of God to grow in the minds of the young, it should be challenged and contradicted with the divine declaration that "the Most High dwelleth not in temples made with hands" (Acts 7:48). It is distressing to think that millions of people, who live in a land of Bibles and who profess faith in Jesus Christ, are passing their entire lives upon earth without once having given thought to the Being of God. The average Christian has no concept of God, let alone a Biblical one.

While we know that God Absolute is incomprehensible and far above all concepts that any man can frame or express, yet, since our goal is to know Him, we must not shrink from the task of forming in our minds a Biblical concept of Him based upon the declarations He has made concerning Himself. Again, let it be stated and received as absolute truth that God is not a man (Num. 23:19), and, therefore, is not limited by any of the laws that are inherent to man.

The first step in the knowledge of God is a giant stride. If comprehended, it will at once put us on the other side of a vast chasm of ignorance; and we will delight in that knowledge which is ever the portion of those who know. This great truth can be simply stated. God is a Being Who can project Himself. Not only can He do it, but He has done so. God Absolute, Who is incomprehensible and invisible, has projected Himself and has in a measure been comprehended and seen as the mighty Jehovah Who walked upon the earth and visited men all through those times of which the Old Testament is the history. He also withdrew this projection of Himself and became a babe in Bethlehem. Yet, as He did this, He maintained the same infinitude and universality as God Absolute that He had before. This is the witness of the Bible, and no text is sufficient to declare it. This is not a truth for those who memorize certain verses. It is truth for those who know the Book.

Of course, there will be readers of these lines who will say that they do not see how God can do this, and others will boldly say that He cannot do it. To admit that we do not understand the power of God is quite all right, but to say that He cannot project Himself and become a babe in Bethlehem is simply to say that God is not God. The facts reveal He has done it. Two thousand years ago He projected Himself and the Jehovah of the Old Testament became the Lord Jesus of the New Testament. "Behold, a virgin shall be with child, and shall bring forth a Son, and they shall call His name Emmanuel, which being interpreted is, God with us" (Matt. 1:23). Thus, God became man; and He did so without diminishing in the least His infinitude as God Absolute.

To illustrate, let us suppose that I am a man of enormous wealth, unlimited wisdom, great power, and vast influence; and in addition to this, I am able to project myself and be a babe, a boy, or a man in another place. "Utterly ridiculous, unthinkable!" I am sure many will exclaim. Then let them admit that this is because I am a man and not God. However, for the sake of the illustration, let it be supposed for the moment that the aforesaid things are true of me. Then let us further suppose that out of a consummate love and compassion for the starving and depressed people of India, and in order to know by experience the depth of their misery, by projection I would cause myself to be born into the family of some untouchable in such manner that this babe would be an extension of myself, while at the same time I would remain all that I ever was in my own country. Furthermore, let it also be supposed that while I would be this, I would feel and experience the hunger, deprivations, and insults that would be heaped upon my representation because of the caste and circumstances into which I had elected that he should be born. If we can imagine this, we might by extension and application begin to understand some of the relationships that existed between God Absolute and His image, the Lord Jesus Christ. Think what amazing light this will throw upon the declaration, "I was cast upon Thee from the womb: Thou art My God from My mother's belly" (Psa. 22:10).

I admit the weaknesses of the illustration I have used. Many objections can be raised concerning it, but let it be remembered that all illustrations are inadequate when we use them to reveal the nature of God. Any likeness we may use will fall far short of its purpose since God is not like anything or anybody. We must ever remember His own challenge, "To whom then will ye liken God? or what likeness will ye compare unto Him?" (Isa. 40:18).

As already mentioned, it is to be expected that many will say they do not understand the idea of God projecting Himself and being another personality in a definite place. However, this may be nothing more than a confession that they know very little about the God Who is revealed in the Bible. Such a confession of lack of understanding could be a good thing, for the acknowledgment of ignorance could be the starting point of a quest for the true knowledge of Him. Whether you, I, or anyone else understands it does not matter. It is still true. It is the subject of divine revelation; it is a part of the record God has given of Himself; it is given to be believed whether fully comprehended or not.

The relationship between the Projector and the Projection is seen in the declaration of the Lord Jesus when He said, "If you had known Me, you should have known My Father also (John 14:7). It is seen again in His words, "He that hath seen Me, hath seen the Father" (John 14:9), and, "Believe Me that I am in the Father, and the Father in Me" (John 14:11). It is fully declared in His words, "I came forth from the Father, and am come into the world: again, I leave the world, and go to the Father" (John 16:28).

All these words are true because He was a projection of God. No man could project himself and be another person in another place, but that which is utterly impossible for man could be a very small matter to God. God can do it, and He has done so. This is our faith in Him. So, "acquaint now thyself with Him and be at peace" (Job 22:21).

The SEED and BREAD Bible-Study leaflets are published as often as time and means permit and are sent free to all names on THE WORD OF TRUTH MINISTRY mailing list. Send us your name. There will be no obligation, solicitation, or visitation. Additional copies of any issue available on request.   ISSUE NO. 51

SEED & BREAD

FOR THE SOWER   ISA. 55:10   FOR THE EATER

BRIEF BIBLICAL MESSAGES
FROM
THE WORD OF TRUTH MINISTRY
339 South Orange Drive, Los Angeles, Cal. 90036

Otis Q. Sellers, Bible Teacher

"TONGUES" ARE "LANGUAGES"

I was seven years of age at the time; and my brother, who was nine, was ahead of me in school. One day he brought home his first language book. With pardonable pride he deposited it prominently on our living room table. Its title was *The Mother Tongue*. With a touch of sibling jealousy, I picked it up and ridiculed anyone who would write such a book on such a subject along with all who would read or study it. However, my mother deflated my ego somewhat when she explained that a "tongue" is a "language" and your "mother tongue" is the language you learn from your parents.

I have never forgotten this in all the years that have passed since then. It was a step forward in the knowledge of truth; and in all I have learned since that day, I have never found anything that indicated my mother was not right. A "tongue" is a "language." This fact was of real value when I first studied the Book of Acts, fifty-five years ago. Apart from all other considerations, anyone who reads the second chapter of Acts and says that the gift described there was not the knowledge of languages that were common to the men out of the seventeen nationalities listed simply stamps himself as an unworthy expositor of the Word of God. "We do hear them speak in our tongues the wonderful works of God" (Acts 2:8,11) was the testimony of the devout men who were there that day.

If one considers the dictionary definition of a *tongue*, he will find many shades of meaning. A dictionary defines words according to the use made of them by men. However, of the many definitions given, there are three that stand out. The first is the muscle in the mouth of most vertebrates, used by man primarily as the organ of articulate speech, and by animals for the purpose of taking and swallowing food. The second definition is "a spoken language," and the third is "unintelligible sounds made in moments of religious excitation and emotional fervor."

If the reader will consider every occurrence of *tongue* (Heb., *lashon*) in the old Testament and every occurrence (Gk., *glossa*) in the New Testament, which I have carefully done, he will find that the first definition is correct and clearly established by Biblical usage. (See Judges 7:5 and Mark 7:33.) He will also find that the second definition is established firmly by the Scriptural occurrences. In fact, the word *tongue* means a *language* in the majority of Biblical passages. However, there is no passage in the Bible that lends any support to the third definition. The word *tongue* in the Bible never means "unintelligible sounds made in moments of religious excitation." If anyone thinks otherwise, then let him point to at least one of the 164 passages where the Hebrew word *lashon* or the Greek word *glossa* appears.

Of course, some will point to the 21 occurrences of the word *tongue* in 1 Cor. 10, 13, and 14, especially those in chapter fourteen where the unwarranted and arbitrary translator's insertion of the word *unknown* before six occurrences has generated much confusion and provided a modicum of support for those who would pass off strange sounds produced by their vocal chords as being the Biblical gift of tongues. This confusion would never have been if church theologians had accepted the simple Biblical facts as to the background of the people to whom the Corinthian epistle was written.

The Corinthians, to whom this letter was addressed, were a great company of Jews who had become believers in the man Jesus as being the promised Messiah to Israel, even their Lord and Savior. That they were Israelites is demonstrated in 1 Cor. 5:1 where Paul states that there was fornication among them, "and such fornication as is not so much as named among the Gentiles." This statement will defy all attempts of honest explanation if those addressed in this epistle are Gentiles.

Paul's language in 1 Cor. 9:13 shows that he is speaking to those who were entirely familiar with the things practiced in the temple in Jerusalem.

In 1 Cor. 10:1-4 Paul addresses those to whom he writes as brethren, and reminds them "how that all our fathers were under the cloud, and all passed through the sea; and were all baptized unto Moses in the cloud and in the sea; did all eat the same spiritual meat; and did all drink the same spiritual drink." Words such as these become sheer nonsense if those to whom he was speaking were Gentiles. These words should settle it for all who settle things by the Word of God. The Corinthian believers were Israelites. If there were Gentiles among them, they are ignored in this epistle.

Strong objections are anticipated in regard to this. Many will say at once: "But what about 1 Cor. 12:2? Does it not state that these were Gentiles?"

My answer to this is, "No it does not." I do not hesitate to say that the phrase, "Ye were Gentiles," is an anti-Semitic translation; and the interpretations based upon it are one more facet of that conspiracy which is determined to get the Jew out and get the Gentile in. The Greek phrase here is *hote ethnē ēte pros*, and it means literally "when nations you were toward." These words could only be applied to Israelites who, due to the dispersion and loss of citizenship toward the nation of Israel, found themselves "toward," that is in relationship to, the nations. In this position they were almost irresistibly led toward involvement in idolatry. It was hard indeed to escape the taint when they were practically submerged in it.

It must always be remembered that the believers to whom this epistle was addressed were Jews in exile, part of the Diaspora that was scattered throughout the Roman empire. In all the colonies of the exiles, it is remarkable how tenaciously the Jews held to their Hebrew language and script. The need for maintaining their original tongue was of the utmost importance; but after seventeen generations in exile, they had to surrender on many points and allow for the translation of the Scriptures into other languages. The best known of these is the Septuagint.

The facts of history, taken from the Talmudic era (the period in which the Talmud was compiled), reveal that the controversy over languages raged constantly in every synagogue and every colony. For example, in Tiberias there was a synagogue that boldly proclaimed its position by taking the name of *Synagogue of Greek-speaking Jews.* However, the use of Hebrew in most areas was constantly reinforced by new arrivals from Palestine; and these newcomers provided fresh fuel for the ancient controversy.

In the end, there being no central authority, each synagogue had to settle for itself what language or languages men could use to pray, speak, or translate the Hebrew Scriptures. As a rule, most prayers were in Hebrew; Scripture readings were in both Hebrew and Greek; and discussions were allowed in any language, as long as it was one understood by some of the participants. A Megillah Mishna, referring to the book of Esther, says that the public reading is not properly done if the language used is one the reader does not understand. It further declares: "It is lawful, however, to read to those who know no Hebrew in a foreign language which they understand." Not all synagogue rulers or rabbis would have been as liberal as this.

The few facts set forth above will give the reader some idea of the controversy concerning languages that raged continually among the dispersed people of Israel, from the dispersion of Israel in 600 B.C. right down to A.D. 54 when Paul first preached in the synagogue of Corinth. This was a seaport and the mixed flow of races that constantly passed through it would keep the controversy alive. A Jew from some distant place might stop in Corinth for weeks or months, and his first inclination would be to seek out his fellow Israelites in their synagogue. But he created a problem if he spoke a language that none of them understood, especially if he insisted on doing so. This was the problem with which Paul dealt with in 1 Corinthians 14. His authoritative conclusions are summed up in these words:

> For if the trumpet give an uncertain sound, who shall prepare himself to the battle? So likewise ye, except ye utter by the tongue words easy to be understood, how shall it be known that is spoken? for ye shall speak into the air. There are, it may be, so many kinds of voices in the world, and none of them is without signification. Therefore if I know not the meaning of the voice, I shall be to him that speaketh a barbarian, and he that speaketh shall be a barbarian unto me. (1 Cor. 14:8-11.)

He concludes the whole matter by saying:

> I thank my God, I speak with tongues more than ye all: Yet among the outcalled I had rather speak five words with my understanding, that by my voice I might teach others also, than ten thousand words in an *unknown* tongue. (1 Cor. 14:18, 19.)

And with these inspired words of Paul, I most heartily agree. The failure to relate 1 Cor. 14 to the ancient controversy concerning languages in Israel, especially among the exiles, and the anti-Semitic error of applying this epistle exclusively to Gentiles has caused much confusion.

As to the present movement in which thousands in all denominations are uttering unintelligible sounds, then insisting that this is the Biblical gift of tongues, the present day believer in Jesus Christ has explicit and co.nplete guidance.

In 1 Timothy 6:20 the Apostle tells Timothy to "avoid profane and vain babblings." The words "vain babblings" are one word in the Greek, *kenophonia,* which is made by combining two words *kenos,*(empty) and *phonia* (sound). The word in its context here can mean nothing else but meaningless sounds. These, we are told to avoid, or turn away from *(ektrempomenos).* The same truth is repeated in 2 Tim. 2:16 where we are told to shun or stand aloof from meaningless sounds.

In view of this, I have my instructions from the Word of God in regard to meaningless sounds. I am to turn away from all such. I an to stand aloof from them. This I have done, and this I will continue to do in the confidence that I will hear His "well done" for having taken Him at His Word and responded accordingly. I refuse to have anything to do with meaningless sounds that are gibberish and with their so-called translations which are pure imagination. These are simply works of the flesh. When this foolishness is attributed to the Holy Spirit, it is a satanic delusion.

The SEED and BREAD Bible-Study leaflets are published as often as time and means permit and are sent free to all names on THE WORD OF TRUTH MINISTRY mailing list. Send us your name. There will be no obligation, solicitation, or visitation. Additional copies of any issue available on request. ISSUE NO. 52

SEED & BREAD

FOR THE SOWER   ISA. 55:10   FOR THE EATER

BRIEF BIBLICAL MESSAGES
FROM

THE WORD OF TRUTH MINISTRY

339 South Orange Drive, Los Angeles, Cal. 90036

Otis Q. Sellers, Bible Teacher

A PSALM FOR TODAY

This title has been given to Psalm 64 inasmuch as it describes conditions and situations that will exist immediately before God assumes sovereignty over mankind, before He deals directly and openly with all the workers of iniquity, and brings about a universal fear of Himself that shall bring great rejoicing from the righteous.

This Psalm is a prayer written by David as God gave him the words. We can rest assured that every God-inspired prayer recorded in the Bible will in due time be answered. All such prayers are in reality prophecies, and as such they will be fulfilled to the letter. It is useless to try to fit this Psalm into the life of David, to make it to have come out of one of his experiences, or to give it any connection with the past history of Israel. The student who is acquainted with both Old and New Testaments can hardly fail to see the close relationship of this Psalm with the conditions and predictions set forth in 2 Timothy 3:1-9. This explains why it can be called a Psalm for today. Both passages describe conditions just before the manifest kingdom of God becomes a reality, and both set forth an event that is a definite part of God's assumption of sovereignty over mankind.

Hear my voice, O God, in my prayer: This Psalm opens with an urgent request for a hearing, an entirely proper procedure for one who would show due respect for the majesty of God. There are matters he would take up with Him, and the established method of communication is prayer. While prayer is important at all times, it takes on a new significance in times of peril and confusion such as that in which we now live. If ever men needed to maintain communication with God, it is in this period of time Paul calls the last days. All who believe should pray without ceasing. We ought always to pray and not to faint.

Preserve my life from fear of the enemy: His petition is direct and to the point, as all petitions should be. He desires preservation from that fear that would cause him to shape his actions and live out his life according to his fear of the enemy. Our lives should be molded by the Word of God. "It is written" should always be our reason for believing as we believe or doing as we do. Men will seek to have us do otherwise; but let us ever remember that our real warfare is not with men, but "against principalities and powers, against the rulers of the darkness of this world, against spiritual wickedness among the most exalted ones" (Eph. 6:12). We will be able to withstand these in this evil day only by taking to ourselves the whole armor of God.(See Eph. 6:11, 17.)

Hide me from the secret counsel of the wicked: A secret counsel is a conspiracy. There is today a conspiracy of evil men whose goal is to make everyone just as wicked as they themselves are. That they are enjoying enormous success cannot be denied. "Get with it; live it up; do your thing; everybody is doing it." These seem to be their battle cries. They have captured the schools, even the seminaries, and most churches. Partial victory will never satisfy them. The presence of righteous men disturbs their serenity. They seek, yea, demand complete conformity to their own evil ways and thoughts. They control the theatres, motion pictures, television, and radio. It is almost impossible not to be influenced by them.

From the insurrection of the workers of iniquity: One wonders if a more perfect and complete description of what we are seeing on every hand today could be put into words. Consider the twenty-one categories of ungodly men who shall rise up in the last days, and ask yourself if these are dominating the present scene (2Tim. 3:1-8). There is a revolt of mankind against everything related to God. They refuse all laws that He has given; they reject all directives He has laid down. They would prevail over God.

Who whet their tongue like a sword: David had certainly seen his soldiers apply the whetstone to their swords in preparation for battle. He now uses this scene to describe the preparation of the minds of evil men as they go into battle against the Truth and men of the Truth. Slander and misrepresentation are often their chief weapons.

And bend their bows to shoot their arrows, even bitter words: Their arrows are words that wound and cause pain. This corresponds to the "false accusers" spoken of in 2 Tim. 3:3. The words of the wicked are always bitter when they are directed against God or His people.

That they may shoot in secret at the perfect: From the security of their positions among men of their own kind, they let fly their belittling, derogatory, and slanderous words against all who seek to live godly in Christ Jesus. Even that morality which one will learn if he reads the Word of God is now slandered as being nothing more than the "Puritan ethic."

Suddenly do they shoot at him, and fear not: They are anxious to hurl their slanders against the Truth and men of the Truth. They are sure of remaining concealed behind their facade of self-imputed righteousness. They do it without any fear whatever. This is especially true under God's present administration of grace.

They encourage themselves in an evil matter: They not only encourage themselves, but also everyone else. The media is filled with articles, advertisements, commercials, programs, and pictures which do nothing but encourage men who are traveling the road of the wicked.

They commune of laying snares privily; They say, "Who shall see them?" To catch unsuspecting prey is the purpose of their schemes. They pride themselves in the fact that their snares are too well covered to be obvious to their victims. Thus, they are led along such paths as to take that drink which ends up making them a slave to alcohol, of placing that bet that makes them a compulsive gambler, of committing that small evil that may lead to a life of iniquity.

They search out iniquities; they accomplish a diligent search: This is certainly a present-day characteristic of a multitude of men. This is called "looking for the action," and cities which offer multiple forms of wickedness soon become tourist attractions and convention centers. The world is searched for new and exotic forms of wickedness.

Both the inward thought of every one of them, and the heart, is deep: Wicked men are not shallow in their wickedness. They execute well-laid plans. Satan has seduced some of the best minds of mankind and turned them against God and His Truth. Their hearts are deep, but not too deep for God, Who knows the heart (Jer. 17:9.)

But God shall shoot at them with an arrow: The pronoun "them" refers to all the wicked ones that have been before us in previous statements. They have shot their arrows of slander and falsehood. They have gained many victories. Nothing has appeared to stop their advance. But, suddenly the whole matter is reversed. God goes into action to plead His own cause against the foolish men who reproach Him daily (Psa. 74:22). He shoots at all the wicked with an arrow. This is the arrow of truth — truth concerning Himself as to Who He is and what He is. This is a poetic description of one aspect of God's assumption of authority over mankind. His lightnings will enlighten the world (Psa. 97:4). "The glory of the LORD shall be revealed, and all flesh shall see it together" (Isa.40:5). "The righteous shall see it and rejoice: and all iniquity shall stop her mouth" (Psa. 107:42).

The day will yet come when with dramatic suddenness every human being upon the earth will know Who Christ is and what Christ is in the sight of God. This is the unveiling of Jesus Christ. It is what the Corinthian saints were waiting for (1 Cor. 1:7).

The words "God shall shoot at them with an arrow" correspond to the statement in 2 Tim. 3:9, where, after a long description of evil men in the last days of God's dispensation of grace, it is declared, "they shall proceed no further." The wicked will be stopped in their tracks when God turns on the light.

Suddenly shall they be wounded: God will not miss. None can hide from Him. All the wicked will be wounded by His Truth.

So they shall make their own tongue to fall upon themselves: They will give themselves a tongue-lashing. "How could we have been so blind; how could we have been so thoughtless; how could we have encouraged and practiced such great wickedness?" may well be their cry against themselves. They now stand face-to-face with the kingdom judgment. (See Issue No. 36.)

All that see them shall flee away: And while it is true that no righteous man will want to be identified with them in that day, yet, this is not what the Hebrew means. "All that see them will shake their heads" is an accurate rendering. This is the great sign of bewilderment at what men will see when the wicked turn their own tongues against themselves.

And all men shall fear: This is that universal awe, respect, and reverence toward God that comes with the divine assumption of sovereignty. It is a truth declared in many places.(See Isa. 59:19.)

And shall declare the work of God: The work that God has done and will be doing will be mankind's chief interest, his main subject of conversation.

For they shall wisely consider of His doing: All His works and actions will be considered logically, not emotionally. One generation will celebrate His works to another, and declare His mighty acts. They will declare His greatness. All His works will praise Him and His saints will bless His Name. They shall speak of the glory of His government and talk of His power, to make known to the sons of men His mighty acts and the glorious majesty of His government. (See Psalm 145:3-12.)

The righteous shall be glad in the LORD, and shall trust in Him: Of course we will! We do now, but it will be more so then. We will join in when all the earth worships Him and sings to His Name (Psa. 66:4).

And all the upright in heart shall glory: Oh happy day! And I expect to be there because of another happy day that fixed my choice on Thee, my Savior and my God.

The SEED and BREAD Bible-Study leaflets are published as often as time and means permit and are sent free to all names on THE WORD OF TRUTH MINISTRY mailing list. Send us your name. There will be no obligation, solicitation, or visitation. Additional copies of any issue available on request.   ISSUE NO. 53

SEED & BREAD

FOR THE SOWER   ISA. 55:10   FOR THE EATER

BRIEF BIBLICAL MESSAGES
FROM
THE WORD OF TRUTH MINISTRY
339 South Orange Drive, Los Angeles, Cal. 90036

Otis Q. Sellers, Bible Teacher

THE FOUR GREAT DAYS

It would be quite simple to show from its usage in Scripture that the word *day* means the period of light between sunrise and sunset. However, if we fixed this meaning upon it and read it into all occurrences, we would end up in great confusion. It would also be easy to show from other occurrences that it means a period of twenty-four hours, and this is usually the first idea that comes to mind when we hear this word. But this word has other meanings, and the most important to the student of prophecy are the occurrences where it is used of a long period of time. There are four of these days named in Scripture, and they set forth four prophetic periods. These are called: (1) Man's Day, (2) The Day of Christ, (3) The Day of the Lord, (4) The Day of God.

These are God-given names. They are not meaningless expressions. Each one marks a separate and distinct period of time. They are of the utmost importance to all who seek to obey God's directive "rightly to divide the Word of Truth" (2 Tim. 2:15). Let us consider each one of these.

Man's Day

This designation is found in 1 Cor. 4:3 where it is almost lost to us due to the faulty translation. The words "man's judgment" here should be man's day," since the Greek word *hēmeras* means "day" and does not mean "judgment." These words appear in connection with a statement made by Paul concerning the attempts of some in Corinth to examine him and come to conclusions as to whether his service was acceptable to the Lord. He declares that he counted it as a mere trifle that he should be examined by them or by man's day. He had not received his commission from them, and he refused to acknowledge their right to examine him. Neither would he be examined "by man's day," since all judgments made on the basis of man's day will need to be revised by the Lord Jesus in the day when He does the judging.

This is somewhat as if a farmer would say, "Do not judge me or my abilities by the appearance of my fields in the winter, for you may have to reverse your judgment when the summer comes."

Man's day had its beginning when Noah and his family came forth from the ark. This was also the beginning of human government and a time when all nations were permitted to walk after their own ways (Acts 14:16). Man's day is a time of human government, the rule of man by man. The highest function of human government is the judicial taking of life (Gen. 9:6), and all other governmental powers are included in this. However, man was not left entirely free to follow his own will or govern as he pleased. They that ruled over men were required to be just, ruling in the fear of God (2 Sam. 23:3). The sword of divine retribution constantly hung over the heads of men and nations, and there are numerous instances in the Biblical record where this sword fell upon them.

Man's day, which is the day of his prominence, exaltation, and glory, reaches its very zenith in this the dispensation of the grace of God. This began with Paul's declaration in Acts 28:28, and since that time all men and all nations have been utterly free to walk after their own ways without any fear of immediate divine retribution. Men commit the basest of crimes; they raise their voices against God every day; yet, He does nothing except show them a love and favor that they do not deserve.

"Does not God care?" "Is He really a God of love?" These are the questions regularly asked in view of the iniquities of mankind that exact such a great toll of suffering from the human race. The answer is that He cares and He loves; yet, because of His present purpose in grace, no sin or transgression receives its just recompense of reward. But this will not always be. Man's day will surely come to an end; and the prayer of the Psalmist will be answered: "Arise, O LORD; let not man prevail: let the nations be judged before Thee. Put them in fear O LORD: that the nations may know themselves to be but men." (Psa. 9:19, 20.)

The Day of Christ

This designation is used in Phil. 1:6, 10 and 2:16. It is ignored by most expositors as they have no room for it in their ideas of things to come. The day of Christ is another name for the Kingdom of God. It will begin on the day when God assumes sovereignty over the earth and its inhabitants, when man's sordid government comes to an end and God's government begins. Then the government will be Jehovah's, and He will govern among the nations (Psa. 22:26-28). The day of Christ is the day of the manifest kingdom of God. It will be the day when Christ will have His way with Israel, with the nations, and with the world. It will be the day of His ascendancy, prominence, and exaltation. He will see the glorious outcome of His death, burial, and resurrection. "He shall see of the travail of His soul, and shall be satisfied" (Isa. 53:11). It has already been declared of Him, "I will be exalted among the nations, I will be exalted in the earth" (Psa. 46:10). "Behold, My Servant shall deal prudently, He shall be exalted and extolled, and be very high" (Isa. 52:13).

The day of Christ is the day of His unveiling (*apokalupsin*), the day of His manifestation (*epiphaneia*). It is the day when the glory of the Lord shall be revealed and all flesh will see it in the same amount and at the same time (Isa. 40:5). In that day, we who are now believing in Him will be privileged to extol the glory of His grace, a task for which He will grace us in the beloved One (Eph. 1:6).

The Day of the Lord

The day of the Lord follows the day of Christ. No certain event is revealed that will mark its beginning since it comes as a thief in the night (2 Pet. 3:10). It begins when God removes all the restraints that He placed upon mankind during the time period of His government. This makes possible a divine testing of all who have lived under and enjoyed the blessings of the kingdom of God. There is a revolt against the kingdom on the part of some. This is described in Psalm 2. However, the "sons of light" will not be in darkness that, that day should overtake them as a thief (1 Thess. 5:2-5).

In this long period of time, we find the final week of Israel's seventy weeks (seven years) as prophesied by Daniel. It comes into full manifestation at the second coming of the Lord Jesus; it includes the entire 1000 years of His *parousia*, the "little season" which follows the *parousia*, and the time period of the great white throne judgment.

The entire Book of Revelation, except the first nine verses and the last two chapters, belongs to the day of the Lord; and it deals with events that will come to pass in that day. Not one word of it deals with anything that will transpire in the dispensation in which we now live, the dispensation of grace; and it has no bearing on the next dispensation, the kingdom of God. This explains why today, we can see the mountain peaks of certain great events in it, but cannot comprehend the valleys in between. We do not face the fulfillment of any of its prophecies at this time. We are facing divine intervention which will result in God's government in and over the earth, and all events in the Book of Revelation are many centuries in the future.

The "day of the Lord" in the New Testament is actually "the day of Jehovah." It is not to be confused with other "days of the LORD" mentioned in the Old Testament. Peter made this distinction clear when he spoke of it as "the great and notable day of the Lord" (Acts 2:20). The word "notable" here is *epiphanēs*, which Robert Young defines as meaning "very manifest," but which I would define as signifying a "blazing forth." Malachi emphasized this distinction when he called it, "the great and dreadful (awe-inspiring) day of the LORD" (Mal. 4:5). It is a definite part of "rightly dividing the Word of Truth" not to confuse these days. This phrase still needs a vast amount of study.

It is in the day of the Lord that "the heavens shall pass away with a great noise, and the elements shall melt with fervent heat, the earth also and the works that are therein shall be burned up" (2 Peter 3:10). This is the process by which God makes all things new and sets the stage for the next great day.

The Day of God

Peter speaks of this great day in his second epistle, chapter 3, verses 12 and 13. In a more exact translation this would read, "Hoping for and hurrying the actual presence (*parousia*) of the day of God, because of which the heavens, being on fire, will be dissolved and the elements will be decomposed with fervent heat. Yet, we, according to His promises, are hoping for a new heavens and new earth, wherein dwelleth righteousness." I do not claim at present a very clear understanding of these words, but I am sure we will all comprehend them perfectly after we have gone through the school of the kingdom of God and the thousand years of His personal presence.

Revelation 21:1 to 22:7 tells us about all that we can now know about the day of God. There we find that it is the day when the tabernacle of God will be with men. The word here for tabernacle is *skēnē* which signifies a center of activity, a headquarters. Never again will men say, "Our father, which art in heaven"; for the center of His activities will have been changed to the earth. This planet made new will become the mediatorial planet to the rest of the universe.

The day of God is the new heavens and new earth. It is a new world, a whole new order which is so far removed from anything we have ever known or experienced that we have no basis for comprehending it. God has made no attempt to tell us what it will be like. I am sure that no eye has ever seen, nor has any ear heard, neither has it entered into the heart of man this glorious condition of things that God has prepared for them that love Him. In view of this, I refuse to speculate about it. All I know for sure is that it will be.

The SEED and BREAD Bible-Study leaflets are published as often as time and means permit and are sent free to all names on THE WORD OF TRUTH MINISTRY mailing list. Send us your name. There will be no obligation, solicitation, or visitation. Additional copies of any issue available on request.   ISSUE NO. 54

SEED & BREAD

FOR THE SOWER   ISA. 55:10   FOR THE EATER

BRIEF BIBLICAL MESSAGES
FROM
THE WORD OF TRUTH MINISTRY
339 South Orange Drive, Los Angeles, Cal. 90036

Otis Q. Sellers, Bible Teacher

THE KINGDOM TITLES

The kingdom of God is the theme of the Bible. Because of this, the spirit of God has seen fit to use numerous appellatives or descriptive titles in order to set forth the many aspects of this great truth.

The name *Abraham Lincoln* is simply a name; and since many men have been so designated, it says very little. But if we add to this name, *The President of the United States*, we have used an appellative that speaks volumes when it is related to one man who bore this name.

Each one of the descriptive titles of the coming kingdom declares and emphasizes a distinct truth in regard to the character of that time when this earth and all who are upon it are governed by God (Psa. 67:4). Each one of these is worthy of the most careful study in view of the truth they express. They should be incorporated into our thinking concerning the kingdom of God. Many of them have been arbitrarily misapplied and misinterpreted. And it may be hard for many, who have long held incorrect ideas as to their meaning, to reconstruct their views in regard to the significance of these appellatives.

As sure as the Bible is true, the day will come when God will assume sovereignty and His government will be a reality upon the earth. The government will be the LORD'S, and He will be the governor among the nations (Psa. 22:28). The dominant and all-embracing title of this glorious time to come (the kingdom of God) has already been dealt with in numerous studies in these Bible-study leaflets; and it is the name by which it should always be designated, unless it is desirable to emphasize some certain aspect.

The kingdom of God. The simplest definition of "the kingdom of God" is that it is God's government, and this title belongs to a future period of time and a condition of things which will be a glorious reality upon the earth. The expectation of being alive and upon the earth in the day when God governs is the "one hope" held out to men in the Word of God. We must not play the part of

Humpty Dumpty with the word *kingdom*. In an incident in Lewis Carroll's book, *Through the Looking Glass*, Humpty Dumpty said to Alice, "When I use a word, it means just what I choose it to mean — neither more nor less." "Kingdom" means "government," even though it is quite proper to use synonymous terms such as *rule, reign, control*, and *sovereignty* in expressing the same idea. See Issue No. 29 for further material concerning this.

The kingdom of the heavens. This title is found only in Matthew, and it is identical in meaning with "the kingdom of God." The Lord Jesus used these two titles interchangeably in Matt. 19:23, 24. The word "heavens" is a synonym for "God," and is so used in many places in the Old and New Testaments. See Issues No. 28 and 34 for additional material on this title.

The regeneration. This title is found in Matt. 19:28. The Greek word is *palingenesia* which means to generate again, and it speaks of the restoration of a thing to its pristine state. Here it speaks of the entire re-creation of the physical and social order under God's government. Think what this will mean to the human brain which, at present, due to the long working of sin and death in mankind, is now working, even in the best minds, at only seven percent of its capacity. What will it be like when we can use our brains at full capacity? (See Isaiah 35.)

The times of refreshing. This is found in Peter's great message in Acts 3:19. Literally translated, the Greek here would say "times of coolness from the face of the Lord." "From the face" is an idiom that means directly from Him, and the word *coolness* spoke volumes to a people who lived with the Mediterranean on one side and the desert on the other. When this "coolness" comes, the world will have respite from the hot winds of sin and death that have seared it for so long.

The times of restitution. This is also found in Peter's message. (See Acts 3:21.) This should read "the times of the restoration," and this is limited to "all things which God speaks through the mouth of His holy prophets." Our Lord declared that, "Elijah truly shall come first and restore all things" (Matt. 17:11), a fact that makes this restoration to precede the second coming of Christ.

The day of Christ. The kingdom of God is the day when Christ will have His way with Israel, with the nations, and with the earth. It is the day of His exaltation. This title of the kingdom is found in Philippians 1:6, 10. See Issue No. 54 for more material on this.

The last days. This title is found in Isa. 2:2, Mic. 4:1, and in Acts 2:17. The word *acharith* in the Hebrew has in it the idea of latter end, sequel, or result. The kingdom of God will be the result of all that God has done preceding the divine assumption of sovereignty. This title must not be confused with "the last days" of God's long display of grace spoken of in 2 Tim. 3:1.

The last day. In Micah 4:1 we read, "But in the last days it shall come to pass"; and this is followed by a description of conditions and blessings which the reader will see to be a picture of Israel and the nations under God's government. However, in Micah 4:6 we read "In that day." Thus, the Spirit of God refers to that period of time by the plural (days) and by the singular (day). In the New Testament we find the singular form six times in John's Gospel, he being the only writer who uses this title. (See John 6:39, 40, 44, 54, 11:24, and 12:48.) In all these occurrences the Greek never varies. It is always "in the last day." The peculiar truth set forth by this title is that the kingdom of God is Israel's final day, there being no night following once this day comes. See Isa. 60:19, 20 for the truth of a glorious day that will have no end. Israel's experience has ever been one of short days followed by long and painful nights; but when the next day comes, it will remain in perpetuity.

The day. This title is used by Paul in Rom. 13:12, and is contrasted with the night period of the kingdom which covered the thirty-three years of which Acts is the history. The coming of "the day" has long been suspended. It will come for Israel and the world when God has completed His present purpose in grace.

The day of judgment. In Isa. 42:4 it is declared of the Lord Jesus Christ that He will not fail nor be discouraged until He has set judgment in the earth. In Matt. 12:18-21 we are told that He will show judgment to the nations (translated "Gentiles" in the K. J. V.), and that this will result in the nations trusting in Him. When this is accomplished, it will then be the day of judgment. In Matt. 12:36 the Lord Jesus said: "But I say unto you, that every idle word that men shall speak, they shall give account thereof in the day of judgment." This passage is commonly interpreted to mean that at some remote future day, men are going to be brought into court to give an account for every idle word spoken during their lifetime. This is not right, and it is not what our Lord meant. It is in the day of judgment that men living then must give an account for each idle word that they speak. The day of judgment is the day of God's due order, and all statements made then which violate that order will make a man liable for disorderly conduct. The day of judgment is the time when God's judgments are in the earth. In that day the inhabitants of the earth will learn righteousness (Isa. 26:9, 10).

The judgment. This title is found in Luke 11:31, 32. It is quite common for a period of time to be called by the name of something which is characteristic of it. Take for example our use of *spring* and *fall* to designate two of the seasons. The kingdom of God is a time when God's judgments will be in all the earth (Psa. 105:7); when He will show judgment to the nations (Matt. 12:18); when He causes judgment to be heard from heaven (Psa. 76:8); when judgment shall run down as waters and righteousness as a mighty stream (Amos 5:24). Beyond all question, the title of "the judgment" is apropos of this period.

The resurrection. This descriptive title of the kingdom of God was used by the Sadducees in Matt. 22:28. The Lord made use of this descriptive title when He answered their question. One of the greatest things that will happen under God's government will be the orderly resurrection of the righteous dead; thus, this time can be properly designated as "the resurrection."

The eon. This title will not be found in most versions of the New Testament, but it should be. The Greek word is *aiōn*; and since there is no word in English that even approximates the true and full meaning, it should be transliterated, Anglicized, and rendered as *eon*. The basic and fundamental idea in this word is flow or outflow. This is based upon its history, usage and development that can be traced out over a period of three thousand years. Galatians 1:4 speaks of "this present evil eon," which means this present evil flow. How appropriate, since the enemy is coming in like a flood (Isa. 59:19). Again, Paul speaks of those who walk according to the eon of this world (Eph. 2:2), which means the flow or current of this world. The translators came very near the truth here when they translated it "course." The kingdom of God is the result, both as to its inception and perpetuation, of His outflowing, when judgment shall run down as waters, and righteousness as a mighty stream (Amos 5:24). In view of this, "the eon" is a most fitting descriptive title for the kingdom of God.

The day of the eon. This expressive title is found in the Greek text of 2 Peter 3:18. The kingdom will be the day of His outflowing, when He gushes forth in judgment, truth, light, and life. Truly this is the day of the eon.

Life This dynamic word is an expressive title of the kingdom of God. To the rich young ruler our Lord said, "If you will enter into LIFE, keep the commandments" (Matt. 19;17). In Matt. 7:14 the Lord Jesus spoke of the narrow way that leads to LIFE. In John 3:36 men are warned that, "he that believeth not the Son shall not see LIFE." Again we find here that the kingdom of God is called by something which is characteristic of it. We now live in a time when death reigns, when its influence is felt by every man, when it dominates the earthly scene. The world to come is to be dominated and controlled by LIFE.

We have considered fifteen of the descriptive titles of the kingdom of God. As said at the start, each one of these terms is worthy of the most careful study. An understanding of each one will greatly advance our appreciation of that glorious time to come when the earth will be governed by God.

The SEED and BREAD Bible-Study leaflets are published as often as time and means permit and are sent free to all names on THE WORD OF TRUTH MINISTRY mailing list. Send us your name. There will be no obligation, solicitation, or visitation. Additional copies of any issue available on request.   ISSUE NO. 55

SEED & BREAD

FOR THE SOWER   ISA. 55:10   FOR THE EATER

BRIEF BIBLICAL MESSAGES
FROM
THE WORD OF TRUTH MINISTRY
339 South Orange Drive, Los Angeles, Cal. 90036

Otis Q. Sellers, Bible Teacher

DISPENSATIONAL TRUTH

"Why call ye Me, Lord, Lord, and do not the things which I say?" (Luke 6:46) These were the challenging words spoken by our Lord Jesus Christ to His disciples, men who had cast their lot with Him. Yet, when I meditate upon these words, I must honestly acknowledge that while I do call Him my Lord, declare that I am a believer in Him, and a follower of Him, I know quite well that I do not do some things He said, that I have never tried to do them, and have no intention of making such an attempt. If I am asked how I can justify my confession with my actions, I will point to the great Biblical principle of dispensational truth.

For example, the One I acknowledge to be my Lord unequivocally declared in Matt. 5:42, "Give to him that asketh thee, and from him that would borrow of thee turn not thou away." I have never made this directive to be a rule of my life, and I do not intend to do so. And while I love to help others, and do help others in their needs, I have always been extremely prudent in such things. Yet, I feel no guilt because of my failure to comply with the words of my Lord, and will accept no criticism for not doing so. Again, I will point to the Biblical principle of dispensational truth.

When the Lord Jesus sent forth His twelve disciples, He commanded them not to take any road that would lead them to the nations, not to enter into any Samaritan city, to go only to the lost sheep of the house of Israel, to herald as they went that the kingdom of heaven was at hand, to heal the sick, to cleanse the leper, to raise the dead, to cast out devils, to do it all without charge, and to take no money of any kind with them (Matt. 10:5-10).

In my own ministry I travel quite a bit; and each time I go forth, I ignore or violate all these commands. Furthermore, it is my personal knowledge that most ministers do the same; and, yet, we feel no guilt in so doing. This is because we believe in and practice dispensational truth. Although, many simply practice it while at the same time ridiculing it and denying any belief in it.

In connection with a warning concerning the deceitfulness of riches, our Lord declared to His disciples, "Fear not little flock; for it is your Father's good pleasure to give you the kingdom. Sell that ye have, and give alms" (Luke 12:32, 33). Now, if anyone who professes to be a follower of the Lord Jesus Christ desires to follow these instructions, it is his privilege to do so; but I have no such intentions. And there is no need for a line to form at my door seeking such gratuities. If any challenge my conduct and charge me with hypocrisy, I will patiently teach them the facts of dispensational truth.

While dispensational truth is ridiculed by many, especially church theologians, I proudly confess that I am a dispensationalist in my handling and interpretation of the sacred Scriptures. Furthermore, I do not believe that anyone can live a consistent Christian life in harmony with the Word of God, unless he is a dispensationalist. This does not mean that I blindly follow such partial dispensationalism as that set forth in *The Scofield Reference Bible*, or that I adhere to a more advanced dispensationalism as that set forth in *The Companion Bible*. I did start out as a Scofield follower fifty-seven years ago, but in time realized that he did not go far enough in a good thing, he being too tightly bound up with the English school of dispensationalism represented by J. N. Darby, F. W. Grant, and C. H. Mackintosh. Their ideas were crystallized, popularized, and practically fixed as absolute truth by Scofield in the footnotes of *The Scofield Reference Bible*. His development of their teachings into a theory of seven dispensations is not a viable interpretation that can be held very long if one continues to study the Word.

While I honor E. W. Bullinger as much as I honor any man who ever put pen to paper to declare the truth; yet, his writings fail to give true direction and leadership to those who would go on in advanced dispensational truth. He made a great change and a positive step forward in his dispensational position about five years before his death, but did not have the time or health to develop and set forth his latest findings. His early writings do not reflect his final dispensational position. This can be partly found in a book called, "The Foundations of Dispensational Truth," which sets forth certain studies he wrote during the last five years of his life. But this book is only an introduction to what he planned to say, and one chapter in it is not even his own work. He was not the writer of the chapter on "Three Spheres of Future Glory."

Bullinger's small pamphlet on "The Mystery" was revised by someone after his death; but who did the revising, I have not been able to find out. *The Companion Bible*, a most excellent production, is his work only as far as the Gospel of John chapter 10; and from this point on, it is so sketchy and weak that it is useless.

The excellent appendixes in the last part of it are all his work, and they make the volume worth whatever it costs. In view of the above facts, let no one say that I am a follower of Bullinger simply because we do come together on the great truth that Acts 28:28 is a dispensational boundary line.

Therefore, without apology, I proudly declare that I am a dispensationalist, one who is not tied up to any fixed dispensational system. I will freely admit that I have gone further than most men in dispensational interpretations. And if this leads anyone to brand me as a "hyper-dispensationalist," I will not bother to deny it. However, I will ask if any man can go too far in a good and true principle of interpretation? And, if one can, then who sets the boundary line and declares that all who cross his predetermined mark are "ultra-dispensationalists"? "Who art thou that judgest another man's servant?" (Rom. 14:4), is still a proper question to ask of all who so say. I intend to go as far in dispensational truth as my studies lead me, and all who know me also know that I will not knowingly go beyond the Word of God.

In my opinion it can truly be said that when the first seeds of dispensational Bible study were sown, many enemies came in and sowed noxious weeds among them. Misrepresentations of dispensational principles have ever been rife. However, the greatest damage was done when excusable errors were made that would have straightened themselves out if men had continued their studies. For example, the erroneous idea of dividing all mankind into three classes, Jew, Gentile, and church of God, based upon the K. J. V. translation of 1 Cor. 10:32, would never have been fixed as a Biblical truth if some leader had checked the original and found that it says Greeks, not Gentiles. Nevertheless, at some point some leader, who probably was afraid of losing face if he admitted his error, would seem to yell "freeze"; and half-studied ideas were locked in permanently. From that time forth all who continued to study or question the idea were disfellowshipped and branded as heretics.

It is also a matter of history that dispensational Bible study started off on the wrong foot due to erroneous and garbled semantics. No one seemed to trouble himself about having a pattern of sound words, as Paul exhorted Timothy to do in 2 Tim. 1:13. The very word *dispensation* was misunderstood and an erroneous definition was fixed upon it, one which ignored altogether the meaning of the elements of the Greek word *oikonomia*. This was defined as being a period of time during which man is tested in respect to obedience of some specific revelation of the will of God. Seven of these periods were set forth, but careful examination caused them to disintegrate. For example, the idea that human government came to an end when God called Abraham is an utterly impossible idea to maintain.

However, as already suggested, the most serious handicap was in the word *dispensation* itself. At the time the *King James Version* was translated, the word *dispense* meant to administer, to regulate, to govern; and the word *dispensation* signified the plan, the method, or the manner of administering or governing. These meanings fit the word *oikonomia* very well, and it is somewhat evident that this is what the translators had in mind when they used the word *dispensation.* But these definitions are now obsolete. New meanings have become attached to both *dispense* and *dispensation,* and these are constantly being read into passages where these words are found. Scofield took the word *dispensation* and used it to describe a new idea of his own, an idea that is in no way related to the Greek word *oikonomia.*

This word is made up of *oikos,* a house; and *nomos,* law. Note that it is "house" not "family." The occurrence of *oikos* in this word has led some to insist that this limits God's dispensational dealings to His household; that is, His children, the members of His family. This is an error which more study would automatically correct, since New Testament usage flatly contradicts the idea. See Romans 16:23 where Erastus is described as being "administrator (*oikonomos*) of the city." Those who would limit *oikonomia* to the administration of a family because the element *oikos* appears in it are guilty of closing their eyes to the Pauline usage of this word as found in the Roman epistle.

A dispensation is therefore, an administration; or to simplify it, a manner or method of dealing. And it can best be understood by asking the questions: What is God's manner or method of dealing with mankind at the present time? or What is God's present dispensation? Does He always reward the good and punish the wicked? Does every transgression and disobedience receive a just recompence of reward? Is He dealing with mankind on the basis of absolute justice administered alike to one and all?

I believe the answers to these questions are obvious. From the Word of God, we know that God's present administration is one of grace (Eph. 3:2). His method of dealing with all men is to show love and favor to the undeserving. He is doing this passively, and He is doing this actively; but if He cannot act in grace, He will not act at all. He has a purpose in this. But that will be the subject of another study.

The SEED and BREAD Bible-Study leaflets are published as often as time and means permit and are sent free to all names on THE WORD OF TRUTH MINISTRY mailing list. Send us your name. There will be no obligation, solicitation, or visitation. Additional copies of any issue available on request.   ISSUE NO. 56

SEED & BREAD

FOR THE SOWER   ISA. 55:10   FOR THE EATER

BRIEF BIBLICAL MESSAGES

FROM

THE WORD OF TRUTH MINISTRY

339 South Orange Drive, Los Angeles, Cal. 90036

Otis Q. Sellers, Bible Teacher

THE DISPENSATION OF GRACE

In our previous study (Issue No. 56) it was declared that a dispensation is an administration, and an administration was further defined as being a method or manner of dealing. This definition is based upon the usage of the Greek word *oikonomia* in the New Testament, the fact that its elements mean house-law, and the fact that at the time the *King James Version* was translated, to dispense meant to administer or manage. And even though this meaning is now obsolete, it is of real help in understanding this word. It should be remembered that in a patriarchal society, house-law was usually the total administration under which a man lived.

The fact that God's administrations change and, therefore, vary from time to time, even varying among people at the same time, is an evident truth to the careful student of God's Word. It is quite plain that God's method of dealing with Israel in the centuries before Christ was based upon a set of principles which had not been imposed upon other nations. In other words, there was no dispensation of divine law that covered all mankind, even though there was one for the nation of Israel. "For what nation is there so great, who hath God so nigh unto them, as the LORD our God is in all things that we call upon Him for? And what nation is there so great, that hath statutes and judgments so righteous as all this law, which I set before you this day? (Deut. 4:7, 8) These were the inspired words of Moses to Israel, which tell us that this one people were under a peculiar divine administration distinct from all others. "You only have I known of all the families of the earth: therefore I will punish you for all your iniquities" (Amos 3:2) was God's message to them.

A reading of Matt. 10:1-4 will show that God's method of dealing with the twelve special disciples was somewhat different from the way He dealt with the majority of those who followed Him. These twelve were given great authority; and, of course, with the authority came great responsibility.

Some men raise their hands in holy horror at the thought of two dispensations operating at the same time, but their response is based upon an erroneous understanding of a dispensation. If it were correctly understood, they should be able to see scores of dispensations operating concurrently. Since a dispensation is a method of dealing with men, and since at one time, some men were apostles, they must have been dealt with as apostles, while at the same time others were being dealt with as prophets and teachers. Inasmuch as we can identify eighteen different gifts in the Acts period, and since each gift constituted a position or calling before God, it would be proper to say that there were an equal number of methods of dealing. Each man had to recognize the gift that God had dispensed to him, and thus, to know his own personal dispensation. In view of this, it is certainly erroneous to divide all time into seven dispensations, and then to place all who lived during one time under the same method of divine dealing.

One lesson we need to learn is that there was never at any time a single method of dealing that covered the whole human race until we come in sacred history to the present dispensation, the dispensation of the grace of God. This is God's first universal method of dealing, one under which all men stand before God on the basis of absolute equality, and under which all are dealt with alike. God's present method of dealing with all mankind, and even all nations, is one of grace. He has a definite purpose in this, and He will not violate His own purpose.

The next dispensation, which is the manifest kingdom of God, will also be universal, and will be one of absolute government under which the will of God will regulate every detail of human life. It will be an administration of perfect justice and righteousness. God will also have a purpose under divine government and He will not deviate from this purpose.

God's dispensation of grace had its beginning with Paul's great pronouncement recorded in Acts 28:28, in about A. D. 66 according to our calendar. To the chief men of the Jews assembled in Rome, he announced that the salvation-bringing message of God had been made freely available to the nations and that it would get through to them. It had been freely available to all Israelites for thirty-three years before this. Now being authorized, or, made freely available to all nations, it places all nations then and all nations now on the basis of absolute equality so far as the gospel is concerned. (See Issues No. 5, 7, and 11 for further truth on this.)

A further pronouncement concerning the dispensation of grace was made by Paul in his Ephesian epistle. The truth of God's present administration had been given to him for proclamation to "you of the nations" (Eph. 3:1, 2). He was bound by the Lord to do this in their behalf. It was not an easy matter for him to declare that which would place his beloved Israel under the same status before God as all others. They had been the most favored nation under God, but this would no longer be true. The descriptive phrase "you of the nations" now includes every member of the human race.

That there would be a dispensation of grace, a long period during which God would do nothing but show favor to the wicked, had been a secret purpose of God, hid within Himself, never revealed in any previous revelation of truth (Eph. 3:3). It was no part of any previous prediction, and the sole revelator was the apostle Paul (Eph. 3:8).

Much confusion has been created due to failure to distinguish between the grace of God as being part of His character, and the dispensation of grace as an absolute method of dealing. He, being the God of every grace, was always showing grace to men from the time He provided coats of skin to cover the nakedness of Adam and Eve. We read that Noah, along with seven others, found grace in the sight of the Lord (Gen 6:8), but it was not an absolute method of dealing with him or the rest of mankind. These were dealt with in strict justice, resulting in God's bringing in the flood upon the world of the ungodly (2 Peter 2:5).

In the Acts period so much grace was shown to men that it could be said that grace reigned (Rom. 5:21), a fact in the life of all who believed. Nevertheless, there were numerous instances when God acted in justice and judgment. The Acts period was no part of God's gracious administration, and we stultify the truth of grace when we try to make it so. Consider the cases of Ananias and Sapphira (Acts 5:1-11), of King Herod (Acts 12:20-23), and of the Corinthian saints who were visited with sickness and death because of their disorderly conduct (1 Cor. 11:30). This was God's dealing in justice and not in grace.

One of the most positive revelations in regard to God's present method of dealing is hidden from the reader of the *King James Version* due to a faulty translation. In Ephesians 4:32 we are exhorted to be kind one to another, tenderhearted, dealing graciously one with another, even as God also in Christ deals graciously with us. In this declaration we have a simple and most positive revelation in regard to God's present method of dealing. The word *charizomai* means to deal graciously; and this is God's declared manner of dealing with us, whether we deal with others in this manner or not.

This statement, it should be noted, is found in an epistle written after Acts 28:28. It would not be speaking the truth if it were found in the Corinthian epistle. God did not deal graciously with those spoken to in 1 Cor. 11:30.

In the Colossian epistle, also written after Acts 28:28, Paul declares that these believers had been saved by God's dealing graciously (*charizomai*) with all their trespasses (Col. 2:13). From these two passages the present-day believer should know that he has been saved by God's dealing graciously with his sins and that he is kept saved by this same gracious dealing. How good it is for those such as we are to be living under God's dispensation of grace!

It needs to be understood that God's grace can be either active or passive. If He does something good for us in view of our sins and needs, then He is actively gracious. If He does nothing in view of our iniquities, then He is passively gracious.

The militant atheist of former years, Robert G. Ingersoll, during the course of his lectures, would shake his fist toward the heavens and cry out, "If there be a God, let Him strike me dead." When nothing happened, it was considered by many to be positive proof of the nonexistence of God. Yet, all that it demonstrated was that God is the God of grace, Who continues to be gracious even in view of wicked challenges.

During the present dispensation, every act of God is an act of grace; so much so, that if He cannot act in grace, He will not act at all. During this time all judgment and punishment is in abeyance. Grace is His present method of dealing with mankind; and in the course of displaying His grace, many, as believers, have found themselves caught up in the flow of it, and have been carried into the very fullness of forgiveness and salvation. God's purpose is to display His grace, and the present-day believer is a by-product of this purpose (2 Tim. 1:9).

The grace that God is now showing is untraceable. It comes to mankind as a part of the outflowing wealth of God. Every good and perfect gift is a part of it. It operates in secret; for His present method of dealing is not only gracious, it is also in secret. Some day it will all be traceable. No act of God's grace in 1900 years has gone unrecorded. The hour will come when the record will no longer be secret. It will be open and available as part of our knowledge of Him.

The SEED and BREAD Bible-Study leaflets are published as often as time and means permit and are sent free to all names on THE WORD OF TRUTH MINISTRY mailing list. Send us your name. There will be no obligation, solicitation, or visitation. Additional copies of any issue available on request.   ISSUE NO. 57

SEED & BREAD

FOR THE SOWER ISA. 55:10 FOR THE EATER
BRIEF BIBLICAL MESSAGES
FROM
THE WORD OF TRUTH MINISTRY
339 South Orange Drive, Los Angeles, Cal. 90036
Otis Q. Sellers, Bible Teacher

EPHESIANS - CHAPTER ONE
THE RESULTANT VERSION
TRUE TO THE GREEK AND TRUE TO THE TRUTH

(1) Paul,[A] a commissioned one[B] of Christ Jesus,[C] through the will of God,[D] to all [E] the saints,[F] the ones being[G] and believing[H] in Christ Jesus:

(2) Grace[A] *be* to you, even[B] peace,[C] from God our Father, even[D] the Lord Jesus Christ.

(3) Exalted[A] *be* the God and Father of our Lord Jesus Christ, Who exalts[B] us in every spiritual[C] exaltation among[D] the most elevated[E] in Christ;

(4) According as He chooses[A] us in Him before founding *His* order,[B] we to be holy and flawless in His sight,[C]

(5) In love designating us beforehand[A] for the place of a son[B] for Himself through Jesus Christ, in accord with the good pleasure of His will,

(6) For the extolling[A] of the glories of His grace, which graces[B] us in the Beloved One,[C]

(7) In Whom we have the redemption through His blood, the forgiveness of sins in accord with the outflowing[A] wealth of His grace;

(8) Which He lavishes toward us in all wisdom and prudence,[A]

(9) Making known unto us the secret[A] of His intention, in accord with His good pleasure which He purposes in Him,

(10) In connection with an administration when the times are ripe for it, to head up[A] all these[B] in Christ, those among the heavens and those on the earth,

(11) In Him, in Whom also our lot is cast, being designated beforehand according to the purpose of Him Who is executing all this[A] according to the counsel of His will,

(12) To the end that we should be for the extolling of His glory, the ones who have hoped in advance[A] in the Christ,

(13) In Whom you[A] also *have hoped in advance,*[B] upon[C] hearing this word of the truth, the good message of your salvation, in Whom even *upon*[D] believing, you were sealed with the Spirit of the promise, the Holy One,

(14) Who is the earnest[A] of our full portion, in relation to the redemption of that which has been purchased for the extolling of His glory.[B]

(15) Therefore, I also, on hearing[A] of this faith of yours[B] in the Lord Jesus, and that in respect to all the saints,[C]

(16) Cease not to give thanks for you, making mention in my prayers,

(17) That the God of our Lord Jesus Christ, the Father of glory, may give you a spirit of wisdom[A] and revelation[B] in the realization[C] of Him,[D]

(18) The eyes of your heart having been enlightened,[A] so that you perceive what is the expectation of His calling,[B] and what the riches[C] of the glory of His portion among the saints,

(19) And what the transcendent greatness of His power for us who are believing,[A] in accord with the working of the might of His strength,

(20) Which is wrought in the Christ, raising Him from among the dead, and seating Him in His right[A] among the most elevated,[B]

(21) Up over[A] every sovereignty[B] and authority[C] and power[D] and lordship,[E] even every name that is named, not only in this eon,[F] but also in that to come,[G]

(22) And subordinates all under His feet, and constitutes[A] Him head[B] over all to the outcalled,[C]

(23) Which is His body,[A] the complement[B] of the One filling all these[C] in all ways;[D]

NOTES ON THE VERSION

1:1 (A) He had two names, Paul and Saul. No evidence that his name was ever changed. See Acts 13:9. (B) The Gk. is *apostolos.* See Issue No. 5 for a study of the verb from which this word is derived. (C) "Not of men, neither by man." See Gal. 1:1. This was a special commission which had to do solely with the writing of this letter. (D) He writes by direct divine appointment. (E) The word "all" (*pasin*) has sufficient manuscript support to justify its place in the text. (F) "Saints" is *hagios,* translated "holy" 161 times, and "saint" 61 times. It means separation, and is always related to service. Every believer in Christ Jesus is a saint. (G) In Greek grammar when an article is followed by a verbal adjective (participle), it becomes a substantive. The article here is plural and is expressed as a substantive by adding the word "ones." (H) A believing man is one who trusts another. A faithful man is one whom another trusts. This letter is addressed to believers in Christ Jesus.

1:2 (A) Grace is favor conferred freely, without any cause whatsoever so far as the recipient is concerned, with no expectation of any return, and finding its only motive in the free-heartedness of the giver. The subject of this epistle is grace. (B) The Greeks used the word *kai* (and) to emphasize identity and to establish apposition. This was a favorite literary device of Paul. The grace he desires for them is peace. (C) The word here is *eirēnē*, a noun from which we get the name *Irene*, from the verb *eirō*, which means to join. A noun derived from a verb cannot mean something different from its parent word. Peace is a perfect union, not a good feeling. (D) There cannot be two sources of divine grace, as the K. J. V. seems to suggest. Source and channel must not be separated.

1:3 (A) "Exalted" much better expresses the meaning of *eulogētos*, from *eulogeō*, made up of *legō* (to speak) and *eu* (good), thus, to speak well of. Our word eulogize comes from this. (B) The aorist tense here denotes an act that happened in one point of time, the effects of which continue. (C) The word *spiritual* designates those things of which God is the author, and that come to us wihout any intervening agency or process. See "spiritual drink" and "spiritual meat" in 1 Cor. 10:2, 3. (D) When used in a plural setting, *en* means "among." (E) Since both *eulogētos* and *ouranos* are used as descriptive titles of God (Mark 14:61 and Luke 20:4) it is evident that these words have relationship. This connection is preserved by translating *en tois epouraniois* by "among the most elevated." See Prov. 25:3.

1:4 (A) This is *eklegomai*, which means to elect, to pick out, to choose, but is always used in the technical sense meaning to choose one for an office or to perform a service. Note this in Luke 6:13. (B) "Before . . . order" is *pro kataboles kosmou.* "His" is supplied since it is God's order (world) that is in view here. (C) This is what God elected us to be. This election or choice took place in our lifetime, before God's founding of His order which is still future, that we might perform a special service in His order.

1:5 (A) These three words translate *proorisas*, aorist, active, participle of *proorizō*, which means to determine or designate beforehand. Our future position, character, and service are determined by God in advance of His establishment of His order upon the earth. (B) These five words are used to translate *huiothesia*, a compound word from *huios* (a son), and *tithēmi* (to place). This is somewhat like our word *antithesis*, which means to place one thing against another.

1:6 (A) Gk. is *epainōs* which suggests praise that exalts. (B) A form of the verb *charitoō*, found only here and in Luke 1:28 where it is translated "highly favored." God will "grace" us for our future service. (C) A new designation for Christ Jesus our Lord.

1:7 (A) God's maintenance and support of our redemption and forgiveness are according to the outflowing wealth of His grace.

1:8 (A) He is not an over-indulgent Father, even in spite of His present grace toward all.

1:9 (A) "Secret" is what *musterion* means. The word *mystery* does not belong in the New Testament, and should have no place in the vocabulary of truth.

1:10 (A) This is *anakephalioō* which most certainly means to head up. (B) "All these" is *ta panta*, an idiom, the meaning of which must be found in its usage. See Col. 3:8 where it is translated "all these," and points to things mentioned in the context. Here it has reference to all who will be placed as sons when God governs the earth.

1:11 (A) This is also *ta panta*, and it refers collectively to the workings of God that have already been set forth.

1:12 (A) "Hoped in advance" is *proelpizō*, a simple and honest rendering of this word. Thayer says this word means, "to repose hope in a person or thing before the event confirms it."

1:13 (A) Note the change from "we" to "you," both plural. Paul is now going to ascribe to this company a unique faith which he cannot ascribe to himself. (B) These words are supplied to fill the ellipsis. They bring forward the thought expressed in the immediate context. (C) They believed "upon hearing." Paul could not say this of himself. (D) The word *pisteusantes* expresses a fact that can be best set forth by supplying the word *upon*.

1:14 (A) The Gk. here is *arabon,* which means anything given by one party to another as a pledge that an agreement will be kept. (B) The long sentence ends here.

1:15 (A) These are not Paul's converts. He knows of their faith only by hearing. They cannot be the Ephesians whom he knew so well and loved so dearly. (B) The Greek here is *tēn kath humas pistin,* which literally reads "the according to you belief," and means "the faith that accords with you." This is a new and different company of believers. (C) This is what the Greek says, and any honest interpretation must begin with these words.

1:17 (A) This would be the capacity to receive revealed truth that would be beyond the grasp of all human minds. (B) This is the capacity to uncover truth. See Prov. 25:2. (C) This is not *gnōsis* (knowledge); it is *epignōsis,* which means full knowledge, accurate knowledge. (D) Don't miss this important point.

1:18 (A) He has already given eyes to their hearts so that out of the darkness, they have found their way to Him. Their commitment to Christ was not one of blind emotion. These believers were divine miracles. (B) This refers to the present position (*klēsis*) of Jesus Christ. Every believer should know fully and enter into the enjoyment of our safety, security, and certainty that comes from His present position. He is the Rock, and we are founded on Him. (C) When *ploutos* (wealth) is used with the genitive, it indicates outflowing wealth of whatever is stated, that is, wealth that enriches others. Note this construction in 1:7; 1:18; 2:7; 3:8, 16.

1:19 (A) The believer has three things operating for his benefit and in his behalf: the present position of Christ, the portion God has given to Christ, the power of God that belongs to Christ. We are not powerless. We are not alone.

1:20 (A) This is what the Greek says, and it should not be rewritten. (B) This is the second occurrence of *en tois epouraniois.* See note on 1:3.

1:21 (A) The word *huperanō* can mean "up over" or "over above," but not "far above." This word is found in Heb. 9:5 where it is used of the position of the cherubim in relation to the mercy seat. (B) This is *archē* which means a first one, a leader. (C) This is *exousia* which means literally, delegated authority. (D) This is *dunamis,* from which we get our word *dynamite.* (E) This is *kuriotes,* from *kurios,* meaning *lord.* These words refer to the most exalted ones among the angelic hosts; yet, Christ is now seated "over above" every one of them. (F) The present evil eon. Gal. 1:4. (G) This is the kingdom of God.

1:22 (A) The Greek here means "give," but is translated "constitutes" here since this is what takes place when one is given an office. (B) A "head" is an outflowing source. (C) All who have a position out of Christ are "outcalled," (*ekklesia*).

1:23 (A) He, the Head, flows into the outcalled and they become His substance or essence. (B) The Gk. is *plērōma,* a word used of the officers and men who made up the personnel of a ship. (C) The Greek here is *ta panta.* It is the outcalled who are filled. (D) This is not the end of the sentence. A bad chapter break occurs here.

The SEED and BREAD Bible-Study leaflets are published as often as time and means permit and are sent free to all names on THE WORD OF TRUTH MINISTRY mailing list. Send us your name. There will be no obligation, solicitation, or visitation. Additional copies of any issue available on request.   ISSUE NO.58

SEED & BREAD

FOR THE SOWER   ISA. 55:10   FOR THE EATER

BRIEF BIBLICAL MESSAGES
FROM
THE WORD OF TRUTH MINISTRY
339 South Orange Drive, Los Angeles, Cal. 90036

Otis Q. Sellers, Bible Teacher

EPHESIANS-CHAPTER TWO
THE RESULTANT VERSION
TRUE TO THE GREEK AND TRUE TO THE TRUTH

(1) Even you,[A] being dead to[B] your offenses and sins,[C]

(2) In which,[A] you, at some time or other[B] walk[C] according to the eon of this world, according to the ruler who is the authority of this atmosphere,[D] the spirit now operating in the sons of disobedience.

(3) Among whom even we[A] all are turned hither and thither[B] at some time or other,[C] in the desires of our flesh,[D] doing the volitions of the flesh and of the mind; and we are,[E] in that which is produced by these forces,[F] children of indignation, even as others;[G]

(4) But God, being rich in mercy, because of His great love with which He loves us,[A]

(5) We also being dead to[A] the offenses, makes us alive together[B] in Christ Jesus, in grace are you saved;[C]

(6) And He raises us together,[A] and He seats us together, among the most elevated[B] in Christ Jesus,

(7) In order that[A] among the eons to come, He might be displaying[B] the transcendent wealth of His grace in kindness toward us in Christ Jesus;[C]

(8) For in the grace are you saved, through faith, and this is not out of you; it is God's gift,[A]

(9) Not of works, so that no one might boast.

(10) For His achievement are we, being created[A] in Christ Jesus for good works, which God prepares beforehand,[B] that we might walk in them.

(11) Wherefore,[A] remember,[B] that at one time[C] you, the nations in flesh,[D] who are called "Foreskin"[E] by the so-called

"Circumcision,"F done by hand in flesh,

(12) That youA were, in that era,B apart from Christ,C having been alienatedD from the citizenship of Israel,E and strangers from the covenants of the promise,F having no expectation,G and without God in the world.H

(13) But now in Christ Jesus, you, the ones at one time being afarA off, are become nearB in the blood of Christ.

(14) For He is our peace,A Who makes the both one,B and razes the middle wall of the barrier,C the enmity in His flesh,D

(15) Annulling the law of the precepts in decrees,A that He might be creating the two, in Himself, into one new man,B making peace,C

(16) And might make congruousA the both to God, in one body through the cross, killing the enmityB in it.

(17) And, coming, He brings the good messageA of peace,B to you the far off, and peace to the near;C

(18) For through Him we both have access in one Spirit to the Father.

(19) Consequently, then,A you are strangers and foreigners no longer; but you are fellow-citizens of the saints,B and of the household of God,

(20) Being built upon the foundation of the apostles and prophets, the capstone being Jesus Christ Himself,

(21) In WhomA the entire building, being framed together, is growing into a holy temple in the Lord:

(22) In Whom you also are being built together for God's dwelling place in Spirit.

NOTES ON THE VERSION

2:1 (A) The italicized words in K. J. V. must be omitted. (B) When the truth of being dead IN sins is set forth in Scripture, the preposition *en* is used. (See John 8:21, 24, and 1 Cor. 15:17.) When the truth of being dead TO sins is set forth, the dative case is used. (Note this in Rom. 6:2, 10, 11, and here.) (C) These words describe the present state of a believer in Jesus Christ. We are dead TO our sins.

2:2 (A) This is *in which* or *in which state*. It is as those who are dead to trespasses and sins that we live and walk in this world. (B) The word *pote* is indefinite, not past. It is a dependent particle related to time. It can be used of the past, but this must be clearly established by the context. Thayer says it means "at sometime or other." It is somewhat like our phrase "now and then." (C) We do, and it is useless to deny it. We have here a divine estimate of our walk. (D) No one can say he is never influenced by his environment and circumstances — "For in many things we all offend" (Jas. 3:2).

2:3 (A) Paul now includes himself. (See Rom. 7:15-25.) (B) Gk. *anastrephō*, which means "turned up and down," (Young); or more literally, "turned topsy-turvy." (C) This is again *pote*, same as in verse two. (D) See

Gal. 5:17. (E) The Gk. is *emetha*, first person, plural, imperfect of *eimi*. (F) "that . . . forces" is a long rendering of the word *phusis*, from the verb *phuō*, which means to sprout. *Phusis*, therefore, is a sprouting. (G) The contrast here is between a believer who now and then lives contrary to the will of God, and the sinner who habitually lives in such manner. The actions described in Eph. 2:1-3 are the sins of the saints. We discover the provision God has made for these as we study on.

2:4 (A) Paul will now show that divine grace meets every demand. This is not the love of God for all mankind as declared in Rom. 5:8, but God's great love for His own who are now believing, as set forth in John 13:1.

2:5 (A) The same dative construction as in 2:1, declaring once more our standing before God. (B) The Gk. is *suzōopoieō*, occuring only here and in Col. 2:13. (C) "Saved" is *sozō*, in which, in this passage, the idea of preservation is preeminent. In grace we are preserved. This speaks of our present salvation.

2:6 (A) "Raises . . . together," is *sunegeirō* which occurs only here and Col. 2:12. (B) "Among . . . elevated" is *en tois epouraniois*, as in 1:3 and 20. This will be our position before God and men when God's government is a reality. We will be among God's nobility.

2:7 (A) These words introduce the great purpose for which God saved us from the guilt of sin, is now saving us from the power of sin, and will yet save us from the dominion of sin. (B) He will display us for His glory, and display His glory in us. (C) We will ever be a living display of the grace He has shown, does now show, and will yet show unto us.

2:8 (A) This gift concerns the whole matter under discussion, our threefold salvation by and in grace.

2:10 (A) "Being created" — the process goes on and will not be complete until we take our place in His kingdom. (B) God has a program for the future which will be worked out to the last predetermined detail.

2:11 (A) The Greek means *wherefore*, or *for which reason*. What is now to be said is based on the truth of the preceding paragraph, which began in 1:15. No one should attempt to interpret this portion until he is familiar with the Biblical history of Israel, and, especially, all the facts related to the great barrier that existed between those in the land and those in the exile. (B) The word *remember* is a demand for close attention on the part of those to whom Paul now speaks. (C) This is the third occurrence in this chapter of *pote*, a word difficult to translate, but one which never points to a definite period of time. (D) They were "nations in the flesh," but not in spirit. This is the only occurrence of this phrase in Scripture and it is a perfect description of the dispersed ones in Israel. (E) The Gk. word is *akrobustia*, which means "foreskin" and nothing else, an epithet that certain Jews in the land hurled at their brethren in exile. It was never used as a derogatory description of Gentiles, even though it was used to factually and truthfully describe them. See Acts 11:3, where the literal translation would be, "You went in to men having foreskin (*akrobustian exoutas*) and did eat with them." (F) There was a self-styled circumcision party in Judea.

2:12 (A) Paul was not one of these. (B) "Era" is *kairos*, a definite period of time having certain characteristics. Here it is the period of the earthly ministry of Christ. The exiles were without Him during those years. (C) Before He came to earth, all the seed of Abraham were apart from Him. After His birth, those in the land had contact; but these in exile were apart from Him. (D) The word *apallotrioō* here is a verb, not a noun. It means *alienated*, not *alien*. (See Eph. 4:18 and Col. 1:21 for the same root word.) "Having been alienated" is the true and honest translation of the form used here. (E) This is that from which they had been alienated. Peter writes to these "expatriates of the dispersion" in 1 Peter 1:1. (F) The phrase "strangers . . . promise" is somewhat like visitors who were no actual part of the family. (G) Their hope was dead and needed reviving. (See 1 Peter 1:3.) (H) They were not "without God" in the absolute sense, but without God in the system or world in which they were forced to live. Israel's divine religion was not transportable. Its rites and ceremonies could not be adapted to foreign manners. They were strictly of Palestine and for Palestine. "An extra-Palestinian Judaism, without priesthood, altar, temple, sacrifices, tithes, first-fruits, Sabbatical and Jubilee years, must first set aside the Pentateuch" (Edersheim).

2:13 (A) See Dan. 9:7 and Acts 2:39 for positive evidence that this description belonged to one company of Abraham's seed. Non-Israelites were not "afar off," as Paul emphatically declares to a Gentile company in Acts 17:27. (B) This is the new status of the dispersed ones in relationship to the Israel of God, a nearness that no physical distance from the land could invalidate.

2:14 (A) This is between the two groups in Israel. (B) Those "near" and those "afar off" are now one. Paul includes himself by use of "our," he being an Israelite who was near. (C) The "middle wall" is the partition wall. If this is razed, no barrier exists. (D) This defines the "middle wall of the barrier." Christ was born in the land, and was circumcised on the eighth day. The barrier that stood between the 2,500,000 Jews in the land and the 5,500,000 outside the land became a fixed matter by His words and actions during the days of His flesh. "Go not into the way of the nations," were His words (Matt. 10:5).

2:15 (A) His death annulled the temporary decrees that were necessary in "the days of His flesh," (B) That He might take these two disparate companies and create them in Himself into one new man. (C) He Himself is the union that binds the two.

2:16 (A) "Make congruous," is *apokatallasō*, formed from three words: *apo* (from), *kata* (down along or parallel with), and *allassō* (to change). Both companies are changed from what they were, down along certain lines, to make them both harmonious to God in one unit. (B) The enmity was between God and the exiles. They were dispersed as a punishment for their sins. However, there was also enmity between the two groups.

2:17 (A) This "coming" was through His appointed representatives. (B) This was a message of perfect, harmonious union. (C) These were the two companies of Abraham's seed, clearly identified by the Word of God in Dan. 9:7 and Acts 2:39; but men have made the Word void here by making these two companies to be Jew and Gentile.

2:19 (A) Paul now brings to a conclusion the statements made in verses 14 to 18. He sums up the results of the work of Christ on the cross, so far as it bore upon the great wall in Israel. (B) This will be in the new Israel which God promised to create (Isa. 66:7-14).

2:21 (A) A pyramid follows the lines of its capstone.

The SEED and BREAD Bible-Study leaflets are published as often as time and means permit and are sent free to all names on THE WORD OF TRUTH MINISTRY mailing list. Send us your name. There will be no obligation, solicitation, or visitation. Additional copies of any issue available on request.   ISSUE NO. 59

SEED & BREAD

FOR THE SOWER   ISA. 55:10   FOR THE EATER

BRIEF BIBLICAL MESSAGES
FROM

THE WORD OF TRUTH MINISTRY

339 South Orange Drive, Los Angeles, Cal. 90036

Otis Q. Sellers, Bible Teacher

EPHESIANS-CHAPTER THREE

THE RESULTANT VERSION
TRUE TO THE GREEK AND TRUE TO THE TRUTH

(1) Of this grace,[A] I Paul, the bound one[B] of Christ Jesus for you of the nations,[C]

(2) Assuming[A] that you surely hear of the administration[B] of the grace of God,[C] which is given to me for you,[D]

(3) For by revelation the secret[A] is made known to me, even as I have written before in brief,

(4) By which you, reading,[A] are able to apprehend my understanding in the secret of the Christ,[B]

(5) Which *secret,* in other generations,[A] is not made known unto the sons of men, as it is now revealed[B] to His holy apostles and prophets:

(6) In Spirit[A] the nations[B] are to be joint-enjoyers of a portion,[C] joint-bodies,[D] and joint-partakers[E] of the promise in Christ Jesus through the good message,

(7) Of which *secret* I became dispenser,[A] in accord with the gift of God's grace, which is granted to me in accord with His powerful operation.

(8) To me, less than the least of all saints,[A] was this grace granted: to herald among the nations[B] the good message of the untraceable[C] wealth of Christ,

(9) Even to enlighten all[A] as to *God's* secret administration,[B] which has been concealed from the eons[C] in God, Who creates all these,[D]

(10) That now to the sovereignties and the authorities among the most elevated[A] may be made known, through the outcalled[B] *One,* the manifold wisdom of God.

(11) In accord with the purpose of the eons, which He makes in Christ Jesus our Lord,

(12) In Whom we have boldness and access with confidence through the faith relating to Him.

(13) Wherefore, I am requesting[A] that you be not despondent at my afflictions for your sake which are your glory.

(14) Of this grace[A] I am bowing my knees[B] to the Progenitor,[C]

(15) Out of Whom every progeny[A] in the heavens and on the earth[B] is named,[C]

(16) That He may be giving you,[A] in accord with the wealth of His glory, to be made staunch with power,[B] through His Spirit, in the inner man,[C]

(17) Christ to dwell[A] in your hearts by faith;[B] that you having been rooted and grounded in love,[C]

(18) Should be strong enough[A] to grasp firmly, with all saints, what is the breadth, and length, and depth, and height,

(19) To know, also, the knowledge surpassing love of the Christ, in order that you may be completed for the entire complement[A] of God.

(20) Now unto Him Who is able to do superabundantly above all that we are requesting or conceiving, according to the power which is operating in us,[A]

(21) To Him[A] be glory in the outcalled[B] One, even in Christ Jesus, for all the generations of the eon of the eons.[C] Amen!

NOTES ON THE VERSION

3:1 (A) The Gk. is *toutou charin*. *Charin* is the accusative form of *charis* (grace), and is used here following the genitive *touto* (of this). It is a peculiar phrase found only three times in the New Testament, Eph. 3:1; 3:14; Titus 1:5. Thus, "this grace" becomes the specific subject; and Paul will enlarge upon it to show that it is God's present method of dealing with mankind and with the nations. (B) Gk. *desmios*, which means a prisoner, but does not always indicate one confined to a jail. He was the bound one of Jesus Christ in relationship to certain great truths; and if he were at the same time a prisoner of Caesar, that would be another matter. (C) This cannot be the same company as those called "nations in the flesh" in 2:11. This description is as broad as the human race. I am "of the nations"; you are "of the nations." All Israelites are, today, "of the nations," even those living in Israel.

3:2 (A) This is not easy to express in English. The aorist (*ēkousate*) is not past, and is here rendered as an indefinite. The facts that are about to be set forth are true and operative whether they have heard of them or not. (B) *Tēn oikonomian* is the Gk. The word "administration" has been used here as it more accurately expresses the meaning of *oikonomia*. (C) He is speaking of God's gracious administration, or God's gracious method of dealing. (D) He speaks of a great truth which he is about to proclaim to them. The word "you" is plural and refers back to "you of the nations" in the previous verse.

3:3 (A) The word *musterion* means "secret," not "mystery." There is no reason for transliterating this word when a good English word is available for its translation.

3:4 (A) They would read; and as they read, they would wonder at his understanding of the things he sets forth. It was by revelation. (B) I understand the genitive here to be that of posession. It was Christ's secret, but He entrusted it to Paul with the direction that he should make it known on behalf of "you of the nations."

3:5 (A) That is, in other revelations of divine truth. (See Issue No. 12 for material on the word *generation*.) (B) Paul was the revelator, and all apostles and prophets needed to be informed of this new administration.

3:6 (A) There is a bad verse break here. These two words belong to verse six. (B) "The nations" now becomes the subject, not individuals of the nations, but nations as such. God's present attitude toward all nations is now to be revealed. (C) These five words translate *sunklēronoma*. A definite portion from God, untraceable and unexplainable, is the portion of every nation. He permits all nations to walk after their own ways, and this freedom is probably one aspect of this portion. (D) The word here is *sussōma*, which is plural. A nation is composed of individuals which, when organized, becomes a body. All nations are bodies; and today, in God's sight, they are joint-bodies, that is, bodies on the basis of absolute equality. This is His present attitude toward the nations. What He does for one nation, He does for all. (E) The word here is *summetocha*, which means partakers together, on the basis of equality. It is no longer "to the Jew first."

3:7 (A) The word here is *diakonos*, one through whom a service flows.

3:8 (A) Paul breaks the rules of grammar and piles a comparative upon a superlative. (B) The nations may ignore it, but the message has been heralded officially. (C) "Untraceable" is *anexichniaston*. The nations today are enjoying wealth flowing from God that cannot be traced back to Him. His present administration is secret.

3:9 (A) This is, "all nations." (B) "God" is supplied here as it is most certainly His administration. Since an administration is a method of dealing, we now have learned that God's present administration is gracious; it is untraceable, and it is in secret. (C) An eon is always a channel. Any being into whom God is flowing, and who in turn flows out to others is a divine eon. For example, see the angel in Luke 2:9-12. In no previous divine eon did God ever give forth the truth revealed in Ephesians 3. (D) The Gk. is *ta panta*, which means "all these," and points to the eons. The words "by Jesus Christ" are not in the original.

3:10 (A) The fourth occurrence of *en tois epouraniois*. (B) *Ek* means "out" and *kaleō* means to position, to designate, or to name (to invite is a secondary meaning). Bring them together in *ekklesia* and we have the "out-positioned," that is, those who have a position out of another. Jesus Christ, whose position or name is out of God, is the preeminent outcalled One. He is the One spoken of here.

3:13 (A) Paul's vigorous ministry has come to an abrupt halt. He is now dwelling in his own hired house, receiving all who come to him, but going out to none. This, along with his miserable physical condition might lead some to think that the cause was hopeless and God's plan defeated.

3:14 (A) This is *toutou charin*, same as in 3:1. (B) The great symbol of submission. (See Gen. 41:43.) (C) This is *patéra* which means Father, but which I have rendered "Progenitor" in order to show the relationship with *patria* (progeny) in the next verse. Rotherham uses "Father" and "fatherhood." The words "by Jesus Christ" are not in the original.

3:15 (A) In order for this to be "the whole family," as the K. J. V. renders it, there would need to be the definite article before *pasa patria*. (B) God is not the Father or Progenitor of all beings in heaven; neither is He the Progenitor of all men upon earth. He is the Creator of all, and all are His creatures. This passage speaks of certain celestial beings and certain human beings to whom God has granted a special measure of His character so that they express Him and He is seen in them. He is the Progenitor and they are His progeny. (C) The word "name" signifies character and standing. (See Luke 6:13, "Whom also He named apostles.")

3:16 (A) Following this statement Paul will list the various aspects of his prayer for them. (B) If the believer experiences this, he will not hesitate to choose the way of truth and stand up for it. He will not become frightened by the contention this may cause. (C) The result of this power will not be seen in outward manifestations. The operation of it will not result in words and works that will alarm the world.

3:17 (A) "To dwell" is to make your home in a place, to have a settled residence. (B) Faith is taking God at His word and responding accordingly. (C) "Having stricken your root deep into the soil of the Love of God, having built your house of salvation firm upon its rock" (Moule).

3:18 (A) The very pettiness of our own personalities can act against us in regard to laying hold of great truths. It is too much to hope that selfish, petty, touchy individuals will ever grasp the truth of the length, breadth, depth, and height of the love of Christ. A change of character must come first. (See Rom. 12:1, 2.)

3:19 (A) These are words so great that it is impossible to fathom them. The translation is correct.

3:20 (A) This is the "untraceable outflowing wealth" of Christ spoken of in 3:8.

3:21 (A) To God be glory. (B) If *ekklesia* means "church," or if it means "all believers," then Paul has placed these ahead of Christ. It is my conviction that "the outcalled" here is "the outcalled One." The word *kai* belongs in the text here and should be translated "even," as I have done. (C) This is a faithful reproduction of the Greek. To find what it means is the work of the student.

The SEED and BREAD Bible-Study leaflets are published as often as time and means permit and are sent free to all names on THE WORD OF TRUTH MINISTRY mailing list. Send us your name. There will be no obligation, solicitation, or visitation. Additional copies of any issue available on request.   ISSUE NO. 60

SEED & BREAD

FOR THE SOWER   ISA. 55:10   FOR THE EATER

BRIEF BIBLICAL MESSAGES

FROM

THE WORD OF TRUTH MINISTRY

339 South Orange Drive, Los Angeles, Cal. 90036

Otis Q. Sellers, Bible Teacher

EPHESIANS-CHAPTER FOUR

THE RESULTANT VERSION
TRUE TO THE GREEK AND TRUE TO THE TRUTH

(1) I am admonishing you, therefore, I, the bound one in the Lord, to order your behavior in a manner worthy of the position[A] in which you have been placed,[B]

(2) With all humility[A] and meekness, with patience, bearing with one another in love,

(3) Giving diligence to safeguard the unity[A] of the Spirit in the uniting bond of peace:

(4) One[A] body[B] and one Spirit,[C] even as you were placed[D] also in one expectation of your position;

(5) One Lord,[A] one faith,[B] one identification,[C]

(6) One God and Father of all,[A] Who is over all, and through all, and in all.

(7) Now to each one[A] of us[B] was[C] given the grace[D] in accord with the measure of the gratuity of the Christ.

(8) For this reason[A] He is saying: "Reascending on high, He captures captivity,[B] and gives gifts to mankind."

(9) Now this, "He reascended," what can it mean except that He first descended also into the lower parts, that is, the earth?[A]

(10) He Who descended is the same Who reascended also, up over all of the heavens,[A] in order to be filling[B] all these.[C]

(11) And this same One indeed constitutes[A] the apostles,[B] the prophets,[C] the evangelists,[D] the shepherds[E] and teachers,[F]

(12) With a view to the proper outfitting[A] of the saints, for the work of dispensing,[B] for the building up of the body of Christ,[C]

(13) Unto the end[A] that we should all attain to the unity of the faith, and the realization of the Son of God, to mature manhood, to the full stature of the complement of the Christ,

(14) That we[A] may no longer be minors, surging hither and thither and being carried about by every wind of teaching, according to men's cleverness, with a view to the methodizing[B] of the error.

(15) But, being true, in love we should be making all grow up into Him[A] Who is the Head, even Christ,

(16) Out of Whom[A] the entire body, being joined closely together and united together through every joint of supply, in accord with the operation of each single part, is making for the growth of the body, for the upbuilding of itself in love.

(17) This, therefore, I am saying and attesting in the Lord that no longer are you to order your behavior as the nations[A] order their behavior, in the futility of their mind,

(18) Being those who have had their understanding darkened, having been alienated from the life of God because of the ignorance that is in them, because of the callousness of their hearts,

(19) Who, being past feeling, in greed give themselves up with wantonness to all uncleanness as a lifestyle.

(20) You, however, have not thus learned the Christ;

(21) Since, surely, Him you hear, and by Him were taught, even as the truth is in Jesus,

(22) To strip off from you, as regards your former manner of life, the old man,[A] which is corrupted in accord with its seductive desires,

(23) And be rejuvenated in the spirit of your mind,

(24) And to put on the new man which, in accord with God, is in truth being created in righteousness and loving-kindness.

(25) Wherefore, putting away lying, let each be speaking truth with his fellow-man, seeing that we are members of one another.

(26) If you are angry, beware of sinning. Do not let the sun go down on your wrath,

(27) And do not leave any room for the adversary.

(28) Let him who is stealing, steal no more;[A] but rather let him be toiling, working with his hands that which is good, that he may have to share with one who has need.

(29) Let no putrid[A] word at all be going forth out of your mouth, but whatever *word* may be good toward needful edification, that it may be giving grace to those hearing.

(30) And do not be grieving the Holy Spirit of God in which you are sealed[A] for the day of redemption.

(31) Let all bitterness[A] and fury and anger and clamor and slanderous speech be taken away from you with all malice;

(32) And become kind to one another, tenderly compassionate, dealing graciously[A] with one another, even as God also in Christ deals graciously with you.

NOTES ON THE VERSION

4:1 (A) This is *klēsis,* which means a position. (B) This is *kaleō,* the verb from which *klēsis* is derived. It means to position, to name, to designate. To invite, or summon is a secondary meaning. These are believers in the Lord Jesus Christ, positioned as individuals in the dispensation of the grace of God. Face up to the fact that this is a very difficult position.

4:2 (A) See James 4:6. We ascribe to God credit for all that we may be or do.

4:3 (A) We do not create this unity of the Spirit. We are asked to safeguard it.

4:4 (A) Paul now declares the seven great principles in which all saints of all callings meet. (B) This is *sōma,* which basically means substance or essence. This is the material out of which a glorious outcalling will be constituted. There never has been and there never will be but one substance that God has given to men. He gives them of what Christ is. (C) This is God's Holy Spirit, the One Who came upon the soldiers of Saul (1 Sam. 19:20), and the 120 at Pentecost (Acts 2). (D) The one common hope held out to all men at all times by the Word is that they can be alive and upon the earth in the day when God governs. There is no other hope (Psa. 37:22).

4:5 (A) This is the Jehovah of the O.T., the Lord Jesus Christ of the N.T. (B) The "one faith" is that in which a man takes God at His Word and responds accordingly. All men of faith meet on this principle. It now centers in the record God has given of His Son. (C) I dare here to translate *baptisma.* This word speaks of an identification, one that involves a merging, includes a commitment, and establishes a relationship. Does the reader have this identification in relationship to Christ? The word *baptisma* is also applied to a water ritual, but this is a secondary and derived meaning which is not in the picture here.

4:6 (A) Every member of God's family at all times and under all dispensations. And while we are a unique company of believers, we are not unique in regard to these seven points of unity.

4:7 (A) At this point Paul looks back and makes known to these believers the divine conditions and arrangements that characterized and operated in the Acts period. (B) We must go forward to verse eleven to find out to whom this plural pronoun applies. It applies to the God-appointed and qualified apostles, prophets, evangelists, shepherds and teachers. For the sake of brevity, Paul omits thirteen other appointments. (C) *Edothē* is the aorist tense and should be rendered *was,* not *is.* (D) This grace was everything needed to fully and properly perform the functions of the position given to them. If they could neither read nor write, and they needed to do so, they were given this ability.

4:8 (A) Paul shows that the unusual gifts of the Acts period were in harmony with O. T. declarations. (B) He took those who were the captives of Satan and made them His own captives. We are not free. We are the bound ones of Christ Jesus.

4:9 (A) This is the genitive of apposition. "Lower parts" is defined by "the earth."

4:10 (A) If "heavens" here means places, then He is not in any heaven, and this would contradict Luke 24:51. These are heavenly beings. He ascended over and above all these. (B) The best place to fill anything is from above. (C) This is *ta panta,* which means "all these," and points back to "the heavens."

4:11 (A) When *didomi* is used of an office or position, it signifies "to constitute." (B) The commissioned ones, the most important office of the Acts period. (C) A prophet is one who speaks the Word of God on any subject. There are no prophets today. To quote Scripture on any subject is not prophesying. Holy men of old spake as they were moved by God. They did not simply repeat or expound Holy Writ as we do today. (D) Men who spoke the evangel or gospel by inspiration. (E) The Gk. is *poimēn*, translated in K J V "shepherd" seventeen times, and "pastor" one time. (F) The instruction put forth by those constituted "teachers" in the Acts period came to them by divine inspiration. It was divine truth from God.

4:12 (A) The Gk. is *katartismos*, which means to be equipped along certain lines. This is why the gifts were given. (B) The Gk. is *diakonias*, from which we get the word "deacon." (C) The essence or substance (body) of Christ was built up on earth by the gifts given to men.

4:13 (A) The Gk. is *mechri*, which speaks of the end in view when God gave gifts to men.

4:14 (A) This refers to the entire outcalled company that will function so perfectly and gloriously in the day when God governs. (B) The Gk. here is *methodeia*.

4:15 (A) This is not the way it is today, but we have God's Word that this will be a future reality.

4:16 (A) He gives of Himself so that the outcalled ones may become what He is.

4:17 (A) The word "other" here in the K J V is an unwarranted addition to God's Word.

4:22 (A) Paul uses figurative language here which we should not change into literal.

4:28 (A) This admonition, along with that of verse 25 indicates that Paul was not writing to the beloved friends spoken of in Acts 20:32-38.

4:29 (A) The Gk. is *sapros* which means rotten, diseased, bad, foul.

4:30 (A) The believer has been sealed, a single past action that continues effectively until the goal is reached.

4:31 (A) A list of the six most common sins, beloved by many, that the Spirit of God stands ready to take away from us if we will only let them go.

4:32 (A) This is one of the most important passages to be found in Paul's final epistles. It declares that God's present method of dealing is gracious. Yet, this great and all-important truth is completely covered and lost by the mistranslation in the K J V. The common word for "forgive" does not appear in this passage. The Gk. is *charizomai*, from the word *charis* (grace) which means to bestow a benefit on one who deserves punishment, i. e. to deal graciously. Paul could not have said this when he wrote to the Corinthians, in view of 1 Cor. 11:30.

The SEED and BREAD Bible-Study leaflets are published as often as time and means permit and are sent free to all names on THE WORD OF TRUTH MINISTRY mailing list. Send us your name. There will be no obligation, solicitation, or visitation. Additional copies of any issue available on request.   ISSUE NO. 61

SEED & BREAD

FOR THE SOWER   ISA. 55:10   FOR THE EATER

BRIEF BIBLICAL MESSAGES

FROM

THE WORD OF TRUTH MINISTRY

339 South Orange Drive, Los Angeles, Cal. 90036

Otis Q. Sellers, Bible Teacher

EPHESIANS-CHAPTER FIVE

THE RESULTANT VERSION

TRUE TO THE GREEK AND TRUE TO THE TRUTH

(1) Become, therefore, imitators[A] of God as beloved children;

(2) And be ordering your behavior[A] in love, even as the Christ also loves you, and gives Himself up for us, an offering and a sacrifice to God for a fragrant odor.[B]

(3) But fornication,[A] and impurity, every kind of it, or covetousness, let these not be named among you, according as is becoming in saints,

(4) And obscenity and stupid speaking or jesting,[A] which are beneath you,[B] but rather thanksgiving.[C]

(5) For this you know absolutely, that no whoremonger,[A] or one impure in thought and life, or covetous person, who is an idolator, has any portion[B] in the kingdom of Christ, even *the kingdom* of God.[C]

(6) Let no one[A] be seducing you by means of empty words,[B] for because of these things, the indignation of God is coming upon the sons of the stubborness.

(7) Stop, therefore, becoming joint-partakers[A] with them;

(8) For you were at one time darkness; yet, now you are light in the Lord. Be ordering your behavior[A] as children of light;

(9) For the fruit of the light is in all goodness and righteousness and truth,

(10) Testing[A] what is well pleasing to the Lord.

(11) And be not joint-participants in the unfruitful enterprises[A] of this darkness; but rather be enlightening them,

(12) For it is a shame even to say what hidden things are done by them.

(13) For all these which are enlightened by the light are made manifest, for everything that is making manifest is light.

(14) Wherefore, He is saying, "Awake! O sleeping one, and arise[A] from among the dead, and Christ shall shine upon you!"

(15) Be constantly observing accurately how you are ordering your behavior, not as unwise ones, but as wise,

(16) Buying up for yourselves the opportune time[A] because the days are wicked.

(17) Therefore, do not become imprudent, but be understanding what the will[A] of the Lord is.

(18) And be not drunk with wine, in which is profligacy;[A] but be filled with the Spirit,[B]

(19) Speaking to yourselves in psalms and hymns and spiritual songs,[A] singing and making melody in your hearts to the Lord,[B]

(20) Giving thanks to God the Father always for all things in the name of our Lord, Jesus Christ,

(21) Putting yourselves in subjection[A] to one another in the fear of Christ,

(22) The wives to their own husbands as to the Lord,[A]

(23) Seeing that the husband is head[A] of the wife even as Christ is Head of the outcalled; *and* He is the Savior of the body.[B]

(24) Nevertheless, as the outcalled is being subject to the Christ, thus, are the wives also to their husbands in everything.[A]

(25) The husbands be loving their wives[A] even as the Christ loves the outcalled, and gives Himself in its behalf,[B]

(26) In order that He should be hallowing[A] it, cleansing it by the bath of water,[B] in the realm of His Word,

(27) In order that He might present[A] to Himself a glorified outcalling,[B] not having spot or wrinkle or any such things, but that it may be holy and flawless.

(28) Thus, the husbands also ought to be loving their own wives as their own bodies.[A] He that is loving His own wife is loving himself.

(29) For no one at any time hates his own flesh, but is nourishing and cherishing it, even as the Christ, the outcalled,

(30) Seeing that we are members[A] of His body.[B]

(31) Corresponding to this, a man will be leaving[A] his father and mother, and will be joined[B] to his wife; and the two will be one flesh.[C]

(32) This secret is great.[A] However, I am speaking in regard to Christ and the outcalled.

(33) Moreover, let each one of you individually[A] be loving his own wife as himself; and the wife, let her reverence her husband.

NOTES ON THE VERSION

5:1 (A) The Gk. is *mimētēs*, from which we get the word *mimic*. The context emphasizes God's gracious dealing.

5:2 (A) The Gk. is *peripateō* which means to walk about. Since it is used figuratively here, an attempt has been made to express this by rendering it "order your behavior." (B) The Gk. is *euodias*, a good odor. God has accepted our substitute, and He accepts us in Him.

5:3 (A) A very common and popular sin in Paul's day, even as it is now in our day. The moral life of the Greco-Roman world had sunk very low, and fornication had long come to be regarded with moral indifference. It was indulged in without shame.

5:4 (A) "The passage does not deal with the play of humor, and wit in general. This is not forbidden in Scripture, and so far as it is the outcome of vigor, gladness, or (in the sense of humor) tenderness, it may be quite in harmony with the strict piety of the gospel" *Moule*. (B) The Gk. is *anēko*, which means "to come up to." It occurs also in Col. 3:18 and Phile. 1:8. (C) The Gk. is *eucharistia*, which could well mean "gracious speech" here. It fits the context.

5:5 (A) Four sins are now mentioned which will bar the practicers from the kingdom of God. (B) The Gk. is *kleronomia* (the law of the lot). It could be translated "allotment." (C) This is one kingdom, not two. It belongs to the Father and the Son.

5:6 (A) The Greek is strong here—"let not even one person be seducing you." (B) "Empty" is *kenos* and this warning is related to that against *kenophonia* (empty sounds) of 1 Tim. 6:20 and 2 Tim. 2:16.

5:7 (A) "Joint-partakers" is *summetochos*, which occurs only here and in Eph. 3:6.

5:8 (A) This is *peripateō*, same as in verse 2.

5:10 (A) The Gk. is *dozimazō* which means putting to the test and, thus, proving.

5:11 (A) These are the rituals, activities, and services in which many well-meaning but unenlightened people would involve us as being the works of God.

5:14 (A) Or, "stand up out from among the dead"—an exhortation to true individualism.

5:16 (A) We should make wise use of every opportunity for doing what God would have us do.

5:17 (A) Not the will of the Lord for us, but simply God's will in accord with His present purpose. It is His will to be gracious, to keep silent, to shut us up to faith. Are we able to accept His will in regard to these things?

5:18 (A) "Profligacy" is a state wherein a man might commit a murder, ruin his life, destroy his reputation, wreck his automobile, or even his home, and excuse it all by saying, "I was drunk." (B) To be filled with the Spirit is to be filled with the things of the Spirit. (See John 6:63 and Gal. 5:22, 23 for examples.)

5:19 (A) These are the sacred compositions of believing men who are taught in the Word and can express the truth in this manner. (B) These words will eliminate all the jazz and jigs that are now so widely used in so-called Christian services. The appeal of these is to the feet.

5:21 (A) The Gk. word *hupotassō* means "being arranged" or "arranging yourselves under one another." If believers did this, they would all be equal and none would be above or over another. Such equality as this would have been impossible in the Acts period.

5:22 (A) Or, "the wives, be arranged under your own husbands, as to the Lord."

5:23 (A) This word *kephalē* (head) has the basic meaning of an outflowing source. For example, Jesus Christ, the Apostle, the Prophet, and the Teacher flowed into Paul, giving him of Himself, thus, making Paul the apostle, prophet, and teacher that he was. He bore in his body the marks of the Lord Jesus. He partook of Christ's substance and, thus, became His body. (B) Even two thousand years in the state of death has destroyed nothing that God gave to Paul, or anyone else who partook of Him.

5:24 (A) The kingdom of God is anticipated in these passages. The loftiest possible concept of the husband and wife relationship is presented here. It would be wise for all who believe to produce some "fruit ahead of season," and see how much of this we can produce now.

5:25 (A) There is nothing in this passage about bridegrooms and brides. The subjects are husbands and wives. (B) He gives of Himself to the outcalled ones that they might become what He is.

5:26 (A) He marks it out for special use and service. (B) "Water" is not a fixed symbol in the New Testament. It can mean the Word of God and it can mean the Spirit of God.

5:27 (A) Or, "set it alongside Himself." (B) If any group, company, or organization claims to be this glorified outcalling, it deceives and the truth is not in it. This glorious outcalling will assume its place and begin its functions when the kingdom of God is a reality. Some materials for it are being collected now.

5:28 (A) Let not the husbands worry too much about what this means. Let them do it.

5:30 (A) A member is a partaker, a participant. He does not make the body. The body makes him what he is. (B) "His body" is His substance, all that he is by investiture from God. "For in Him dwells all the fulness of the Deity in essence." (Col. 2:9.)

5:31 (A) This is *kataleipō*, to leave behind, to depart from. (B) This is *proskallō*, to glue upon, to glue to, to join oneself to another closely. (C) They must make it so. It is not automatic.

5:32 (A) Indeed it is a great secret! One that is only partly uncovered. And we must not stultify the truth here by applying Paul's words concerning the *ekklesia* to anything that is in existence today. A glorified outcalling is the goal of God. We are not it, but we are some of the threads which someday will be woven into the great tapestry that already exists in the mind and purpose of God. The relationship that will exist between Christ and the outcalled is still a secret. We get some glimpses of what it will be, but we cannot now conceive the picture as a whole.

5:33 (A) The universal duty in the marriage relationship, from which no husband is exempt. If he will not fulfill verse 33, he cannot claim the privileges of verse 23.

The SEED and BREAD Bible-Study leaflets are published as often as time and means permit and are sent free to all names on THE WORD OF TRUTH MINISTRY mailing list. Send us your name. There will be no obligation, solicitation, or visitation. Additional copies of any issue available on request.   ISSUE NO. 62

SEED & BREAD

FOR THE SOWER   ISA. 55:10   FOR THE EATER

BRIEF BIBLICAL MESSAGES

FROM

THE WORD OF TRUTH MINISTRY

339 South Orange Drive, Los Angeles, Cal. 90036

Otis Q. Sellers, Bible Teacher

EPHESIANS-CHAPTER SIX

THE RESULTANT VERSION

TRUE TO THE GREEK AND TRUE TO THE TRUTH

(1) The children, be hearkening submissively[A] to your parents in the Lord; for this is right.[B]

(2) "Honor[A] your father and mother," which is the chief[B] precept in connection with a promise.

(3) "That well with you it may be, and you may be a long time on the earth."[A]

(4) And the fathers,[A] do not be provoking[B] your children to anger, but be nurturing them in the discipline and admonition of the Lord.

(5) The slaves,[A] be hearkening submissively[B] to your masters according to the flesh, with fear and trembling, in the singleness of your heart as unto the Christ,

(6) Not with eye-slavery[A] as man-pleasers, but as slaves of Christ, doing the will of God from the soul,

(7) With good will, slaving as to the Lord and not to men,[A]

(8) Knowing that whatsoever good each one should be doing, for this he will receive back from the Lord,[A] whether slave or free.

(9) And the masters, be doing the same toward them, refraining from threats, knowing that their Master, as well as yours, is in *the* heavens; and there is no respect of persons with Him.[A]

(10) In conclusion,[A] my brethren, be empowering yourselves in the Lord, and in the might of His strength.

(11) Put on the complete armor[A] of God to enable you to hold your ground against all the strategems[B] of the adversary;[C]

(12) For our wrestling[A] is not against blood and flesh,[B] but

with the sovereignties, [C] with the authorities,[D] with the world-rulers[E] of this darkness, with the spiritual forces[F] of wickedness among the most elevated.[G]

(13) Therefore,[A] take to yourself the complete armor of God in order that you may be able to stand in the wicked day,[B] and having done all this, to stand.

(14) Stand,[A] therefore, having girded[B] your loins[C] with truth,[D] with the breastplate[E] of righteousness[F] in place,

(15) And your feet shod with the readiness[A] of the good message of peace.[B]

(16) In addition to all these, having taken up the great shield[A] of faith[B] by which you will be able to extinguish all the fiery arrows of the wicked one,

(17) Also receive the helmet[A] of the salvation-bringing *message*,[B] even the sword of the Spirit which is God's utterance,

(18) With all prayer[A] and supplication, praying in every season, in Spirit, and thereunto watching with all perseverance and supplication for all the saints,

(19) And on behalf of me, that to me expression may be granted in the opening of my mouth with boldness to make known the secret[A] of the good message,

(20) In behalf of which I am conducting an embassy in a chain,[A] that in it I may be speaking boldly as I must speak.

(21) Now in order that you may be acquainted with my affairs, and what I am doing, all will be made known to you by Tychicus, the beloved brother and faithful servant in the Lord,[A]

(22) Whom I send to you for this same purpose, so you will know the things concerning us, and that he might be encouraging your hearts.

(23) Peace be to the brethren, and love with faith, from God the Father, even the Lord Jesus Christ.

(24) The grace be with all who are loving our Lord Jesus Christ in incorruptibility.[A]

NOTES ON THE VERSION

6:1 (A) The Gk. is *hupakouō*, which indicates to listen, hearken, submit to. Note this word in Heb. 11:8. (B) The Gk. is *dikaios*, not *euarestos* (well pleasing as in Col. 3:20).

6:2 (A) "Honor" is *timaō*, which means to estimate, fix the value, determine the worth. (B) So translated in order to be true to the truth. The second commandment also had a promise connected to it.

6:3 (A) An inspired paraphrase of the Old Testament precept and promise. This cannot mean that every obedient child will have a long life and that the life of the disobedient will be cut short. The actual facts of human experience and observation deny such an interpretation. Verses 2 and 3 declare a condition that was true in Israel before the covenant was broken, and it anticipates conditions in the coming kingdom of God.

6:4 (A) This is addressed to the father, as the head of the family, the pilot of the household. (B) A common sin of many fathers who irritate and exasperate their children, making obedience and honor impossibilities.

6:5 (A) The word here is *doulos,* which means a slave. These were slaves who were also believers in the Lord Jesus Christ. Slavery was an established institution in the Roman Empire. They far outnumbered the freemen. They abounded by the millions, chattels to be bought or sold as their masters saw fit. They had no rights of any kind. In fact, slavery was so woven into the fabric of Roman society that to abolish it would have torn the Empire into shreds. Paul makes no attempt to correct this injustice or inequality, but tells the slaves how to live within it, and gives instructions as to the conduct of masters who are believers. (B) The same Greek word as in verse one.

6:6 (A) "Eye-slavery" is service performed only when one is under the eye of the master for the sake of escaping blame or incurring undeserved favor.

6:7 (A) Strange as it may seem, Paul's directive is that the slave should serve the human master as if he were serving the Lord Jesus.

6:8) (A) The encouragement for doing this is found in the fact that whatever good the slave does for his human master shall be rewarded by Christ.

6:9 (A) In verses 5 to 9, slavery is accepted as an institution that existed. It is neither condemned nor approved. Neither Paul nor the Lord Jesus engaged in social reform. To change the world was not their commission.

6:10 (A) The Gk. is *loipon* which means "in respect to the rest." "Finally" is a good translation, but I prefer "in conclusion."

6:11 (A) "Complete armor" is *panoplia,* from which we get our word "panoply." (B) "Strategems" are "methods," or "change of ways." (C) The adversary is the devil.

6:12 (A) The word "wrestling" indicates a personal, individual, hand to hand conflict. Don't organize a team to fight these enemies. (B) "Blood and flesh" stand for men of all kinds and abilities. (C) The Greek is *archē.* (D) The Gk. is *exousia.* (E) The Gk. is *kosmokratōr,* from *kosmos* (world) and *krateō* (to have strength). (F) "Spiritual" is *pneumatika,* which is accusative, plural, neuter. "Wickedness" is *ponēria,* which is genitive, singular. These two words do not agree and cannot be used together. (G) The Gk. here is *en tois epouraniois,* same as in 1:3, 1:20, 2:6, and 3:10. It is a plural adjective. It means "the most elevated ones." However, these are not "in Christ" as they are in 1:3, and 2:6.

6:13 (A) Because the fight is with such powers, we need to take up and put on the whole armor of God. (B) We, as none before us, are living in an unusually wicked day, due to the fact that evil men and seducers have continually waxed worse.

6:14 (A) God expects us to stand, and not surrender or lie defeated before the enemy. (B) The participles show that the armor is to be put on before we attempt to stand. (C) The Gk. is *osphus,* meaning hip, loins, the part of the body surrounded by the girdle. We are to surround ourselves with that which is the truth. "Thy Word is truth" (John 17:17). (D) The Lord Jesus said, "I am the truth" (John 14:6), and "Thy Word is truth" (John 17:17). This is first mentioned in this list of equipment, because the living Word and the written Word are of the utmost importance. (E) The word for "breastplate" is *thorax* which means both breast and breastplate. It always means the latter in the New Testament. (F) This is the genitive of apposition and means "the breastplate which is righteousness." This is Christ Who is our righteousness.

6:15 (A) This word (*hetoimazō*) was used in Classical Greek in the sense of a firm foundation. (B) The good message that set forth the basis for a true and proper union with God.

6:16 (A) The word here is *thureos,* from *thura,* a door, because it was shaped like a door. (B) Faith is taking God at His Word and responding accordingly. An ever present faith in the Lord Jesus Christ is needed for victory over all the fire-tipped arrows of the wicked one.

6:17 (A) "Helmet" is from two words, *peri* (around) and *kephale* (head). (B) The word which I have translated "salvation-bringing" is *soterion,* an adjective; and "message" is supplied because no adjective ever stands alone. For a full examination of this word, see Issue No. 8, a portion of which I repeat here: "In this passage 'the helmet' equals 'the salvation-bringing,' for they are appositional—one defines the other. And then by a further apposition, these are defined as 'the sword of the Spirit' which in turn is described as being 'a declaration from God.' In view of this, we should read here, 'And take the helmet of the salvation-bringing declaration (the gospel).' And let it not be thought strange that the salvation-bringing declaration of God is both the believer's helmet and the Spirit's sword. There is no mixing of metaphors here, but two distinct metaphors setting forth two separate uses of the same thing. It is my firm opinion that the salvation-bringing declaration of God is the gospel according to John, the only book in the Bible that was written so that men might believe that Jesus is the Christ, the Son of God, and believing have life through His name (John 20:31). The one who is not securely grounded upon this message will not be able to stand against the wiles of the devil. We need this helmet."

6:18 (A) Prayer is a believer's weapon that is of prime importance. Constant, earnest, believing prayer is necessary for a victorious warfare against the enemy. The other weapons in our hands will not work well without it. Nevertheless, we should not make a religion out of prayer.

6:19 (A) There is a secret truth related to the gospel, and Paul is making this known.

6:20 (A) The truth revealed to him was indeed a strong chain that bound him to a duty that had to be performed.

6:21 (A) In regard to service, I take this to be the highest title to which any man can aspire in this dispensation.

6:24 (A) This is a glorious word, and it stands as the last word of this magnificent epistle. The word "Amen" does not belong here.

The SEED and BREAD Bible-Study leaflets are published as often as time and means permit and are sent free to all names on THE WORD OF TRUTH MINISTRY mailing list. Send us your name. There will be no obligation, solicitation, or visitation. Additional copies of any issue available on request.   ISSUE NO. 63

SEED & BREAD

FOR THE SOWER   ISA. 55:10   FOR THE EATER

BRIEF BIBLICAL MESSAGES
FROM
THE WORD OF TRUTH MINISTRY
339 South Orange Drive, Los Angeles, Cal. 90036

Otis Q. Sellers, Bible Teacher

GOD'S PRESENT PURPOSE

With the one exception of knowing from the Word that he is a child of God through his faith in the person and work of Jesus Christ, there is no truth that is of more importance to the believer than to know the present purpose of God. If we would walk worthily of the position in which God has placed us, we must not be ignorant of this great truth. Many, indeed, are working at counter purposes with Him because they do not know it. There is no experience in knowing that will bring tranquility of mind, courage of heart, and inward peace like that which comes from realizing and living harmoniously with God's present purpose. Every professing Christian needs to ask and then seek the answers to these pertinent questions: What is God's present purpose? What is God doing now? Is He failing or succeeding?

Without any further words of introduction to the subject, permit me to say decisively and emphatically that God's present purpose is to write into the history of His long dealings with the human race a complete record of the grace that is inherent in His character.

By contrast we can say that God is not now demonstrating His power, majesty, justice or judgment. He is demonstrating His grace. This is His present purpose.

This purpose began when God suspended His kingdom purposes by issuing through His herald, the Apostle Paul, the proclamation recorded in Acts 28:28 (see Issue No. 11). It has continued for more than 1900 years and will continue until the record of His grace is complete to His own satisfaction. He will then assume sovereignty over the earth and all its inhabitants, and His administration (dispensation) will change radically from one of absolute grace to one of absolute government.

In Luke 6:35, after exhorting His disciples to love their enemies, declaring that, by so doing, they would be sons (true expressions) of the Highest, the Lord Jesus went on to make the amazing declaration that, "He is kind unto the unthankful and to the evil."

The concept of God that is set forth in these words is contrary to the view which is held by practically all religions and religious men today. They hold and teach that He is kind only to the good, measuring out nothing but wrath to the ungrateful and wicked. To show kindness to the ungrateful and wicked is most certainly grace in action, and such an act would automatically flow from those who are gracious. The Scripture record from Genesis 1 to Acts 28:28 gives witness to the fact that God is gracious and to innumerable acts of grace that flowed forth from Him even though He did act in justice and wrath on many occasions. However, He is now writing into the history of all His dealings with mankind an absolute, unquestionable record of the truth of the words spoken of Him in Luke 6:35, "He is kind unto the unthankful and to the evil."

When God has finished His present demonstration of grace, never again can anyone question His grace. If they should, we can point to the record which will ever be positive proof that He is "the God of every grace" (1 Pet. 5:10). This demonstration of His grace is now taking place in an administration of grace, in which every act of God is one of love and favor to the undeserving, so much so, that if He cannot act in grace, He will not act at all. He will allow nothing to enter into His present work or ways that will spoil His record of grace. And even though we cannot now read or trace out the record of the grace that He is showing, all His present works of grace being untraceable (Eph. 3:8), yet, every day is one of God's grace to the world and one of special grace to we who are now believing.

It will greatly help us to appreciate God's present purpose if we remember that the words *grace* and *government* declare the polarity of God's character. He is "the God of every grace" (1 Peter 5:10), and He is "the Judge of all the earth" (Gen. 18:25). As the Judge of all the earth, He must do what is right, that is, administer justice and righteousness. As the God of every grace, He will show forth grace. Yet, these are such totally different principles that He cannot do both at the same time in regard to any one thing. Since, in times before Acts 28:28, God had not committed Himself to any specific manner of dealing with mankind, He was free to show grace or administer justice. Many examples can be shown of both.

God has now committed Himself to act in grace. He has declared this through His chosen apostle, Paul; and we will do well to take Him at His word and think accordingly. This is the great truth revealed in Paul's final epistles, especially Ephesians and Colossians. (Note Eph. 3:2.)

If God is not recognized as being both the God of grace and the God of government, we will have a lopsided concept of the character of God, one that comes from believing only a part of the truth. When men argue that because of the great love of God, no man will ever be punished, they are ignoring one pole of His character. They are putting all the emphasis on the God of grace and ignoring the God of government. He has punished in the past, and He will punish in the future. The obvious fact that He is not punishing men today is clear proof of His present administration in which He deals graciously with all. It does not indicate that He has ceased to be the Judge of all the earth, Who will do what is right in that day when every sin and transgression receives its just recompence of reward (Heb. 2:2; 12:23).

Mankind is yet going to see and experience a complete and open demonstration of the government of God. He will experience its power and principles, its methods and morals, its justice and judgment, its light and life, its healing and health, its benefits and blessings. These will all be seen in manifest operation. "All men shall declare the work of God, for they will wisely consider of His doing" (Psa. 64:9). Under an administration of divine government, men will come to know from experience the Judge of all the earth and that He does right. They will in that day be able to make a full comparison between God's government and man's government and will repudiate the latter forever.

This is what the world would have seen and experienced if God had not suspended His kingdom purposes at the close of the Acts period. The foundation was laid in that thirty-three years for the full revelation of God's righteous government, the manifest kingdom of God. The blade and ear stages (see Mark 4:26-29) of the kingdom were finished. The time for "the full grain in the ear" stage had arrived (see Issue No. 48). But all this was suspended by God in order to fulfill another purpose that is supremely essential if men are ever to know the God of grace. This purpose was a secret known only to God until He revealed it to the Apostle Paul.

God is now creating within the history of mankind a total and complete record of the graciousness of His character. He is doing this in an administration (dispensation) of grace under which all His government or kingdom purposes are in abeyance.

God's present purpose is succeeding every day and in every way. He is not failing in anything that He purposes to do. Every passing day on the calendar adds one more page to the record of His grace. This record is not open to us today. All His operations are secret. His works are untraceable. However, a day is coming when the secret workings of God in this dispensation will be opened for inspection. Then, when we stand with eyes that can truly see and look back over 1900 years of divine history, we will know and cause the world to know that He was indeed the God of every grace.

Since God's present administration is one of grace, as Paul so definitely proclaims in Ephesians 3:2, then it cannot be an administration of divine government, even in part. In Eph. 4:32, Paul declares that God is dealing graciously with us, a great truth that is buried under the erroneous translation of *charizomai* in the K J V. This word is found twice in this passage. It means "to deal graciously," a fact that most translators ignore because of their ignorance of God's present dispensation of grace, His method of dealing with mankind in it, and His present purpose in such a lavish display of grace as this passage declares.

Another important passage in connection with God's present

purpose is 2 Tim. 1:9. This passage is also so poorly translated that its great message is stultified. In a more accurate and literal rendering, this would read: "Who saves us and places us in a holy position, not in accord with our works, but in accord with His own purpose, even the grace which is given to us in Christ Jesus before eonian times."

We are the by-products of God's present display of grace. He is being gracious to all in order to produce the record of His grace. As definite acts of grace, He has acted and moved in relationship to us, tenderly knocking upon the door of our hearts. If we slam the door in His face, if we turn our backs upon Him, His gracious acting toward us will still become a part of the record and, in due time, will speak of the grace that is inherent in Him.

The explanation of God's long toleration of evil, His present silence in the face of multiple and manifest wrongs, and His toleration of the works of Satan can be explained only when we realize that God is fulfilling another purpose. This purpose of His is one that greatly concerns Him and the full revelation of His character toward men. What He is doing now is for the sake of His own name.

God is now doing all that is necessary to forever establish beyond all question that He is the God of every grace. This is what He is now doing. This is His present purpose.

The SEED and BREAD Bible-Study leaflets are published as often as time and means permit and are sent free to all names on THE WORD OF TRUTH MINISTRY mailing list. Send us your name. There will be no obligation, solicitation, or visitation. Additional copies of any issue available on request.   ISSUE NO. 64

SEED & BREAD

FOR THE SOWER   ISA. 55:10   FOR THE EATER

BRIEF BIBLICAL MESSAGES
FROM

THE WORD OF TRUTH MINISTRY

339 South Orange Drive, Los Angeles, Cal. 90036

Otis Q. Sellers, Bible Teacher

CHRISTIAN INDIVIDUALISM

The God-inspired declaration of the Apostle Paul tells us that all who determine to live godly in Christ Jesus shall suffer persecution (2 Tim. 3:12). In most lands today, this persecution will usually take the form of disfellowshipping, ostracism, separation, and misrepresentation and misunderstanding of one's high and holy purpose. Along these same lines, I would add that if anyone does determine to live godly in Christ Jesus, he will have to do it as an individual. The one who gives his time searching for some group or company that is living godly in Christ Jesus, and to which he may attach himself, is doomed in advance to failure and disappointment. Put it down for a positive fact that the average professing Christian is not interested in living godly in Christ Jesus. He spends most of his time seeking for ways to live worldly in Christ, to make a "fun thing" or a "money thing" of his professed connection with the Lord.

A most positive aspect of living godly in Christ Jesus is that the one who has so determined has "chosen the way of truth" (Psa. 119: 30). He joins the Lord Jesus in saying, "Thy Word is truth" (John 17:17). And once this choice has been made, the only question that can ever be asked concerning any teaching or practice is, "Is it the truth?" If it is, it must be embraced and declared; if not, it must be repudiated.

It should be understood in advance that the determination to live godly in Christ Jesus, and the choice of "the truth way" rather than "the church way" is not an easy road to travel. It could be a very lonesome road. So, if one cannot decide in advance that, through the help of Jesus Christ, he can accept the isolation, the ostracism, and the misunderstanding that may come from following such a course, he had better not start upon it. He would probably be happier if he simply cast his lot with some like-minded group of "food, fun, and fellowship" seekers. If one is going to be miserable living the life of a Christian individualist, he had better find some other way of life.

If, among those who read these lines, there are those who have had a true encounter with the Lord Jesus Christ; if they have judged themselves as sinners and received Him as their Savior; if they have come face-to-face with the fact of God's Truth versus man's error; if they have chosen the way of Truth, and it has become their determination to grow in grace and in the knowledge of Jesus Christ — they will find it necessary to find a way of life in Christ Jesus that will allow them to live out to the limit the relationship which they now bear to God through Him. If Jesus Christ, rather than some sect or denomination, is to be the molder of their lives, I recommend to them *Christian Individualism* as being the true and best way of life for the active believer in Christ Jesus.

The believer whose knowledge of the Bible is ever increasing, whose appreciation of the person and work of Jesus Christ is ever growing, with this resulting in a determination to give Him the preeminence in all things, will find that he quickly becomes *persona non grata* (an unacceptable person) in any church today. His unwillingness to go along with the popular schemes and make-work activities of today's religions will cause him to be branded as a divisive factor, and any protests he makes will bring the charge that he is a troublemaker.

The churches want bodies to help swell the attendance; they welcome purses that will help with the finances, but they insist that everything that means so much to the active believer in Christ must be forgotten and left at home. He can play and he can pay but is allowed nothing to say. And if he insists in raising his voice in protest, he can expect a visit from the board of deacons who will insist that he keep quiet and conform or else face a more drastic action. This can be such a frightening prospect to many that they will seek to avoid it at any cost. So, they become amenable and complacent, usually giving as an excuse that they are doing it for the sake of their families.

However, for many others, such compromises are impossible. The truth as it is in Christ Jesus means more to them than any organization, and they cannot remain silent when grievous errors and practices are promulgated. Thus, the only course open to them is one of Christian individualism. This means a commitment to Christ and to His Word while standing apart from any commitment to any religious body.

It has been my joy to recommend this way of life to many believers in Christ. It is my belief and my experience that it is the privilege of any individual to establish relationship with Jesus Christ in which all that He can ever be to any man in this dispensation, His rich blessings, and fellowship can be enjoyed wholly apart from any institution called a church. Such things as nearness to God, likeness to Christ, devotedness to His Word, and separation from the world can all be attained and maintained by the individual believer in Jesus Christ without his being any part of an organized company. The believer can be attached to Christ, to His Name, to His Word, yes, even to His people, without being any part of any church. I offer my own life as proof of this.

The primary value of Christian individualism is that it permits a faithful presentation of Jesus Christ to others. It permits one's eye to be single when he seeks to win men to Christ. There is no demand upon him to bring men to Christ and also into some church.

He is able to plead God's cause and feels no need of pleading the cause of any church or denomination.

Christian individualism lifts a man to a position of sublime independence of all the religions of this world. The Christian individualist knows that a man can be joined to God through Jesus Christ, and that he does not need to face or become involved in all the divergent issues created by religious organizations. He knows the satisfying value of having gone directly to God, knowing no intermediary but Jesus Christ, His Son, and no other authority save the written Word of God. He smilingly refuses the officious cries of churchmen who declare that he cannot have Christ as his Savior until he has first acknowledged and received them.

The Christian faith was from the very first the personal faith of individuals. This is clearly seen in the declaration of Paul who tells us that after God's dealings with him on the Damascus road, he did not confer with any human being. Neither did he go up to Jerusalem to them that were apostles before him; but he went into Arabia, then later came back to Damascus (see Gal. 1:15-19).

The believers of the Acts period were not always scattered; and wherever possible, they moved and acted as a fellowship of individuals. But when one of them found himself cut off from all others, he stood alone, finding his all in Christ.

Before determining to live godly in Christ Jesus, before choosing the way of truth, before starting out on the path of Christian individualism, the believer had better make sure that he can "go it alone" spiritually. It may be necessary for him to do this. Let him be determined in advance that he is able to say with godly Asaph of old: "Whom have I in heaven but Thee? and there is none upon earth that I desire beside Thee" (Psalm 73:25).

Christian individualism is a way of life, not a way of escape. It consists of that which an active believer in Christ does, not what he does not do. Therefore, let no careless, loveless, prayerless, antisocial individual take refuge in it. Let no sports enthusiast, Sunday-morning golfer, fisherman, or television addict adopt it in order to free himself for the pursuit of his pleasures. Let not the stingy use it as a way to stop all giving. Let no one take this high and holy position unless his life, from that day on, is to be lived for the glory of Jesus Christ.

Quite a few believers who have considered Christian individualism as a way of life have asked about fellowship with other believers. And to this there is only one answer — fellowship with others to the very limit. Christian individualism is not an anti-social way of life. Do not hesitate to go anywhere, where you can find and be of help to other believers. However, if you find that such associations are causing you to compromise or keep quiet in regard to things you know to be the truth, better withdraw from them at once. Remember, "Our fellowship is with the Father, and with His Son Jesus Christ . . . . If we say we have fellowship with Him, and walk in darkness, we lie, and do not the truth. But if we walk in the light, as He is in the light, we have fellowship one with another, and the blood of Jesus Christ His Son cleanseth us from all sin" (1 John 1:3-7).

So, after all has been said, and all arguments pro and con have been exhausted, there is only one method of dealing with God in this dispensation; and that method is personally and individually. This is the way we must start, and this is the way we should continue. In this way of life, we can best fulfill our position as believers in an unbelieving world, as godly men in an immoral world, as students of God's Word in a world that is Biblically illiterate.

The SEED and BREAD Bible-Study leaflets are published as often as time and means permit and are sent free to all names on THE WORD OF TRUTH MINISTRY mailing list. Send us your name. There will be no obligation, solicitation, or visitation. Additional copies of any issue available on request.   ISSUE NO. 65

SEED & BREAD

FOR THE SOWER   ISA. 55:10   FOR THE EATER

BRIEF BIBLICAL MESSAGES

FROM

THE WORD OF TRUTH MINISTRY

339 South Orange Drive, Los Angeles, Cal. 90036

Otis Q. Sellers, Bible Teacher

WHEN HE SHALL COME

I desire to say, and to have it on record, that I believe in the personal, visible return of the Lord Jesus Christ to the earth. I believe this because it is declared in the Word of God. I believe this as an individual and would hold it to be the truth even if I were the only one on earth who did so. There is no compulsion from any other source that requires me to believe this. It is not the creed of any group with whom I fellowship. I believe this just because it is written that, "This same Jesus which is taken up from you into heaven, shall so come in like manner as ye have seen Him go into heaven" (Acts 1:11). In fact, I hesitate not at all to make the boast that there is no man on earth who believes any more strongly than I do in the personal, visible return of Jesus Christ to the earth. I am a believer; believing is my business; it is my way of life; and I do not stumble at any detail, once I can settle in my mind that it is what the Word says.

Furthermore, I believe that this personal and visible return of Jesus Christ is with the purpose in view that He shall be personally present upon the earth for a thousand years. I do not agree with those who make everything of Christ's coming and little or nothing of His personal presence. The fact of His presence is the important truth, not the journey that brings Him back.

I believe that His thousand-year personal presence will be a thousand-year *parousia*. A personal presence is not necessarily a *parousia*. Most men who have studied this word have terminated their studies prematurely, and they have finished with the erroneous conclusion that this word means naught but personal presence. While this is the basic idea in it (a *parousia* is not possible apart from a personal presence), yet, a personal presence may or may not be a *parousia*. (See Issues No. 24 and 25 for full examination of this word.)

My firm belief in the personal return and presence of Christ does not include all the ideas connected with it that have been concocted by the emotional and illogical preachers of prophecy. I have no time at all for the thousand-and-one events, past and present, that have been set forth as signs that the return of the Lord is imminent. Neither do I believe the oft-repeated idea that the Christians of the first century expected the return of Christ before death would overtake them. If this had been their expectation, they would have had to have been led to expect it by the Holy Spirit; and this theory could only point to the conclusion that He led them wrong. While many passages are cited to prove that the first followers of Christ expected His return at any moment, I believe that all such passages have been misinterpreted, misunderstood, and misapplied. Some, like 1 Cor. 1:7 which is constantly used, have been mistranslated.

The Bible does not teach the possibility of the Lord Jesus returning to the earth today, tomorrow, this week, or this year. If He did return today, it would make a shambles of God's own revealed order of events. This order of events may not be crystal clear in all its details, but the main events are clear enough to establish the truth that many things must precede the return of Jesus Christ to the earth.

For example, Elijah must come first and restore all things (Matt. 17:11). This is not an independent event, as it follows God's assumption of sovereignty; and the work of Elijah is all done within the time period of the kingdom of God. Furthermore, in due time, a "man of lawlessness" must be unveiled who will seat himself in "the temple of God, shewing himself that he is God" (2 Thess. 2:4). Since this one will be destroyed by the blazing forth of His *parousia*, it is evident that the *parousia* cannot take place until the "temple of God" has been rebuilt. Israel's great new temple will be rebuilt in the kingdom of God.

It has, for more than a half-century, been my purpose to know and to believe all that the Bible teaches concerning the return and personal presence of Jesus Christ. Most things revealed are very pleasant and easy to believe; but some things declared are not so pleasant; yet, these must also be believed. For example, it is my conviction that 2 Thess. 1:7-10 refers to His actual coming in person to be present upon the earth. Here we read:

And to you who are troubled rest with us, when the Lord Jesus shall be revealed from heaven with His mighty angels, In flaming fire taking vengeance on them that know not God, and that obey not the gospel of our Lord Jesus Christ: Who shall be punished with everlasting destruction from the presence of the Lord, and from the glory of His power; When He shall come to be glorified in His saints, and to be admired in all them that believe (because our testimony among you was believed) in that day. 2 Thess. 1:7-10.

I have examined this passage in the original Greek, looked at it in at least twenty versions of the New Testament, and consulted many writers, wondering if someone had found a way of translating or interpreting this passage that would ameliorate this exceedingly drastic punishment that will be visited upon "them that know not God, and obey not the gospel of Jesus Christ." The search has been in vain, for the words here are plain and highly expressive. This passage describes the fate, not just of unusually wicked men, but of ignorant men and those disobedient to the gospel, "when He shall come."

From all this, it is evident that if the second coming of Christ takes place while the world is in its present state of darkness and disobedience, then the overwhelming majority of living humanity will be exterminated. This is such a radical action, that I, for one, cannot justify it on the part of God, the One Who so loved the world that He gave His Son for its salvation.

However, let there be a long period of time when men live under the beneficent effects of divine government (Psalm 67:4), of divine enlightenment (Psa. 97:4), of the manifestation of Jesus Christ (Col. 3:4[1]), of an unveiled Christ (1 Cor. 1:7[2]), of a world filled with "the knowledge of God" (Isa. 11:9) — then if they shut God out of their thoughts and refuse to obey the gospel of Jesus Christ, any punishment visited upon them would be just and right.

If Jesus Christ were to come back tonight, it would completely upset the divine timetable, scramble the Word of God, and make impossible the fulfillment of at least a hundred glorious promises that God has made concerning Israel and the nations. There are today upon the earth about 13 million Jews, whose chief characteristic for 1900 years has been their rejection of every claim concerning Jesus Christ, both as to His mission and message. What would happen to them if Christ should return today? Would not Israel as a living people be destroyed? How then would God fulfill all the glorious promises He has made to them? Consider, for example, the promise made concerning them in Ezekiel 34:11-15:

For thus saith the Lord GOD; Behold, I, even I, will both search My sheep and seek them out. As a shepherd seeketh out his flock in the day that he is among his sheep that are scattered; so will I seek out My sheep, and will deliver them out of all places where they have been scattered in the cloudy and dark day. And I will bring them out from the peoples, and gather them from the countries, and will bring them to their own land, and feed them upon the mountains of Israel by the rivers, and in all the inhabited places of the country. I will feed them in a good pasture, and upon the high mountains of Israel shall their fold be: there shall they lie in a good fold, and in a fat pasture shall they feed upon the mountains of Israel. I will feed My flock, and I will cause them to lie down, saith the Lord GOD. Eze. 34:11-15.

When this prophecy is linked up with two more of like nature in Ezekiel 20 and 28 (note 20:30, 42, 44; 28:25; 34:27), it will be seen that Israel comes to know the Lord as the result of all this beneficent activity in their behalf.

The truths declared in the prophecies of Israel's restoration and that declared in 2 Thess. 1:7-10 are so opposed to one another that they are mutually exclusive. If Jesus Christ came back to earth today, the event described in 2 Thess. would make impossible the fulfillment of these prophecies.

The divine vengeance of 2 Thess. 1:8 is of such nature that divine justice would require that certain other things must be true before it can be righteously executed. Remember, this vengeance is not the penalty of those who have lived their lives in sin and disobedience. It is the portion of those who know not God and who obey not the gospel of Jesus Christ. Therefore, before this divine vengeance could be righteously executed, there would first of all need to be an unquestioned opportunity given to every living man to know God. Since this divine vengeance concerns only those who are living upon the earth "when He shall come," they should at least be treated equally with the Pharisees of whom the Lord said: "If I had not come and spoken unto them, they had not had sin: but now they have no cloke for their sin." "If I had not done among them the works which none other man did, they had not had sin: but now have they both seen and hated both Me and My Father" (John 15:22, 24).

Once such an opportunity is given to men to know God, then any punishment meted out to those who know not God would be fully deserved and its justice cannot be questioned. How thankful we should be that there is to be a long period of time before the second coming of Christ when the glory of the LORD shall be revealed, and all flesh shall see it together (Isa. 40:5). This will be in the kingdom of God, a period time that precedes His return to the earth.

[1]The word "appear" in the KJV is from the Gk. *phaneroō* and should be translated "be manifested."

[2]The word "coming" in the KJV is from the Gk. *apokalupsis,* "unveiling."

The SEED and BREAD Bible-Study leaflets are published as often as time and means permit and are sent free to all names on THE WORD OF TRUTH MINISTRY mailing list. Send us your name. There will be no obligation, solicitation, or visitation. Additional copies of any issue available on request.   ISSUE NO. 66

SEED & BREAD

FOR THE SOWER   ISA. 55:10   FOR THE EATER

BRIEF BIBLICAL MESSAGES

FROM

THE WORD OF TRUTH MINISTRY

339 South Orange Drive, Los Angeles, Cal. 90036

Otis Q. Sellers, Bible Teacher

A FORETASTE OF THE KINGDOM

What will the kingdom of God be like? What will it be like to live upon this earth in the day when it is governed by God? These questions have exercised many. Believing, as I do, that at any moment, God may speak in heaven and assume sovereignty over all mankind, both the living and the dead, I find myself wondering what it will be like to live upon this earth when God governs.

These questions have both a general and a specific answer: general, so far as one's being a subject of the kingdom of God is concerned; and specific, so far as one's being a son of God, a part of the nobility, and performing a special service. This study will deal only with the general.

My interest in this has caused me to seek a greater degree of familiarity with that part of the Old Testament that extends from the Psalms to Malachai. I believe that these books deal primarily with a time to come when God is going to establish His own order or system upon the earth. This will be vastly different from anything that man has ever experienced in the past or is experiencing at present. It will be a new method of dealing with mankind, a new dispensation, a new administration.

The world to come will be one in which absolute justice will prevail. In its dominion, it will always be well for the good and ill for the wicked (Isa. 3:10, 11). Some would like to think that it is this way today, but the obvious facts tell us that we are not now living in a moral universe where sin always carries its own penalty and righteousness always brings its own reward.

In the order of things to come, mercy, love, and forgiveness will be available to men; but grace will no longer characterize God's dealings with men. (See Issue No. 57.) Grace is the opposite of government, and grace is not possible under a system that has as a part of its constitution the rule that every sin and disobedience will have its just recompense of reward. The coming order is to be a time of absolute government in contrast with the present time of absolute grace. Under God's government, no one will ever suffer except what they justly deserve to suffer. The innocent will never suffer, but the guilty certainly will.

In God's coming order, all that is good becomes permanent; and all that is evil will be only for the moment. Under such a system, the good will ever increase in number; and the evil will decrease as men find that sin does not pay—not even a momentary gain. Truly, "In His days shall the righteous flourish" (Psalm 72:7).

Thus, we realize and believe that the advent of the kingdom of God will have a profound effect upon the morals of men; but we must also realize and believe that God's government will have a profound effect upon the physical aspects of mankind. A government that is not concerned about the health and physical welfare of its subjects is not fit to be called a government. God's government will be concerned about the health of all the earth's people. This truth is epitomized for us in the simple declaration, "And the inhabitant shall not say, I am sick" (Isa. 33:24).

A very important revelation concerning this can be found in a declaration made by our Lord. The Pharisees had spoken blasphemy against His miracles. They said He performed them by the power of "Beelzebub the prince of the devils." In His answer to them, the Lord said in part: "But if I cast out devils by the Spirit of God, then the kingdom of God is come unto you" (Matt. 12:28).

Since we know and fully believe that He did cast out demons by the Spirit of God, can we do nothing else but believe that the kingdom of God had come to these blaspheming Pharisees? This creates numerous difficulties.

Not long after this, the Lord said to His disciples: "But I tell you of a truth, there be some standing here, which shall not taste of death, till they see the kingdom of God" (Luke 9:27). Then in connection with Joseph, the man who made the arrangements and provided a place for the burial of the Lord Jesus, we are told that he was one, "who also himself waited for the kingdom of God" (Luke 23:51).

The reader will quickly see the discrepancy in these three statements. If the kingdom of God had come to the Pharisees, how then could it be said to be coming before all the disciples had died; and why would Joseph still be waiting for it?

Critics have questioned my teaching that the kingdom of God will be a future condition of things upon this earth after God has assumed sovereignty. They have bombarded me with quotations of the passage in Matt. 12:28, in order to prove that His kingdom was a reality during the earthly ministry of Jesus Christ.

Whenever there are apparent discrepancies, or when a passage is to be used to build a doctrine or to refute a man's teaching, the translation should always be carefully checked to make sure one is standing on a solid foundation. Hundreds of Biblical discrepancies and misunderstandings have been created by inadequate or erroneous translations in the King James Version of the New Testament.

When a check is made of Matt. 12:28, the difficulty in rendering the original Greek is seen at once. This is apparent in the efforts of the translators to express it. Here are some examples:

"the kingdom of God has burst out above you." Fenton
"the kingdom of God has overtaken you." Goodspeed
"the kingdom of God is already upon you." Montgomery
"the reign of God has reached you already." Moffatt
"hath come upon you unawares the kingdom of God." Rotherham
"the kingdom of God outstrips in time to you." Concordant
"the kingdom of God has swept over you unawares." Phillips

A variety of renderings such as these indicates that the original must be checked before the careful student can come to any conclusion.

The translator's problem here is in the Greek word rendered "is come." This is *phthanō*, the exact form here being *ephthasen* (aorist). An interesting and illuminating occurrence of this word is found in 1 Thess. 4:15, where it is translated "prevent," which all students will recognize at once as an old English word that has changed its meaning. It comes from the Latin *prae* (before) and *venire* (to come). In the days when the K J V first made its appearance, *prevent* meant to go before, that is, precede. This occurrence, in the light of its context, gives us a good grip on the meaning of *phthanō*. It means "to move ahead of"; and a literal rendering of Matt. 12:28 would be, "the kingdom of God moves ahead to you." Although this may sound awkward, it becomes our task to get the meaning, not to rewrite it. I believe it means that the Pharisees and all who witnessed it had seen a preview of one aspect of the kingdom of God, or that they had a foretaste of it. An honest paraphrase of the Greek here would read: "But if I cast out demons by the Spirit of God, you have a foretaste of the kingdom of God."

By the process of logical deduction and projection, we have every right to believe that every beneficent miracle performed by the Lord Jesus was a foretaste of the kingdom of God. Further proof of this is found in Matthew 10:7, 8, where we find that when the Lord sent forth His twelve disciples to herald the nearness of the kingdom of the heavens (Matthew's name for the kingdom of God, see Issue No. 28), He commanded them in connection with this proclamation to, "heal the sick, cleanse the lepers, raise the dead, cast out devils." Each one of these acts was a foretaste of the kingdom, a preview of what could be expected from God in the day when He governs the earth.

Of course, any such "foretaste" could be a "savor of life or a savor of death." No man could witness or be the beneficiary of such a miracle without becoming responsible to God to act upon its evidence. This is what our Lord had reference to when He said: "If I had not come and spoken unto them, they had not had sin:

but now they have no cloke for their sin. If I had not done among them the works which none other man did, they had not had sin: but now have they both seen and hated both Me and My father" (John 15:22-24).

If we examine this particular miracle which brought forth the statement, "you have a foretaste of the kingdom of God," we find the following facts. Someone had "brought unto Him one possessed with a devil, blind, and dumb" (Matt. 12:22). Our Lord healed the man immediately and completely so that this demon-possessed, blind, deaf-mute both spake and saw. In this man's afflictions, we see some of the things that have come upon mankind because Adam sinned and brought sin and death into the world. Our Lord came to do the work that would remove this curse with all its effects, and here we have a preview of how this will be done. Wholly apart from any act of the demon-possessed man, the Lord made him whole. Thus it will be when the foretaste becomes "a feast of good things unto all people," when the preview becomes the reality.

Our Lord made the lame to walk, caused the blind to see, cleansed the lepers, gave hearing to the deaf, restored sanity to broken minds, caused the dumb to speak, cast out demons, healed the sick, restored severed members to the body, fed the hungry multitudes, yes, and even raised some who were dead. Each one of these was a foretaste of the kingdom.

The Bible reveals that God ushers in His kingdom by bringing blessings to all mankind. In the previews of the kingdom, we find such words as, "He healed all that were sick" (Matt. 8:16), "healing every sickness and disease among the people" (Matt. 9:35), "great multitudes followed Him and He healed them all" (Matt. 12:15). He made no exceptions or distinctions; and, thus, He provided a preview of the healing, health, and soundness that will be the immediate portion of all mankind when God assumes sovereignty. It is entirely fitting that God's long dispensation of grace should end with a public display of grace such as the world has never seen before.

The SEED and BREAD Bible-Study leaflets are published as often as time and means permit and are sent free to all names on THE WORD OF TRUTH MINISTRY mailing list. Send us your name. There will be no obligation, solicitation, or visitation. Additional copies of any issue available on request.   ISSUE NO. 67

SEED & BREAD

FOR THE SOWER   ISA. 55:10   FOR THE EATER

BRIEF BIBLICAL MESSAGES

FROM

THE WORD OF TRUTH MINISTRY

339 South Orange Drive, Los Angeles, Cal. 90036

Otis Q. Sellers, Bible Teacher

THE CHRISTIAN FAKERS

It may seem somewhat inelegant to use the word *Christian* to describe a certain class of fakers, but the words in this title state precisely what I have to say in this study. In all fields of endeavor, there are millions of fakers; and among these are the thousands who practice their deceptions under the cloak of Christianity. These delude themselves into thinking that since they profess to be Christians, they could not possibly be deceivers. Since they make much use of the name of Christ, they feel that this frees them from every taint of deception; especially so, since they are acclaimed by Biblically illiterate masses as being God's servants doing His work and His will. Thus, they deceive not only themselves; but they deceive others as well and are described in 2 Tim. 3:13 as displaying one of the prominent characteristics in the concluding days of God's present dispensation—"deceiving and being deceived."

Yet, there are many today who refuse to even think that there are present and prominent in professing Christian circles those who are fakers, even though the words of Christ tell of them. All who profess to follow Him should know that He spoke of this class of deceivers when He said: "Many shall come in My name, saying, I am Christ; and shall deceive many" (Matt. 24:5). In view of these words, how can anyone think that there are no such things as Christian fakers?

The full force of this warning has been obscured in this passage by an inadequate translation. It is a well-known fact that the Greek word *christos* means "anointed"; and even though it is translated "Christ" in all its 569 occurrences, we lose much truth in many passages by always translating it this way. In this passage it could be better rendered, "Many will come in My name, saying, I am the anointed one," thus claiming that they have been designated or appointed by God to perform some great service or function. Our Lord warned that there would be "many" of these, and that they would be well received since "they will deceive many" (Matt. 24:5).

Following this, our Lord declared: "For there shall arise false

Christs (*spurious anointed ones*), and false prophets, and shall shew great signs and wonders" (Matt. 24:24). If all believers in the Lord Jesus Christ would take Him at His word here, they would once and for all banish from their minds the popular superstition that anyone who can foretell future events, or those who can produce signs and wonders, are of necessity in close relationship with God. Let this truth be burned into our minds—that supernaturalism is never in itself an index of divine activity, since it is by means of the supernatural that evil forces gain their greatest victories.

We need to note carefully the words of Paul that tell us that the presence of the Antichrist is "after the working of Satan with all power and signs and lying wonders" (2 Thess. 2:9). It is imperative in these days for the true servants of God to warn all professing Christians of the danger of being deceived, not by that which is obviously evil, but by that which has all the outward appearances of good. Beware of the Christian fakers! They surround us on every side.

However, the words from Scripture which we have been considering are declarations that mostly have to do with a future time, the great tribulation (Matt. 24:21); and we need to examine those that have a more direct application to the time in which we now live. The words spoken by our Lord in Matt. 7:15-23 do have a direct application to the present time. It is a time immediately preceding the divine assumption of sovereignty, the advent of the kingdom of God upon the earth. He said: "Beware of false prophets, which come to you in sheep's clothing, but inwardly they are ravening wolves" (7:15).

Then, in the time of which Matt. 7:21 speaks, it is evident that the kingdom of God has become a reality upon earth, the judgment of all living men is in progress (2 Tim. 4:1), and many are pleading their cases before the Judge of all the earth. They speak on earth and are heard in heaven. He speaks in heaven and is heard upon the earth. They are seeking to be allowed to continue to live upon the earth where all the blessings of God's beneficent government are starting to be enjoyed.

Concerning them, our Lord said: "Many will say to Me in that day, Lord, Lord, have we not prophesied in Thy name? and in Thy name have cast out devils? and in Thy name done many wonderful works?" (Matt. 7:22). These people are so deceived by their own supernatural works that they dare to present them as evidence to God for the reason that they think they should find a place in His kingdom. Nevertheless, the Lord replies to them, "I never knew you: depart from Me, ye that work iniquity." In view of these words, the warning needs to be repeated, "Beware of false prophets, especially those who perform supernatural works!"

It is generally believed that a prophet is demonstrated to be false if his predictions fail to come true, but this is not the way it is presented to us in Scripture. There, if the prophecy comes to pass and he uses his apparent success to aggrandize himself and lead people away from the Lord, the fact is pure and simple, he is a faker. The venerable Moses said: "If there arise among you a prophet, or a dreamer of dreams, and giveth thee a sign or a wonder, and the sign or the wonder come to pass, whereof he spake unto thee, saying, Let us go after other gods, which thou hast not known, and let us serve them; Thou shalt not hearken unto the words of that prophet, or that dreamer of dreams: for the LORD your God proveth you, to know whether ye love the LORD your God with all your heart and with all your soul" (Deut. 13:1-3).

Could it not be that also in our day, God is testing our profession of love toward Him by proving us to see if we will hold fast His simple and explicit declaration of "One Mediator between God and men, the man Christ Jesus" (1 Tim. 2:5); or will we accept as mediators all great and small miracle workers that come along? Will we allow some self-styled prophetess, like Jeanne Dixon, to use her few successful predictions to lead us away from finding our all in Jesus Christ, and into the worship of sun, moon, and stars as little gods to stand between us and our great God, and to be the real controllers of our lives to which we must pay due homage before any movement we might make? She attempts to do this in her syndicated newspaper column on astrology. And since she brings into all this the name of Christ, she becomes a most pertinent example of Christian fakery.

Another outstanding example is found in the revelations of Marjoe Gortner, who now repudiates his hypocrisy. Exploited by his mother, he was ordained a minister at the age of four and performed a marriage ceremony one year later—an incident that created a wave of notoriety which he was able to ride for the next ten years. However, by the age of fifteen, the "adorable child" had become an awkard, unattractive adolescent whose career quickly went into eclipse. After a few obscure and lean years, he decided to try a comeback and enjoyed a measure of success on the holiness and pentecostal circuits. He carried with him grosses of bandannas stamped, "Marjoe's Miracle Handkerchief," which he sold at meetings for ten dollars each. He painted a cross on his forehead; and as he perspired, it would appear and disappear. Men and women adored him, fell at his feet, and showered him with money. All this is according to his own words.

Feeling the need of some new gimmick in his ministry, he worked hard to perfect his ability to make people faint, a hypnotic routine that had emerged in holiness circles and was claimed to be a manifestation of the power of God. This demonstration was one developed to perfection by the late Kathryn Kuhlman, the foremost practitioner of this (miracle?).

In a meeting in Detroit, Gortner asked everyone who did not feel the power of God within them to stand. Sixteen men and women stood up. He called them forward, lined them against a wall, and kept them standing there through a long sermon. In the sermon he declared that the wicked would stand fast in their sins, but the saved would yield. Following this preconditioning of mind and body, he jabbed his finger at them; and they fell to the floor like a row of dominoes. This was declared to be the power of God coming upon them, a visitation of the Holy Spirit.

This gimmick of making people faint is certainly one of the most crass bits of fakery practiced by the Christian fakers, especially when it is set forth as being a supernatural visitation of God. It has no basis in Scripture, and there is not one line in the Bible to support it. It is nothing whatsoever but religious hypnotism such as any practitioner of the art can easily duplicate. All the elements required for successful results by a hypnotist are present—the pre-conditioning by song and sermon, the willingness of the subject, and his anxiety for a successful outcome. A professional hypnotist, one well-known by his stage appearances, declares that in an hour or so, he can teach a bright fourteen-year-old boy the trick of making people faint.

"I do not know how I do it." This was the constantly repeated exclamation of Katherine Kuhlman as one of her subjects would fall backward to be lowered to the floor by the ever present "catcher." If she truly did not know, then she was very ignorant of hypnotic processes and the power of suggestion upon a preconditioned person. She was utterly blind to any fact that threatened the validity of her ministry.

The deception in this fainting routine was clearly revealed in a ninety-minute television program entitled, "Kathryn Kuhlman in Las Vegas," the only time one of her public services was recorded for later television showing. A middle-aged woman, who was supposedly smitten by the power of God, was lowered to the floor by the "catcher"; but in doing so, he clumsily pulled his arm over her head and caused her wig to slide forward until it completely covered her face. This brought her out from under the supposed power of God immediately. She tried to replace the wig without raising her head, but could not do so. Finally, she raised herself into a ridiculous squatting position and replaced the wig, but, lacking a mirror, got it on crooked. The sharp eye of the television camera revealed all of this, and it also revealed the fakery of the whole performance.

In this study it has been necessary to name names; but in doing so, it has not been my purpose to charge any individual with being a faker. My task has been to sound an alarm and to declare certain facts that I have seen, facts that I have heard, and facts that have been published. Uppermost of all, I have set forth certain facts written in the Word of God. The reader can now from these make his own judgments. Finally, I say, beware of Christian fakers!

The SEED and BREAD Bible-Study leaflets are published as often as time and means permit and are sent free to all names on THE WORD OF TRUTH MINISTRY mailing list. Send us your name. There will be no obligation, solicitation, or visitation. Additional copies of any issue available on request.   ISSUE NO. 68

SEED & BREAD

FOR THE SOWER   ISA. 55:10   FOR THE EATER

BRIEF BIBLICAL MESSAGES

FROM

THE WORD OF TRUTH MINISTRY

339 South Orange Drive, Los Angeles, Cal. 90036

Otis Q. Sellers, Bible Teacher

THE LOVE OF THE TRUTH

The Apostle John declared to the "wellbeloved Gaius" that he "rejoiced greatly, when the brethren came and testified of the TRUTH that is in thee, even as thou walkest in the TRUTH"; and he followed these words by a much stronger statement declaring, "I have no greater joy than to hear that my children walk in the TRUTH" (3 John 1:3, 4).

There can be no doubt but that these words express the mind of the Apostle John; nevertheless, we believe that John wrote by divine inspiration, saying only such things as God would have him say, so that in these words he was also expressing the very mind of God. Thus we have it, loud and clear, that God has no greater joy than to hear that His children walk in the TRUTH. Does the reader accept this? Does he believe it? Or has he accepted the popular idea that many other things bring greater joy to God than for the believer in Jesus Christ to walk in the TRUTH that He has given?

It is written and we believe that there is joy in heaven over one sinner that repents (Luke 15:7), but we must also believe that this is not God's greatest joy. He has declared otherwise, and it becomes faith on our part when we take Him at His Word and think and respond accordingly.

The words found in John's third epistle should be enough to establish the importance of TRUTH in God's sight, and the reader must admit that whatever is important to God should be just as important to him. Moreover there is something to be found in almost every book in the Bible that emphasizes the importance of TRUTH in the sight of God. We will consider several examples from the prophecy of Jeremiah.

When the small kingdom of Judah faced the threat of invasion from strong forces that would most certainly end in defeat and captivity, God spoke to Jeremiah saying: "Run ye to and fro through the streets of Jerusalem, and see now, and know, and seek in the broad places thereof, if ye can find a man, if there be any that executeth judgment, that seeketh the TRUTH; and I will pardon it" (Jer. 5:1).

Think upon this—one man seeking for the TRUTH would be sufficient cause for Jehovah to pardon the nation and preserve it from invasion and certain defeat. Here we learn, not only the importance of TRUTH, but also the importance of one man seeking it. He would be the one grain of salt that would preserve the nation. It seems tragic that there was no one man in Jerusalem who could step forward and say, "Lord, I am weak and insignificant, but all my life I have diligently sought for Thy TRUTH." But no such man existed in Jerusalem, a fact that causes us to wonder how many cities in the world could lead forth and present such a man today.

We live in a time when men have turned their ears from the TRUTH and turned them to fables (2 Tim. 4:3,4). They heap to themselves teachers who will tell them exactly what they want to hear. They are even as Jeremiah said of the men of Judah: "They bend their tongues like their bow for lies: but they are not valiant for the TRUTH upon the earth; for they proceed from evil to evil, and they know not Me, saith the LORD" (Jer. 9:3).

The total absence of men in Jerusalem who sought after the TRUTH caused Jeremiah to cry out in anguish: "O LORD, are not Thine eyes upon the TRUTH" (Jer. 5:3). To this there can be only one answer—the eyes of God are most certainly upon the TRUTH. He wants to see what men are doing with it, how they are treating it, and what it means to them. "His eyes behold, His eyelids try, the children of men" (Psa. 11:4). What pleasure then can it bring to God when singers repeat over and over the same lie that some Biblically illiterate composer has incorporated into some song—one sung not because it expresses any Biblical TRUTH, but because it has become popular with the masses. Can God find joy in their saying they "came to the garden alone," and claiming that while there, God walked with them, and talked with them, and told them they were His own, as one popular song declares? They know and I know that this never happened; but since they put sentiment and wishful thinking above the TRUTH, they sing this over and over again.

What has already been said brings us face-to-face with the most famous question ever asked, that which Pilate asked of the Lord Jesus Christ, "What is TRUTH?" It is hardly possible to read his question without detecting the note of weariness and skepticism of one who had persuaded himself that there is no such thing as TRUTH. He did not wait for an answer. He broke off the conversation with his question and turned away.

At that moment, TRUTH was very near to him, literally, standing in front of him. If he had waited for an answer, he might have found it. If he had asked as an honest inquirer, as a lover of TRUTH, our Lord might have repeated in his presence the very words He had spoken to His disciples a few hours before—"I am the TRUTH" (John 14:6). Before him was the very embodiment of TRUTH; before him was TRUTH personified. To lay hold of Him was to lay hold of the TRUTH.

"But," someone is sure to ask "is it reasonable to expect that when He becomes our Lord and Savior, the TRUTH is in our possession?" Yes, this is reasonable and also possible; for when we lay hold of Him, we lay hold of the fountain of all TRUTH. We are then connected with the Source, and TRUTH can flow unto us.

But will we, if we receive Him, have all knowledge, the answers to all questions, solutions for every problem? Are we then ready to serve Him in TRUTH with all our heart? The answer is no, for this One Who is the TRUTH must be apprehended by us. He must be "put on" (Rom. 13:14). And as we discover Him, as we learn what God's Word has to say concerning Him, we will be discovering and learning the TRUTH—"taught by Him even as the TRUTH is in Jesus" (Eph. 4:21). In Him, we will find, in God's due time, the answer to every question, the solution of every problem.

And yet, this forces upon us the question, how is this to be? What is the secret of "putting on the Lord Jesus Christ"? The answer to this is found in another statement. The One Who said, "I am the TRUTH," also said, "Thy Word is TRUTH." We need to face up to this declaration, for the Word we know is the TRUTH we know.

It is evident that many who make constant use of the word *truth* need to look it up in the dictionary. They seem to have no definition of it. Their only concept of *truth* is one of telling it or not telling it as they speak of the affairs of life. *Truth,* to them, has no bearing on the things of God and no relationship to Him. "It makes no difference what one believes as long as he is sincere" is their philosophy. The fact that God has spoken means nothing to them, and they care not what He has said. They have no love for the TRUTH.

The basic definition of truth is: that which accords with the facts in the case. This definition is so simple and honest that it is apt to be ignored. It needs to be fixed in our minds. As an illustration, I was born in a certain year, a fact that cannot be changed and one that is fixed by government records. If I should say that I am younger than I am, my statement would not accord with the facts and it would not be the truth.

God's TRUTH is established by the facts recorded in the Word of God. "Thy Word is TRUTH," said our Lord. "To the law and to the testimony: if they speak not according to this Word, it is because there is no light in them." These were the words of Isaiah (8:20) in regard to this.

Every direct statement in the Bible sets forth a positive fact concerning the subject of the declaration. It is our duty to discover these facts by diligent study. We must take the individual words, phrases, and sentences, draw out of them their precise meaning, and apply them only after we have established of whom or what they were spoken, at what time, to what intent, and have given full consideration to the context in which they are found. This is "rightly dividing the Word of Truth" (2 Tim. 2:15), and anyone who suggests that "right division" is of no importance has no love for the TRUTH and stamps himself as an unworthy interpreter.

Consider, for example, the Biblical facts concerning death. In its first occurrence, it is presented to us as being a divine penalty for certain sins. It is declared to be an enemy, and one that shall in due time be destroyed (abolished). In view of these facts, when we hear anyone speak of death as a friend, when they make it to be an angel that leads us into the presence of God, they are not speaking the TRUTH. What they say does not accord with God's simple facts.

In his second letter to the Thessalonians, Paul speaks of those who "received not the love of the TRUTH, that they might be saved" (2 Thess. 2:10). From this we know that the love of the TRUTH is a gift from God, a disposition wrought in man by the Spirit of God. It is an act of His grace that can be received or rejected. God will not force a love for His TRUTH upon anyone.

The Psalmist prayed, "Create in me a clean heart, O God," a prayer that we all need to utter today. And since we know that God has no greater joy than to hear that His children walk in the TRUTH, it would also be appropriate for all believers in the Lord Jesus Christ to pray along these lines:

"Create within me, O God, a pure love for Thy TRUTH. Indeed, Thou art a God of TRUTH; and You desire TRUTH in our inward parts. Give me the wisdom and courage to choose the way of TRUTH, even in the day when so few plead for the TRUTH, when TRUTH has fallen in the street, yea, when TRUTH faileth. Do this for me that I may serve You in sincerity and in TRUTH." (See Deu. 32:4; Psa. 51:6; Psa. 119:30; Isa. 59:4, 14, 15; Josh. 24:14).

As a young believer, I prayed after this manner many, many times. I had the Savior; with Him I was satisfied, and I loved to serve Him. But I lacked a real love for His Word which is His TRUTH. MY PRAYER WAS ANSWERED. Today, I ask only one question in regard to anything in the realm of divine matters—"Is it the TRUTH?" If it is, I will believe it; I will embrace it; I will proclaim it; and I will accept all the consequences that come from following such a course. I will recognize no other authority but the One Who is the TRUTH, the Lord Jesus Christ; and that which is the TRUTH, the written Word. These are my standards in regard to all I say or do.

The SEED and BREAD Bible-Study leaflets are published as often as time and means permit and are sent free to all names on THE WORD OF TRUTH MINISTRY mailing list. Send us your name. There will be no obligation, solicitation, or visitation. Additional copies of any issue available on request.   ISSUE NO. 69

SEED & BREAD

FOR THE SOWER   ISA. 55:10   FOR THE EATER

BRIEF BIBLICAL MESSAGES

FROM

THE WORD OF TRUTH MINISTRY

339 South Orange Drive, Los Angeles, Cal. 90036

Otis Q. Sellers, Bible Teacher

GOD'S EARTH

It is written in the opening declaration of Scripture that: "In the beginning God created the heaven and the earth" (Gen. 1:1). Without argument, there is room here for some diversity of opinions as to what is indicated by the word "heaven"; so for the sake of this study, I am going to say that it must mean the most important "heaven" in the universe, that place where God has prepared the throne (seat) of His government (Psa. 103:19), the place where Elijah was taken (2 Kgs. 2:11), the place to which the Lord Jesus ascended and where He is now seated (Mark 16:19, Heb. 9:24). In regard to what is meant by "the earth," there can be no diverse opinions. It means the planet upon which we now live and make our home.

Thus, the Bible declares that in the beginning, God created two places, one called "heaven" and the other called "earth." So we have before us the perfect Workman and His perfect works, for we cannot conceive of God doing anything that is imperfect or incomplete. All His works praise Him. When these two creations came from His hand, they were perfect in every detail, creations worthy of their Creator. One was as perfect and beautiful as the other. They satisfied Him; and if He had spoken concerning them, He would have pronounced them good.

If in the beginning, God had exhibited both of these places to man and permitted him to make a choice of the one on which he would live his life, he could not have made the decision. He would have had to acknowledge that both were so wonderful, beautiful, and glorious that he could not choose between them. In the end he would have appealed to God to make the choice for him. As we look upon the earth today, this is hard to believe; but if the reader will carefully consider it, he will know that this is true.

Considering the present condition of the physical earth, we see much that is glorious and beautiful. Men will travel many miles just to gaze upon earthly scenes. And yet, the greater part of its land mass is totally unfit as a proper dwelling place for man. Its climate is such that in places, it is unbearably hot; while in other parts, it is bitterly cold. One only needs mention such places as Antarctica, the Amazon jungles, Siberia, and the Sahara, where life is either impossible or so difficult that only a few people live in these vast areas. Man naturally seeks out the most favorable places; but this, along with an ever-increasing population, has caused such over-crowding that in these, the struggle for existence is most difficult.

If we consider the earth from the moral standpoint of its human inhabitants, we are forced to admit that it is not a suitable place for peaceful, honest, moral, and industrious men to live. In the past few decades alone, it has become characterized and overrun by terrorists and murderers, by fierce and cruel men, by selfish men and money lovers, by slanderers and calumniators, by evil men and seducers who constantly wax worse and worse, by lovers of pleasure, by blasphemers, by alcoholics, by sex perverts, by rapists and sodomites.

Every child that is born upon this earth is brought forth into a system that is characterized by sin and iniquity, and no one is able to say in advance how he will be affected by this environment. Evil forces will work upon him to shape his life; and he must ever struggle against a flood of false principles, teachings, opinions, practices, customs, and purposes that make up the atmosphere which he will inhale almost every moment of his life. This is not the way it should be, but it is a reality to be faced and nothing is to be gained by denying it.

Present conditions upon the earth, both physical and moral, have come about from many factors, the greatest one being the adverse judgment (curse) that came upon both mankind and the earth when Adam transgressed. His disobedience opened the door and permitted the principle of sin to enter into the world. Then death entered through sin; and death passed through to all mankind, so that all members of the human race are mortal (Rom. 5:12); that is, death is working in us and we are dying. We are not born sin-ners; but we are born mortal; and the death process that ever works in us will respond to the sin that is in the world, even as the strings of a piano or harp will vibrate in harmony when one or the other is played in the same room.

Certain additions to this adverse judgment were made after the flood of Noah's day, and a further addition came after the tower of Babel. All this has been further complicated by man's inability to govern, by his determination to exclude God from his thoughts, by the fools who make a mock of sin, by man's determination to walk after his own ways, and by the tolerance of God that permits him to do so for a time (Acts 14:16).

When the incarnation, death, resurrection, and ascension of Jesus Christ, the Savior of the world, became accomplished facts, everything was done that needed to be done in order to reverse and remove all these adverse judgments or curses from the earth, even the removal of the curse of Adamic sin and death from the world. Indeed, He is the Lamb of God that taketh away the sin of the world (John 1:29). And even though all this has been long delayed while God accomplishes His present purpose in grace (See Issue

No. 64), it will become a blessed reality in that day when God speaks in heaven, assumes sovereignty, and divine government becomes a fact in the earth.

There is nothing too hard for our God (Gen. 18:14). There is nothing wrong with this earth that God cannot make right. There is nothing bad that He cannot replace with good. He can bring this earth back to the condition it was in at the end of His six days of creative work: "And God saw everything that He had made, and, behold, it was very good" (Gen. 1:31). And when He does all this, there will be no place in the universe where it is better for man to live and serve than this planet, God's earth.

The first astronauts who journeyed to the moon furnished mankind with some of the most amazing photographs ever taken. These now permit us to see the whole sphere in one glance. As we gaze upon these beautiful pictures, we are able to borrow words from Scripture and say, "O, earth, glorious things of thee are spoken." And we could say this on the authority of God's Word; for concerning this earth, God has spoken and its future is glorious.

For many centuries men have been guilty of discounting or ignoring every declaration that God has made as to the glorious future of the earth. It seems they have been afraid to declare what God has said for fear that men might be attracted to the earth and lose interest in the traditional heaven of hymnology. To them, this planet has no future but to be burned up. In fact, this is a vital principle in one great theological system. It teaches that the time will come when this planet will have ceased to exist, and all mankind will be either in heaven or hell.

It is true that many devout students of the Word have lost all interest in heaven as being their future home once they have learned the glories of the redeemed earth. As Patrick Fairbairn said more than a century ago: "Why may not, why should not, that which has become for man, as fallen, the house of bondage and the field of ruin, become also for man the habitation of peace and the region of pre-eminent delight . . . and were I left to choose, out of all creation's bounds, the place where my redeemed nature is to find its local habitation, enjoy its Redeemer's presence, and reap the fruits of His costly purchase, I would prefer none to this." (*The Typology of Scripture*, page 411.)

The objective study of the Word of God is sure to bring the conviction that all of God's purposes in relationship to man are in some way related to the earth. All the glorious promises of the Bible have the earth as their subject. The earth has a glorious future, and in its future we will have a part.

The first stage of earth's glory will begin when God assumes sovereignty, takes to Himself His great power, and governs this planet and all who are upon it. And since heaven is His throne and the earth is His footstool, we can rest assured that His government will be from the throne and not from the footstool. The redemption, restoration, and renewal of the earth is not in any way related to Jesus Christ coming back again. It is not preceded by the great tribulation; and it is not introduced by Armageddon, as so many dispensers of the gospel of fear and frightfulness would have us believe. It could begin at any moment. There is no event that precedes it.

If God should decree it today and His government should begin; if the constantly repeated prayer, "Thy kingdom come," should suddenly be answered, it would result in the most blessed and startling events on every hand. Jesus Christ would immediately be unveiled to the world. It would know the One Who has become King of the earth. The *apokalupsin*[1] (unveiling) would become a glorious reality (1 Cor. 1:7). The glory of Jesus Christ would thus blaze forth, making His promised *epiphaneia*[2] to be a fact of history (Titus 2:13). The whole earth would be filled with the knowledge of the glory of the Lord (Isa. 11:9). Jesus Christ would be manifested[3], and we would be manifested[3] with Him (Col. 3:4). The world would know Who Jesus Christ is and what He is in God's sight, and the world would know the glory of the believer in God's sight. The redemption and restoration of Israel would begin and quickly become a miraculous reality.

Under God's government, the curse of Adamic death and all the ills that flow out of it would immediately be lifted from the earth. Life would work in men instead of death; and the death processes would at once be stopped, even in the most advanced cases. Death would then come upon men because of their personal sins, never again because Adam sinned (Jer. 31:29, 30).

Under God's government, the curse that now rests upon the physical earth will be removed. The creation is to be delivered from the bondage of corruption (Rom. 8:21, 22). The earth will become an ideal place for men to live and work. Every acre of it will become habitable and fruitful. As long as men give due reverence to God, every part of the earth will receive the sun and rain that it requires, at the time it is needed. It will be an ideal place for family life. All marital unions will be the result of God joining two people together, an ideal situation for rearing children.

When one has discovered all this from the Word of God, it is bound to create a desire to see it, to experience it, to be a part of it. It has for me. This earth is my home, the only home I have ever known. If death should overtake me before God assumes sovereignty, I will be buried in it. But when God has made His judgment of me, I will come forth from it to take my place and stand in my lot upon God's earth. Will I see you then and here?

[1]*Apokalupsin*, "unveiling" is translated "coming" in KJV, 1 Cor. 1:7.
[2]*Epiphaneia*, "blazing forth" is translated "appearing" in KJV, Titus 2:13.
[3]*Phainō*, "be manifested" is translated "appear" in KJV, Col. 3:4.

The SEED and BREAD Bible-Study leaflets are published as often as time and means permit and are sent free to all names on THE WORD OF TRUTH MINISTRY mailing list. Send us your name. There will be no obligation, solicitation, or visitation. Additional copies of any issue available on request.   ISSUE NO. **70**

SEED & BREAD

FOR THE SOWER   ISA. 55:10   FOR THE EATER

BRIEF BIBLICAL MESSAGES
FROM
THE WORD OF TRUTH MINISTRY
339 South Orange Drive, Los Angeles, Cal. 90036

Otis Q. Sellers, Bible Teacher

EARTH'S GLORIOUS FUTURE

In considering the Biblical doctrine of the future of the earth, we must not limit our thoughts to the planet itself. We must include in our thinking the world, and mankind as living in the world and upon the earth. These three are so intertwined, that while we need to make clear distinctions between them, we must keep them locked together when we speak of the future of any one of them. This principle is clearly seen in the great declaration of Psalm 24:1: "The earth is the LORD'S, and the fulness thereof; the world, and they that dwell therein."

We will need to keep in mind that the earth is the planet; the world is the order, system, ecology, or environment that is upon it; and mankind is the inhabitant to whom this earth has been given (Psa. 115:16) and for whom the world was made. There would be no world apart from the planet, and the world is essential to man's well-being. The destruction of either the earth or the world would mean the end of mankind. This is why so many have become highly exercised, and rightly so, about the pollution of the environment in which we live.

There is at present great anxiety among men concerning the future of the earth, the world, and mankind. Predictions are being made that the earth will in time become a lifeless planet, that the world will be destroyed by man himself, while others are assuming that it will be destroyed by God. But this will never be; for we can say with certainty that, concerning the earth, the world, and mankind, God has spoken; and their future is glorious.

The truth of this can be epitomized in the fact that this planet is set forth as being the future location of "the holy city, new Jerusalem," the place of God's future tabernacle (center of activity), and as the place where He will dwell with men (Rev. 21:2, 3). The day is coming when men will no longer say, "Our Father, which art in heaven"; for the center of all God's activities will be upon the earth; and it will become the mediatorial planet of the universe. However, all this is far in the future, in that time period called "the new heaven and new earth," the most important thing made new, so far as mankind is concerned, being the earth itself.

The final state of things, "the new heaven and new earth," is something so inconceivable that it cannot be described to us; and God makes no attempt to do so. There are no terms of present experience that can be used to portray it. We know that it will be a reality and that it will be glorious, and in this our faith rests. However, before that state is reached, there will be two preceding states of glory for this earth, first under God's government and then under the thousand years of the personal presence of Christ. The sad and extreme error of Bible students during the past 175 years has been to eliminate altogether the pre-advent kingdom of God and to make the next state of things to be the advanced conditions that will be the rule during His personal presence. In so doing, they have eliminated one glorious segment of earth's future, dumping everything that pertains to it into the millennium.

In the theology that came out of the reformation, this planet and its world were given no future. Martin Luther was loathe indeed to take up the subject of eschatology and steadfastly refused to give any consideration to the Biblical message of future events. Thus, the Protestant movement was handed a garbled mess of Roman Catholic tradition, with very little modification as to what the future of the earth would be. John Calvin, who assembled into one body of doctrine the scattered opinions of the reformation period, avoided coming to grips with the great eschatological problems of the Scriptures. Thus, the reformers did very little but generalize about the future and left the Protestant world an almost childish version of things to come.

In the reformation theology, the earth, the world, the nations, and Israel simply have no future. All the Biblical promises to them are considered to mean nothing, most of these being explained as speaking of "the church" in heaven. As to the future, this theology holds that there is to come a great day of judgment. This is equated with and said to fulfill all declarations in regard to the second coming of Christ. At this, all mankind, past and present, are to be personally assembled and divided into two companies, the righteous and the wicked. The righteous are then given a permanent dwelling place in heaven and the wicked either sent to or returned to a place called hell, where they are to be tormented forever. Then the earth and all that pertains to it are to be destroyed.

The translators of the *King James Version* were rigid followers of the reformation theology. This explains why a simple Greek phrase such as *suntelias tou aiōnos* (the consummation of the eon) was translated "the end of the world" (Matt. 24:3). They were translating their crude concept of the future of the world into the Word of God, and now many readers of this version suffer the consequences of this corruption of Biblical truth.

Even the casual Bible reader should be able to see the conflict and contradiction between "the end of the world" and the words of Jesus Christ: "God sent not His Son into the world to condemn the world; but that the world through Him might be saved" (John 3:17), also, "I came not to judge the world, but to save the world"

(John 12:47). Furthermore, we have the inspired words of John: "The Father sent the Son to be the Savior of the world" (1 John 4:14).

In view of these statements, we can declare upon the authority of God's Word that this world is savable and that it is going to be rescued, delivered, and made safe from all that afflicts it. "The world also shall be established that it shall not be moved" (Psa. 96:10). And even though a multitude of prophets of doom, both secular and religious, are now armed with scientific opinions and economic tables that declare its early demise, this world is not going to end, neither at the hands of men nor the hand of God. It is going to be rescued and delivered by He Who is "the Savior of the world" (John 4:42), even the Lord Christ Jesus.

In addition to this, it needs to be declared that it is not the message of the Bible that this planet's deliverance from the bondage of corruption (Rom. 8:21, 22) and the salvation of the world come only after God has torn the world and its inhabitants to pieces by internecine warfare, nuclear holocausts, and the imagined revival of a ten-nation Roman Empire. All this is dramatically asserted by Hal Lindsey and his sensational ghost writer Carol Carlson in their book *The Late Great Planet Earth*. This has had an enormous sale due to its exploitation of man's present anxieties. Now that it is to be made into a movie, its claim that the Bible sets forth certain signs that are now present and which "herald man's doomsday" will become more and more the popular delusion of the Biblically illiterate masses.

Permit me, as an assiduous Bible student for fifty-seven years, to say that God's Book does not set forth any signs which herald man's doomsday, the end of the world, or the extinction of mankind. Furthermore, that which is heralded as "the most important sign of all"—the Jew returning to the land of Israel—is an event of no present significance whatsoever. In every prophecy of Israel's return and restoration, without exception, the return is a divine miracle wrought by God alone and one that results in immediate, unparalleled blessings for Israel, for the world, and for mankind. See Eze. 11:16-21; 20:33-44; 28:25, 26; 34:11-31; and 37:19-28 for a sample of the actual prophecies of Israel's restoration and the results that follow. The present return of certain Jews to Palestine does not fulfill any prophecy in the Word of God. If any think otherwise, let them point out which one does so.

This earth has a glorious future, and its glory could begin before this day is over. The salvation of the world could become a reality within the hour. There is not one thing more that God needs to do but decree it. There is no prophecy that needs to be fulfilled in advance of God's assumption of sovereignty. Every prophecy and promise in the Scripture that is yet unfulfilled will have its final and definitive fulfillment either in (1) the kingdom of God, (2) the great testing, (3) the thousand year parousia of Jesus Christ, (4) the little season, or (5) the new heaven and new earth (see Issue No. 23).

The prophesied glorious future of the earth will come about (1) under God's government, (2) under the personal presence of Christ, (3) in the new heavens and new earth. Inasmuch as its next state is under God's government, we will look briefly at the earth after Jesus Christ takes to Himself His great power and is governing the earth and all men upon it.

Should God assume sovereignty among the nations today, by tomorrow His spokesmen (whom He would commission) would be proclaiming among the nations that Jehovah has become King, that He has readjusted the world, that it cannot be altered or shaken, and that He will dispense judgment unto the peoples with equity. This is the message of Psalm 96:10.

As the Lord judges among the nations and enlightens the people, they shall beat their swords into plowshares and their spears into pruning hooks; nation shall not lift up sword against nation; neither shall they learn war any more. This is the message of Isa. 2:4.

Under God's government, great and beneficent physical changes will occur in the earth in harmony with man's needs and progress. The Lord will open rivers in high places and fountains in the midst of valleys. He will make the wilderness a pool of water and dry lands springs of water. Great amounts of arable land will be added to the earth's surface when the Lord does such things as "utterly destroying the tongue of the Egyptian sea." Isa. 41:18 and 11:15 give testimony to this.

When God governs, the earth will be filled with the knowledge of the glory of the Lord as the waters cover the sea. This is the result of the glory of the Lord having been revealed and all flesh having seen it in the same amount and at the same time. Because of this, none shall hurt or destroy in all God's holy government. This is revealed in Isa. 11:9 and 40:5.

In that time there will be multitudes upon the earth who have experienced death, have been in the state of death, and have come out of it through resurrection. Each one of these will be like a page or chapter in an encyclopedia that can be turned to for information on any part of history which they experienced. Old friendships will be renewed, and fellowships that were broken in death can be restored. Numerous writers give witness to this. (See Job 14:14, 15; Ezekiel 37:5, 6; Daniel 12:2; Luke 11:31, 32; Luke 20:37; John 11:25.)

Truly, "Eye hath not seen, nor ear heard, neither have entered into the heart of man, the things which God hath prepared for them that love Him" (1 Cor. 2:9). A work of God's Spirit is required for one to appreciate earth's glorious future.

The SEED and BREAD Bible-Study leaflets are published as often as time and means permit and are sent free to all names on THE WORD OF TRUTH MINISTRY mailing list. Send us your name. There will be no obligation, solicitation, or visitation. Additional copies of any issue available on request.   ISSUE NO. 71

SEED & BREAD

FOR THE SOWER   ISA. 55:10   FOR THE EATER

BRIEF BIBLICAL MESSAGES
FROM
THE WORD OF TRUTH MINISTRY
339 South Orange Drive, Los Angeles, Cal. 90036

Otis Q. Sellers, Bible Teacher

THE SALVATION OF THE WORLD

"This is my Father's world." Thus spoke the poet, and his words are in complete harmony with those of the Psalmist who declares that God has said, "the world is Mine, and the fullness thereof" (Psa. 50:12). He is its Founder; He is its Maker; and He so loved it that He put His only Son into it, thus creating the arrangement that whosoever in the world believes in Him should not perish but have eternal life (John 3:16, John 1:10). In these truths we can rest and proclaim with confidence that He will never allow His world to slip out of His hand. It will never come to an end, nor will it ever be destroyed.

In a previous study (Issue No. 71), it was declared that the world is the arrangement, order, system, ecology, or environment that is upon the earth. In fact, it is the sum total of everything that constitutes an orderly and proper habitation for man. It includes all that is essential to man's well-being.

Since the word *kosmos* basically means order, system, or arrangement, it is possible to use it of other systems, great and small. We know from the Bible that man has created many worlds which at present we must use and in which we are forced to live (1 Cor. 7:31), although some of these we must hate and shun. However, these will not be dealt with in this study, as our present task is to consider the salvation of the world that God made and loves.

In the theologies of Christendom, there is no place for the salvation of the world. Even believing men can see no further than the salvation of individuals. Some are able to see the salvation of Israel, as Paul so emphatically declares in Romans 11:26; but even this is usually limited to the redemption of a number of Israelites, a remnant that will later be established as a nation. Thus, they deny what they affirm and do not really believe that, "All Israel shall be saved."

It is to be carefully noted here that Paul does not say "all Israelites," since it is a fact that the salvation of Israel will be accomplished by the elimination altogether of some Israelites. Ezekiel declares this when speaking of the regathering and deliverance of Israel: "And I will purge out from among you the rebels, and them that transgress against Me: I will bring them forth out of the country where they sojourn, and they shall not enter into the land of Israel: and ye shall know that I am the LORD" (Ezek. 20:38).

From what has been said above, let no one think or suggest that I believe in some future universal salvation of every Israelite that ever descended from Jacob. I am sure that restored Israel will be a far better nation if such men as Ahab (1 Kgs. 16:33) and Judas Iscariot are forever eliminated from among the people. And it will be a far better nation when such men as Abraham, Isaac, and Jacob are again a part of it (Matt. 8:11).

While the salvation of the world may have no place in the theology of Christendom, it does have a prominent place in the Word of God. One of the most important declarations in regard to this is found in John's Gospel: "For God sent not His Son into the world to condemn the world; but that the world through Him might be saved" (3:17). This glorious promise has been stultified in the *Scofield Reference Bible* by a marginal note that says *kosmos* here equals "mankind," a note that was wisely deleted by the Editors of the *New Scofield Reference Bible*. Later, our Lord declared: "I came not to judge the world, but to save the world" (John 12:47). And as if to epitomize this great truth in one statement, the Apostle John declared: "The Father sent (Gk. *apostellō* — commissioned) the Son to be the Savior of the world" (1 John 4:14).

The passages cited in the paragraph above are simple and plain statements of truth, and they should not be nullified by erroneous interpretations. In fact, they are so direct that certain enemies of Christ are now using them to argue that both Jesus and John were deceivers who, if followed, would lead men astray by false promises. They point to the world nineteen hundred years after these declarations were made; and there is nothing to indicate that it has been saved, or that it is being saved from the bondage of sin, corruption, and pollution that strangles it more and more each passing day. Of course, these Christ rejectors know nothing at all about the present parenthetical dispensation of the grace of God, a period of time during which God is writing into the history of His long dealings with mankind a record of the grace that is inherent in His character. This record will be a precious deposit that God will place in the world after He does His great work of salvation.

The flippant will say, "There is nothing wrong with the world; it is the people in it." But this is false. There is something wrong with the world, yes, something very seriously wrong with the system or order into which everyone is born and in which all of us must live. Malignancies have insinuated themselves into every part of the environment which is man's home.

The world today is desperately ill—so seriously ill that many wonder if it can be saved. The putrid eruptions that are seen in every land are only the tip of the iceberg. "The dark places of the earth are full of the habitations of cruelty" (Psa. 74:20). Men do what they can to alleviate these openly festering spots, at times achieving some small degree of success; but they soon break forth again in a more virulent form in the same or another place. Thus, the world that God made as a proper habitation for man becomes increasingly inhospitable to all who live in it. A malignancy is rampant in the world, from which the world needs to be saved.

As stated before, the average Christian today knows nothing about the salvation of the world. It is no part of his thinking, and it forms no part of his hope. And since with so many, nothing is true except what they already know and believe, they quickly deny and repudiate all Biblical declarations concerning the salvation of the world. No matter how much Biblical evidence may be marshaled in support of this great truth, they steadfastly refuse to add to their faith this knowledge.

That the Greek word *kosmos* has to do with order, arrangement, and system is a fact that is well-known to all students and one to which all lexicons will give witness. Nevertheless, by its usage in the New Testament, it is evident that in its most exalted meaning, it has to do with an order, system, and arrangement which is what it is because it was so determined by a Master Mind, a Peerless Arranger, a Supreme Architect. This is called "creation's order" in Rom. 1:20 (from the Gk. *apo ktiseōs kosmou*), and this is the world of which I am speaking when I proclaim the salvation of the world.

From the Bible we know that it was an ideal system or environment which God provided for man, even before his creation. "And God saw that it was good," is the fourfold repeated statement that God made before He created the first member of the human race. Man was expected to utilize and enjoy the world that God had made for him. However, certain things went wrong, and they have grown progressively worse mostly because man has chosen it to be this way.

The most revealing statement concerning what happened to God's world is found in Romans 5:12: "Wherefore, even as through one man the sin entered into the world, and through the sin the death, even so the death passed through into all mankind, on which all sinned" (TRV). Thus, if we believe God, it was by one man (Adam) that the principle of sin (singular) entered into the world and became then, and still is, the origin of all the acts that are classified as sins (plural). Sin is the root and sins are the fruit. For example, murder is not sin; it is one of the sins that has its source in the sin that came in through Adam. I make this statement at the risk of being misquoted and misunderstood.

The fact of sin in the world is a fact to be faced and reckoned with. Sin is a prime mover that results in many motions, all of which are sins. When sin entered the world, it opened the door to death; and now sin is transmitted through death. We are not born sinners, but we are born dying; that is, death is working in every member of the Adamic race and it produces all the illnesses, diseases, and infirmities that exist among men today.

If the world is to be saved, if it is to be rescued, delivered, and made safe as a proper habitation for mankind, then sin as a principle will have to be removed from it. However, this is a definite part of God's overall plan of redemption, even as John the Baptist boldly announced: "Behold the Lamb of God, which taketh away the sin of the world" (John 1:29).

In this passage the word "world" should not be stultified by making it to mean mankind or some out of mankind who receive Christ, nor should it be made to mean every member of the human race. This passage has nothing to do with the sins of men, and it is not to be equated with Rom. 5:8 or 1 Cor. 15:3—passages which do have to do with your sins and my sins.

Jesus Christ in His death has done all that is necessary to remove the principle of sin from the world. One man, Adam, did all that was necessary to bring sin and death into the world; and another man, the God-man Christ Jesus has done everything that is necessary to get it out. This removal has long been delayed, but it is sure and certain. When that moment comes in God's time-table for the removal of sin, it will be done; and this will also mean the removal of Adamic death and all the ills that flow out of it.

The removal of the companion principles of sin and death from the world does not mean that none will ever sin again or that none will ever die. But it does mean that never again can any man be a "federal head" who, by some act of his, brings the principle of sin back into the world, or that death or mortality can be transmitted from generation to generation. It will then be in the world even as Jeremiah has declared it will be in Israel. (See Jeremiah 31:29, 30.)

The salvation of the world is one great segment of the work of God that will result in the kingdom of God becoming a reality upon the earth. God's government is to function in a world that He has rescued, delivered, and made safe. He will save the world first, and then He will judge the world in righteousness by that One Whom He has ordained, even Christ Jesus.

The SEED and BREAD Bible-Study leaflets are published as often as time and means permit and are sent free to all names on THE WORD OF TRUTH MINISTRY mailing list. Send us your name. There will be no obligation, solicitation, or visitation. Additional copies of any issue available on request. ISSUE NO. 72

SEED & BREAD

FOR THE SOWER   ISA. 55:10   FOR THE EATER

BRIEF BIBLICAL MESSAGES
FROM
THE WORD OF TRUTH MINISTRY

339 South Orange Drive, Los Angeles, Cal. 90036

Otis Q. Sellers, Bible Teacher

INHERITING THE EARTH

"For evildoers shall be cut off: but they that wait upon the LORD, they shall inherit the earth" (Psalm 37:9).

The passage quoted above is the first direct statement in the Bible that speaks of the future portion and blessing of those who wait upon the Lord. Its importance demands careful consideration. The first important word in it is "wait." This is a flexible word that can have numerous shades of meaning. It is the Hebrew word *qavah,* which, when considered in all its occurrences, shows that it means to wait, to expect, to look for—but all the time serving according to God's directives while these actions are taking place. Isaiah 26:8 gives us a good example of this extended meaning: "Yea, in the way of Thy judgments, O LORD, have we waited for Thee." Therefore, no one is truly waiting on the Lord unless he is doing what God has said he should do.

It hardly needs to be pointed out that what God expected the Israelite to do while he waited is quite different from what God expects of you and me while we wait upon Him. In relationship to the present dispensation of God's grace, it is His revealed and declared judgment that there is a supreme work that we should do. This was made known when certain ones asked Him, "What shall we do that we might work the works of God?" (John 6:28). His explicit answer to them was "This is the work of God, that ye believe on Him Whom He hath sent" (John 6:29). And there is no later word spoken by our Lord or written by His apostles that changes this in the least.

It is also the revealed and declared judgment of God that one book in the Bible was written so that men might "believe that Jesus is the Christ, the Son of God; and that believing ye might have life through His name" (John 20:31). Then in God's final revelation He gave for our instruction, we are told to "Proclaim the Word, to keep at it in season and out of season, make the facts known, rebuke, and entreat with all patience and teaching" (2 Tim. 4:2, TRV).

So, while we wait upon the Lord, we will give great diligence and thought, above all things, to be believers in the Lord Jesus Christ, to the assiduous study of every word that the Gospel of John reveals concerning Him, and to the faithful proclamation of His Word. All this is a part of our waiting on the Lord.

The next word that demands consideration is "inherit," a word used many times in connection with the promises of God. It should be noted that in order to inherit, one must be given the place of an heir; and he must in due time receive a portion which becomes his as an allotment to enjoy. Thus, in every occurrence of the word "inherit," we should see the idea of one having a place and enjoying a portion. The Old Testament word (*yarash*) means to occupy, to possess; and the New Testament word (*klēronomeō*) means to obtain and enjoy an allotment.

The final word of importance is "earth." This is the Hebrew word *erets*, a word from which one could easily cite numerous occurrences to show that it means "land"; but just as many could be brought forth to show that it means "the planet earth." Note the occurrences in Gen. 1:1 and 1:10. In the first it means the planet and in the second it means the land. Every occurrence must be defined by the context in which it is found.

In view of these facts, it becomes plain that the first great declaration in the Word (excluding Psalm 25:13) concerning man's future home is that, if he waits upon the Lord, he will have a place and enjoy a portion in the earth. This declaration is immediately repeated in the same Psalm.

"For yet a little while and the wicked shall not be: yea, thou shalt diligently consider his place, and it shall not be. But the meek shall inherit the earth; and shall delight themselves in the abundance of peace" (Psalm 37:10, 11).

These verses, with the one that precedes them, emphatically declare the fate of the wicked and the future of the righteous. Evildoers will be cut off; but the meek shall have a place and enjoy a portion in the earth, and in the abundance of peace they will find delight.

The "meek" are the submissive, the yielded, the humble. We are exhorted to: "Humble yourselves therefore under the mighty hand of God, that He may exalt you in due time" (1 Pet. 5:6). This we will do. We will submit to God and to His Word. We will yield to Him in all things. But not for one moment will we yield or submit to men, to their creeds, to their organizations, or to their crude and puerile theologies. We will take our place with the meek in all things that pertain to God and His Word.

The declaration that those who are given a place and a portion in the earth shall "delight themselves in the abundance of peace" may have to do with the fact that God "will speak peace to His people" (Psa. 85:8) and cause "wars to cease to the end of the earth" (Psa. 46:9). Of course, this will be a source of great delight;

however, I feel there is more in this passage than this.

Our word "abundance" comes from the Latin *ab*, meaning "from," and *unda*, meaning "wave"; and it speaks of wave upon wave of something that rolls in upon us. The Hebrew word for "peace" is the familiar *shalom*, and it is used interchangeably with *eirēnē* in the New Testament. Thus, according to the law of divine interchange, these two words are the same in value and meaning. The word *eirēnē* is a noun which comes from the verb *eirō*, "to join." And since a noun derived from a verb cannot mean something entirely different from its parent word, both *shalom* and *eirēnē* suggest a perfect union. This gives us another facet of earth's glorious future. It will be a place characterized by wave upon wave of things that are joined to God. This will fulfill the prayer of Amos: "But let judgment run down as waters, and righteousness as a mighty stream" (Amos 5:24). Then we will say: "How excellent is Thy loving-kindness, O God! therefore the children of men put their trust under the shadow of Thy wings. They shall be abundantly satisfied with the fatness of Thy house; and Thou shalt make them drink of the river of Thy pleasures. For with Thee is the fountain of life: in Thy light shall we see light" (Psa. 36:7-9).

A further statement in this Psalm is most revealing. "For such as be blessed of Him shall inherit the earth; and they that be cursed of Him shall be cut off" (Psalm 37:22).

Indeed, many will be blessed of Him; and all who are blessed of Him will have a place and enjoy a portion on the earth. All places will not be the same, neither will all portions be equal. The declared destiny of the twelve apostles is an example of this. Of these it has been said, "Ye also shall sit upon twelve thrones judging the twelve tribes of Israel" (Matt. 19:28). This will be their portion in this earth, and this place is exclusive to the twelve.

Those who qualify as believers in the Lord Jesus Christ in this present dispensation are to enjoy the allotment of being "blessed with every spiritual blessing among the most elevated in Christ" (Eph. 1:3, TRV). But even these great blessings will be our portion in this earth.

When the Lord Jesus was upon the earth, He confirmed the promises made in the Old Testament (see Rom. 15:8) and declared: "Blessed are the meek: for they shall inherit the earth" (Matt 5:5). He confirmed and did not contradict in any manner the promises made by the Psalmist, and there is nothing in anything spoken in His later words or the words of any writer that in any way nullifies the Biblical witness as to man's future place and portion. The Word of God does not change—all who are blessed of Him will have a place and enjoy their portion in the earth.

The testimony of Scripture is that God brings salvation and blessing to men upon the earth, and this should not be contradicted by the Greek philosophy that all the benefits of the work of Christ are to be gained by a flight from this world into heaven.

At present, the earth is in such condition that many will say they want no place or portion in it. And such dire things are now being predicted by men (not by God), in regard to the future of the earth, that they fain would fly from it. And we must admit that conditions on the earth are such today that at times we are inclined to say with the Psalmist: "Oh that I had wings like a dove! for then would I fly away, and be at rest. Lo, then would I wander far off, and remain in the wilderness. I would hasten my escape from the windy storm and tempest" (Psa. 55:6-8).

The Bible, throughout, acknowledges the present condition of the earth; and it is epitomized in one neat phrase, "the bondage of corruption" (Rom. 8:21). Scripture enlarges upon this, saying, "For we know that the whole creation groaneth and travaileth in pain together until now" (Rom. 8:22). The time of its deliverance is set as being the same as the unveiling of the sons of God, and we know that the manifestation of the sons of God is simultaneous with the manifestation of the Lord Jesus Christ. (See 1 John 3:2 where "appear" is *phaneroō* and means "to manifest." See also Col. 3:4). The unveiling and the subsequent manifestation of Jesus Christ will take place when, "The glory of the LORD shall be revealed, and all flesh shall see it together" (Isa. 40:5). This will result in the earth being full of the knowledge of the Lord, as the waters cover the sea (Isa. 11:9). This is God's next move; it is next in His order of events, and it is in no way dependent upon or related to His personal return to the earth to be personally present for a thousand years.

It seems that for every malignant and evil condition of the earth, there is a beneficent promise. It would make an interesting study to trace these out, but this cannot be done within the limits of space that remains. It is sufficient for now to say that when God governs the nations upon the earth (Psa. 67:4); when the whole earth is filled with His glory (Psa. 72:19); when the heavens declare His righteousness, and all the peoples see His glory (Psa. 97:6); when God opens His hand and satisfies the desire of every living thing (Psa. 145:15, 16); when God's judgments are in the earth, and the inhabitants of the world are learning righteousness (Isa. 26:9); when no inhabitant of the earth shall say that he is sick (Isa. 33:24); when God opens rivers in high places, and fountains in the midst of valleys (Isa. 41:18); when the desert shall blossom as the rose bush blossoms (Isa. 35:1);—I want to be on earth, see all this, and be a part of it. I want to be where the action is.

The SEED and BREAD Bible-Study leaflets are published as often as time and means permit and are sent free to all names on THE WORD OF TRUTH MINISTRY mailing list. Send us your name. There will be no obligation, solicitation, or visitation. Additional copies of any issue available on request.   ISSUE NO. 73

SEED & BREAD

FOR THE SOWER   ISA. 55:10   FOR THE EATER

BRIEF BIBLICAL MESSAGES
FROM
THE WORD OF TRUTH MINISTRY
339 South Orange Drive, Los Angeles, Cal. 90036

Otis Q. Sellers, Bible Teacher

THE BELIEVER'S DESTINY

After many years of careful observation, I am convinced that the fundamentalists, the dispensationalists, and the premillennialists have no real conviction in regard to where God's people are going to be in the future, what we are going to be doing, or how we are going to spend our time. They have not, up to this time, come forth with any real, solid Biblical truth in regard to this matter. And if any other group, sect, or denomination has done so, I have failed to detect it in their writings which have been examined.

On a recent Sunday morning I watched, for a time, part of the televised broadcast of the morning service of a great church which prides itself on being Biblical. The pastor was outlining what his church believed, and he said in part: "We believe that the Lord is coming back; and when He does, His church will be caught up into the air to meet Him. We will be with Him there for seven years while the earth is being cleansed by the fires of the great tribulation, after which we will return to the earth with Him to help set up His kingdom. And then we will rule and reign with Him for a thousand years."

Exactly one week later I listened to the same program and heard this same man say: "The day will come when the Lord will descend from heaven; and we will be caught up to meet Him in the air, from which He will take us with Him back to heaven where we will be forever with Him."

Such statements as these are almost typical of the contradictions spoken by many who claim the Bible for their authority. They simply have not faced up to the facts as to what the Word of God has to say about the future home of God's people.

If the Bible is carefully examined from Genesis to Malachi, there will not be found one single hint, suggestion, or intimation that anyone ever expected or even desired to go to heaven. The Hebrew word for heaven (*shamayim*) is found 419 times in the Old Testament and is translated "heaven" in 398 passages and "air" in 21. Yet, even in all this wealth of references, each one of which I have examined with assiduous care, there cannot be found a hint that a home in heaven was the expectation of any man, that any man expected to go there at death, or that it would be his home when he was raised from the dead. God never promised anyone a place in heaven in any of the thirty-nine books that make up the Old Testament. In fact, a distinctly opposite truth is set forth in its pages, as the Spirit of God declared through David in Psalm 37:9, 11 and 22. (See Issue No. 73.)

There is nothing in the Old Testament which in any way contradicts the expectation that the Psalmist held out to the righteous. The experiences of Enoch and Elijah have no bearing on this subject, and they should not be used to nullify the Word of God. They are two special cases of Godly men who were taken alive into heaven in connection with some special purpose of God. The expectation of rightous men from Adam to Christ was that when they arose from the dead, they would live upon and enjoy the earth under God's government. This is beautifully expressed in the stirring testimony of Job:

For I know that my Redeemer liveth, and that He shall stand at the latter day upon the earth: And though after my skin worms destroy this body, yet in my flesh shall I see God: Whom I shall see for myself, and mine eyes shall behold, and not another; though my reins be consumed within me (Job 19:25-27).

When we come to the New Testament and examine the four gospels, we find that Jesus Christ confirmed the testimony of David, holding forth the same hope: "Blessed are the meek; for they shall inherit the earth" (Matt. 5:5). These words were spoken in the sermon on the mount. They are one of the beatitudes, which many people have memorized, but which very few believe. And while it is true that in the same message, He told His disciples to lay up treasures in heaven, this cannot mean that He was promising them heaven as their future home. These words were spoken to the same men to whom He had just held out the hope of inheriting the earth and to whom He would later declare that they would sit upon twelve thrones judging the twelve tribes of Israel. These were positions and services related to the earth. There is simply nothing in the four Gospels that would lead anyone to think that their future life is to be lived out in heaven.

Of course, many will dispute this and point to John 14:1-6, as positive testimony that a place in heaven was the hope of these men. This is done in spite of the obvious fact that heaven is not the subject of this passage, and no mention is made of it. However, I am well able to sympathize with all who may think that this is the first mention of "a hope of heaven," there being a time in my early ministry when I proclaimed this same "hand-me-down" idea. When the time came that I made an honest study of this passage, I found I was reading ideas into it that were not there. This passage has for so long been tangled up in the emotional reasonings of men that logical thought concerning it is almost impossible. This comes from the fact that this portion of Scripture is used in most funeral services where it is related to death, heaven, and destiny—matters with which it does not deal.

There are certain truths concerning these words of our Lord that need to be fearlessly faced. They were spoken personally and privately to eleven very special men, each one of whom was destined to sit upon a throne and judge a tribe of Israel. And while every believer can read these words and profit from them, he must honestly recognize that the promises in them belong to the apostles to whom they were spoken. Any application of these words to our own lives will simply confuse the witness of God and our understanding of it as well.

If we examine verses 12, 13, and 14 of this same chapter, we will find other promises made that can apply only to the apostles. If we attempt to claim these as promises to us, we are doomed to disappointment. True, we believe on Him; but we cannot do the works that He did — let alone still greater works, as He declared in verse twelve. We have no blanket promise that if we ask anything in His Name, He will do it, as the apostles certainly had, according to verse thirteen and fourteen. In fact, these promises have nothing to do with prayer. They established an unlimited drawing account for these eleven men who were to serve Him in a very special manner.

We need to take a closer look at John 14:1-6. The Lord declared, "In My Father's house are many mansions." This is immediately seized upon by careless readers and incompetent interpreters who say that "the Father's house" is heaven, and the "mansions" are many grandiose buildings in heaven that are being prepared for our occupancy. All who handle this passage should learn to interpret Scripture by Scripture, a method which usually consists of finding the identical term in a place where its meaning is crystal clear, then applying it to occurrences that may not be so clear or may be in dispute.

The term "My Father's house" is found only two times in the New Testament. Both occurrences are in the Gospel of John, and both came from the lips of our Lord. In John 2:16, He said: "make not My Father's house an house of merchandise." Here the phrase can mean nothing else but the temple in Jerusalem, a temple that will someday be rebuilt and be the center of all life, government, and divine religion in the nation of Israel when God governs. This phrase cannot have one meaning in John 2:16 and another meaning in John 14:2. If so, then anyone can make God's Word to mean whatever he wants it to mean.

The Greek word *monē*, which is translated "mansion" in this passage, is difficult to express in English. We lack a word that corresponds with it. It is found only twice in the New Testament, both occurrences being in this chapter. It is translated "mansion" in verse 2 and "abode" in verse 23, which shows that the K J V translators did not know what to do with it. After much study, I am now convinced that our word "station" best expresses this word, providing we understand "station" to mean position, sphere of life, duty, or occupation.

Thus, the Lord declared to His disciples that in His Father's house were many stations, such as positions, duties, and occupations. Then, He declared in 14:23 that those who loved Him and kept His words would find the Father and the Son stationed with them and working through them.

His next statement was: "I go to prepare a place for you." Of course, the place was in the Father's house. And these words cannot mean that He was going to heaven to sweep it out, clean it up and refurbish it as a dwelling place for them, as much childish theology declares. This is sheer foolishness. He meant that He was going to the Cross and to the Tomb; and by His death and resurrection, a place would be made for them. Before this, He had said to them: "Except a grain of wheat fall into the ground and die, it abideth alone: but if it die it bringeth forth much fruit" (John 12:24).

Our Lord did go to the Cross and He returned from the state of death. The words, "I will come again, and receive you unto Myself," do not refer to His second coming. They speak of His return from the journey into death. The Lord would not have consoled His disciples by promising them participation in an event none of them ever experienced and which is still future after more than 1900 years.

This "coming" refers to that spoken of in John 14:18 and 23. He said to them: "I will not leave you comfortless: I will come to you." In considering this, only two alternatives are possible. He either made good His promise and came to them, or He broke His word and left them comfortless. It is my conviction that He came to them and received them unto Himself as recorded in John 20:19-23, a fact that became manifestly public on the day of Pentecost.

There is nothing in John 14:1-6 that would rightfully lead anyone to think that the destiny of the twelve apostles was a place called heaven. Their destiny was an exceedingly high station in the Father's house, the future temple of Israel. Even as David declared long before: "Blessed is the man whom Thou choosest, and causest to approach unto Thee, that he may dwell in Thy courts: we shall be satisfied with the goodness of Thy house, even of Thy holy temple" (Psa. 65:4).

As those who are now believing, a place in the Father's house is not our destiny. We will enjoy our own special place and privileges in this earth when God governs.

The SEED and BREAD Bible-Study leaflets are published as often as time and means permit and are sent free to all names on THE WORD OF TRUTH MINISTRY mailing list. Send us your name. There will be no obligation, solicitation, or visitation. Additional copies of any issue available on request.   ISSUE NO. 74

SEED & BREAD

FOR THE SOWER   ISA. 55:10   FOR THE EATER

BRIEF BIBLICAL MESSAGES
FROM

THE WORD OF TRUTH MINISTRY

339 South Orange Drive, Los Angeles, Cal. 90036

Otis Q. Sellers, Bible Teacher

THE EARTH - OUR FUTURE HOME

The subject of this study declares a conviction that has been mine for twenty-five years. It is a conviction that was forced upon me by my own studies in the Word of God. I now regret that I did not see and understand this tremendous truth during the first thirty-two years of my Christian experience and Bible study. I had come upon intimations of this Biblical message many times as I searched the Word, but was somewhat reticent to really look into it. I now admit that I shrank back from further investigation when, early in my studies of man's destiny, I began to see what the Bible really said as to our future home. But it was only a momentary pause to catch my breath, and now my studies have continued in this subject for a quarter-century.

As a result of these studies, I have come to realize more and more that when you carefully search out something for yourself, piecing all the clues together, facing up to every question and problem the study raises, it creates a conviction that is much deeper than one that has come from simply accepting some hand-me-down traditions. Such a conviction will always be equal to any onslaught of doubt from any source, it being protected by the whole armor of God's Word.

Of course, very few men indeed will want to even consider that an idea might be the truth when it will demand that they re-examine and rethink all that they have ever been taught from childhood. Could it be that they know that the Word of God is powerful, especially when it comes to "casting down imaginations," and that every imaginary idea about heaven is sure to fall if one persists in searching the Scriptures to see what the Bible reveals concerning it?

When I was a small boy, we were taught a song, one line of which said, as best I can remember, "I love to think about heaven, and the joys that await me there." We sang this at the top of our childish voices; but we did not know what we were saying; and what we said was not the truth. We probably wondered about heaven, since there was so much talk about it; and we were constantly being promised that someday, if we were good, we would go there. But it could not have been true that we actually thought about it. This would have been impossible, since we had nothing whatsoever to think with.

I do not mean by this the brain, since we all possessed a brain. Neither child nor man thinks with his brain. He thinks with the facts that are recorded by the brain and stored there for future recall and use. If the facts are not there, or if they cannot be recalled, we cannot think, no matter how hard we try. If the facts are there, they can be assembled and sorted out so as to form proper and right ideas. The exhortation to "use your brain" is an exhortation to act upon and make use of facts you already know. In order to think properly, we must be in possession of certain facts which we have gained and verified. So, since we did not possess any knowledge of heaven and were in possession of very few facts concerning it, it was impossible for us to think about it. We accepted the few things we were taught about it, usually by inadequate and incompetent instructors; but that was all we could do.

Inasmuch as young and active minds like to collect and store away facts, we often sought information about heaven from our parents, Sunday-school teachers, or pastors. I now feel that it was not easy for them to acknowledge their ignorance of the subject, so they often manufactured something on the spot to tell us about it. As one mother confessed to me, "My child asked me question after question about heaven; and since I knew nothing about it, I felt impelled to make something up. And I finished up believing what I had manufactured to tell my child." Even so, we were loaded down with a lot of imaginary ideas concerning heaven.

As I reviewed all this later in life and sought to separate the true from the false, I saw that only three things I had been told about heaven could be verified by the Word of God: (1) heaven is a place, (2) Jesus Christ is now located there, and (3) it is the dwelling place of a host of angelic beings. These were the only truths about heaven that I could verify.

I can now honestly say that I have added to these facts. In the course of my studies in the Word of God, careful consideration has been given to every one of the 419 occurrences of the Hebrew word *shamayim* (the Hebrew word for heaven), and the 268 occurrences of the word *ouranos* (the Greek word for heaven). These have been carefully examined in their contexts; and as a result, I am now in possession of many more facts about heaven that have come from the Word of God. These facts now regulate, circumscribe and order all my thinking in regard to heaven. Now, when I hear a speaker on the radio say, "The Bible says," and he then follows this with some imaginary or traditional statement about heaven, I am forced to answer, "Not *my* Bible."

The messages which I have spoken and written on this subject over the past twenty-five years have sent hundreds of people scurrying to the Bible, fully confident that they could turn up hundreds of passages that would support the idea that heaven is our future home. Many were amazed at what they found there, and they reported their experiences to me. Most all of them confessed to great difficulty in understanding how an idea could be so widely held and taught throughout Christendom and, yet, have nothing in the Word of God to support it. This is not hard to explain.

When the Egyptian and Greek ideas of "the immortality of the soul" became the almost universal belief of mankind, along with all the related errors that make up the Platonic philosophy of man's nature, it was necessary for them to have someplace for these "immortal souls" to go when they departed from the body. So, the Greeks had their "Elysium"; the American Indian had his "happy hunting ground"; the Hindus had their "Nirvana"; and the Norse had their "Valhalla." All of these were places where "immortal souls" were supposed to go at death.

When the church of the Latin and Greek fathers (not the simple fellowship of the apostles) adopted the Platonic philosophy as to man's nature, that hybrid, which took the name of Christianity, took the Biblical word "heaven" to describe the place where "immortal souls" were supposed to go at death.

The Bible-taught believer does not find himself in any such quandary. He knows that death is a reality, that it is an enemy yet to be abolished, that it is the end of this life, and that resurrection from the dead is the beginning of the life to come. Thus, he has no need for some imaginary place with a Biblical name for "immortal souls" to go between the time of death and resurrection. There is no such thing as an "immortal soul" in the Bible; and the very idea is flatly contradicted by Ezekiel 18:4, "The soul that sinneth, it shall die."

Of course, the position I take in regard to our future home is highly controversial. Strong reactions are to be expected. One who takes an unpopular position must expect it to be denied, ridiculed, and misrepresented. I am prepared for this in mind and spirit. However, after twenty-five years I am still waiting for someone to bring forth from Scripture positive facts that will show I am wrong and that the popular view is right. Meanwhile, there is one misrepresentation that constantly amuses me. Over and over some are saying, "Mr. Sellers does not believe in heaven." In answer to this, I will simply say that Mr. Sellers takes second place to no man living or dead in believing in the reality of a place called heaven. In fact, my insistence upon heaven being a place has brought to light the fact that many do not believe that heaven exists at all.

When one says that heaven is a place, it is a meaningless statement unless we define the word "place." Let us consider that an airport is a very definite place upon the earth. We go to this place when we wish to travel by plane. When the plane is 35,000 feet above the earth, there is no place in the air for the plane to stop. If anything happened, the plane would not stop until it came to someplace upon the earth.

Heaven is not a place upon the earth, but it is a very definite place in space. It is the place where "the man Christ Jesus" is now located, the place where Enoch and Elijah now are. Heaven is a place in space, just as the earth is a place in space.

There are those who say that "heaven is a place beyond all space," but this is a meaningless statement that defies analysis.

Others say that "heaven is a place beyond the reach of man's greatest telescopes," but that is the same kind of guesswork as if one should say that heaven is the planet Pluto. For all we know, when we train our telescopes upon some distant and giant star, we may be looking at the sun of another solar system; and one of its planets may be the place that the Bible calls heaven. If heaven is a place, and I believe that it is, then it is a place somewhere in this universe.

It is also said that my views of heaven are too "materialistic." Those who say this insist that heaven is "a spiritual place," but such a declaration says nothing and means less. To them the opposite of "spiritual" is "material," but this is a part of the Platonic philosophy and it is not Biblical. I challenge anyone to write as much as three meaningful statements about an "immaterial" place called heaven. Heaven is just as much a material place as is the earth.

It has to be acknowledged that today heaven is a much better place than the earth. Conditions there are certainly far better than they are here. However, every possible criticism that anyone can make of the earth or of the conditions upon it has to do with something that is to be changed or removed.

It is my conviction that this earth, not heaven, is the future home of God's redeemed. In taking this stand and in teaching it to others, the words of Carl Sandburg, spoken in regard to another matter, come to my mind: "If I had not faithfully plodded through every last piece of material I could lay my hands on that concerned the essential record, I would feel guilty." But far more important are the words of the Psalmist:

The heaven, even the heavens, are the LORD'S: but the earth hath He given to the children of men. (Psalm 115:16.)

The SEED and BREAD Bible-Study leaflets are published as often as time and means permit and are sent free to all names on THE WORD OF TRUTH MINISTRY mailing list. Send us your name. There will be no obligation, solicitation, or visitation. Additional copies of any issue available on request.   ISSUE NO. 75

SEED & BREAD

FOR THE SOWER   ISA. 55:10   FOR THE EATER

BRIEF BIBLICAL MESSAGES
FROM

THE WORD OF TRUTH MINISTRY

339 South Orange Drive, Los Angeles, Cal. 90036

Otis Q. Sellers, Bible Teacher

WHAT IS MAN?

The question asked in the title of this study is certainly Biblical. It is one of great importance, but very few who call themselves Christians have ever given it any consideration. Yet, it is one that must be asked and answered if we expect to understand anything the Bible declares concerning us, concerning our resurrection, and our destiny.

The Psalmist asked, "What is man, that Thou art mindful of him?" (Psa. 8:4); and the Apostle Paul repeated the same question in Hebrews 2:6. Today, it seems that when this question is asked, the world and the church springs into action with a ready-made cliché for an answer. "Man," they say, "is a tripartite being composed of a body, a soul, and a spirit," hurriedly pointing to 1 Thess. 5:23 where "spirit, soul, and body" are mentioned together in the benediction that closes that epistle. From this supposedly impregnable fortress they call upon all who think otherwise to lay down their arms and meekly surrender. However, before we do, and face the firing squad for having resisted the edicts of orthodox theology, we would like to ask a pertinent question.

Why do they pass so quickly over Luke 10:27 and make the seven-league jump to 1 Thess. 5:23? If they had hesitated for a moment and meditated upon the Luke passage, they would have seen how simple it would be to prove from one isolated text that man is a quadripartite being composed of four parts: "heart, soul, strength, and mind." Why do they begin their studies with the eight hundred and thirty-third reference to the soul in the Word of God? Does not their action indicate that they selected the passage which seems to say what they already believed and passed by all others that would seem to contradict it? Furthermore, did they set themselves to find an honest interpretation of 1 Thess. 5:23 in order to find out what Paul said and why he said it?

It is my conviction that neither Luke nor Paul was presenting truth in regard to what man is, and the use of 1 Thess. 5:23 for this purpose reveals that they who do so have applied themselves to Scripture for the sole purpose of proving a predetermined and foregone conclusion. If we take the elements of these two passages

(Luke 10:27 and 1 Thess. 5:23) and link them together, we will have heart, soul, strength, mind, spirit, and body. This is enough to show that these words are expressing various aspects of a man, and they are not dealing with his constitution.

If we are going to enter into possession of the Biblical answer to the question, "What is man?" we must go to the words of his Creator, the One Who is best able to inform us of the work of His hands. When He first spoke concerning man, He declared that it was his purpose to make him in His Image and after His Likeness (Gen. 1:26), a statement which has troubled many who pay little attention to the exact words used in a divine communication. They think that "image" means "shape" and that "likeness" means a "look-alike." The truth is that the Deity had an Image (See Col. 1:15) and a Likeness, and man was created in this Image and after this Likeness. However, the point to be noted here is that it was a man, a human, or as most would be inclined to say, a human being.

In the Biblical revelation, three great classes of beings are set forth: human beings, angelic beings, and spirit beings. The human being, having been made in the Image and after the Likeness of the Deity, is positively the highest order of all created beings. Man is not an angelic being and he never becomes one. In fact, for a human being to become an angelic being or spirit would be a positive loss, a step downward. We are human by birth, we are human in life, we will be human in death, and we will be human in resurrection. Any idea that human beings by any process ever become angelic beings or spirit beings is entirely foreign to the Word of God.

In Genesis 2:7 we find the first and the most important statement in the Word of God concerning the nature of man. There the Creator tells us of the creature that He made: "And the LORD God formed man of the dust of the ground, and breathed into his nostrils the breath of life; and man became a living soul."

Here we have a direct statement concerning the subject we are considering. It is not the complimentary close of an epistle from which we must draw inferences. It is cause for thanksgiving that it is so simple and direct, and that no serious objections can be raised concerning its translation. It has been rewritten by many who have tried to harmonize it with the Platonic theory of man's nature, but the Hebrew wording has withstood all assaults. This passage tells us how man was made, it tells us of what he was made, and it tells us what he became, and what he is. It is the testimony of the Maker in regard to the work of His hands. And it cannot be denied, that the Maker of man is the One best able to inform us as to the nature of that which He made. All who receive this testimony can rest assured that they are in possession of and are believing the Truth of God.

Since Genesis 2:7 is the earliest and fullest account that God has given concerning the nature of man, this passage demands our close scrutiny. It should be noted carefully that we are told the LORD God "formed man." It was a human being He formed. This can be received and believed, or it can be twisted and altered to fit some human opinion. It was not a soul, it was not a spirit being, it was not an angelic being that God formed. It was a man. It was not a habitation or a house for man to move into. It was not a garment to cover a man. It was a man.

Many there are who insist that it was not a man that God created but only a body. And while we freely admit that it was a body, yet, God says it was a man; and this is what we must believe. God could have said "body," but He did not do so. He had the word for "body," but he did not use it. He used the word "man," and that is exactly what He meant.

We are also told in this passage that God formed man of the dust or soil of the ground. He was not created out of nothing. God used material, and this was soil. This truth is emphasized and enforced by the words God used in Genesis 3:19: "till you return unto the ground, for out of it you were taken; you are dust, and unto dust you shall return." (RSV)

In view of this divine testimony, it is plain that, that which God formed from the dust was the man. It is useless to deny this and insist that man was something else — something not made of soil. If we do this, we break with the Word of God in its opening chapters; and this throws us out of harmony and into conflict with all the rest that God has spoken. If man refuses to be taught by the Word of God in Genesis 2, any further study will be of doubtful value. If he rejects God's earliest statement concerning man, he will have to rewrite and twist all later statements. Let us believe God! He says He formed "man" of the dust of the ground. This is the truth, and he who believes it is believing God's Truth.

But, alas, there are many who do not believe this. The Platonic view of man's nature has been so thoroughly incorporated into Christian theology that, to many, Plato's view of man is thought to be just as much a part of divine revelation as is the birth of Christ in Bethlehem and His death upon the cross of Calvary.

According to Plato, man was not formed out of the dust of the ground. Man, to him, was a soul, which for some reason, had become united to a body. This soul, he held, was the real and true man; and its union with the body was considered by him to be a great calamity. He regarded death as a positive blessing, inasmuch as it freed the soul from its undesirable union with the body. The idea of Plato that the soul is the real and true man is one that has pervaded Christianity to the very core, and this has been the foundation of an amazing amount of false doctrine.

It is from God's Word, from its first use of the word "soul" (nephesh), that we learn that "the soul" is something that man became. As originally created, he had only a bodily phase or aspect; but by a further act of God, he became a living soul. Thus, the Biblical Truth is not that man has a soul, but that he is a soul, and that he became this by the divine act of inbreathing life into the man.

There are many who will make no attempt to understand the meaning of the words used in the above statement. They will deliberately stumble over the distinction of "having" and "becoming." But in order to help those who earnestly desire to know, a further explanation and illustration will be given.

Since the man that God had made became a living soul by a further act of God, it is evident that the word "soul" describes an aspect or an attribute of the man. Consider the following illustration. I am fundamentally and basically a man, a human being; but in one aspect of my being, I am a husband. I was not always a husband, but I became one when I took to myself the woman who has been my wife for more than a half century. In another aspect of my life, I am a father, something which I became when our daughter was born. I became a grandfather when our daughter became a mother. Yet, all the time I remain a man, for only a man can be these things. And it should be noted that there is no way that these aspects of my being can be separated from me and exist apart from the one who is them and who displays them. If I die, the husband, the father, and the grandfather will die with me. All these are founded upon a living man, and they cannot exist apart from him.

Even so it is with the many phases of man that are set forth in the Word of God such as heart, soul, strength, mind, spirit, and body. And while it is common to speak of man having these things, no definition is ever given of this wealthy being called man who possesses them. If they follow the Platonic idea that the true man is a separable soul, then they are saying that the soul has a soul. I do not believe that a single logical statement can be made of man unless it presupposes a body. It was a man that God made from the soil, and no subsequent addition of the breath of life that made man a living soul can be said to supersede and become the true man. It is an absurdity to suppose that any of man's aspects such as spirit or soul can, apart from the body, be a man.

Thus, from the Word of God, we learn what man was when created and what he subsequently became. He was earth; and while beautifully fashioned, he was as lifeless as any clump of earth. However, into this lifeless earth, God breathed the breath of life. This made man a living soul, and this he remained until that breath of life went back to the One Who gave it. "And all the days of Adam were nine hundred and thirty years: and he died" Gen. 5:5). And there is nothing but resurrection that will ever remove him from this condition.

The SEED and BREAD Bible-Study leaflets are published as often as time and means permit and are sent free to all names on THE WORD OF TRUTH MINISTRY mailing list. Send us your name. There will be no obligation, solicitation, or visitation. Additional copies of any issue available on request. ISSUE NO. 76

SEED & BREAD

FOR THE SOWER   ISA. 55:10   FOR THE EATER

BRIEF BIBLICAL MESSAGES

FROM

THE WORD OF TRUTH MINISTRY

339 South Orange Drive, Los Angeles, Cal. 90036

Otis Q. Sellers, Bible Teacher

WHAT IS THE SOUL?

In any study of the human soul, one should begin by recognizing and admitting that whatever this quality is that is called "soul," it is something that was attributed to animal life four times before it was used of man. This pertinent fact is covered up in the *King James Version*, due to the fact that its translators were completely committed to the Platonic theory of man's nature, which made the true and real man to be a separable soul, which for some reason had been united to a body. These "learned men" approached the work of translating the Bible thoroughly saturated with the Greek view of human nature in general and the soul in particular. They fully believed that the soul was a person dwelling within the human body.

The Hebrew word for soul is *nephesh*. It is found 754 times in the Hebrew Old Testament, and it is translated at least thirty-three different ways in the *King James Version*. This seems to have been done in order to try to make the Word square with the ideas of men who carried Plato's philosophy into their work of translating; and when they could not square it, they confused it. When they came to the first occurrence of *nephesh* (Gen. 1:20), which certainly attributes the quality of soul to lower forms of life, they either omitted it or else translated it "life." There are two words in this passage, *chaiyah* and *nephesh*; and we cannot say today which one was ignored and which one was translated "life." However, from this first occurrence of the word *nephesh*, we learn that God called the living and moving things of the sea "living souls" before He applied this term to man. Anyone who possesses a copy of *Young's Analytical Concordance* can discover for himself, that when Moses in Gen. 1:20, 21, 24, and 30 speaks of the nature of the lower creatures, and when in Gen. 2:5 he speaks of the nature of man, he uses identical Hebrew terms of both one and the other.

The study of the word *nephesh* is not an easy one, but some have made it. We have examined with care every passage in which this word is found, marked them in our Bibles, considered their contexts, and tried to arrive at some true Biblical understanding of this very important word. Our studies are not yet finished, and they never will be in this life; but one thing we know for certain is that the translators of the *King James Version* gave us a rewrite of their own when they came upon the word *nephesh*. In rendering it, they used such terms as "life," "soul," "dead," "appetite," "lust," "mortally," and "fish," (fish?).

The Greek word for "soul" is *psuchē*. It occurs 105 times and is translated seven different ways: "soul," "life," "mind," "heart," "you," "heartily," and "us." I do not believe that any honest Bible exegete would even try to defend all this confusing and unfaithful treatment of these Hebrew and Greek words. So we have reason to thank God that, in the study of Scripture, the language barrier has been broken; and we can go to the original words that God used. Every occurrence of *nephesh* will be found listed beginning with page 829 of *The Englishman's Hebrew and Chaldee Concordance*, and every occurrence of *psuchē* will be found on page 807 of *The Englishman's Greek Concordance*.

From the five occurrences of *nephesh* in Genesis 1 and 2, we will know that man can claim no preeminence over the beast so far as being a living soul is concerned. Furthermore, we will see at once the utter absurdity of supposing that the soul apart from the body is the real man. We will know that the soul is not an entity that can do all that man does and be all that he is.

The soul, according to many, can see without eyes, can reason and think without a brain, can walk without legs, and speak without tongue, teeth, or vocal chords. All these abilities are attributed to something men say is the soul. And while all this is in harmony with Plato's philosophy, it is not taught in the Word of God.

Those who make a full study of the word *nephesh* will have to admit that its most important occurrence is the one where it is first used in connection with man. In Genesis 2:7 we are told: "And the LORD God formed man of the dust of the ground, and breathed into his nostrils the breath of life; and man became a living soul."

This passage, if believed, actually separates the Biblicist from the Platonist. It denies the Platonic philosophy in its totality. Here we must choose between the Word of God and the ideas of Plato. And the reader should recognize in advance that if he chooses the Word of God, it will put him outside the mainstream of what is called "orthodox theology."

It is, therefore, the opening testimony of the Bible that the whole man as a living sentient being is a soul. At one point he was only a body made of soil; and as created by God, he had every organ that the body has now. He had a brain, eyes, ears, nose, hands, and feet. But the brain could not reason, the nose could not smell, the eyes could not see, the ears could not hear. Man, as created, lacked no organ; but he needed yet something from God to make these operative, to make him a living soul. He needed "the breath of life," and this he received by a divine operation from the Creator who had made him. As a result, he became something that he was not before. He became a living soul. Before God breathed the breath of life into his nostrils, he was only a beautifully fashioned and wonderfully organized portion of the soil of the ground, a lifeless figure. In his origin he was only dust; but in the perfection to which the second work of God brought him, he became a living soul. We must believe this, since God Himself tells us of it.

The truth that one learns from Genesis 2:7 is reaffirmed in the New Testament where Paul declares: "And so it is written, the first man Adam was made a living soul" (1 Cor. 15:45). The simplicity of the account of creation can be demonstrated in the following manner: A. The LORD God formed man of the dust of the earth; B. He breathed into the man's nostrils the breath of life; C. The man became a living soul. Thus, act A plus act B resulted in C. There is no record of the creation of the soul in the Bible. It was the whole man that became a living soul and not some separable part of him.

What man became and what man is as a living soul depends for its continuance upon God. If the breath of life is withdrawn, man will become a dead soul. He will sink back into the soil from which he came, and nothing but resurrection can bring him out of this state. When this is understood, the fact of resurrection from the dead becomes one of supreme importance.

Any attempt to provide a one-sentence definition of the soul is simply trying to define the indefinable. However, an enormous amount of truth concerning it can be gained by considering all that God has said about it and from all the uses made of it by the Spirit of God.

From God's Word we know that "soul" is attributed to all animal life, and that "soul" is what the man made of the soil became when God breathed into his nostrils the breath of life. We know that man remains a living soul as long as the breath of life is in him, and he becomes a dead soul when it is taken from him. These are basic truths and they cannot be denied by texts taken from other places in Scripture. God's Word does not contradict itself. The study of every occurrence of *nephesh* and *psuchē* must begin with these fundamental truths in mind, since they are the first that God revealed. And if we would arrive at God's Truth concerning the soul, we must at the very outset of our studies purge our minds as far as possible of the entire Platonic theory concerning souls and their nature. We must give God a clean slate to write upon.

The soul of man is not the man himself. It is not another entity, a second person, or another ethereal man existing within an outer man. It is not something that is immortal. It dies when the man dies, as it is declared in the classic passage of Ezekiel 18:4: "Behold, all souls are mine; as the soul of the father, so also the soul of the son is mine: the soul (*nephesh*) that sinneth, it shall die." A million arguments can be found in theological books for "the immortality of the soul"; but when we search the Word, we fail to find even one passage that declares it. Many texts are brought forward which are supposed to imply this, but none can be found that declares it. In fact, the very opposite is asserted in the Scriptures, a fact that the translators have successfully concealed. Leviticus 24:17, 18 states in the Hebrew: "He that kills the soul of a man shall surely be put to death; and he that kills the soul of a beast shall make it good, soul for soul." This is what God says; and even as Abraham believed God, I, too, believe God.

There is no detachable part of man that survives physical death. The Bible states nothing of the immortality of a detached and independent soul, or of our future state as one of disembodied blessedness. The idea that the soul is a detachable part or substance, capable of existing independently of the body, is an idea adopted from Greek philosophy and incorporated into Christian thought by the so-called church fathers. This started in the third century and was fully developed by the thirteenth century. The Reformation did nothing to clear this up; so today in Reformed Theology, we find a mixture of Greek and Biblical ideas, with the Greek ideas predominating. And so for centuries, Platonic philosophy has been propagated under the Christian label.

Let no one think that the writer, in coming to the conclusions already set forth, has failed to consider such passages as 1 Kings 17:21, 22 and Matt. 10:28. No passage has been neglected or ignored in search of the truth. Any interpretation of these passages must be in complete harmony with the Biblical definition of the soul and with all other truth revealed concerning it. Furthermore, Matt. 10:28 shows that the soul is subject to destruction; and we must remember that if man cannot kill a soul, then the command of God with its severe penalty recorded in Numbers 35:30 is about the same as if our government should make it punishable by death for any man to interfere with the rising of the sun.

Many passages that relate to the soul are worthy of being dealt with at length, and this will be done in later issues of these Bible-study leaflets.

The SEED and BREAD Bible-Study leaflets are published as often as time and means permit and are sent free to all names on THE WORD OF TRUTH MINISTRY mailing list. Send us your name. There will be no obligation, solicitation, or visitation. Additional copies of any issue available on request.   ISSUE NO. 77

SEED & BREAD

FOR THE SOWER   ISA. 55:10   FOR THE EATER

BRIEF BIBLICAL MESSAGES

FROM

THE WORD OF TRUTH MINISTRY

339 South Orange Drive, Los Angeles, Cal. 90036

Otis Q. Sellers, Bible Teacher

THE BREATH OF LIFE

The first mention of "the breath of life" (*neshamah chayim*) is found in Genesis 2:7. There we are told that it was breathed directly into the nostrils of the man whom God had created, and this resulted in man becoming a living soul (*chaiyah nephesh*). Thus, the first truth we learn of "the breath of life" is that it is a direct emanation from God. The study and the understanding of this term is therefore of the utmost importance, since it is this breath of life that gives life to everyone of us and makes us living souls.

In considering the two aspects of a living man that constitute him a living soul, we note first that there is a body. This was created out of something already in existence, the dust or soil of the earth. A man may love his body, care for it, protect it, and nurture it; and it is good if he does. Yet, it is just so much soil; and at death, it will return to the soil from which it was taken. Since God could, if He so desired, raise up from stones children unto Abraham (Matt. 3:9), we must not consider ourselves to be of such great value. God could duplicate each one of us a thousandfold. And while it is true, we are of more value than many sparrows; but how much is a sparrow worth?

The second thing that makes man a living soul is "the breath of life." This is spoken of in Scripture as being God's gift to man. Man is not this "breath"; it is God's gift to him. When we read in Scripture of "the breath of the LORD," we are reading of the same breath that made man a living soul. Man was once without it, yet, he was man; and before it was given to him, it was residing in the fulness of the Deity Himself. After it entered into man and became a part of him, it still belonged to the LORD and is regarded by God as being His own breath.

In the phrase "breath of life," we need to recognize that "of" is the sign of the genitive; and here it is the genitive of apposition, a figure of speech in which the second noun defines the first. We should, therefore, understand this as telling us that God breathed into man's nostrils the breath, that is to say, life. Thus, it was actually life that God breathed into man, and this constituted him a living soul.

In studying the Hebrew words to discover the nature of man, we will find three words appearing again and again. These are *neshama* which means "breath," *chaiyim* which means "life," and *ruach* which means "spirit." These three words are all used of the same thing. They are not used of three different things, but set forth the same thing by using three terms. The breath that God breathed into man is his life, and this life is man's spirit. All one needs to do is compare Gen. 2:7 with Eccl. 12:7 and he will discover that "the breath of life" which God gave to man is one and the same with man's spirit, which, when a man dies, must return unto God Who gave it. And while this "spirit" is sometimes spoken of as belonging to man, it remains always God's spirit and must return to Him.

The most positive help in identifying the breath of life (*neshamah chaiyam*) with man's spirit (*ruach*) is found in the book of Job. I trust the reader knows that Job is Hebrew poetry, and that in Hebrew poetry the rhythm is not achieved by a repetition of sounds, but by a repetition of sentiments and ideas. This is called parallelism. In this we find passages of two clauses in which the second clause is identical with the first, but expressed in different words. Note this in the following passages.

All the while my breath (*neshama*) is in me, and the spirit (*ruach*) of God is in my nostrils. Job 27:3.

The spirit (*ruach*) of God hath made me, and the breath (*neshamah*) of the Almighty hath given me life. Job 33:4.

But there is a spirit (*ruach*) in man: and the inspiration (*neshamah*) of the Almighty giveth them understanding. Job 32:8.

If He set His heart upon man, if He gather unto Himself His spirit (*ruach*), and (even) His breath (*neshamah*); All flesh shall perish together, and man shall turn again unto dust. Job 34:14, 15.

Thus saith the LORD . . . He that giveth breath (*neshamah*) unto the people upon it, and spirit (*ruach*) to them that walk therein. Isa. 42:5.

An examination of all passages that bear upon the subject will show that "breath" (*neshamah*), "life" (*chaiyim*), and "spirit" (*ruach*) are different designations of the same principle; and they are not the names of three different things. Do not stumble over this fact. If the Eskimo requires 600 terms to describe snow, do not think it strange if the Hebrew used five or six to describe the life principle in man.

"But why is 'spirit' called 'breath'?" someone is sure to ask. The question is a proper one and, in its answer, we will find much truth.

In the Word of God, there are certain things that we could never understand if God had not made them plain by the use of figures. These figures become illustrations of things that are imperceptible to the senses; therefore, man lacks the faculties for entering into them.

Take, for example, the matter of death. The divine figure or illustration of death is sleep. Man can know nothing of death since he has never experienced it; but he does know much about sleep, which he has experienced many times. Thus, God has chosen the figure of sleep to picture death to us. Death is not sleep, no more than sleep is death. But sleep is the name given to and is the figure of death, and the reality is often called by the name of the figure.

This is true also of the soul. The divine figure and illustration of the soul is the blood. (See Gen. 9:4, 5 where the word "life" is *nephesh*.) It is not that the soul is the blood, but that blood is the divinely chosen figure to make the soul comprehensible to us.

Then there is the subject of our study, the breath of life or spirit of man. This is beyond the comprehension of any of our senses, so God has seen fit to use the breath as a divine figure or illustration. And if we wonder why the breath should be chosen as a figure and ask what we are to learn from this, we will need to begin with the familiar, man's breath, and work to the unfamiliar, man's spirit. Thus, we begin with the figure and work up to the fact.

Consider a goldfish bowl containing water and fish. The bowl of water is the world in which those fish live. Each fish is constantly drawing in the water and expelling it, even as man inhales and exhales the air he breathes. When the water is drawn into the gills of the fish, it is at no time cut off from the water in the bowl, for it ever remains a part of it.

Now let us go from the fish in the bowl to man upon the earth. This planet, *on* which we live is covered with a coat of air *in* which we live and *by* which we live. We actually live at the bottom of a great invisible ocean; but the ocean is one of air, not of water. The atmosphere that covers the globe is a unit; and if any part of it is separated from the whole, it will become poisonous and destroy the creatures that live in it. This air is constantly entering into and going out of every living being or soul; and, thus, it unites every living soul upon the earth. How plain it becomes, then, that if God should gather unto Himself His spirit, even His breath, all flesh would perish together (Job 34:14, 15). Even as Paul declared it: ". . . seeing He giveth to all life, and breath, and all these things" (Acts 17:25).

God has given one air to all men, but all that a man can personally have of it is just what his needs require. No man can draw in from the atmosphere, say that this breath is his own and that he is going to keep it. Let him try this and in a few seconds his whole system will rebel and expel his breath in spite of himself. When a man draws in breath from the air, it is never cut off from the atmosphere as a whole.

As already stated, the breath is God's figure or illustration of the life or the spirit of man. The source of every man's spirit or life is God, just as the source of every creature's breath is the atmosphere. Man's spirit or life is a direct emanation from God Himself, and it flows from God to every living soul. Each one has that portion of life or spirit from God which he needs for his purposes. All things that live, live only in and by His life. Life has no other source but God. He originates and sustains life in all by giving it out of Himself. This was the explicit testimony of Paul to the men of Athens in Acts 17:28: "For in Him we live, and move, and have our being" (our existence).

During the few brief moments that man's breath is in his body, he has every right to call it "his breath," even though it remains a part of and is never severed from the air as a whole. Likewise, during the days or years that the spirit or life from God may be in man, he has every right to call it "his spirit" or "his life," even though it is never severed from and remains a part of the life of God. But when man's breath leaves his lungs, it must return to the air from which it came; even so, when man's spirit or life leaves the man, it must return unto God Who gave it. "Then shall the dust return to the earth as it was: and the spirit shall return to God Who gave it" (Eccl. 12:7).

In making the study of man's spirit, we must guard against two errors. That spirit which God loans to man for a time is not the Holy Spirit. This is made plain by the qualifying word "Holy." Also, we must never forget that man's spirit is not a spirit being. Before man came into possession of "the breath of life," which is fully identified in Scripture as being "man's spirit," it was a part of the divine nature, residing in God's fulness. When it returns to Him, it will again be a part of His nature and will find its place in His fullness.

Man's spirit has no personality, no individuality, no separate existence. All these things are attributes of the man, and they are the result of life or spirit entering into him and making him a living soul. Many there are who think that, in death, man becomes a "disembodied spirit"; but this is an idea that has no basis in the Word of God.

The central idea of Pantheism is that God is in everyone and everything. There is a definite element of truth in this, and we may not deny truth itself. But the great error of Pantheism is that everything is God and that there is no personal God. This is a deadly error. God's spirit or life is in every living thing, but we cannot find God by looking into things. He is to be found only in His Son Jesus Christ.

The SEED and BREAD Bible-Study leaflets are published as often as time and means permit and are sent free to all names on THE WORD OF TRUTH MINISTRY mailing list. Send us your name. There will be no obligation, solicitation, or visitation. Additional copies of any issue available on request.   ISSUE NO. 78

SEED & BREAD

FOR THE SOWER   ISA. 55:10   FOR THE EATER

BRIEF BIBLICAL MESSAGES
FROM
THE WORD OF TRUTH MINISTRY
339 South Orange Drive, Los Angeles, Cal. 90036
Otis Q. Sellers, Bible Teacher

WHAT IS DEATH?

The present interest among men in the subject of death is somewhat surprising, since discussion of this subject has been on the taboo list for many centuries, especially among professing Christian people. Reports continue to be heard of college and university students who have requested lectures and discussions of this matter, much to the chagrin of some of their professors, who have had to speak out of their vast ignorance concerning it. The widely circulated magazine *The Reader's Digest* devoted a large section of a recent issue to this theme, and an advertisement on the front loudly proclaimed that the article would present scientific proof of life after death. The entire presentation was made up of reports from people who, due to many causes, had come very near to death and others who had even been pronounced clinically dead but had revived. They told what they imagined they had seen and heard; but a logical person reading these reports which were supposed to be "scientific proof" would be inclined to say to the writer, "You have to be kidding."

I was myself surprised upon going into a large evangelical bookstore and finding one bookcase separated from the rest with a sign over it proclaiming, "Books About Death." These were written by psychiatrists, sociologists, medical doctors, liberal thinkers, and a few by evangelical writers. I welcomed the opportunity to look them over, reading a page here and there; but I bought none of them. I cannot afford to waste money on books written by men who have no facts to support their theories, or evangelicals who are so spoiled by the Platonic philosophy that they think it is taught in the Word of God. I left the store convinced that if there ever was a time when professed Bible-believing expositors should be writing on what has been the one taboo subject for centuries, it is now. However, they are not able to measure up to this challenge when all their efforts are given to trying to make the Bible say the same as Greek philosophy set forth by Plato.

Plato's view of death, as epitomized from the *Phaedo*, was that our bodies are only an outer garment, ill-fitting as a covering for the soul, which prevents our souls from living and moving freely in harmony with their proper eternal essence as long as we live.

man be more just than God? shall a man be more pure than his Maker" (Job 4:17). However, if Adam did not fully understand it at first, it was made unmistakably plain by the words that God spoke after he had sinned: "In the sweat of your face you shall eat bread till you return to the ground, for out of it you were taken; you are dust, and to dust you shall return" (Gen. 3:19 RSV).

In view of the directness and simplicity of this declaration, I do not hesitate to say that anyone, who does not believe that Adam is in the dust awaiting resurrection, is one who does not believe the Word of God.

It is from this passage that we learn the true meaning and nature of death. The dictionary defines it as being the cessation of all vital functions; and this being true, we accept it. The Platonist defines it as being the separation of the soul from the body and holds that death affects only the bodily aspect of man. Thus, "separation" is the prominent word in all his declarations concerning death. But the Biblicist declares that death is a return. Man is soil and he returns to it. He was given the breath of life, which becomes his spirit; and at death that breath which is his life or spirit returns unto God Who gave it.

At Adam's death the work of creation went into reverse. He was made from the soil and then given the breath of life which caused him to become a living soul. This was man's creation; and if the process is reversed, you will have man's death. This is the plain testimony of Ecclesiastes 12:7 where, after four things are mentioned which symbolize death, Solomon says: "Then shall the dust return to the earth as it was: and the spirit shall return to God Who gave it."

At death, no part of man or the man as a whole enters into any new, strange, or unknown condition. The man came from the soil, and he returns to it. The spirit (breath of life) came from God, and at death it will return to the One Who gave it. And there is nothing that can bring man back from this condition except the experience of resurrection, worked by the One Who is Himself the Resurrection and the Life.

If there were no resurrection of the dead, then death would be the end of man. It would mean the loss of all that he ever was: "For if the dead rise not, ... then they also which are fallen asleep in Christ are perished." (1 Cor. 15:16, 18).

If it were not for resurrection, death would be man's destruction. God would lose nothing, but man would lose everything. Nothing but resurrection can take man out of the state into which death working in him finally brings him. Our hope is in resurrection, not in death.

The SEED and BREAD Bible-Study leaflets are published as often as time and means permit and are sent free to all names on THE WORD OF TRUTH MINISTRY mailing list. Send us your name. There will be no obligation, solicitation, or visitation. Additional copies of any issue available on request.   ISSUE NO. 79

SEED & BREAD

FOR THE SOWER   ISA. 55:10   FOR THE EATER

BRIEF BIBLICAL MESSAGES
FROM
THE WORD OF TRUTH MINISTRY
339 South Orange Drive, Los Angeles, Cal. 90036

Otis Q. Sellers, Bible Teacher

CONCERNING RESURRECTION

It will be my purpose in this study to exercise great care in order that all words shall be used accurately, so that Paul's admonition in 2 Timothy 1:13 to "hold fast the form of sound words" will be obeyed.

The great truth of "the resurrection of the dead" is a divine truth. It is not found in man's religions or in his religious beliefs, unless these have come in contact with the Word of God. Even then they are corrupt and bear little resemblance to the Truth of Scripture. Therefore, in dealing with these things, they must be presented in harmony with the principle set forth in 1 Cor. 2:13: "Which things also we speak, not in the words which man's wisdom teacheth, but which the Holy Ghost (Spirit) teacheth."

In Christendom we find the phrase "the resurrection of the body" used continually. This fits in well with the Platonic theory of man's nature, but it is a phrase that is never found in the Word of God. The phrase used consistently in the Bible is "the resurrection of the dead." This teaches us that it is the one who died that is raised and not just some part or aspect of him called the body.

In insisting upon the use of the God-breathed words "the resurrection of the dead," this does not mean that I believe that resurrection is not literal and actual. I do believe that man is raised from the dead, actually, literally, and bodily. I am insisting only that since it is a man that dies, it is a man that is raised from the dead.

I will never permit anyone to take from me the words that God has used and put into my mouth the words they use. Over and over, the Spirit of God inspired men to speak of "the resurrection of the dead." He never led them to speak of "the resurrection of the body." This fact makes it quite simple to choose the path of faithfulness to His words and to obey the admonition of Jeremiah, "he that hath My word, let him speak My word faithfully" (Jer. 23:28). I well know that Scripture states, "it is raised a spiritual body." I fully believe this, but this has no bearing on the matter before us. We are dealing with man's phrase, "the resurrection of the body," which is used to imply that it is only the body that is dead, and God's phrase, "the resurrection of the dead." It is my choice to speak God's thoughts after Him, and in His own words.

In answering the question, "What is resurrection?" one that is seldom asked, we can say by the Word of God that resurrection is the restoration of life to one who is dead; it is an act of God that takes one from among the dead and places him among the living. If one is not dead, then resurrection would be needless and impossible. It is positively not the resuscitation of someone who is apparently dead or the reviving of one who is very near to death. It is not reincarnation, wherein something, called "the soul" by some and "the spirit" by others, returns to the body from which it supposedly moved out. The facts concerning resurrection are supported by every instance of restoration to life recorded in the Word of God. We will consider one such record.

In Luke 7:11-15 we have the divine report of the raising of the widow's son. It is a narrative of facts, and from it we can learn much about resurrection. Each word needs to be carefully considered.

And it came to pass the day after, that He went into a city called Nain; and many of His disciples went with Him, and much people. Now when He came nigh to the gate of the city, behold, there was a dead man carried out, the only son of his mother, and she was a widow: and much people of the city was with her.

And when the Lord saw her, He had compassion on her, and said unto her, Weep not. And He came and touched the bier: and they that bare him stood still. And He said, Young man, I say unto thee, Arise. And he that was dead sat up, and began to speak. And He delivered him to his mother.

The words, "there was a dead man carried out" are an exact expression of what took place. These are not the words of man's wisdom. They are words of the Holy Spirit. They are not the carelessly chosen words of man. They are the inspired words of God. When the Lord spoke to the dead man, He said, "Young man, I say unto thee, arise." And the inspired record tells us that "he that was dead sat up."

In the light of these emphatic statements, certain questions should be asked and honestly answered. Was this a dead man or merely a body from which the man had departed? Was our Lord speaking to a "young man" or to a body when He said, "Young man, arise"? But most important of all, was this man dead or alive? If anyone insists he was alive, let them tell that to the Lord in the day when men shall give an account for every idle word.

This record will show plainly that all illustrations of resurrection such as the trees putting forth their buds or the flowers springing up from bulbs or seeds in the ground, so common in sermons at that time of the year that the world and the church call Easter, bear no likeness to resurrection whatsoever.

God's answer to death is resurrection. Whatever death is, resurrection is the undoing of it. Therefore, what one believes concerning death will have a profound influence on his belief concerning resurrection. If we are in possession of God's truth concerning death, we can go on and possess God's truth concerning resurrection. If we are in error in regard to the nature of death, we will then have to wrest the truth concerning resurrection to make it fit our false ideas. God's truth concerning death appears very early in Scripture.

The orthodox idea that is prevalent throughout Christendom is that in death the body is but a garment laid aside from use, or a dwelling abandoned while the dweller in the house has gone elsewhere. But this is not what we find in God's Word. A directly opposite view is there set forth. The body, dead and lifeless though it may be, is always looked upon as the man. This is the uniform, unvarying testimony of Scripture. Thus, when we read of death and burial in the Bible, it is always the man who is laid in the grave. Sarah, Abraham, Jacob, and Moses were buried. The Bible does not speak of them as having gone somewhere else or as being anywhere alse except in the grave. The person, the individual, the man, he who was once alive is spoken of as lying in the grave. (See Gen. 23:2, 19; 25:8, 9; 50:26; and Deut. 34:5, 6.)

God's truth concerning death, like His truth concerning sin and future punishment, is not pleasant truth. He never intended that man should find any consolation, not in sin and death, but in Christ our Savior from sin and our Redeemer from death. He would turn our eyes toward the One Who is our Resurrection and our Life. Our entrance into His presence will not be by means of the enemy death, but by means of resurrection through Jesus Christ.

The very fact of resurrection tells us that death is not man's end. Death is only for a time. It is not eternal, and it is not man's destruction. I accept without question the testimony of the Bible that my history as a living soul will come to an end at death. I will return to the soil and the life that God allowed me to have for all these years will return to Him Who gave it. He gave it to me with every breath I have ever drawn, but I have no assurance that my next breath will not be my last. No line will be added to my history, no matter how long I am in the state of death. I will do no work; I will gain no knowledge; I will have no experiences. However, my history will begin again on the day of my resurrection. Glorious day! I will then take up where I left off.

False teaching has led many to believe that the day we die is actually the day we begin to live, that death is a door that leads to a greater and fuller life. God forbid that I should believe this lie of Satan; for if this were true, resurrection would be wholly unnecessary.

Of course, I know from experience that many who read this study will say: "Then you belive that the soul sleeps between death and resurrection"; so I will here state emphatically that I do not believe any such thing. My understanding of the soul makes such a belief impossible. Others will say, "Then you must believe that the dead are unconscious." And again I must say that I do not believe this. I do not believe in "soul sleep," and I know that the words *conscious* and *unconscious* can only be applied to the living. I believe that a man can be alive and conscious or alive and unconscious; but when he is dead, he is neither *conscious* nor *unconscious*. He is dead, and only resurrection will remove him from this state.

In the Biblical record of the death of Christ, we find the statement that Joseph begged the body of Jesus from Pilate; and after receiving permission, he came and took the body of Jesus. Some would make out of this wording the idea it was no longer Jesus, it was only His body. However, this is false; for as if to expressly guard against any such idea, it further declares: "Now in the place where He was crucified there was a garden; and in the garden a new sepulchre, wherein was never man yet laid. There laid they Jesus" (John 19:41, 42). When Mary came to the tomb on the morning of His resurrection, she reported to Peter and John, "They have taken away the Lord out of the sepulchre, and we know not where they have laid Him" (John 20:2). When the disciples were sore perplexed at this strange turn of events, two heavenly messengers appeared and said to them: "Why seek ye the living among the dead? He is not here, but is risen" (Luke 24:5, 6). And if we ask why He was not among the dead, the answer comes back, "Because He had risen." If He had not risen, He would still be among the dead.

Over and over again, Christian people make the firm declaration, "We do not worship a dead Christ." This is true, we do not worship One Who is dead. Our Savior is a living, active, working Savior. But it must always be kept in mind that the one reason we have for making such declarations is because He arose from the dead. Apart from resurrection, He would not be alive. And once any man enters into the state of death, he will never live again apart from resurrection.

Truth at times may be bitter, but it is never disappointing. We must face the facts. If there is no resurrection of the dead, our loved ones have perished. We can chisel on their tombstones "NO HOPE," if the dead rise not (1 Cor. 15:16-19). But before we take this radical step, let us hear the words of our Lord Christ Jesus:

I am He that liveth, and was dead; and, behold, I am alive forevermore. Rev. 1:18.

These things saith the First and the Last, Which was dead, and is alive. Rev. 2:8.

Because I live, ye shall live also. John 14:19.

The SEED and BREAD Bible-Study leaflets are published as often as time and means permit and are sent free to all names on THE WORD OF TRUTH MINISTRY mailing list. Send us your name. There will be no obligation, solicitation, or visitation. Additional copies of any issue available on request.   ISSUE NO. 80

SEED & BREAD

FOR THE SOWER　　ISA. 55:10　　FOR THE EATER

BRIEF BIBLICAL MESSAGES
FROM
THE WORD OF TRUTH MINISTRY
339 South Orange Drive, Los Angeles, Cal. 90036

Otis Q. Sellers, Bible Teacher

CONCERNING RESURRECTION

It will be my purpose in this study to exercise great care in order that all words shall be used accurately, so that Paul's admonition in 2 Timothy 1:13 to "hold fast the form of sound words" will be obeyed.

The great truth of "the resurrection of the dead" is a divine truth. It is not found in man's religions or in his religious beliefs, unless these have come in contact with the Word of God. Even then they are corrupt and bear little resemblance to the Truth of Scripture. Therefore, in dealing with these things, they must be presented in harmony with the principle set forth in 1 Cor. 2:13: "Which things also we speak, not in the words which man's wisdom teacheth, but which the Holy Ghost (Spirit) teacheth."

In Christendom we find the phrase "the resurrection of the body" used continually. This fits in well with the Platonic theory of man's nature, but it is a phrase that is never found in the Word of God. The phrase used consistently in the Bible is "the resurrection of the dead." This teaches us that it is the one who died that is raised and not just some part or aspect of him called the body.

In insisting upon the use of the God-breathed words "the resurrection of the dead," this does not mean that I believe that resurrection is not literal and actual. I do believe that man is raised from the dead, actually, literally, and bodily. I am insisting only that since it is a man that dies, it is a man that is raised from the dead.

I will never permit anyone to take from me the words that God has used and put into my mouth the words they use. Over and over, the Spirit of God inspired men to speak of "the resurrection of the dead." He never led them to speak of "the resurrection of the body." This fact makes it quite simple to choose the path of faithfulness to His words and to obey the admonition of Jeremiah, "he that hath My word, let him speak My word faithfully" (Jer. 23:28). I well know that Scripture states, "it is raised a spiritual body." I fully believe this, but this has no bearing on the matter before us. We are dealing with man's phrase, "the resurrection of the body," which is used to imply that it is only the body that is dead, and God's phrase, "the resurrection of the dead." It is my choice to speak God's thoughts after Him, and in His own words.

In answering the question, "What is resurrection?" one that is seldom asked, we can say by the Word of God that resurrection is the restoration of life to one who is dead; it is an act of God that takes one from among the dead and places him among the living. If one is not dead, then resurrection would be needless and impossible. It is positively not the resuscitation of someone who is apparently dead or the reviving of one who is very near to death. It is not reincarnation, wherein something, called "the soul" by some and "the spirit" by others, returns to the body from which it supposedly moved out. The facts concerning resurrection are supported by every instance of restoration to life recorded in the Word of God. We will consider one such record.

In Luke 7:11-15 we have the divine report of the raising of the widow's son. It is a narrative of facts, and from it we can learn much about resurrection. Each word needs to be carefully considered.

And it came to pass the day after, that He went into a city called Nain; and many of His disciples went with Him, and much people. Now when He came nigh to the gate of the city, behold, there was a dead man carried out, the only son of his mother, and she was a widow: and much people of the city was with her.

And when the Lord saw her, He had compassion on her, and said unto her, Weep not. And He came and touched the bier: and they that bare him stood still. And He said, Young man, I say unto thee, Arise. And he that was dead sat up, and began to speak. And He delivered him to his mother.

The words, "there was a dead man carried out" are an exact expression of what took place. These are not the words of man's wisdom. They are words of the Holy Spirit. They are not the carelessly chosen words of man. They are the inspired words of God. When the Lord spoke to the dead man, He said, "Young man, I say unto thee, arise." And the inspired record tells us that "he that was dead sat up."

In the light of these emphatic statements, certain questions should be asked and honestly answered. Was this a dead man or merely a body from which the man had departed? Was our Lord speaking to a "young man" or to a body when He said, "Young man, arise"? But most important of all, was this man dead or alive? If anyone insists he was alive, let them tell that to the Lord in the day when men shall give an account for every idle word.

This record will show plainly that all illustrations of resurrection such as the trees putting forth their buds or the flowers springing up from bulbs or seeds in the ground, so common in sermons at that time of the year that the world and the church call Easter, bear no likeness to resurrection whatsoever.

God's answer to death is resurrection. Whatever death is, resurrection is the undoing of it. Therefore, what one believes concerning death will have a profound influence on his belief concerning resurrection. If we are in possession of God's truth concerning death, we can go on and possess God's truth concerning resurrection. If we are in error in regard to the nature of death, we will then have to wrest the truth concerning resurrection to make it fit our false ideas. God's truth concerning death appears very early in Scripture.

The orthodox idea that is prevalent throughout Christendom is that in death the body is but a garment laid aside from use, or a dwelling abandoned while the dweller in the house has gone elsewhere. But this is not what we find in God's Word. A directly opposite view is there set forth. The body, dead and lifeless though it may be, is always looked upon as the man. This is the uniform, unvarying testimony of Scripture. Thus, when we read of death and burial in the Bible, it is always the man who is laid in the grave. Sarah, Abraham, Jacob, and Moses were buried. The Bible does not speak of them as having gone somewhere else or as being anywhere alse except in the grave. The person, the individual, the man, he who was once alive is spoken of as lying in the grave. (See Gen. 23:2, 19; 25:8, 9; 50:26; and Deut. 34:5, 6.)

God's truth concerning death, like His truth concerning sin and future punishment, is not pleasant truth. He never intended that man should find any consolation, not in sin and death, but in Christ our Savior from sin and our Redeemer from death. He would turn our eyes toward the One Who is our Resurrection and our Life. Our entrance into His presence will not be by means of the enemy death, but by means of resurrection through Jesus Christ.

The very fact of resurrection tells us that death is not man's end. Death is only for a time. It is not eternal, and it is not man's destruction. I accept without question the testimony of the Bible that my history as a living soul will come to an end at death. I will return to the soil and the life that God allowed me to have for all these years will return to Him Who gave it. He gave it to me with every breath I have ever drawn, but I have no assurance that my next breath will not be my last. No line will be added to my history, no matter how long I am in the state of death. I will do no work; I will gain no knowledge; I will have no experiences. However, my history will begin again on the day of my resurrection. Glorious day! I will then take up where I left off.

False teaching has led many to believe that the day we die is actually the day we begin to live, that death is a door that leads to a greater and fuller life. God forbid that I should believe this lie of Satan; for if this were true, resurrection would be wholly unnecessary.

Of course, I know from experience that many who read this study will say: "Then you belive that the soul sleeps between death and resurrection"; so I will here state emphatically that I do not believe any such thing. My understanding of the soul makes such a belief impossible. Others will say, "Then you must believe that the dead are unconscious." And again I must say that I do not believe this. I do not believe in "soul sleep," and I know that the words *conscious* and *unconscious* can only be applied to the living. I believe that a man can be alive and conscious or alive and unconscious; but when he is dead, he is neither *conscious* nor *unconscious*. He is dead, and only resurrection will remove him from this state.

In the Biblical record of the death of Christ, we find the statement that Joseph begged the body of Jesus from Pilate; and after receiving permission, he came and took the body of Jesus. Some would make out of this wording the idea it was no longer Jesus, it was only His body. However, this is false; for as if to expressly guard against any such idea, it further declares: "Now in the place where He was crucified there was a garden; and in the garden a new sepulchre, wherein was never man yet laid. There laid they Jesus" (John 19:41, 42). When Mary came to the tomb on the morning of His resurrection, she reported to Peter and John, "They have taken away the Lord out of the sepulchre, and we know not where they have laid Him" (John 20:2). When the disciples were sore perplexed at this strange turn of events, two heavenly messengers appeared and said to them: "Why seek ye the living among the dead? He is not here, but is risen" (Luke 24:5, 6). And if we ask why He was not among the dead, the answer comes back, "Because He had risen." If He had not risen, He would still be among the dead.

Over and over again, Christian people make the firm declaration, "We do not worship a dead Christ." This is true, we do not worship One Who is dead. Our Savior is a living, active, working Savior. But it must always be kept in mind that the one reason we have for making such declarations is because He arose from the dead. Apart from resurrection, He would not be alive. And once any man enters into the state of death, he will never live again apart from resurrection.

Truth at times may be bitter, but it is never disappointing. We must face the facts. If there is no resurrection of the dead, our loved ones have perished. We can chisel on their tombstones "NO HOPE," if the dead rise not (1 Cor. 15:16-19). But before we take this radical step, let us hear the words of our Lord Christ Jesus:

I am He that liveth, and was dead; and, behold, I am alive forevermore. Rev. 1:18.

These things saith the First and the Last, Which was dead, and is alive. Rev. 2:8.

Because I live, ye shall live also. John 14:19.

The SEED and BREAD Bible-Study leaflets are published as often as time and means permit and are sent free to all names on THE WORD OF TRUTH MINISTRY mailing list. Send us your name. There will be no obligation, solicitation, or visitation. Additional copies of any issue available on request.   ISSUE NO. 80

SEED & BREAD

FOR THE SOWER   ISA. 55:10   FOR THE EATER

BRIEF BIBLICAL MESSAGES

FROM

THE WORD OF TRUTH MINISTRY

339 South Orange Drive, Los Angeles, Cal. 90036

Otis Q. Sellers, Bible Teacher

INTERPRETATION OF MATT. 10:28

Professing Christians who hold the Platonic theory as to the nature of man are quite firm in their belief that the soul is a detachable and separable part of man that lives on as a true and complete man after the body is dead. And most of these seem to find the greatest comfort and support for this theory in the words spoken by our Lord to His disciples when He said:

And fear not them which kill the body, but are not able to kill the soul: but rather fear Him which is able to destroy both soul and body in hell. Matt. 10:28.

This passage is said to declare the inherent immortality of the soul, its everlasting character, along with all the ideas that accompany the Greek body-soul dualism that arises out of such a belief. To the Platonist this verse declares that there is a detachable part of man that survives the death of the body, and that this part is the real and true man who is just as well off without a body as he is with one.

This interpretation can be easily and readily accepted by the superficial Bible reader who has never made a logical study of all the Biblical material that concerns the soul — a study that can be made by anyone who has access to an analytical concordance (Young's or Strong's). Even a cursory study will bring the conviction that the Hebrew word for soul is *nephesh*, and that this word is used interchangeably by the Holy Spirit with the Greek word *psuchē*, the word for "soul" in the New Testament. Compare Isa. 42:1 with Matt. 12:18; Deut. 6:5 with Matt. 22:37; and Psalm 16:10 with Acts 2:27. Thus in harmony with the law of divine interchange of Hebrew and Greek words we can declare with full confidence that these two words are identical in meaning and of equal value.

In view of these facts we know that Matthew 10:28 is only one of the 859 passages in the Word of God that gives testimony in regard to the soul. And to borrow the phrasing of our Lord, we can properly say that one should not build his convictions on one occurrence of a word, but on every occurrence of that word that has proceeded from the mouth of God (See Matt. 4:4).

Whatever conclusions one may come to in regard to Matt. 10:28, whatever doctrine he may build upon it, or ideas he may seek to prove by it, all these must be in harmony with the great mass of divine truth given in the word of God concerning the soul, also in harmony with the Biblical definition given of it. The human soul is what the man became when God breathed into his nostrils the breath of life (Gen. 2:7). We must reject flatly, firmly and once and for all any interpretation or use made of this passage which puts it into direct conflict with other clear passages. No interpretation can be accepted that makes Scripture to be contradictory and confusing.

Having made an assiduous study of the Hebrew word *nephesh* in all its occurrences, I have entered into certain truths that I can never forget, ignore, or lay aside. For example, it is positive truth that the Hebrew original of Lev. 24:17, 18 reads: "He that killeth the soul of a man shall surely be put to death, and he that killeth the soul of a beast shall make it good, soul for soul."

The word *nephesh* is found four times in these two passages, but the *King James* translators well knew what an accurate rendering would do to their treasured Platonic philosophy, so they took care of the matter by ignoring two occurrences altogether and rendering the other two by the word "beast."

Any student can verify the 'fact that in Numbers 35:30 the Hebrew says: "Whosoever killeth any soul, the murderer shall be put to death;" and that Numbers 6:6 actually speaks of a "dead soul" (*muth nephesh*).

Thus it is crystal clear that the Spirit of God in the Old Testament speaks of men killing the soul, while in Matt. 10:28 it seems that the Lord Jesus speaks of men not being able to kill the soul. Therefore, on the principle of mutual exclusivity, both of these ideas cannot be true; and I, for one, will not accept any understanding or interpretation of Matt. 10:28 that places Jesus Christ in the position of being in direct conflict with the Old Testament. For if man is not able to kill the soul, then the commandments of God with their severe penalties given in Lev. 24:17, 18 and Num. 35:30 make about as much sense as if our government should make it an offense punishable by death if anyone interferes with the rising of the sun in the morning.

As one who publicly professes to love the truth, to hold it, and to proclaim it, I would not be able to sleep at night if I set forth the interpretation of Matt. 10:28 that most men are giving today. Therefore, I, for one, must find an honest interpretation of this passage, one that will be in harmony with the definition of the soul given in Gen. 2:7, and it must also be one that will not make ridiculous the divine laws given in Lev. 24:17, 18, and Num. 35:30.

A comparison of this passage with the parallel passage in Luke's Gospel should be made. Luke gives an explanatory rendering of this passage in which the soul is not mentioned. There we read: "And I say unto you My friends, be not afraid of them that kill the body, and after that have no more that they can do. But I will forewarn you whom ye shall fear: Fear Him, which after He hath killed hath power to cast into Gehenna; yea, I say unto you, Fear Him" (Luke 12:4,5).

From this passage it seems clear that if the thrust of truth in Matthew 10:28 was to set forth "an immortal soul," or "a never-dying soul," or "an indestructible soul," as so many insist, this would not have been omitted by Luke. He would not cut the very heart out of this passage if "an immortal soul" is the heart of it.

This passage deals with whom the disciples shall not fear and Whom they shall fear. They are not to fear men who can kill only the body but cannot go beyond this, but they are to fear Him which after He has killed, can destroy both soul and body in Gehenna. These words from the lips of our Lord are remarkable, inasmuch as they were spoken at a time when Greek philosophy taught that the true man was an eternal soul that could not die, could not be killed, and was indestructible. These ideas were almost universally held, and were so prestigious that the Greeks classified all men as barbarians who did not hold them. This philosophy had permeated into the thinking of many in Israel, but our Lord negated this whole system of thought when He flew into the face of all Greeks who taught this and all in Israel who assented to it when He said: "Fear Him who is able to destroy both soul and body in Gehenna." A soul that can be destroyed is certainly not eternal or immortal.

The *King James* translators, whose thinking had been deeply permeated by the Platonic philosophy, solved most problems of conflict by translating most of the Old Testament in harmony with their views. However, the man who has committed himself unalterably to the truth cannot allow himself any such liberties with the original words spoken by God. And, beyond all question, the commonly accepted interpretation and use made of Matt. 10:28 throws it into direct conflict with many clear passages in the Old Testament. To avoid this we must pay close attention to all the words that God has used. This will be the key that solves the problem of Matt. 10:28.

The New Testament word for "murder" is the verb *phoneuō*. From this is derived the noun *phoneus* which means a murderer. This verb has a fixed meaning as examination of its twelve occurrences will show. It is never used of a judicial killing, what we call "capital punishment."

Another word is *apokteinō*, which is a more flexible word, but it is the word that is always used when a legal or judicial deprivation of life is in view. Its exact meaning is regulated by its context, and when the context supports it, it always means to put to death by judicial decree. See Matt. 16:21, John 16:2 and 18:31 as examples of this. The word *apokteinō* is found twice in Matt. 10:28

and twice in Luke 12:4,5. With these facts in mind we will examine the context of this passage.

In the section that makes up Matt. 10:16-28 it is plain that the Lord Jesus is looking far into the future, while at the same time He is applying His words to the immediate experiences of His disciples. He warns them concerning men who will deliver them up to the councils and scourge them in their synagogues, tells them that they will be brought before governors and kings for His sake, and that they would be hated and persecuted. But when and if this comes upon them they are not to cease their testimony. What He had told them in darkness, they were to speak in light; and what He had whispered in their ears, they were to proclaim from the housetops. And at no time were they to allow their actions to be shaped by the fear of men, not even the most powerful men. These can only kill the body, and afterward have no more that they can do, But they are to fear Him who is able to destroy both soul and body in Gehenna.

Thus it is evident that the word "kill" in this passage has to do with the judicial sentencing of a man to death, so that by a legal process his life, his labors, his influence, and his testimony are all brought to an end. Such judges would probably rub their hands in glee, congratulate one another, and say: "A good work, that troublemaker is dead and done for!" But, we ask, is he? The answer has to be, "No, by no means." That man will be heard from again — not because he survived death, or that his soul lives on, but because of the great fact of resurrection from among the dead.

It is probable that the real key to the meaning of Matt. 10:28 is found in the fact that in Hebrew thought, the word "soul" regularly stands as a simple personal pronoun and is used in places where we would use *I, myself,* or *me.*

Our Lord was a Hebrew, not a Greek, and the men He spoke to were Hebrews. It is in harmony with this fact that we find the true meaning of His words in Matt. 10:28. The powerful rulers who would sentence the Lord's apostles to death could only bring them to an end as animated bodies, but they could not bring an end to the apostles themselves. Of all that the Father gave the Son He would lose nothing. Not because they were still living after having been killed, but because He would raise them up in the coming day (John 6:39).

This passage does not teach the Greek idea of a detachable and immortal soul. But it does declare a future life for one that evil judges thought was gone forever.

The SEED and BREAD Bible-Study leaflets are published as often as time and means permit and are sent free to all names on THE WORD OF TRUTH MINISTRY mailing list. Send us your name. There will be no obligation, solicitation, or visitation. Additional copies of any issue available on request.   ISSUE NO. 81

SEED & BREAD

FOR THE SOWER   ISA. 55:10   FOR THE EATER

BRIEF BIBLICAL MESSAGES

FROM

THE WORD OF TRUTH MINISTRY

339 South Orange Drive, Los Angeles, Cal. 90036

Otis Q. Sellers, Bible Teacher

WHAT DOES SHEOL MEAN?

The word *sheol* is a Hebrew word that is found sixty-five times in the Old Testament. It is an important and significant word to which very little studious attention has been given. Translators have used it and abused it in order to get the word and the ideas of "hell" into the Hebrew Scriptures. It has been translated three ways in the *King James Version* as follows: "Grave," 31 times; "hell," 31 times; "pit," 3 times. This arbitrary and inconsistent treatment of the word *sheol* prompts the following conclusions. If *sheol* means "grave," then it does not mean "hell," and if it means either of these, then it does not mean "pit." It appears that the *King James* translators rendered it "grave" when it spoke of a good man going there, and "hell" when it spoke of an evil man departing this life. As to why they translated it "pit" is anybody's guess.

The truth is that *sheol* does not mean grave, hell, or pit. This fact was recognized by the translators of the *American Standard Version* (Nelson, 1901). They admirably solved the problem imposed by this word, one for which there is no English equivalent, by carrying over the word *sheol* in every occurrence. However, when the ASV was revised in 1952 and became the *Revised Standard Version,* the revisers reverted to the word "grave" in 1 Kgs. 2:9 and Song of Solomon 8:6, which did no more than create a bit of translational foolishness and inconsistency.

The word *sheol* is a noun, and in view of the prevailing grammatical illiteracy, some may need to be reminded that a noun is the word that tells what one is talking about. A noun is a word that means something. Thus the question before us is, what is it that is called *sheol*, what idea did the Spirit of God desire should come into our minds when we come upon this word in Scripture?

Since the meaning of any word is established by its usage, it follows that the meaning of Biblical words should be established by the use made of them in Scripture. An examination in situ of the sixty-five occurrences of this word should bring a definite conviction as to its meaning. If this will not do it, then there is no possible way in which it can be defined, and we may as well forget the whole matter, and let each attach to it a meaning according to his own imagination. Having made this examination many times, I believe that *sheol* is a name for the state of death. It signifies the state into which one comes as a result of the process of death having worked in him until it gained the victory. There is a state of life and there is a state of death. The Hebrews had a name for this state into which the death process is constantly bringing men, and that name was *sheol*.

If we should say that a man lived eighty years and then died, we would be speaking the truth as we see it. However, it would be just as true to say that this man was dying for eighty years until at last death gained its victory. This truth is set forth in an accurate grammatical rendering of 1 Cor. 15:22 which declares: "For as in Adam all are dying, even so in Christ shall all be made alive." The word "dying" here is present tense, and the words "made alive" are future. Because of what Adam did, all men are dying now; and because of what Christ has done and will yet do all will be made alive. In that time that may elapse between the conclusion of death working in us and our being made alive we will be in the state of death, a condition that the Hebrews called *sheol*.

Scripture speaks of the living and it speaks of the dead (2 Tim. 4:1). We enter into the company of the living by birth, and we enter the company of the dead when the breath of life (our spirit) goes out of us. The Lord Jesus was in the state of death (*sheol*) for three days and three nights, and He would still be there if He had not been raised from among the dead. In the Psalms He said prophetically of Himself: "Thou wilt not leave My soul (Me) in the state of death; neither wilt Thou suffer thine Holy One to see corruption "(Psa. 16:10).

The definition that has been given of the word *sheol* can be tested by every occurrence in the Old Testament. It will be found to be viable, and if the passages where it is found are examined without prejudice, it will enlighten each verse in which it occurs. Only a few of these can be examined in the space available in this leaflet.

The occurrence in Gen. 37:5 is important because it is first. Jacob believed that an evil beast had killed his beloved son Joseph, and mourned for him many days. His sons and daughters sought to console him, but he refused to be comforted, declaring that his sorrow would continue until he had joined his son in the state of death (*sheol*).

In Gen. 42:38; 44:29, 31 we find three occurrences which along with the one cited above have been used to prove that *sheol* is a place of mourning and sorrow. This is apparently done to make this word to mean a place of frightfulness, and thus get minds ready for the further idea that *sheol* means "hell;" that is, a place of torment and suffering.

The sorrow of Jacob over the loss of Joseph seems to have been eased in some measure by his delight in Benjamin. When his brothers sought to take him into Egypt to confirm the truth of their statements made to Joseph, Jacob was loath for him to go, out of fear that something evil would happen to him on the journey. He declared that if any evil should befall him that he would go into the state of death (*sheol*). In other words, he said he would die of a broken heart.

Since Jacob spoke of going "down" into *sheol*, his statements have been used to support the theory that it is a place downward, and is located somewhere inside of the earth. However, *sheol* is not a place. It is a state or condition, and when we compare the state of the dead with the state of the living, the word "down" properly describes its character. In all the Old Testament the word *sheol* is never related to life, to a place of life, or a state of life.

Hannah, in her inspired prayers after the birth of Samuel, declares: "The LORD killeth, and maketh alive: He bringeth down to *sheol* and bringeth up" (1 Sam. 2:6). This being Hebrew poetry, we find a repetition of ideas. Here "killing" is the equivalent of bringing down to *sheol*, and "making alive" is the equivalent of bringing up from *sheol*. Hannah's conception of *sheol* was one of death, not of life.

David set forth the same idea of *sheol* in telling of his own experiences: "When the waves of death compassed me, the floods of ungodly men made me afraid; the sorrows of *sheol* compassed me about; the snares of death prevented (had confronted) me about" (2 Sam. 22:5,6). This is a theme which is repeated many times in the Psalms. In Psa. 30:3 we read: "O Lord Thou hast brought up my soul from *sheol*: thou hast kept me alive from going down into the pit." David was never in *sheol*, but apart from divine intervention he would have been. Therefore, he spoke of his experience as if it had been real.

In the Old Testament *sheol* and *death* are used synonymously; they are always linked together as being one and the same. *Sheol* is beyond all doubt the state of death. Therefore, those in the state of death cannot be alive, and there is no release from this state except by resurrection. "For if the dead rise not . . . . Then they also which are fallen asleep in Christ are perished" (1 Cor. 15:16, 18).

Among the passages that need to be considered because they give explicit information in regard to those who are in the state of death (*sheol*) is Psalm 6:5: "For in death there is no remembrance of Thee: and in *sheol* who shall give Thee thanks." Again in Psalm 89:48 the question is asked: "What man is he that liveth, and shall not see death? Shall he deliver his soul from the hand of *sheol*?" Solomon urged, "Whatsoever thy hand findeth to do, do it with all thy might, for there is no work, nor planning, nor knowledge, nor wisdom in *sheol* whither thou goest." Eccl. 9:10.

A note on Isaiah 14:9-17 is necessary as the word *sheol* is found three times in this portion, verses 9, 11, and 15; and the passage is used to prove that there are conversations in *sheol*. In considering this passage we must not forget that the prophecy of Isaiah is Hebrew poetry, and as is usual in poetry the language is highly figurative, going even to the point of poetic license. This is certainly done in 14:8 where we are told that trees are speaking. I am convinced that the language of this portion is the most highly figurative in the Old Testament. A note from F. C. Jennings is apropos here: "We must most surely not assume with some, that we have here a simple prosaic revelation of the world of the dead, any more than that in the previous verse we are told with prosaic literalness that the trees talk. In both cases the language is intensely poetical, and yet nothing could more graphically bring before our minds the height from which this king of Babylon had fallen, and the depth to which that fall had taken him."

The difficult nature of this passage must not be minimized, yet the idea that it sets forth life as it is in *sheol* is absurd.

The witness of good King Hezekiah is most important. In Isaiah 38 we find that he was sick unto death and had been told by the prophet to set his house in order, for he was to die and not live. This is proof that life and death are opposites, and that death cannot be life in another place. The King made this a matter of earnest prayer, bringing to God's attention his life and walk before Him, and the Lord answered his prayer by promising him fifteen more years of life. When he recovered from his illness he wrote of his dealings with God wherein he said: "I said in the cutting off of my days, I shall go to the gates of *sheol*, I am deprived of the residue of my years. I said, I shall not see the LORD, even the LORD, in the land of the living, I shall behold man no more with the inhabitants of the world" (Isa. 38:10, 11). Furthermore, he declared, "For *sheol* cannot praise Thee, death cannot celebrate Thee: they that go down into the pit cannot hope for Thy truth. The living, the living, he shall praise Thee, as I do this day" (Isa. 38:18, 19).

May all the living who read these words be generated of God to make an honest study of this important word.

The SEED and BREAD Bible-Study leaflets are published as often as time and means permit and are sent free to all names on THE WORD OF TRUTH MINISTRY mailing list. Send us your name. There will be no obligation, solicitation, or visitation. Additional copies of any issue available on request.   ISSUE NO. 82

SEED & BREAD

FOR THE SOWER   ISA. 55:10   FOR THE EATER

BRIEF BIBLICAL MESSAGES
FROM
THE WORD OF TRUTH MINISTRY
339 South Orange Drive, Los Angeles, Cal. 90036

Otis Q. Sellers, Bible Teacher

IF A MAN DIE?

The question that forms the title of this study is one from the Word of God. It was asked by the patriarch Job as he was giving an answer to his three friends. Seeing it set forth in bold type, many will be inclined to say: There is no "if" about it. It is appointed unto men once to die, as the writer of Hebrews boldly declares (Heb. 9:27). However, the title above is only part of the question, for the thrust of Job's query is in the second part. The full question is: "If a man die, shall he live again?" (Job 14:14).

To the adherents of traditional, orthodox theology, who accept without reserve the Platonic theories of death and life, Job's question must sound quite foolish. Since, according to their views, no one ever dies, they simply leave their bodies to live on some higher plane of existence, why ask the foolish question, "If a man die," there being to them no such thing as death. And why ask if he shall live again, since the dead are always alive? As one prominent minister of traditional orthodoxy declares it: "The true man is a soul, and once it is created it is immortal and will continue forever, either in bliss or in torment."

But where in God's Word do we find anything about the creation of an immortal soul? We read of the creation of man in Genesis 2:7, and we also find that this man became a living soul by a further act of God. Therefore, since it was a man that God created, and if this man dies, how can the living soul which he became continue to live? Furthermore, why ask the question, "Shall he live again?" if the man is not dead?

The Biblicist, who has purged himself of Plato's philosophy, will recognize immediately that Job's question is a sensible and proper one. We answer it in the affirmative, declaring that if a man dies he will live again — not because he survives the experience of death, but because of the fact of the resurrection of the dead, the only thing that can bring anyone forth from the state of death.

Resurrection is God's answer to death. It is not a natural process, but an eminently supernatural and miraculous one. There is no such process in nature as a resurrection from actual death. Men may find some faint analogies to resurrection in one awakening from sleep, in the budding of trees in the spring, in the quickening of seeds in the ground, or in the transformation of the grub into a winged butterfly. However, these are all living processes. There is no actual death in any of these. A dead tree never lives again, dead seed will not sprout, and a dead grub will never develop into a butterfly. And, even so, if a man dies and that man lives it will be because of supernatural power that transcends all natural laws that raises him from the dead and makes him a living soul once again.

It is certainly logical and reasonable to say that if a man dies, then that man is dead. There is no value in denying this, and Scripture most certainly affirms it. Even as Peter declared in his inspired message on the day of Pentecost: "Let me freely speak to you of the patriarch David, that he is both dead and buried, and his sepulchre is with us unto this day" (Acts 2:29).

In considering the question "If a man die?" we need to make a clear distinction between "dying" and "death." Paul declares that "in Adam all are dying," which is an honest translation of the Greek of 1 Cor. 15:22. This truth is based upon the divine record of the entry of death into the world. And in view of the fact that death was threatened to Adam as the penalty for disobedience, we need to seek and find an honest answer to the question: "What was the 'death' that was threatened, and what was the 'death' that was incurred?" In the KJV it reads:

And the LORD God commanded the man, saying, of every tree of the garden thou mayest freely eat: But of the tree of the knowledge of good and evil, thou shalt not eat of it: for in the day that thou eatest thereof thou shalt surely die. Gen. 2:16,17.

These words raise the question, Did God mean that a complete cessation of life would immediately follow the act of disobedience? There are those who argue that since Adam did not "drop dead" on the day that he ate of the forbidden fruit, that the word "death" here has some other meaning than we usually give to it. It is said here to mean "spiritual death," and this is defined as being "separation from God." However, there is no such thing as "spiritual death" in the Bible, and there is no evidence that Adam was separated from God. The next thing recorded after he had sinned is that God was seeking fellowship with him (Gen. 3:8,9).

While the word "death" is used in a figurative sense in the Bible, these occurrences are quite clear and should not be used to define literal death. God made it very plain to Adam what He meant by "death" when He repeated and interpreted the nature of Adam's punishment after he had transgressed.

Because thou hast hearkened unto the voice of thy wife, and hast eaten of the tree, of which I commanded thee, saying, Thou shalt not eat of it: . . . . In the sweat of thy face shalt thou eat bread, till thou return unto the ground; for out of it wast thou taken: for dust thou art,

and unto dust shalt thou return. Gen. 3:17-19.

Thus we see that while something drastic happened to Adam on the day that he transgressed, it was not the sudden cessation of life. The key to what happened is found in the Hebrew original of Genesis 2:16-17 where the verb "die" is repeated in two different forms. The phrase should read "dying thou shalt die." Thus on the day that Adam sinned, death began to work in him and it continued to work until he reached the age of 930 years. This is an enormous life-span, but the first man was of such perfect physical health that it took the working of death a long time to wear him out.

The Apostle Paul enlarges upon this truth in his great declaration: "Therefore, even as through one man sin entered into the world and death through sin, and thus death passed through into all mankind, on which all have sinned" (Rom. 5:12). So we can truthfully say that if a man die, death has been working in him from the day of his birth. Much of the time it has probably been quite dormant, and again it may have manifested itself in active ways: illness, diseases, deformities, aging, but it works on until man keeps that appointment that none can cancel.

In this day when many who have been near to death are using their aberrational experiences and illusions to establish the nature of death, even to prove that death is a continuation of life, it will be good for all who love the truth to look away from all such experiences and consider the case of one who actually died as it is recorded in the Word of God. We find the record of the actual death and resurrection of Lazarus as set forth by the Holy Spirit. We have, therefore, a more exact view than if we had been present and saw it with our own eyes. Open your Bible to John 11.

Lazarus, who lived in Bethany with his two sisters, Mary and Martha, was sick. The process of death, which ever worked in him even as it does in all men, had suddenly flared up. The smoldering fire of death which slowly but surely consumes every man had burst into an open flame. It was evident to the sisters that this was no ordinary illness, so they sent to the Lord Jesus saying that the one whom He loved was sick.

When Jesus heard this He said: "This sickness is not unto death, but for the glory of God" (11:4). He did not say that Lazarus would not die, but only that the illness was not unto death. Since Lazarus was on the verge of death, we see that by these words He did not promise natural healing or miraculous healing, but the miracle of resurrection that would bring Lazarus back to life. That which does not end in death must end in life for there is no middle ground.

We know that the Lord loved Lazarus, Mary, and Martha; still He remained in the same place for two more days; after which He said to His disciples, "Let us go into Judea again." This brought a protest from the disciples due to the great personal danger it involved for all of them. Our Lord reassured them, and then declared: "Our friend Lazarus sleepeth: but I go, that I may awake him out of his sleep," using one figure of speech to describe death, and another figure to speak of resurrection from the dead. Death is not sleep, no more than sleep is death. As Rudolf Stier has said: "Since the days of old, men on earth, and among them the children of Israel, used this euphemism in speaking of dreadful death because of the outward similarity and in order to cast a soft veil over the grave; but in the mouth of the Lord this figure of speech turns into reality." Sleep is a good figure of death, since normal sleep is without sensation, without knowledge, and should be of unbroken oblivion.

The disciples, loath to face the fact that Lazarus was dead and that the Lord had permitted it, took the figure as a statement of fact and said, "Lord, if he sleep, he will do well," for they took it that the Lord spoke of taking rest in sleep. But our Lord corrected this at once, and dropping all figures of speech said unto them plainly, "Lazarus is dead."

In view of this direct statement we can ask every reader of these lines the question, "Was Lazarus dead or alive?" And by the answer they give we can divide the truth lovers from the tradition lovers, the believers from the twisters, the faithful from the faithless, and the Biblicist from the Platonist.

When Jesus arrived in Bethany, He asked to be shown the grave, and then requested that the stone which closed the tomb should be rolled away. This brought a protest from Mary that Lazarus had been dead for four days, that decomposition was well advanced, and that the whole scene would be offensive to smell and sight. Nevertheless, the stone was removed, and the Lord cried out, "Lazarus come forth!" And the faithful record tells us that, "he that was dead came forth."

This record of the death and resurrection of Lazarus provides a full answer to the Biblical question, "If a man die, shall he live again?" The man Lazarus died. He was in the state of death for four full days. He came out of the state of death when his name was spoken by the Lord Jesus. Of his experiences while in the state of death, he said nothing, and we are told nothing. This demonstrates the truth of Ecclesiastes that: "There is no work, nor device, nor knowledge, nor wisdom, in the grave (*sheol*) whither thou goest" (Eccl. 9:10).

The SEED and BREAD Bible-Study leaflets are published as often as time and means permit and are sent free to all names on THE WORD OF TRUTH MINISTRY mailing list. Send us your name. There will be no obligation, solicitation, or visitation. Additional copies of any issue available on request.   ISSUE NO. 83

SEED & BREAD

FOR THE SOWER   ISA. 55:10   FOR THE EATER

BRIEF BIBLICAL MESSAGES
FROM
THE WORD OF TRUTH MINISTRY
339 South Orange Drive, Los Angeles, Cal. 90036

Otis Q. Sellers, Bible Teacher

IS IT GAIN TO DIE?

It has been my practice for many years to ask God that He preserve me in life, and also to thank Him for having done this very thing. This has been no empty request, and the thanks that I give Him are honest and sincere. I am appreciative of the fact that He has preserved me in life, already beyond the Biblical span of "threescore and ten," because I do not believe that to die is gain.

Certainly God has not cheated me by preserving me in life; yet I would have to think this if I believed there was any profit in death. Yet, over and over, I hear Christian people say and insist that it is gain to die. The leading evangelist of our time says over and over, "The Bible says to die is gain."

Of course there will be those who will say: "Why do you ask such a question? Does not the Bible plainly state that to die is gain? Since you profess to believe that the Bible is the Word of God, why not just accept what it says and let that settle the matter?"

To all who ask such questions I would say that while the words "to die is gain" are found in the Bible, that is not what the Bible teaches about death. Death, in the Bible, is set forth as being the loss of the most precious gift that God has given to man. Moses, speaking God's word to Israel, declared, "I have set before you life and death, blessing and cursing: therefore choose life, that both thou and thy seed may live" (Deut. 30:19). The prophet Jeremiah, after setting forth the sins of Israel and the punishment that would be theirs because of their persistence in iniquity, declares that this would be of such severity that it would bring about an abnormal desire for death among the people that did not immediately perish in the holocaust. He proclaimed: "Death shall be chosen rather than life by all the residue of them that remain of this evil family" (Jer. 8:3).

These words set forth a truth that is also demonstrated by personal observation. Under certain conditions the state of death is preferable to the state of life. But such a preference is not natural; it is abnormal, one brought about by conditions over which the suffering one has no control. The normal God-implanted desire of men is to live, for life is ever to be preferred to death, and normal men under normal conditions do not believe that death is better than life, or that to die is gain.

The Bible in its first mention of death sets it forth as being the divine penalty threatened, and later imposed, upon the first man because of his disobedience (Gen. 2:17). The second reference shows that Eve understood it to be dire punishment that would come from disobeying God's command (Gen. 3:3), and the third occurrence came from the lips of Satan who insisted that it would never take place (Gen. 3:4). All occurrences that follow in the Old Testament show that death is a calamity of no small kind, and it teaches us that if life is a priceless blessing, then death, which is the deprivation of life, is an incalculable loss.

In the New Testament we learn that death is a calamity, a tragedy (Matt 2:18), that it entered into the world riding piggyback on the principle of sin (Rom. 5:12), and that it is an enemy that is to be destroyed (1 Cor. 15:26). Without hesitation it can be said that Scripture teaches us that the death of a man is the loss of his life, that because of it that which was once a man becomes a dead soul, that death visits every descendent of Adam irrespective of his position or character, that death reigns in a measure from the day of one's birth until the day of his death when it begins its reign in full power, that death is a curse and not a blessing. Furthermore, what the Scripture tells us about death is not spoken in obscure, doubtful, hesitating language, but it speaks with clarity and authority.

However, the prevalent theology of Christendom is a systematized denial of all of this. It is at variance with the Scripture on all these points, and it speaks a confused and contradictory language when it deals with the subject. It actually presents death as being the hope of the faithful, setting it forth as a thing to be desired; and all these erroneous views are supported by inferences drawn from texts that have been separated from their contexts. Death is made to be the door that will usher the faithful into the presence of God, thus eliminating any need for resurrection from the dead. And, one perverted statement that is always called upon to testify that death is all these glorious things is four words extracted from Philippians 1:21, "to die is gain."

Over and over this is repeated. Nevertheless, it is my conviction that no normal person really believes this, for if they did, then the strength of this belief would be the strength of the death wish of the one who holds it. This would be abnormal. In fact, it would be diagnosed as a form of mental derangement. Yet, very few have been courageous enough to ask if the Bible really teaches this. I, for one, say that it does not, and that these four words have been severed from their context and made to be one more spider web to support Plato's theory that death is a blessing.

Some devout Christians have told me that the high value they put upon staying alive was an actual contradiction of the Biblical words "to die is gain." I would calm the fears of all such by saying that the Bible says no such thing. It says:"For to him that is joined to all the living there is hope: for a living dog is better than a dead lion. For the living know that they shall die: but the dead know not anything, neither have they anymore a reward, for the memory of them is forgotten" (Eccl. 9:4,5).

Personal experience over many years has shown me that when truth from God's Word is presented concerning death, a question that will come from the average listener is: "But what about Paul's words, 'to die is gain'?" And to this my answer must ever be: Paul never said that. These are merely four of his words, taken out of the sentence in which he placed them. And only by a most ruthless amputation from the body of truth can these words be made to teach that death is profitable, something to be gained, an experience to be desired.

In the interpretation of any passage of Scripture the first and foremost principle is that the interpreter must reproduce with exactness the sense of the writer; that is, the thoughts which the author had in mind when the passage was written. Furthermore, the thought of the writer must be interpreted in connection with the context in which it is originally found. To ignore the context is bound to lead to misinterpretation. Philippians 1:21 is a passage of such nature that it demands explanation, interpretation, or exegesis. This I shall attempt to honestly do.

In the statement that immediately precedes this passage Paul declares that it is his earnest expectation and hope that Christ should be magnified in his body, whether it be by life or by death. This should be noted carefully, for these are his words just before he makes the declaration: "For to me to live is Christ, and to die is gain." We must never lose sight of this context, the grand theme of which is the magnification of Christ.

The word *magnify* means: to increase the importance of; to increase the value of; to enlarge; to amplify; to extoll. Paul could not do this Godward, but he could do this toward men. The magnification of Christ would be the result of his service if he lived, and it would also be the result if they put him to death. Following this he makes the statement which reads in the original: "For to me to be living Christ, and to be dying gain," a fact that can be verified easily by anyone able to follow a Greek interlinear.

Thus it is quite evident that something is missing from both parts of this passage, an ellipsis which the KJV translators recognized and tried to supply by two insertions of the verb "is," which did not work out too well, for the words, "For to me to live is Christ" do not form a complete statement. If taken as it stands it would make Paul guilty of egotistical boasting. In order for this statement to set forth what Paul had in mind, his words must be extended by filling in the ellipsis. But who has the authority to do this? The answer is that no one has. Let all men keep their hands off this statement! If it must be extended then let this be done by the simple, honest process of carrying into it the thought from the immediate context. Then it will say: "For to me to be living is the magnification of Christ."

In the full passage we have two figures of speech. The first is an *ellipsis*, which means that words have been omitted which are obviously indicated from the context, and the second is a figure called *chiasmos*, which means that there is intended to be a crossing over of ideas. Since the word "gain" is not a totally separate idea from "magnify," it carried the same force as the declaration in the context. Thus, in Phil. 1:21 Paul actually says:

> For to me to be living is gain for Christ,
> And to me to be dying is gain for Christ.

Since, before this Paul had said to the Corinthians, "I am dying daily" (1 Cor. 15:31), he may have had references to the physical price that he paid in order to serve the Lord. However, the translation I have given is in complete harmony with the subject of the portion and the context. Nothing is added that is not already there, and it accurately fits into the flow of thought. An honest paraphrase of this portion will show this:

> This is in accord with my earnest expectation and hope, that I shall never have reason to be ashamed; but with all boldness, as it has always been before, even so now, Christ shall be magnified in my body, whether through life or through death. For to me to be living is gain for Christ, and to me to be dying is gain for Christ. But if I continue to live in the flesh, the magnification of Christ will be the fruit of my own labors. Phil. 1:20-22.

Some will strenuously object to any addition to the words of Phil. 1:21, and will charge me with violating the spirit of Prov. 30:6. Yet they gladly accept the two additions of the word "is" that were inserted by the *King James* translators.

In conclusion let me say to all who continue to insist that "to die is gain," how about showing your faith by your works and laying hold of this gain?

The SEED and BREAD Bible-Study leaflets are published as often as time and means permit and are sent free to all names on THE WORD OF TRUTH MINISTRY mailing list. Send us your name. There will be no obligation, solicitation, or visitation. Additional copies of any issue available on request.   ISSUE NO. 84

SEED & BREAD

FOR THE SOWER   ISA. 55:10   FOR THE EATER

BRIEF BIBLICAL MESSAGES
FROM

THE WORD OF TRUTH MINISTRY

339 South Orange Drive, Los Angeles, Cal. 90036

Otis Q. Sellers, Bible Teacher

PAUL'S DESIRE TO DEPART

In the Philippian epistle many truths spring forth, and Paul does not deal with these at length. Exceedingly important statements are made within the flow of the message which are new and different. We often wish for more introductory words to lead us into the truths, also more explanation following, but it is not given. This can be clearly seen in Paul's declaration in 1:22 where suddenly he brings up the matter of a choice that is open to him, and declares that what his decision will be he is not making known. He did not want to close his options by stating what his choice would be.

The word *choose* is a common word, used every day in ordinary conversation, and it requires no defining. The Greek word here has to do with what one prefers as being the basis of a selection. However, a matter to be decided is before Paul, and if we go back to discover what this might be we find nothing that fits into the picture. He has been speaking of life and death in the previous passages, but it cannot be that in these two great issues he had any choice. This can be seen by asking if he will die if he chooses death. And we might further ask if he chooses death, will he make the choice effective by committing suicide? It is bordering on the ridiculous to interpret this choice as if Paul were playing Hamlet and mulling over the question "to be or not to be?"

As we go forward from Paul's statement, "Yet what I shall choose I am not making known," we discover at once what he is talking about. His selection is limited to one of two things: 1) to depart and be with Christ, or 2) to abide (remain) in the flesh. Thus, the choice is between departing and remaining, and not between living and dying, for "departing to be with Christ" does not mean death. It is tragic that this beautiful phrase has been taken and used as a description of death in the ritual of funeral services.

Of course this is bound to bring forth the question, "If departing to be with Christ does not mean death, then what does it mean?" This is asked as if there were no alternatives. And this can best be answered by pointing out three other departures in Scripture, none of which had any connection with the death of the one who departed.

There is the case of Enoch. We are told that "Enoch was not, for God took him" (Gen. 5:24); and this is further interpreted by the declaration: "By faith Enoch was translated that he should not see death; and was not found, because God had translated him" (Heb. 11:5). Thus he departed and was in the presence of the LORD of heaven, but this was in no way related to death.

Then, there is the departure of Elijah. We are told in Scripture that "Elijah went up by a whirlwind into heaven" (2 Kgs. 2:11). This plain and direct statement should not be contradicted by the words of our Lord in John 3:13, where all three occurrences of "heaven" mean God. See Issue No. 34 for a fuller treatment of this.

Finally, there is the departure of the man Christ Jesus, as recorded in Acts 1:9-11. This was by ascension, and not by death.

These three departures of living men are sufficient to show that the words "to depart and be with Christ" do not mean death, and that Paul was not expressing a death wish when he said that this was his desire. For it is from these words that we learn that one of the unique privileges that God gave to Paul was the right to leave this earth and ascend into heaven where he would be with Christ. These words concern Paul, and him alone, for he was the only one who could choose if he so decided to depart and be with Christ or to remain upon the earth.

It will probably be difficult for those who are Biblically illiterate to understand how this privilege could be given to Paul and to none other. They will ask why this should be true of him alone. Questions such as these can only be answered by establishing certain truths about God's greatest apostle, the man Paul.

Of that which we know about Paul, certain great facts that were true of him are revealed to us in very few words. These must be believed on the basis of these terse statements as there is no corroborating testimony. He declares: "I have fought with beasts at Ephesus" (1 Cor. 15:32); "of the Jews five times received I forty stripes save one" (2 Cor 11:24); "thrice I was beaten with rods" (2 Cor. 11:25); "thrice I suffered shipwreck" (2 Cor. 11:25); "caught up to the third heaven" (2 Cor. 12:2). The five statements alone are sufficient to show that certain great experiences in the life of Paul are made known by and must be believed on the basis of very few words. Furthermore, there are certain great truths that were true of him alone which must be believed on the basis of one terse statement. We will consider five of these.

Paul states he was "one born out of due time" (1 Cor. 15:8); that he was "the chief of sinners" (1 Tim. 1:15), a fact that can be true only of one; he was "a pattern to them which should hereafter believe" (1 Tim. 1:16); there was given to him "a thorn in the flesh, a messenger of Satan to buffet me" (2 Cor. 12:7); and he bore in his body "the marks of the Lord Jesus" (Gal. 6:17). All these were true of him alone.

With the foregoing examples in mind, we are ready to consider Paul's desire to depart and be with Christ, a truth exclusively true of him. This unique privilege of his is revealed in one statement. There is no additional testimony. His terse statement reveals that it was within his power to elect at any time to depart from this earth and to be with Christ. He spoke of not making known what he would choose, so he must have had the power of choice.

Enoch departed from this earth, but he had no choice in the matter. Elijah departed to heaven in a whirlwind, but to choose this was not his privilege. So, there are three in heaven who have been men on earth. Paul could have made this four, if he had chosen to do so, for it was his privilege, not to live or die, but to depart and be with Christ. It follows then that if on the basis of very few words we can believe that Paul was shipwrecked three times and that three times he was beaten with rods, why then cannot we believe that it was possible for Paul to "depart and be with Christ" on the basis of one simple statement made in Phil. 1:22.

The problem that so many have in believing the actual declaration made in this passage is based upon the fact that men have long taken the words "to depart and be with Christ" and used them to describe the death of God's people. This allows them to be used to support the orthodox theory as to what happens when a man dies, holding that at death he is immediately ushered into the presence of Christ. But, if this be true, of what value then is resurrection?

The question as to why, out of all others, this privilege was given to Paul is bound to arise. Why did he have this power of release and deliverance if he ever desired to use it? The answer to this is not difficult to find.

When Paul became the instrument of the Lord to bear His Name before the nations, and kings, and the sons of Israel (Acts 9:15), God declared that He would "show him how great things he must suffer" for His name's sake. From this we know that he was given a preview of the rest of his life, so far as his sufferings were concerned. Before Paul was given his divine commission, he knew that as he carried it out every year would be one of intense suffering; Just how much he suffered is not revealed to us, but we can be sure that his afflictions have no parallel in history. We do get one quick look in his words in 2 Cor. 11:23-27:

In labors more abundant, in stripes above measure, in prisons more frequent, in deaths oft. Of the Jews five times received I forty stripes save one. Thrice was I beaten with rods, once was I stoned, thrice I suffered shipwreck, a night and a day I have been in the deep; in journeyings often, in perils of waters, in peril of robbers, in perils by mine own countrymen, in perils by the nations, in perils in the city, in perils in the wilderness, in perils in the sea, in perils among false brethren; in weariness and painfulness, in watchings often, in hunger and thirst, in fastings often, in cold and nakedness.

There is no other man who has served the Lord save Paul who could write a catalog of sufferings such as these. He was the pattern believer, and as such he was the one chosen by God to demonstrate to all men just how much a man would willingly and joyfully suffer when he knew to what these sufferings were related. And Paul knew! For after God had given him a preview of his life of suffering, He caught him away to the third heaven, even unto paradise, giving him a view of the ultimate goal of all of God's purposes for the universe. What he saw was for him alone, since he was not permitted to tell what he had seen or heard (2 Cor. 12:1-4).

Since no one else has ever been called upon by God to suffer what Paul did, no one else stood in need of hearing and seeing the things he saw and heard. He alone could speak from experience when he said: "The sufferings of this present time are not worthy to be compared with the glory that shall be revealed in us" (Rom. 8:18).

In order that Paul's sufferings should be endured willingly, rather than being something forced upon him, and from which there was no way out, God made it possible for him at any moment to make the choice of being done with it all and departing to be with Christ. This, no doubt, must have been a continual desire upon his part. As he stood on the deck of a ship that was soon to be torn to pieces by tempestuous waves, how tempting it must have been to "call it quits" and depart and be with Christ, rather than to be plunged into the raging sea. As blow after blow rained down upon his bleeding back, what a temptation it must have been to have told God he had taken all he could (God would understand), and have departed to be with Christ. If he would have so chosen, he would have vanished from the earth before another blow fell upon him.

But, he did not do this, and the question arises at once, "Why did he not do this?" If he had this power, then why did he not use it? The answer is at hand. This would have taken him away from his work of magnifying Christ, and of ministering the Word of God to His people. He told the Corinthians: "You are in our hearts to die and to live with you" (2 Cor. 7:3). He would not abandon God's people.

Many centuries before Paul, King David was experiencing a period of suffering which was more than he could bear. He describes this by saying, "Fearfulness and trembling are come upon me, and horror hath overwhelmed me;" following which he cried out:

Oh that I had wings like a dove! for then would I fly away, and be at rest. Lo, then would I wander far off, and remain in the wilderness. I would hasten my escape from the windy storm and tempest. Psa. 55:6-8.

David did not have these "wings." He had to stay there and see it through. But Paul, figuratively speaking, did have them. And it is to his glory that he never made use of them, giving as his reason: "To abide in the flesh is more needful for you" (Phil. 1:24).

The SEED and BREAD Bible-Study leaflets are published as often as time and means permit and are sent free to all names on THE WORD OF TRUTH MINISTRY mailing list. Send us your name. There will be no obligation, solicitation, or visitation. Additional copies of any issue available on request.   ISSUE NO. 85

SEED & BREAD

FOR THE SOWER   ISA. 55:10   FOR THE EATER

BRIEF BIBLICAL MESSAGES
FROM
THE WORD OF TRUTH MINISTRY
339 South Orange Drive, Los Angeles, Cal. 90036

Otis Q. Sellers, Bible Teacher

THE SIGNS OF THE TIMES

The familiar and often used phrase "the signs of the times" came to mankind from the lips of the Lord Jesus Christ. These words, when spoken by Him, had nothing to do with His second coming. Nevertheless, many generations of the "prophets of doom" have used these words to bolster their own wild predictions concerning the future of mankind and the soon anticipated coming of the Lord Jesus Christ. Thus, the phrase "the signs of the times" has been forced into an unholy alliance with a thousand-and-one sensational events, all of which are declared to be the most positive signs of the imminent return of Christ. When this phrase is restored to its context, the honest sudent will readily admit that these words had no such meaning when first spoken by our Lord.

Consider the circumstances that brought forth these words. The Pharisees and Sadducees were enemies, but they found common ground in their rejection of Jesus as being the Christ. Together they came to Him and asked that He show them a sign from heaven. In answer He spoke of their custom of looking at the Palestinian sky, reading the signs there, then predicting the weather. He then denounced them as hypocrites since they could not discern "the signs of the times." (See Matthew 16:1 - 3.)

This makes it evident that our Lord was not speaking of any signs that would precede and point to His second coming. The reality of His first coming and presence upon the earth was the fact that was before them. His second coming was not yet in the picture. So, it would have been most unfair for the Lord to have publicly branded these men as hypocrites because they could not discern signs that pointed to His return to the earth. There could have been no such signs at that time. How absurd it would have been for the Pharisees, or even His faithful disciples, to have looked upon certain strange events and accepted them as signs of His second coming. Furthermore, the 1900 years of history that have passed since these words were spoken reveal how mistaken anyone would have been, had they judged anything that transpired in that day to have been a sign of His second advent.

When we face the facts, there can be no other conclusion —

the phrase "the signs of the times," as it came from the lips of the Lord Jesus and as it now comes to us from the Bible, has no connection with the second coming of Christ.

In the past 150 years, many who professed to be preachers of the Bible's prophetic message have practiced a great deception upon themselves and upon their hearers by taking the unusual, spectacular, and sensational events that are always transpiring, and presenting them, after much embellishment, as positive signs of the imminency of the second coming. The passage of time has proven that they were completely wrong, never right, always mistaken. Others, who have been as consistently wrong, have been the date-setters, who, by a hundred different methods of calculation, have set the date for the return of Christ. The history of the past has demonstrated they were always wrong, and future events will continue to show their errors. And this is and will continue to be just as true of those who have presented some outstanding event as a sign that the coming of Christ is imminent. I have been a close personal observer of this for 60 years, since 1916 when I first heard of the second coming; yet, in spite of the thousands of things that have been presented as the most positive signs, the Lord has not yet come. Nevertheless, there is still a good market for each new book of which claims are made that a new set of signs are presented that indicate the Lord is coming soon.

Had the Pharisees discerned "the signs of the times," they would have known that they were living in the days of the Son of God upon the earth. The appearance upon the earth of God's Anointed One, the Christ, had long been prophesied. Certain definite signs were to give witness to the reality of His presence, and these were manifest in that day. The man Nicodemus, one of the Pharisees and a ruler, spoke for all his group when, after considering these signs, he declared: "We know that Thou art a teacher come from God: for no man can do these miracles that Thou doest, except God be with Him" (John 3:2).

The miracles performed by our Lord were the signs of those times — signs that spoke eloquently and proclaimed the presence of the Son of God upon the earth; but the Pharisees had failed to listen to their message. These signs did not point to some future event. They spoke of a then present reality.

Those who today profess faith in the Lord Jesus Christ should earnestly seek to avoid the mistake made by the Pharisees. They could not discern the signs of their times. We will make the same mistake if we fail to discern the signs of our times. There are signs of the times in which we live, signs which we need to discern and heed, signs that reveal to us the character of the time in which we live.

We do not live in the days of the Son of God upon the earth, and the signs that gave witness to that fact and truth are not seen today. They would be out of place and give false witness if they were a common occurrence. Neither do we live in that unique and strange period of thirty-three years of which the book of Acts is the history. In that time God always confirmed His Word with signs following (Mark 16:20, Heb. 2:4). In the Acts period, the kingdom of God was then in the blade and ear stage, like growing grain (see Issue No. 48); and all the signs of that time gave witness to this. We are living in a time and under a condition when all of God's kingdom purposes have been suspended. We are living under a distinct and new dispensation or administration. This is the administration or dispensation of the grace of God, and there are signs on every hand that give witness to this fact. If we close our eyes to these, we will make the same mistake as did the Pharisees.

An administration or dispensation is a method of dealing. Neither word has to do with a period of time, even though they take place in a period of time. But what doesn't? God's administrations are God's methods of dealing with mankind or with some portion of mankind which He has marked out, such as Israel (Amos 3:2). God's present administration, His present method of dealing, is entirely gracious. It makes no difference whether one is a saint or a sinner, God is dealing with Him only in grace (see Issue No. 57). This fact is known from a divine secret revealed to Paul, which was then made known by him for those for whom it was intended, the nations (Eph. 3:1, 2). Today, if God cannot act in grace, then He will not act at all. This is witnessed to by almost 1900 years of human history, by every fact of human life and experience, and by the signs that abound on every hand.

Let the reader consider his own life as an example. Has God rewarded you according to your sins? Has God dealt with you according to your iniquities? Has each sin and transgression of yours brought their just recompence of reward? Has God dealt with you in strict justice? What has been God's method of dealing with you?

To these questions there can be only one answer. You have not been dealt with according to your sins. You have not been dealt with in strict justice. You have been dealt with in grace — in that love and favor that God shows to the undeserving. You may have thought at times that God was punishing you; but, if so, you were mistaken. You may have thought you were experiencing a display of divine wrath, but you were wrong. God has not punished you, and His wrath has not been displayed. To think so, or to make such statements, is to slander the grace that He is continually showing. God has, for the present, ignored your sins in order that He might display His grace toward you. Every day of your life gives witness to this. These are the signs of our times. It is tragic that so many fail to discern this.

We must not be so childish as to think that a sign must be some stupendous miracle. Great progress will have been made when one has learned with Elijah that God may not be in the wind; He may not be in the earthquake; and He may not be in the fire; but He may be in the still small voice (1 Kgs. 19:11, 12). But still greater progress will be made when we realize that God can speak by means of absolute silence. If silence is golden and if silence can be eloquent, then we are today face-to-face with a golden eloquence to which every ear should be in tune.

If we read the signs that exist on every hand today, we will know that God's present method of dealing is worked in secret. He operates in secret, and this has caused many to conclude that He is not acting at all, and some to suggest that He is dead. To act in secret is always proper when one is acting in grace, but all acts of justice must be evident and in the open. You have every right to secretly slip a twenty-dollar note under the door of your needy neighbor, but you have no right to take twenty dollars from him unless you publicly invoke the due processes of the law. By acting only in grace and always acting in secret, God is steadily and fully accomplishing His present purpose to write into the history of His long dealings with mankind a complete record of the grace that is inherent in His character (see Issue No. 64). Every sign today tells us we are living in a time of God's silence and under an administration of grace. And were it not for the truth that God gave in His final revelations through Paul, this would be one of the greatest mysteries of our existence.

On every hand, there are voices that make the claim that God is speaking to and through them. Yet, in all the nineteen centuries since God became silent, not one thing has come forth from anyone that has added one iota to man's knowledge of God. Men may imagine that God is speaking, but the facts of life demonstrate that He is silent. We may not like it this way; and in their dissatisfaction, men may implore God to break His silence. But God will not do this until His present purpose in His present silence is complete. If God should speak, then He must back up His word with acts of justice; and this would end His long display of grace.

The Word of God which we possess, especially that truth contained in God's final revelation to the Apostle Paul, should lead us to see that we are living in a time when God's method of dealing is entirely gracious, when every act of His is one of love and favor to the undeserving, a time when He maintains a strict silence, and a time when He operates in secret. The Bible tells us this, and every fact and experience of our lives give witness to it. These are our signs. They tell us of the times in which we live. Let us discern the signs of our times.

The SEED and BREAD Bible-Study leaflets are published as often as time and means permit and are sent free to all names on THE WORD OF TRUTH MINISTRY mailing list. Send us your name. There will be no obligation, solicitation, or visitation. Additional copies of any issue available on request.   ISSUE NO. 86

SEED & BREAD

FOR THE SOWER   ISA. 55:10   FOR THE EATER

BRIEF BIBLICAL MESSAGES
FROM
THE WORD OF TRUTH MINISTRY
339 South Orange Drive, Los Angeles, Cal. 90036

Otis Q. Sellers, Bible Teacher

WHAT DOES KALEO MEAN?

The Greek word *kaleō* might well be one of the most significant words in the New Testament. It is the basis or root of seventeen other very important words, among which are *klēsis* (calling), *klētos* (called), *parakaleō* (entreat, exhort, comfort), *paraklēsis* (entreaty, exhortation), *paraklētos* (an advocate, intercessor), and most important of all, *ekklēsia* (church, outcalled). If the verb *kaleō* is not honestly defined and objectively understood, then all the words of which it is the basis will probably also be misunderstood; and the passages in which they are found will fail to speak God's Truth to us. It is my conviction that *kaleō* has never been accurately defined and that its full meaning has been deliberately stultified in order to maintain a certain traditional meaning of *ekklēsia*.

Many words have primary and secondary meanings, and this is true of *kaleō*. However, when the secondary or derived meaning of a word is exalted to the preeminent place and the primary meaning is ignored and stultified, great confusion will be the result. In most lexicons *kaleō* is said to mean "to call," that is, "to invite or to summon." One lexicon, which is before me as I write, gives as a complete definition of this word: "Call those within range of the voice for immediate action, invite those at a distance for a future occasion." Another lexicon says it means: "To call, summon; to call to one's house, to invite; to call, name, call by name."

Such definitions as these ignore the primary meaning of this word altogether. And while it is true that *kaleō* does mean in some occurrences "to call" in the sense of inviting, summoning, or bidding, it is also true that in at least ninety-five occurrences of this word in the New Testament, it simply cannot have this meaning.

This word is found 146 times in the New Testament. Thus, the facts in the case are that in about two-thirds of its occurrences, it cannot have the meaning of to call, to bid, to invite, or to summon, while in one-third it does have this meaning and should be so translated. These facts alone are sufficient to show that "to call" is not the primary meaning of this verb, and another meaning must be discovered and fully recognized if we are to faithfully interpret all passages where it is found.

A clear example of the twofold meaning of this word can be seen by consulting two separate chapters in Luke's Gospel. In Luke, chapter one, the word *kaleō* is found ten times; and in none of these occurrences, can it be given the meaning of to bid, to summon, or to invite. (See Luke 1:13, 31, 35, 36, 59, 60, 61, 62, and 76.) In Luke, chapter fourteen, it is found eleven times; and in each occurrence it will be found to mean to bid, in the sense of inviting; and it is correctly translated in the K J V. (See Luke 14:7, 8, 8, 9, 10, 10, 12, 13, 16, 17, and 24.)

When all occurrences of this word are carefully considered in their context (and if this will not provide the true and full meaning, nothing else will), it will be found by the law of usage that this word primarily means to appoint, to place, to position, to designate or to name, and that to call, summon, invite or bid are derived and secondary meanings.

The first occurrence of this word is found in Matt. 1:21, where it says, "And thou *shalt call* His name Jesus: for He shall save His people from their sins." (The italicized words are *kaleō*.) The word *Jehosua* (*Jesus*) meant Savior, and He was to bear this designation since this was the work He would do. His name described His position and work. And as the angel continued his message to Joseph, he declared: "And they *shall call* (*kaleō*) His name Emmanuel, which being interpreted is, God with us" (Matt. 1:23). This designation was a most proper one, for God had projected Himself and was present upon the earth in the person of Jesus Christ. God could do this without sacrificing one bit of His infinitude and universality.

These first two occurrences alone are enough to show that *kaleō* does not always mean to call, in the sense of inviting, bidding, or summoning. Of course, it would be quite simple to take other occurrences in Matthew and show that it does mean this, for example, Matt. 22:3, 4, 8, 9; but the fact remains that in two-thirds of its 146 occurrences, it cannot possibly have this meaning.

It should be carefully noted that while the word *kaleō* means to appoint, to place, to designate, to position, or to name (all these terms being synonymous), as well as to invite, bid, or summon, the Old English word "call" had both of these meanings. Our modern English word "call" does not now signify the ideas of appointing, designating, placing, positioning, or naming. Today, we would say, "The President has not yet named the Secretary of State." If we would say, "The President has not yet called the Secretary of State," it would mean something quite different. However, there was a time when the king's call or invitation to serve was equal to appointment to the position, since none dared refuse the call of his monarch. This is how *kaleō* got the secondary meaning of to call, in the sense of inviting or bidding.

Today, the word "call" as meaning to designate, to appoint, or to name to a certain position has become utterly obsolete. Yet, traces of this meaning still remain in our word "calling." When we say that a man's calling is law, medicine, or education, by this we mean the work that he does and the position he holds. In Ephesians 4:1 we would have a much clearer communication if we would translate it, "order your behavior in a manner worthy of the position (*klēsis*) in which you have been placed" (*kaleō*). This would preserve and emphasize the very close relationship that exists between *klēsis* and *kaleō*, and provide pertinent advice to all in Christian service or in government.

If the primary meaning of *kaleō* is seen to be to appoint, to designate, or to name, it will be of immeasurable help in gaining clear and correct interpretations of passages where words occur that are derived from this verb. For example, translators and commentators have often struggled with the three occurrences of *klētos* in 1 Cor. 1:1, 2, and 24. I believe it becomes quite simple when we translate 1:1 as saying, "Paul, a designated apostle of Jesus Christ," 1:2 as saying "designated as saints," and 1:24 as saying, "But to them that are designated, both Jews and Greeks." Some may prefer the word "named" or "positioned" here, but this is a minor matter.

Matthew 22:14, which reads, "For many are called, but few are chosen," has always been a difficult passage, part of which is due to the occurrence of the word *eklektos* (chosen) which means "elected." This should read "For many are designated, but few are elected." See Luke 6:13 for a clear example of this, where many were designated as disciples, but only twelve were elected (chosen), and these were named apostles.

Jude 1:1 becomes much clearer if we read it "Beloved by God the Father, preserved by Jesus Christ, and positioned."

Rev. 17:14 glows with a new light when we read it, "They that are with Him are designated ones, chosen ones; and they are faithful."

The exhortation in 2 Peter 1:10 is freed from all difficulties when we read it, "Give diligence to confirm your designation and your choice."

Hebrews 3:1 speaks a new message when we read it, "Wherefore, holy brethren, participants of a most exalted position."

The primary meaning of *kaleō* and of the two cognate words that come out of it *klētos* and *klēsis* is of great help in understanding 2 Tim. 1:9 which will read as follows: "Who saves us and places (*kaleō*) us in a holy position, not according to our works, but according to His own purpose and grace."

Most important of all is the light that a true definition of *kaleō* and *klētos* sheds upon the difficult passage of Romans 8:28 - 30. I doubt if very many will want to accept my interpretation of this portion; but that matters very little, it being my duty to set forth my finding after having fully studied the passage. My reward will come from the proclamation and not from the number who accept it.

This portion begins with the familiar declaration: "And we know that all things work together for good to them that love God." This passage is quoted by many who have "things" working in their behalf instead of God Himself. Some go on to quote the rest of the passage, but disregard altogether what it says. In the K J V this reads, "To them who are called according to His purpose." But according to my understanding, it should read, "To them who are positioned in harmony with His purpose."

Now, as to loving God. I believe I can qualify; but as to being positioned in harmony with God's purpose, I hesitate to make this claim.

I consider the positions of the Acts period believers and know that, "God has set some in the outcalled, first apostles, secondarily prophets, thirdly teachers, after that miracles, then gifts of healings, helps, governments, diversities of tongues" (1 Cor. 12:28). And, yet, none of these things is true of me; and all that I can claim to be is a sinner saved by grace. I fully believe that God worked all things together for good for men such as these, but far too many "things" have worked to my harm for me to recklessly apply Rom. 8:28 to myself.

The passage then goes on to say that, "Because whom He knew in advance, He also designates beforehand to be conformed to the image of His Son, so that He (the Son) might be Sovereign among many brethren. Moreover, those whom He designated beforehand, them He also appointed; and whom He appointed, them He also declares righteous, and whom He declares righteous, He also glorifies" (Rom. 8:29-30, Resultant Version). This all has to do with the positions held and services performed by God's saints. It has nothing to do with the salvation of a sinner. Since God was for all such as this, resistance against them was useless.

I leave the rest to students of the Word and hope I have pointed the way to truth by a clearer understanding of *kaleō*.

The SEED and BREAD Bible-Study leaflets are published as often as time and means permit and are sent free to all names on THE WORD OF TRUTH MINISTRY mailing list. Send us your name. There will be no obligation, solicitation, or visitation. Additional copies of any issue available on request.   ISSUE NO. 87

SEED & BREAD

FOR THE SOWER   ISA. 55:10   FOR THE EATER

BRIEF BIBLICAL MESSAGES
FROM
THE WORD OF TRUTH MINISTRY
339 South Orange Drive, Los Angeles, Cal. 90036

Otis Q. Sellers, Bible Teacher

WHAT DOES "SPIRITUAL" MEAN?

It is a well-known fact that certain Greek words were selected by the Spirit of God and used in a special and restricted way in the New Testament. This meaning of the word is established by God's usage of it. This is not at all strange since men constantly do this with words, and they have every right to do it. When it becomes apparent that the Spirit of God has done this with a Greek word, its meaning must then be determined by the way in which it is used by New Testament writers. The Greek word *pneumatikos*, which is always translated "spiritual," is one of these.

The English word "spiritual" is one that is in very common use; and it is my conviction that there is no word in the Christian vocabulary that is as misused, abused, and misunderstood as this one. Most of the time it is used as a ritualistic word, having no meaning and carrying no information to those who hear it.

The incorrect use and the abuse of this word have given rise to a flood of errors that have done great harm by creating misunderstandings of God's revealed Truth. If we purpose to "walk in the Truth," then we will need to be in harmony with the Spirit of God, both in our understanding and use of this word.

As a teacher of the Word of God, and as one who permits his hearers to ask questions at the close of each class, I know quite well how many Biblical problems have been created due to misunderstandings of the meaning of the word "spiritual." Over and over the same questions are asked that would never need to be asked if the questioner had any conception of the Biblical usage and meaning of this word.

Usually framed as objections to something I have said, some of these questions are: "But, Mr. Sellers, aren't we spiritual Israel?" "Isn't it a spiritual kingdom?" "Aren't our blessings spiritual?" "Isn't heaven a spiritual place?" or, "Won't we have spiritual bodies?"

In attempting to deal honestly with such questions, it is necessary to ask, "What do you mean by the word 'spiritual'?" I seldom get an answer to this; and if the questioner does attempt an answer, it always demonstrates a complete lack of understanding of the usage of this word in the Word of God. It also reveals that he has adopted, without question, the Platonic concept that the opposite of spiritual is material and that material things are never spiritual.

In the writing and thinking of the Greek philosopher Plato and all who follow him, it is evident that the word "spiritual"(*pneumatikos*) is used to describe things that are not material or physical, that is, incorporeal, having no substance. This was Plato's use of the word and these are the ideas he intended to convey; but this is not the way the Spirit of God uses it, and these are not the ideas conveyed by it.

Since dictionaries define words according to the way in which they are currently used by men, the definition based upon Plato's usage is the one we will find in them. However, it must be remembered that man's usage is not the same as that in the New Testament. What men mean when they use this word is not what the Spirit of God means when He uses it. No man can claim that he has "overcome the world" as long as he is mouthing the ideas of the world in regard to the word "spiritual." I would be doing nothing but mouthing the concept of the Mormons if I used the word "gentile" to designate a non-Mormon. That is the way they use it and that is what it means to them, but it will never mean that to me. Even so, the word "spiritual" may be used by the church and the world to designate that which is not physical or material; but I refuse to follow them in this.

The Greek word with which we must deal in considering the meaning of "spiritual" is *pneumatikos*. This is an adjective which comes from the noun *pneuma*, and it is found 26 times in the New Testament. It is translated "spiritual" in every occurrence, so the student is not troubled with discordant renderings. There is also an adverb (*pneumatikōs*) that is cognate with this adjective. It is found only two times and is translated "spiritually" in both occurrences.

As a simple Greek adjective, derived from the noun *pneuma* (spirit), it is entirely correct to define *pneumatikos* as meaning "of the spirit," or "having the qualities of spirit"; but, as already stated, this is a word which the Spirit of God has chosen, used in a specific way, and given a specific meaning. This is in harmony with Paul's declaration: "Which things also we speak, not in the words which man's wisdom teacheth, but which the Holy Spirit teacheth" (1 Cor. 2:13).

In determining the meaning of a word by New Testament usage alone, the proper process is to find an occurrence where the meaning is unmistakably clear, then to try out this meaning in all other occurrences. If this meaning fits, if it makes the passage clearer, if it enlightens the passage, we can then feel assured that we have the idea which the Spirit of God intended to convey when He inspired the writer to use this term.

Certain occurrences of this word in the writings of Paul are so crystal clear in meaning that it has caused some scholars to speak of the "special Pauline use of this word," inferring that Paul gave this word a sense not found in other writings. But it is right here that they miss the truth, since twenty-four of the twenty-six occurrences of this word are found in Paul's writings, as reference to a concordance will show. The two occurrences found in Peter's epistles are in complete harmony with Pauline usage.

In 1 Corinthians 10:3, 4, we find three occurrences of this word in a familiar and plain context.

And did all eat the same spiritual meat; and did all drink the same spiritual drink: for they drank of that spiritual Rock that followed them: and that Rock was Christ.

In this passage we can identify three actual, material, physical things that are called "spiritual": the manna, the water, and the rock, nullifying once and for all the idea that the material cannot be spiritual.

The manna was actual food. In shape it was round, and in color it was white. It was gathered in containers, and it could be baked or boiled. It spoiled quickly, would breed worms, and give an offensive odor if kept too long. It had many of the same qualities which we attach to many foods today. When taken into the mouth, it was chewed and swallowed the same as any other food. It filled the stomach, caused hunger to cease, and gave the digestive process something on which to work.

Thus, we have an actual, physical, and material thing that is called spiritual. And if we ask why the Spirit of God so describes it, there is only one answer. It is called spiritual because it was produced directly by God Himself without any natural instrumentality.

The water they drank was actual water, two parts hydrogen and one part oxygen in a liquid form. The people drank of it; the cattle drank of it; the women did the family washing in it; the children waded in it and gleefully splashed it on one another. It was real, literal, material water; yet, it is called "spiritual" by the Spirit of God. And again, if we ask why, there is only one answer. This water was produced directly and by the sole power of God without any intervening, natural instrumentality. There was no evaporation, no clouds, and no precipitation; yet there was water.

From Paul's threefold use of the word spiritual in 1 Cor. 10:3, 4, we are able to say that when anything is produced by God, when it comes directly from God, when it can be attributed directly to Him without any natural instrumentality, and when it is something for which He is directly responsible, then it can be called spiritual. The manna, the water, and the rock fit all these descriptions; therefore, they are called spiritual by the Spirit of God. In order to further clarify this definition, let us consider several illustrations.

Take for example an earthquake. These are usually caused by natural forces such as volcanic explosions in the earth, by the faulting of the rocks, or the movement of the earth along a fault.

Any earthquake caused by these natural instrumentalities could not correctly be called "spiritual"; but one produced by the direct and sole power of God could be so designated, according to the New Testament usage of this word. Thus, the earthquake recorded in Acts 16:26 can be called a spiritual earthquake. It is not so designated in Scripture, there being no discussion as to its nature there.

In Judges 6:36 - 40, we read of Gideon, who sought evidence in regard to God's purpose to use him by asking permission to put a fleece of wool on the ground and to know that it was God's purpose to deliver Israel through him if the dew wet only the fleece and the earth around it remained dry. As further proof the sign was reversed so that one night it was wet fleece and dry earth, and the next night it was dry fleece and wet earth.

Now, according to the inspired usage of "spiritual" in the New Testament, we have every right to say that the wetness and dryness of the fleece were spiritual conditions. It would have been a simple matter for a man to have made the fleece wet and just as easy for him to have kept it dry. But such wetness or dryness would have been human conditions. The wetness and dryness of Gideon's fleece were spiritual conditions — they were produced by God.

In 1 Corinthians 15:44, we read, "it is raised a spiritual body." The followers of the Platonic philosophy jump in quickly here and say that this means we will have "immaterial bodies," which, they say, can pass through solid objects such as doors without opening them. This is childish thinking to say the least, since the very words "immaterial bodies" are contradictory. There cannot be a body unless there is material and substance. One may as well speak of "bodiless bodies."

I do not know how a babe is produced within its mother, but I do know it is produced there by natural processes that God has ordained and established. Truly, we are born "after the flesh"; and the body that is ours was not produced solely by an act of God without any intermediate processes. However, when we are raised from the dead and given a body as it "pleaseth Him," it will be one produced solely by God and without any human participation. It will be produced in an atom of time, and the nine months required for the natural process will be eliminated. Our bodies in resurrection will be actual, physical bodies, composed of flesh and bones, even as today; yet, they will be spiritual since they will be produced entirely and only by a direct act of God.

The SEED and BREAD Bible-Study leaflets are published as often as time and means permit and are sent free to all names on THE WORD OF TRUTH MINISTRY mailing list. Send us your name. There will be no obligation, solicitation, or visitation. Additional copies of any issue available on request.   ISSUE NO. 88

SEED & BREAD

FOR THE SOWER   ISA. 55:10   FOR THE EATER

BRIEF BIBLICAL MESSAGES
FROM
THE WORD OF TRUTH MINISTRY
339 South Orange Drive, Los Angeles, Cal. 90036

Otis Q. Sellers, Bible Teacher

"SPIRITUAL"—A WORD STUDY

In the previous study, the word "spiritual" was shown to be an adjective used specifically by the Spirit to designate things produced by the Spirit of God, which came directly from God without any human instrumentality or natural processes intervening. I believe that this definition will shed light on every passage in which the word is found, and it is my plan to demonstrate this in this second study.

To emphasize this definition further, let me say that it is my firm conviction that when Adam was created, he had a spiritual body. No man and woman came together in order to produce him. He did not pass through the birth processes, even as you and I. He was never a babe, had no father or mother; but he was every inch a man. Since he was produced entirely by God without human instrumentality or natural processes, he was spiritual. We will now see how this definition fits in the passages where the word *pneumatikos* is found.

Romans 1:11. "Some spiritual gift." The message which was proclaimed by Paul was not according to man; he had not received it from men; he was not taught it in any school; nor did he learn it from other apostles (Gal. 1:11, 12). It was therefore a "spiritual gift" which he desired to pass on to those in Rome.

Romans 7:14. "The law is spiritual." Many prohibitions and directions in the law of Moses were not new. Men had seen the need of these restrictions; conscience told them they were right; and rulers before Moses had decreed them for their subjects. However, the law of Moses was a divine production. Even Moses was only the deliveryman. Indeed, the law was spiritual. It came from God apart from any human instrumentality.

Romans 15:27. "Their spiritual things." Israel's spiritual things, of which the nations became partakers, were entirely out of God. They had nothing worthwhile to give to anyone except what they had received from Him.

1 Corinthians 2:13. "Comparing spiritual things with spiritual." In the context of this passage, Paul tells of speaking "wisdom among them that are perfect" (1 Cor. 2:6). Here he speaks of matching that which is spiritual with those who are spiritual. He took God-produced truths and gave them to God-produced believers.

1 Corinthians 2:15. **"He that is spiritual."** The contrast here is between the soulish (*psuchikos*) man and the spiritual (*pneumatikos*) man. The chief characteristic of the soulish man is that he rejects the things of the Spirit of God, neither can he know them for they are spiritually discerned. In contrast, the God-produced believer receives the things of the Spirit of God.

1 Corinthians 3:1. **"I could not speak unto you as unto spiritual."** As believers who had been produced by the Spirit of God, they were spiritual. Yet, because of shortcomings, Paul could not speak to them as such.

1 Corinthians 9:11. **"If we have sown unto you spiritual things."** The things that the apostles had planted in these Corinthians were most certainly things produced by the Spirit of God.

1 Corinthians 10:3, 4. **"Spiritual meat . . . spiritual drink . . . spiritual rock."** This passage is the basis for my definition of the word "spiritual." In John 6:1 - 14, we read of the feeding of about five thousand men. Our Lord began with five barley biscuits and two sardines, a boy's lunch. This was material food, produced by natural means, which, in the case of the barley biscuits, required the planting of seed, time for growth, harvesting, threshing, grinding, and baking. The Lord Jesus produced barley biscuits apart from all this. Those biscuits which the boy brought could not be called spiritual. Those which the Lord produced could be called spiritual. They were produced by Him apart from all natural processes.

1 Corinthians 12:1 and 14:1. **"Spiritual gifts."** The word "gifts" in both of these passages is supplied by the translator. Some noun is certainly needed to complete the sense. "Gifts," "endowments," "manifestations," and "persons" have been used by various translators. The word "endowments" appeals to me more than any other. But whatever Paul may have had in mind, we know he was speaking of something produced solely by God's Spirit.

1 Corinthians 14:37. **"If any man think himself to be a prophet, or spiritual."** I do not think that I am a prophet, and neither do I claim to be spiritual. Many men are prone to think of themselves as being spiritual, and they readily ascribe spirituality to others who conform to their mold. I do not claim spirituality for myself, and neither will I ascribe it to any other man. However, I do claim that as a theogenic believer in the Lord Jesus Christ, I am in possession of many things that are very definitely spiritual. I have faith in the record God has given of His Son. I have a forgiveness that is entirely of God. I have redemption and all that comes under the heading of salvation, and these are things of which God is the author and for which He is entirely responsible. No priest has absolved me; no blood of bulls and goats has redeemed me. The things I claim as a believer are entirely spiritual. They are out of

God. In the present dispensation, one person cannot be more spiritual than another. Some are more devoted, more faithful, and more diligent, yes, even more prayerful and careful; but all believers are now in Christ Jesus and none can claim spiritual possessions that are not the joint property of all.

1 Corinthians 15:44 - 46. "Raised a spiritual body . . . there is a spiritual body." If we try here to read the Platonic concept of "immaterial" into the word "spiritual," then the two words "spiritual body" flatly contradict each other. It would be like saying "cold heat" or "hot ice." There are no such things. When Jesus Christ was raised from the dead, He invited His disciples to handle Him, saying, "A spirit hath not flesh and bones, as ye see Me have" (Luke 24:39). Thus, in resurrection He had a material body; and we can expect to have the same.

Galatians 6:1. "Ye which are spiritual." These were men of flesh; yet, they are described as spiritual.

Ephesians 1:3. "All spiritual blessings." The usual cliche, which men utter when they come to this passage, is that, "Our blessings are spiritual in the heavenlies, while Israel's blessings are to be material upon the earth." Such a statement implies that the opposite of spiritual is material and that Israel is to have no spiritual blessings. How can these men make such a declaration in view of the words spoken by Jeremiah: "I will put My law in their inward parts and write it on their hearts; and will be their God, and they shall be My people" (Jeremiah 31:33)? These are most certainly great spiritual blessings. The Ephesian passage speaks of "every spiritual exaltation," and designates exaltations of which God alone is the author — exaltations that will be our portion apart from any human agency or process. The Pope of Rome may be very highly exalted by men now, but will he ever be so exalted by God?

Ephesians 5:19. "Spiritual songs." This would have to mean songs of which God is the author. Truly, He "giveth songs in the night." (Job 35:10).

Ephesians 6:12. "Against spiritual wickedness in high places." It would seem as if all I have said as to the meaning of "spiritual" is contradicted by the occurrence here. But not so, for there is a very faulty rendering of the Greek here. "Spiritual" is *pneumatika*, which is accusative, plural, neuter. "Wickedness" is *ponēria*, which is genitive, singular. These two words do not agree in case and number and cannot be used together. Since there is no substantive here, one needs to be supplied. The phrase should read: "with the spiritual *forces* of wickedness among the most elevated." It is these forces against which we wrestle. Understanding the word "force" to mean the power to act effectively and vigorously, or the power to persuade and influence, and seeing Satan as the prime example, it is not difficult to understand the use of the word "spiritual" here. Where did Satan get his wisdom, skill, and ability? Was he not endowed with these when he was created as one of the cherubim? Did he lose all these when he fell? As much as we dislike to admit it, we must acknowledge that Satan is in possession of forces of which God was the author and giver. God never intended that these abilities should be used by him the way they are being used today. Satan has prostituted all his God-given powers in ways that are contrary to the will of God. These are the forces against which we must now wage war.

Colossians 1:9. "Wisdom and spiritual understanding" Solomon urged his children saying: "Wisdom is the principal thing; therefore get wisdom: and with all thy getting get understanding" (Prov. 4:7). Wisdom can be obtained in many ways by natural processes. We can memorize passages in the Bible and quote them freely; but if we ever understand them, understanding will have to be given by God. And as Paul declares: "For what man knoweth the things of a man, save the spirit of man which is in him? Even so the things of God knoweth no man, but by the Spirit of God" (1 Cor. 2:11). Such knowledge and such understanding are indeed spiritual.

Colossians 3:16. "Spiritual songs." See comments on Eph. 5:19.

1 Peter 2:5. "A spiritual house." A good commentary on this will be found in Hebrews 3:1 - 6.

1 Peter 2:5. "Spiritual sacrifices." A spiritual sacrifice would be one provided wholly by God.

There are two occurrences of the adverb that need to be considered. In 1 Cor. 2:14 we are told that the things of God are "spiritually discerned." This means that comprehension and understanding of that which is divine is wholly dependent upon God and must come from Him. In Revelation 11:8 we are told that Jerusalem "spiritually is called Sodom and Egypt." This means that this is a divine designation. It is called this by God.

It has not been my intention to expound or explain all these passages. I have deliberately avoided trying to do so. My purpose has been to show that my definition of the word "spiritual" is in harmony with, and is not contradicted by, any passage in the New Testament.

We commit an offense against the Word of God when we take the word "spiritual" and force it to serve us, making it mean what we want it to mean. To a certain extent, this word is a Pauline word, since practically all its occurrences are found in his epistles. Let us use it as he did and give it the meaning which he gave it. In doing so, we will be holding fast the form of sound words which we have learned from him (2 Tim. 1:13).

The SEED and BREAD Bible-Study leaflets are published as often as time and means permit and are sent free to all names on THE WORD OF TRUTH MINISTRY mailing list. Send us your name. There will be no obligation, solicitation, or visitation. Additional copies of any issue available on request.   ISSUE NO. 89

SEED & BREAD

FOR THE SOWER   ISA. 55:10   FOR THE EATER

BRIEF BIBLICAL MESSAGES
FROM

THE WORD OF TRUTH MINISTRY

339 South Orange Drive, Los Angeles, Cal. 90036

Otis Q. Sellers, Bible Teacher

THE TRUTHS GOD CALLS SECRET

There are many who claim to be dispensationalists, even advanced dispensationalists, who are trying to build a theology of their own on the English word "mystery." They talk much about "the dispensation of the mystery," "the church of the mystery," and "the gospel of the dispensation of the mystery." However, when we talk to them about these things or read their writings concerning them, everything seems to vaporize and vanish, or else becomes lost in a torrent of words and phrases. We search in vain for something Biblically solid that we can embrace. It becomes somewhat like trying to pick up a ball of mercury with the fingers, a parallel that all will recognize who have ever tried it. In my own opinion, these men have gone far beyond anything warranted in Scripture. They have taken a mistranslation and tried to build a body of truth upon it, all the while promising a very special place and extraordinary future blessings for all who will repeat their teachings as articles of faith.

To these men, those who believe the record God has given of His Son (a belief that has for its foundation the Gospel of John, the book that was written so that men might believe that Jesus is the Christ, the Son of God) are only "John believers." We are relegated to a lower class of believers. But those who have "believed the gospel of the dispensation of the mystery," which they say is in Ephesians, are first-class believers who are to enjoy special blessings in a special place called "the heavenlies."

I have talked to these men and tried to find out exactly what is the content of "the gospel of the dispensation of the mystery," supposed to be found in Ephesians. I would like to "examine myself" by it to see if I am in the faith, in the spirit of 2 Cor. 13:5. I have read every word in Ephesians hundreds of times; I have examined every word of it in the original language; I have taught it to many classes; I have translated it and published my translation for public inspection; and, most important of all, I have believed every word of it. Yet, according to their judgments, I do not qualify for membership in this elite group. One of them said to me, "You are in the faith, but not in the mystery." Further questioning brought forth the declaration that the members of this exclusive group have been "initiated into the mystery," so that one does not get in by believing, but by initiation. To all this I say poppycock, tommyrot, and balderdash. You are not fooling anyone but yourselves. You have built a pyramid from the point upward, and even the point does not exist. The word "mystery" does not belong in the Bible.

The word translated "mystery" in the New Testament is *musterion*; and while they may sound alike, *musterion* does not mean "mystery." The dictionary tells us that a "mystery" is something that has not been or cannot be explained, something incomprehensible and uncomprehended. However, there are no such ideas in any occurrence of the Greek word in the New Testament.

The honest student of God's Word should face up to the fact that the word *musterion* has been mistranslated in every occurrence and that we should be done with the word "mystery" once and for all, so far as its being useful in communicating God's Truth.

Of course, some will be very loath to do this, for then they can no longer mysterize (cultivate a mysterious air) and indulge in mysteriosophy, giving the gullible the impression that they have entered into esoteric understandings which are not known to the ordinary believer, especially to those who have only found the Christ revealed in the Gospel of John. I am convinced that some of these are following the practice recommended to the young man in Gilbert and Sullivan's operetta *Patience:*

> **You must lie upon the daises and discourse in novel**
> **Phrases of your complicated state of mind.**
> **The meaning doesn't matter if it's only idle chatter of a**
> **Transcendental kind.**
> **And every one will say,**
> **As you walk your mystic way,**
> **"If this young man expresses himself in terms too deep for me,**
> **Why, what a very singularly deep young man**
> **This deep young man must be!"**

The word *musterion* is found twenty-seven times in the New Testament. It means "secret" in every occurrence and should always be so translated. Examination of every passage in which it is found will show that it always refers to truths being revealed of which no previous mention has been made in Scripture. In the past, these truths had been hidden in God and could not therefore be known. And, yet, after they were made known, they could be understood by all who had ears to hear. Today, any individual or group claiming exclusive knowledge or possession of the truths God calls "secret" have deceived themselves.

In the parallel passages of Matthew 13:11, Mark 4:11, and Luke 8:10, the Lord Jesus speaks of "the secrets of the kingdom of heaven," or "the secrets of the kingdom of God." These secrets had to do with truths that had not been revealed before, no mention of them having been made in previous revelations; but they were then being made known to His disciples. Thus, these things were no longer secret. They were understood by His disciples; for when they asked Him why He spoke to the multitudes in parables, He answered: "Because it is given unto you to know the secrets of the kingdom of heaven, but to them it is not given" (Matt. 13:11). Following this He said: "But blessed are your eyes, for they see: and your ears, for they hear" (Matt. 13:16). Today, the believer can have the same understanding if he will do the work that is necessary to arrive at this goal. These truths are not "mysteries"; they never were "mysteries." They were "secrets" which have now been told and written, and they can be understood by any believer whose goal is the truth.

The two occurrences of the word *musterion* in Paul's Roman epistle are highly illuminating. In Romans 11:25 he declares that he would not have them to be ignorant of this secret: that a hardness (*pōrōsis*) in part has happened to Israel, until the full number of the nations have come in. At the time these words were written, God was paying a visit to the nations to take out of them a people for His name (Acts 15:14). This was to be a short work (Romans 9:28), and it certainly was. It was all completed in the twenty-five years that elapsed between Acts 10 and Acts 28:28. The declarations in Rom. 11:25 and Acts 15:14 do not describe God's present purpose or His present work.

The other occurrence of the word *musterion* in Romans is found in 16:25, but the truth is obscured here due to very careless translation. I have labored long on this passage and I believe it literally reads: "Now to Him Who is able to establish you in accord with my gospel and the heralding of Christ Jesus, in accord with the revelation of a secret, hushed in eonian times, yet, manifested now through prophetic Scriptures also, in accord with the command of the eonian God, being made known to all nations for the obedience of faith."

The full interpretation of this passage presents many difficulties. But there are certain things in it of which we can be sure. In the Acts period, the proclamation of the salvation-bringing message and the presentation of Jesus Christ was always the outcome of a new and fresh revelation to the herald. Consider Peter's message in Acts 2, and compare it with his second message in Acts 3. Then, compare these two messages with that of Stephen in Acts 7, and with Philip's to the Ethiopian eunuch in Acts 8. Follow on through Peter's message in the house of Cornelius (Acts 10), and Paul's messages to the Jews in Pisidian Antioch (Acts 13), to the Philippian jailer in Acts 16, to the Thessalonians (Acts 17), on Mars' hill (Acts 17:22 - 33), to the multitude (Acts 22), to the Sanhedrin (Acts 23), to Felix (Acts 24), to Festus (Acts 25), and to Agrippa (Acts 26).

Careful examination of all these messages will reveal that in each one, the gospel was preached, Jesus Christ was proclaimed, and that each one was a divine communication. Yet, they are all different in scope and content. They met with exactitude the needs of the hearers; each one of them was inspired by God (1 Thess. 2:13); and all of them were the revelation of a secret. These messages had never been heard by any man before. However, at the time Paul wrote Romans, the gospel of Jesus Christ was beginning to shine forth through prophetic Scriptures, of which the Roman epistle became another one.

We need to remember that in the Acts period, no man could hear the gospel without a herald (Rom. 10:14), and no man could herald except he be divinely commissioned as such (Rom. 10:15). Furthermore, the message he gave had to be provided by God for every occasion; and every message given was the revelation of a secret by God to the herald. When all these facts are taken into consideration, we can better understand Paul's statement that his gospel, even the heralding of Jesus Christ, was in accord with the revelation of a secret.

Lack of space makes impossible the examination of every passage in which *musterion* is found, so we will go at once to two very important occurrences in Ephesians 3:3,4. As the chapter opens, Paul declares that he is "the bound one of Jesus Christ for you of the nations"; and he assumes that they have surely heard and are hearing of the administration of the grace of God, the truth concerning which had been given to him for them, that is, "you of the nations." This description, after Acts 28:28, is as broad as the human race. Even Israelites today are "of the nations," including those living in Israel. He further declares that it was by revelation that the secret, the truth that God's method of dealing had become totally gracious, was made known to him, a matter of which he had already spoken in brief. It had been "Christ's secret," but He had told it to Paul with the stipulation that he should make it known to the nations. One aspect of the secret concerning the administration of grace was that, as it runs its course, the nations (it is plural) are to be treated by God as joint-bodies (also plural), that is, bodies on the basis of absolute equality. There are no "most favored nations" with God in this dispensation.

Ephesians 3:3, 4 has nothing to do with the individual believer. It has nothing to do with the *ekklēsia,* and nothing to do with the body of Christ. The "secret" here has to do with nations. That is the subject and we have no right to change it and insert some idea of our own. Neither does it have to do with "Gentiles" being formed into some special body. To read this idea into it is just one more facet of the great theological conspiracy to get the Jew out and get a Gentile church in. (See Issue No. 45.) If we translate it "the nations," we include Israel. For that is what Israel is today, just one of the nations.

The SEED and BREAD Bible-Study leaflets are published as often as time and means permit and are sent free to all names on THE WORD OF TRUTH MINISTRY mailing list. Send us your name. There will be no obligation, solicitation, or visitation. Additional copies of any issue available on request.   ISSUE NO. 90

SEED & BREAD

FOR THE SOWER   ISA. 55:10   FOR THE EATER

BRIEF BIBLICAL MESSAGES
FROM
THE WORD OF TRUTH MINISTRY
339 South Orange Drive, Los Angeles, Cal. 90036

Otis Q. Sellers, Bible Teacher

THE MISSION OF ELIJAH

In Galatians 3:16 we are emphatically told that to Abraham and his seed were the promises made, and in Romans 9:4 that the promises belong to Israel. The Old Testament closes with one of the greatest promises to Israel to be found in the Word of God. It is a promise that is yet to be kept by God. Through the prophet Malachi He declared: "Behold, I will send you Elijah the prophet before the coming of the great and dreadful day of the LORD: And he shall turn the heart of the fathers to the children, and the heart of the children to their fathers, lest I come and smite the earth with a curse" (Mal. 4:5,6).

These are the glorious words that close the Old Testament, and even though the meaning of certain statements made in this promise are somewhat obscure, its leading features are quite plain. We are told that before "the great and dreadful day of the Lord" comes, Elijah the prophet will be sent to the people of Israel, and he will accomplish a far-reaching work of spiritual nature. It is also declared that if it were not for this great work, it would be necessary for the Lord to smite the earth with a curse when He comes.

The Lord is of purer eyes than to behold iniquity. If He returned to earth today, He, according to His word, would "take vengeance on them that know not God, and that obey not the gospel of our Lord Jesus Christ" (2 Thess. 1:8), and since people like this make up the overwhelming majority of mankind, His action would be one of smiting the earth with a curse. But we can rest assured that He will not need to do this, for before He comes He will send Elijah who will do a work that will make such far-reaching vengeance unnecessary.

The phrase "turn the heart of the fathers to the children and the children to their fathers" is somewhat obscure as to its exact meaning. However, we can say with certainty that these words indicate a work of great spiritual value and importance, first for Israel and then from them a blessing for all families of the earth. Furthermore, we know that in God's order the family is the one unit He has established, and that these words indicate a full return to the family system when God governs the earth. In the family the father is supposed to be the head and the teacher of the children. Today, the average father is incapable of being either head or teacher, and at the best the children regard the father as a well-intentioned nincompoop whose chief function is to bring in the money. The ministry of Elijah is going to make fathers to be what they should be, and he will do the same for the children.

The words of the angel of the Lord to Zacharias, the father of John the Baptist, shed further light on the meaning of this phrase. Concerning John he said: "And he shall go before Him in the spirit and power of Elijah, to turn the hearts of the fathers to the children, and the disobedient to the wisdom of the just; to make ready a people prepared for the Lord" (Luke 1:17).

The ministry of John the Baptist did not fail. It prepared many in the land of Israel for the first advent of Christ. The work of Elijah in a coming day will prepare all Israel for the second advent of Christ. When He comes again He will find a nation fully ready for Him. There should not be even as many as one who will need to be eliminated because he knows not God. "For they shall all know Me, from the least of them unto the greatest of them, saith the Lord: for I will forgive their iniquity and I will remember their sin no more" (Jer. 31:34). This is God's promise to them.

The words of Christ emphasize still further the far-reaching spiritual nature of the work Elijah is to do: "And His disciples asked Him saying, Why then say the scribes that Elijah must first come? And Jesus answered and said unto them, Elijah truly shall first come and restore all things" (Matt. 17:11). From this we know that the work of Elijah is not to be insignificant. He will "restore all things," and this will be done before the beginning of the great and notable day of the LORD.

It must be noted here that Elijah does his great work in the time period and under the conditions brought about by the divine assumption of sovereignty which inaugurates the government of God upon the earth. He is the one who will indicate the exact boundaries of the land God promised to Abraham, the boundaries of the land allotted to each tribe, the division of Israel according to their tribes, the identification of the Aaronic family, the three divisions of the tribe of Levi, the restoration of the judges and counselors as promised in Isa. 1:26, the identification of historical sites, the restoration and proper observance of the feasts. Today no one knows how passover was observed in the time of Christ. All this will be restored by Elijah when God governs the earth.

The prophecies of Malachi and the words of the Lord Jesus concerning the coming and ministry of Elijah have proved embarrassing to many students of the prophecies of things to come. They do not know what to do about a coming of Elijah and his great work before the return of the Lord. They have no room for such a grand event within the limits of their tight systems of prophetic interpretations.

Some get around it by making Elijah to be one of the two witnesses described in Rev. 11:3-12. But this cannot be true for Elijah does a great work of "turning." He turns the hearts of both fathers and children. The verb *turn* which appears twice in the Malachi prophecy is the Hebrew word *shuv*, and it denotes the kind of turning that denotes the conversion of the heart. See Psalm 51:13, Psalm 19:7, and Isa. 6:10 where this same word is translated converted. Since the two witnesses in Revelation are smiting both the earth and men upon it, we cannot say that they are doing a work of converting men so that the Lord will not need to smite the earth with a curse when He comes.

Others get around the direct prophecy of Malachi by saying that it was fulfilled in John the Baptist. They feel they have solid ground for this position. And since this is the way they want it to be, they steadfastly refuse to consider any truth that would make their position impossible. Furthermore, they refuse to see that if proven true the idea would break the Word of God. In considering the teaching that John the Baptist and his ministry fulfilled the Malachi prophecy of the coming of Elijah, certain facts must be faced.

When the priests and the Levites asked John if he were Elijah, his emphatic answer was, "I am not" (John 1:21). This should be enough to settle the question for all who permit the Word of God to speak in matters in dispute. John the Baptist certainly knew who he was and the nature of his mission, and he declared that he was not Elijah.

In the Malachi prophecy we have the direct statement of the LORD that He would send "Elijah the prophet." Since John declared that he was not Elijah, he could not have been the one God promised to send. Even though he came in the spirit and power of Elijah, he did not fulfill the Malachi prophecy. God made a promise and we have every right to believe He will fulfill this promise. We do not need to settle for John the Baptist. To do so would break the Word of God.

The language of Matthew 17:10,11 seems to indicate that the scribes were justifying their "do nothing" attitude toward the Lord Jesus by quoting the prophecy of Malachi. They insisted that He did not have Elijah as His forerunner. This led the disciples to ask: "Why then say the scribes that Elijah must first come" (Matt. 17:10). And even though John the Baptist had come, had completed his ministry, and had been beheaded, the Lord Jesus said in answer: "Elijah truly shall first come, and restore all things" (Matt. 17:11).

Thus our Lord made the coming of Elijah and the restoration of all things to be still future events, even after the death of John the Baptist. However, He added: "But I say unto you, That Elijah is come already, and they knew him not, but have done unto him whatsoever they listed. Likewise shall also the Son of man suffer of them. Then the disciples understood that He spake unto them of John the Baptist" (Matt. 17:12,13).

This is the passage that many use to prove that John was Elijah. At first glance it would seem to teach this, but many of us have learned to take more than one glance at a Scripture passage. We know that Elijah never died, and that John was "born of a woman." If John were Elijah, then we would have here a clear case of reincarnation. But if this be so, what became of that Elijah who "went up by a whirlwind into heaven" (2 Kgs. 2:11)? Furthermore, when Elijah appeared with Moses on the mount of transfiguration, it was Elijah and not John (Matt. 17:3). What then did our Lord mean when He said, "Elijah is come already."

Since the scribes were using the fact that Elijah had not yet come as proof that Jesus was not the Messiah, it is evident that His words were directed against them. If they did not recognize John as one sent from God, they would not recognize Elijah if he were sent by God. If Elijah had come they would have treated him just as they treated John, since John came in the spirit and power of Elijah. I believe that the Lord here used a figure of speech that is familiar to all of us. We speak of the need for "a Lincoln" or "a Gladstone" or "a Solomon." Our Lord was telling the disciples that *an* Elijah had already come and the scribes had rejected him. Would it have been any different if *the* Elijah had come?

In an earlier reference to John and Elijah our Lord had said: "And if ye will receive it, this is Elijah which was for to come" (Matt. 11:14). The truth here is expressed in the same manner as we find in Matt. 26:26 where the Lord said: "This is My body" meaning "this represents My body." Thus, in Matt. 11:14 our Lord declared to all who received him, John represented Elijah, and he would do for them individually what Elijah will do for Israel as a nation. So, by the words "Elijah, who is about to come," our Lord confirmed the fact that Elijah's coming was a future event even though John was then upon the earth.

There is one group in the United States that has made so much of the coming of Elijah to restore all things that they have built a small denomination upon this principle. They would have all believers looking for and waiting for Elijah. This is wrong. Elijah will make no appearance until after God has assumed sovereignty. All his work will be done within the parameters of the kingdom of God. We must put first things first and continue to live looking for the blazing forth of the glory of our great God and Savior the Lord Jesus Christ (Titus 2:13). Elijah will not come until this great manifestation has taken place.

The SEED and BREAD Bible-Study leaflets are published as often as time and means permit and are sent free to all names on THE WORD OF TRUTH MINISTRY mailing list. Send us your name. There will be no obligation, solicitation, or visitation. Additional copies of any issue available on request.

ISSUE NO. 91

SEED & BREAD

FOR THE SOWER   ISA. 55:10   FOR THE EATER

BRIEF BIBLICAL MESSAGES

FROM

THE WORD OF TRUTH MINISTRY

339 South Orange Drive, Los Angeles, Cal. 90036

Otis Q. Sellers, Bible Teacher

THE SEVEN MILLENNIUM THEORY

In the quarter century that preceded the year 1000 A.D. the minds of many were dominated by the idea that the year 1000 would mark "the end of the world." There were no sound reasons for this belief. Its only support was that "1000" was a nice round number, and that it would be appropriate for God to end the world at that time. This view spread like a prairie fire. It was even accepted by the ungodly, resulting in a wave of immorality almost without parallel. Men determined to have their final fling before the holocaust descended. But the year 1000 came and went, and nothing out of the ordinary happened.

Since that time, in the religious world, date setting has been the favorite occupation of many. These attempts to "fix the time" have as a rule been related to something called "the battle of Armageddon," the second-coming of Christ, and the beginning of the millennium. Men have set their dates, supported them by elaborate charts, and shouted them from the housetops. In the past two centuries thousands of men have set as many positive dates for the return of the Lord, but when the date arrived, nothing happened. Thus, on the basis of experience alone, a teacher of God's Word should not be faulted when he emphatically denies relationship to any other teacher who attempts to set a date for the end of the dispensation of grace, or for the second advent of Christ, or for the beginning of the millennium. I, for one, cannot extend sympathy to any man who claims to have knowledge of the times and seasons which is greater than that which the Lord Jesus gave to His twelve apostles (Acts 1:7).

Twenty-five years ago (1953) I wrote a study on this same subject repudiating the ideas of certain dispensationalists who were setting the year 2000 A.D. as being the date for the beginning of that glorious millennium of human history when Satan will be bound and Jesus Christ will be personally present upon the earth. Their theories were not new to me. I had first come upon them in

1923 and as a young student was momentarily intrigued by them. But after careful study I rejected them, feeling they were founded solely upon inferences and not upon any direct teaching in the Word of God. They were linking an erroneous human calendar with the errorless Word of God.

These theories hold that God's complete program for the human race, so far as it is revealed, is to be worked out in seven millenniums; that is, in seven one-thousand-year periods. It is held that from the creation of Adam to the beginning of the new heavens and new earth is to be exactly seven thousand years, and that the last of these would be the thousand years that follow the return of Jesus Christ. Since, according to the commonly accepted chronology, as established by Archbishop Ussher, 5982 years have now passed since the creation of Adam, this leaves only eighteen years until the first day of the seventh millennium begins. And since these men readily admit that there is a seven year period, the seventieth week of Israel's seventy weeks, this now leaves just eleven years before the covenant is made that marks the beginning of that seven-year period, and for the complete setting of the stage for the acting out of the great drama of that seventieth week. Israel must be restored, the temple of God must be rebuilt on its ancient site where a Mohammedan mosque stands today. So, all this means that an enormous amount now has to be accomplished in the next eleven years. Could it be that the "temple of God" which the man of sin desecrates (Matt. 24:15, 2 Thess. 2:4) is jerry-built?

At the time I wrote on this subject twenty-five years ago, some of the brethren who were advocating this theory were then allowing 33 years for the setting of the stage, and others were allowing only 16, but both of these groups have now run out of years and their charts and schedules now mock them. And, it was because that some of these brethren were so sold on these theories that they rejected without consideration my discovery that there would be a long period of divine government for Israel and for the world before the second coming of Christ. There was simply no room for such a time before the year 2000 A.D., according to their charts and calculations.

The major argument that was then and still is being presented for the beginning of the seventh millennium in 2000 A.D. is taken from 2 Peter 3:8. There we read: "But beloved, be not ignorant of this one thing, that one day is with the Lord as a thousand years, and a thousand years as one day." There are some who see in this passage a mathematical formula, some sort of a code-breaker for determining when an event will take place. They think that God is here establishing fixed values. Then they go to the first two chapters of Genesis where they find God actively working for six days and resting on the seventh, and *presto* this gives them the theory that God's program for man covers seven days or seven thousand years. And since the seventh day was the sabbath, it follows in their reasoning that the seventh one-thousand year period has to be the millennium. Now the flood gates of imagination are opened and out flows outrageous and anti-biblical results.

I am not able to put my eye to the keyhole of a simple passage such as 2 Peter 3:8 and see the far-reaching propositions that these men claim they see. Furthermore, I know that what they are presenting is not taught in this passage, even when it is combined with the opening chapters of Genesis. I have studied and expounded many times the chapter in which this passage appears, and in it have found many truths such as: 1) A divine promise is as certain of fulfillment in a thousand years as it is in one day. A human promise always become weaker the longer it remains unfulfilled. 2) Time with God has none of the limitations that it has with us. With us a day is a day and a thousand years is exactly that. 3) A long time with God may be a very short time with us, and a short time in God's sight may be a very long one in ours. 4) God can either execute in a day or spread out over a thousand years any purpose of His mind or action of His hand. 5) In Psalm 90:4 we are told that a thousand years in God's sight are but as yesterday when it is past, even as a watch in the night. A "watch in the night" among the Hebrews would have been four hours. Therefore, a thousand years can be either twenty-four hours or four hours. Thus, the Spirit of God has set up a safeguard so that none would think He was establishing fixed values.

The proponents of the seventh millennium theory also hold that the seven days of Genesis 1 and 2 are typical of the seven millenniums of earth's history, six of which have already about run their course, and that the creation week has a prophetic character. But if each day is examined as to its character, and the six one-thousand-year periods of human history are examined, it will be found that there is no correspondence in any of them. This is especially true of the seventh day when it is compared to the prophesied character of the personal presence of Jesus Christ for a thousand years — the time usually called "the" millennium.

On the seventh day God ended His work and rested (Gen. 2:1). This we are told is a foreview of the millennium. But when the facts are faced there is no correspondence, likeness, or identity of character between these two. Whatever the character of the millennium will be, it is not in any sense a sabbath. This thousand-year period is inaugurated by the second coming of Jesus Christ. This coming will result in His parousia or personal presence for a thousand years. The Greek word *parousia* indicates a personal presence when one is present because of who he is and what he does. Thus, His coming will not be in order to rest but to begin a glorious new work. (See Issues No. 24 and 25 for more on this glorious event.) This event does not end God's work; it will mark the beginning of what is probably the greatest period of divine effort. In this thousand years, Christ will work and we will work. It will not be a sabbath for God, and it will not be a sabbath for man. In fact, if there is no work to be done, I would not want to be there. I believe in work, and I love to do it. The millennium has no correspondence with the seventh creation day when God rested.

Space does not permit the examination of other passages which are called into the witness box to give testimony in support of this theory. Nevertheless, when these passages are carefully examined it becomes plain that they have been misinterpreted and do not support the theory being advocated. One of these is Hosea 6:1,2 where the people of Israel say: "Come and let us return unto the LORD: for He hath torn, and He will heal us; He hath smitten and He will bind us up. After two days will He revive us: in the third day He will raise us up and we shall live in His sight." The "one day equals a thousand years" equation is applied to this passage, and in order to make it come out right these "two days" or two thousand years are started with the birth of Christ. However, it is my conviction that these two days are two twenty-four hour periods that begin with God's assumption of sovereignty and Jesus Christ is unveiled. Israel will then know the One whom they have so long rejected, and this will begin two days of mourning and depression as they wait to discover what will happen to them. It is not until the third day of divine rule that they are revived and begin to live in His sight.

In this study, solely for the sake of discussion, I have accepted the years of the commonly accepted chronology (Ussher's) as being correct. However, this is not my personal view. I know that when the dates are computed from the Septuagint Version of the Old Testament, 1465 years must be added between Adam and Christ. If the Septuagint contains the correct figures, it indicates that man has been on the earth for 7447 years. The witness of the Septuagint cannot be dismissed with a wave of the hand. Its chronology could be the correct one.

The reader is asked to take into consideration the fact that this study was written in January 1978.

The SEED and BREAD Bible-Study leaflets are published as often as time and means permit and are sent free to all names on THE WORD OF TRUTH MINISTRY mailing list. Send us your name. There will be no obligation, solicitation, or visitation. Additional copies of any issue available on request.   ISSUE NO. 92

SEED & BREAD

FOR THE SOWER   ISA. 55:10   FOR THE EATER

BRIEF BIBLICAL MESSAGES

FROM

THE WORD OF TRUTH MINISTRY

339 South Orange Drive, Los Angeles, Cal. 90036

Otis Q. Sellers, Bible Teacher

CONCERNING "BORN AGAIN"

The phrase "born again" has suddenly become one of great popularity. This, to a great extent, has resulted from the present President of the United States declaring that he is a "born-again Christian." From his use of this descriptive term it seems that he means that he is a Christian whose commitment to Jesus Christ has made a definite change in his thinking and way of living. This is good, and I applaud it. However, in spite of the popularity of this term, permit me to say that I would not want to hang one minute of my almost sixty years of Christian life and experience upon it. I could easily adopt it, as so many have done, and could apply it to myself as well as anyone to signify a higher quality of Christian life and commitment than that of the average run-of-the-mill church member. But if I did I would have to cease all study of this term, for I know that Biblical research would cause it to vanish into the realm of meaningless, ritualistic terminology.

We are exhorted by Paul in 2 Timothy 1:13 to "hold fast the form of sound words," or, as it could be more accurately translated to "have a pattern of sound words." It is my conviction after careful study that the words "born again" are not sound words, that they do not truly represent any words in the original Greek, and since they have no real foundation in Scripture, anyone can take them and make them to mean anything he wants them to mean.

After hearing one of my radio messages on the importance of believing in the Lord Jesus Christ, a woman wrote to me and said: "I am a believer in the Lord Jesus, but I want to be born again. I am so dissatisfied with myself and so unhappy. Please help me."

Of course I would very much like to help this lady, but it is evident that someone has caused her to think that there is some experience that will produce within her a new personality with which she will be quite satisfied and happy. There is no such experience set forth in the Bible, even though thousands are now claiming to have experienced it. However, I wonder what it will be like for them if they ever truly get into the Word and find in their own lives that "tribulation or persecution ariseth because of the Word." Will they still want the difficulties that involvement in the truth will bring?

As a result of careful investigation I am convinced that the words "born again" were forced into the *King James Version* in order to lend support to a gross and profane misrepresentation of truth called "baptismal regeneration." It was to Nicodemus, a Pharisee, one of the rulers of the Jews, that the Lord declared, according to the translators of the *King James Version,* "Verily, verily, I say unto you, except a man be born again, he cannot see the kingdom of God" (John 3:3).

It is strange indeed how many people quote this verse, and claim to have been "born again," yet they do not "see the kingdom of God," they have no definition of this term, and no understanding of what it means. The criticism of many Jews today is justified when they charge that the Christians took the Old Testament concept of the kingdom of God and twisted it into a concept of "the church in heaven." The very purpose for which one is "born again" has not been realized in the lives of most professing Christians. Tell them God's truth concerning the kingdom of God, and they will say, "I cannot see it," or, as one said, "It leaves me cold."

The exact wording here in the Greek for "born again" is *gennēthē anōthen*. Since President Carter reads his New Testament in the Greek, he should be able to see at once that this means "generated from above," and not "born again." The root word is *gennaō*, and it is not too far out of line to translate it by the word "born," if it is understood that "born" is the past participle of "bear" and means to produce. However, *gennaō* means to generate, and in all honesty this is the way it should be translated.

The word *anōthen* does not mean "again," not by any stretch of the imagination. It means "above," and I doubt if this word would ever have been translated "again" in this verse if it had not been for the determination of some translator who wanted it to mean this. He was probably a spiritual descendent of Humpty Dumpty and paraphrased his words to say: "When I consider a Greek word it means just what I choose it to mean — neither more nor less." This translator revealed that he knew the true and exact meaning when he rendered it "above" in the thirty-first verse of this same chapter. Such discordant translating is inexcusable, and while no one today can say why it was done, we do know that these translators were all ministers in the *Church of England,* and were completely subservient to that Church and the King who had appointed them. One of the most important doctrines and practices in that denomination was that of "baptismal regeneration."

This doctrine held that every child born by natural generation belonged to the fallen race that started with Adam, and that Adam's sin must banish it to the torments of hell, unless by regeneration it is brought within the family of God. However, by the simple ritual of sprinkling a few drops of water upon the child's head, he was relieved of his guilt and brought into the family of God, providing of course that this ritual was accompanied by the utterance of a few cabalistic words.

There is good reason to believe that these translators wanted to render this in some fashion so that the generating work spoken of here could be removed from the absolute divine realm and lowered to be something that one human being, properly accredited of course, could do for another. They wanted this work to be something that a clergyman could do for an infant, thus securing the child's salvation if death should seize upon it. This self-assumed power gave the church and its clergy an unwarrantable hold upon the parents, especially upon the mother, to whose Biblical illiteracy was left the direction of religion in the family. Since there was very little Scripture that could be twisted into support for this idea, they laid hold of this portion because "born of water" could be made to mean the water ritual which they performed. But they could not do this if *anōthen* were translated "above," so, some other meaning must be given to it. Thus, it was translated "again," which is contrary to all reason.

The Greek word that means "again" is *palin*. This is found 142 times in the Greek New Testament, and it is translated consistently "again" in every occurrence. This is the word the Spirit of God would have led John to use if He had intended to set forth the idea of "again," or, "a second time." But He did not use *palin*, He used *anōthen*, which means "above" and is so translated in every occurrence except the two found in this portion.

There are those who insist that *anōthen* is translated "again" in Gal. 4:9 where, they say, "again" is its evident meaning. But this is totally wrong. The word translated "again" in the Galatian passage is *palin*, and the word *anōthen* which follows it is left untranslated. Most translators since the KJV have followed this example, except Rotherham who renders it, "the weak and beggarly elementary principles unto which over again ye are wishing to come into servitude." However, this occurrence of *palin* and *anōthen* together shows clearly that *anōthen* does not mean again.

Compilers of lexicons have earnestly sought to find evidence that *anōthen* can mean "again," hoping to justify the translators of the *King James Version*, but they have failed. Moulton and Milligan cite certain examples from the papyrus of which they somewhat feebly say, "the meaning 'again,' 'a second time' seems best to suit the context." However, a student with no axe to grind will see that the rendering "above all this" best suits the examples they have given. In view of all this evidence, I repeat, I do not want to hang one moment of my Christian life and experience on the words "born again." I say it is not a sound expression, that it defies any exact definition that can be backed up with Scripture, so it is useless so far as declaring any exact Christian truth is concerned.

From past experience I suppose that this leaflet will bring letters declaring that I am a lost soul, and that I am barred from the kingdom of God since I have never been "born again." Some will even charge me with having committed an unpardonable sin because

I have denied the validity of this term. I will answer these in advance by a word of personal testimony.

It has now been fifty-nine years since I became related to God through believing in the Lord Jesus Christ. I stand firmly upon the divine declaration that "As many as received Him, to them gave He authority to become the children of God." I do not believe that this act of receiving Him consists in "going to the front," "praying the sinners' prayer," or being worked over by some personal worker. To me this receiving of Him has been defined by God as "believing on His name" (John 1:12). Today, I know that fifty-nine years ago God moved in relationship to my life. I did not at that time understand what He was doing, and I do not fully comprehend it even now, but I do know that He moved in relationship to my life to make Himself a part of it. I was a sinner, and He was the Savior of sinners, and He was seeking sinners in order to become their Savior. He wanted me to be saved. As a result of His efforts, I became a believer in the Lord Jesus Christ, starting out by believing the small amount of truth concerning Him that was available, but seeking every day to add to my faith.

I know that from the day I became identified with Him, strange and miraculous changes began to take place in my life. My interests, my motives, my purposes, my desires, my likes and dislikes, my language and conversations — yes, almost everything that made up my life began to move in a strange new direction. All this was because I was living a new life in Christ Jesus, and was living it as a confessed believer in Him. Therefore, I fully believe in the metamorphosis that takes place in one when he enters into relationship with the Lord Jesus Christ. However, I do not believe that this should be called a "new birth" or that it is wise to refer to it as being "born again."

I know that in evangelical circles many would describe my experiences as being "born again," but I reject any such description. I am a child of God through personal faith in the Lord Jesus Christ. Because I received Him I have the authority to say, "God is my Father and I am His child." Because I am a believer I have received from God the sealing of the Holy Spirit of promise, which is the earnest of my inheritance until the day comes that God redeems His purchased possession (Eph. 1:13, 14). I believe that this portion of God's Spirit is the possession of all who believe. I will not seek for it, neither will I pray for it, since I feel this would be a lack of faith in His Word upon my part. I believe that this was given to me, not to get me worked up or excited, but in order that I might know the things freely given to us of God.

The SEED and BREAD Bible-Study leaflets are published as often as time and means permit and are sent free to all names on THE WORD OF TRUTH MINISTRY mailing list. Send us your name. There will be no obligation, solicitation, or visitation. Additional copies of any issue available on request.   ISSUE NO. 93

SEED & BREAD

FOR THE SOWER   ISA. 55:10   FOR THE EATER

BRIEF BIBLICAL MESSAGES

FROM

THE WORD OF TRUTH MINISTRY

339 South Orange Drive, Los Angeles, Cal. 90036

Otis Q. Sellers, Bible Teacher

GENERATION FROM ABOVE

In the study on "Concerning 'Born Again'" (Issue No. 93) it was demonstrated by infallible proofs from Scripture that the Greek phrase *gennaō anōthen* does not mean "born again" as it is translated in John 3:3, 7; and that the simple, honest, and objective meaning of this phrase is "generated from above." This being true, then we all owe it to God to find out as much as we can from His Word just what "generated from above" means.

Jesus Christ said to His disciples: "Without Me ye can do nothing" (John 15:5). This was true of the apostles to whom this was declared, and it is still true of every one of us today. However, it must be acknowledged that there is much that a capable or talented person can do even in the religious realm that has no real relationship to Him. In conferences on "church growth" you will be told of a thousand gimmicks you can use and schemes that can be worked in order to assemble great crowds. One of these is to hire the best musical director you can obtain, organize and train a choir of four hundred voices, and this will guarantee an attendance of at least 1200 people, 1600 if the choir is counted. But all this will prove to be just so much wood, hay, and stubble in the day when every man's work shall be made manifest.

Paul declared: "For what man knoweth the things of man, save by the spirit of man which is in him? Even so the things of God knoweth no man, but the Spirit of God" (1 Cor. 2:11). This tells us that while all human things can be searched out and known by human intelligence, no mater how complex they may be, yet divine things can be known only by divine enabling.

In view of such declarations as these from the Word of God, it is evident that there has to be a work of God that makes possible every acceptable thing that anyone ever does in relationship to Him. This would need to be an enabling work, an empowering work. That there is such a work is declared in many places in Scripture, and the term that best describes this work is "divine generation." This most important truth is one which is only feebly understood by many, due to the fact that the passages which declare it are forced either by mistranslation or misinterpretation to support traditional ideas that are not in them.

It has been said that quite often we make our own troubles, after which we are troubled by the troubles we have made. This is certainly true in the case of many passages into which men have read the theological ideas of "regeneration," or the so-called "new birth." In all theology this is supposed to be a one-shot thing, experienced instantaneously at the moment of conversion, settling once and for all one's place as a child in the family of God. It is held that as by a first and natural birth one becomes a child of human parents, even so by a second divine birth he becomes a child of God. Those who say they have experienced this usually lay claim to having been "born again." However when they come upon the passage that emphatically declares: "Whosoever is born of God doth not commit sin; for His seed remaineth in him: and he cannot sin, because he is born of God" (1 John 3:9), they are greatly troubled. While they insist they have experienced this birth, they are too honest to claim they have reached the stage of sinlessness.

So the problem they have created calls for the manufacture of other theological doctrines in the hope of solving the problem and dispelling the trouble. Some who have a very low estimate of the character of sin are able to claim such sinlessness inasmuch as they have ceased from certain obvious vices, or have given up the use of certain things which their sect calls sinful. Thus, measured by their own private yardstick they are sinless. Further claim is usually made that this sinlessness was produced by some other experience which is described by various terms such as sanctification, eradication, second-blessing, or the baptism of the Holy Spirit. But there are many Christians who have a much keener sense of the nature of sin, and who live lives of much greater commitment, devotedness, and service than the self-acclaimed pietist and perfectionist, yet would never think of claiming sinlessness.

There are others who have developed a doctrine called "the two natures of the child of God," a "sinful nature" which is the result of natural birth, and a "divine nature" which they attribute to being "born of God." It is further held that all sin in our lives is the outflow of our "sinful nature," and that no sin at all is ever out of the divine nature. This is supposed to take care of John's difficult declaration, since it is held that he is speaking of the divine nature when he said, "He that is born of God doth not commit sin."

This is one way out of the difficulty, but it will not stand the test of constant examination by the white light of God's Word. In it we have only one nature, which is our human nature. And while we have become partakers of the divine nature, we must remember that it is a human being that becomes a partaker of this, and that it comes from believing in the Lord Jesus Christ (2 Pet. 1:4).

In the meaningful study of any passage of Scripture we must first of all ask, "What does it say?" This must be answered wholly without any input from those doctrines that have been built upon it, and which are supposed to be demonstrated by quoting it. And if our question sends us to the original Greek, then to the Greek we will go. Furthermore, if the mere suggestion of "going to the Greek" frightens anyone, then he does not know that in Bible study the language barrier has been broken, and that every fact that is available to anyone is also available to you and me.

In the passage we are now considering (1 John 3:9), everything depends on the meaning of the word "born." The Greek word is *gennaō*, one of a large family of words which has the root *gen* as a base. This root is also carried over into English usage, providing us with many words that use *gen* as a prefix or root, all of which have the idea of producing in them.

The basic meaning of *gennaō* is to generate, or to produce, especially in the sense of giving origin to. The lexicons, usually following one another, are prone to say that *gennaō* means "to beget," but this presents no problem if we keep in mind that *beget* and *generate* are synonymous terms, and that they come into comparison in the sense that they both have in them the idea of "to give origin to," that is, "to produce." Of this word Herman Cremer says: "Peculiar is the use made by Paul in some passages of the word to denote an influence exerted on someone, moulding his life, as in Gal. 4:24." However, I do not think that these are peculiar uses at all. What Paul said in the Galatian passage was that the Sinai covenant "gendereth (*gennaō*) to bondage," which means that the law generated slavery, not freedom.

The idea of generating is a basic meaning that must always be kept in mind in considering any occurrence of *gennaō*. John declares that, "Whosoever is generated of God does not commit sin," and enforces this by saying, "we know that whosoever is generated of God sinneth not, for His seed remaineth in him, and he cannot sin for he is generated of God."

The lesson to be learned here is that the generating work of God never produces sin as a result. It cannot lead to the committing of sin. John does not say that the children of God never transgress. Indeed, in an earlier passage he freely admits the possibility of sin in the believer's life, telling him that if any man does sin he has an Advocate with the Father, Jesus Christ the righteous. It does not seem that God would have made such marvelous provision for His sinning children if it were impossible for them to sin.

What the Holy Spirit is telling us in 1 John 3:9 is that the generating work of God will never produce sin. Even when sin is committed by the Christian, it will never be the outcome of divine generation. God's generating work always has a specific purpose, a definite end in view. It is likened to a man planting seed. If a farmer wants wheat, he plants the seed that produces wheat. All seeds bring forth only after their kind. The seed God plants remains within us. It does not change into something else. He never plants a seed that produces sin. If His generating work produces nothing in our lives, His seed remains and will be a witness against us when God judges the living and the dead. Even as the Lord

Jesus declared: "The word that I have spoken, the same shall judge him in the last day" (John 12:48).

As already noted, when we recognize that *gennaō* means to generate, or to produce, all passages in which this word occurs will shine forth with a new light and reveal greater and more positive truth. Take as an example 2 Tim. 2:23 where Paul instructs Timothy to avoid foolish and unlearned questions "knowing that they do gender (*gennaō*) strifes." How simple this passage becomes when we use the word *generate* as a translation.

In Matt. 1:18 we read: "Now the birth (*gennēsis*) of Jesus Christ was after this manner." The word *gennēsis* is a verbal noun derived from *gennaō* and should be translated "generating." Joseph had no part in the generating or producing Jesus the Christ. His incarnation was entirely a work of the Holy Spirit. Then in Matt. 1:20 we read that the angel of the Lord said to Joseph: "Fear not to take unto thee Mary thy wife, for that which is conceived (*gennaō*) in her is of the Holy Spirit." This shows that *gennaō* has more to do with all that took place in the womb of Mary in the nine months before birth rather than with the actual birth (coming forth) of the babe itself. The proper understanding of *gennaō* in this passage will produce a better appreciation of the virgin birth.

Another passage from 1 John is of the utmost importance. It is emphatically declared that: "Whosoever believeth that Jesus is the Christ is born (*gennaō*) of God (1 John 5:1). A quick look at this passage might cause one to think that belief in Christ is the cause, and that "born of God" is the result, but this is not the truth being declared here. If any use it as proof of this, he had better end his studies then and there, for if he continues he will find two other statements in this epistle that make such an interpretation impossible. These are: "Ye know that every one that doeth righteousness is born (*gennaō*) of Him" (1 John 2:29); and "For love is of God; and every one that loveth is born (*gennaō*) of God" (1 John 4:7).

These passages tell us that belief in Jesus Christ is God-generated. There would be no believers apart from this. Some who say they will believe when they get "good and ready" had better give due heed here. How do they know that the generating work of God will be there at their convenience? We also learn that love is the result of divine generation. Apart from this all men would care only for their own, and none would care for another. Righteousness which is acceptable in God's sight is also generated by Him.

I believe I have pointed truth lovers to an avenue of truth down which they can walk and enjoy the beauty of truth as they go.

The SEED and BREAD Bible-Study leaflets are published as often as time and means permit and are sent free to all names on THE WORD OF TRUTH MINISTRY mailing list. Send us your name. There will be no obligation, solicitation, or visitation. Additional copies of any issue available on request.   ISSUE NO. 94

SEED & BREAD

FOR THE SOWER ISA. 55:10 FOR THE EATER

BRIEF BIBLICAL MESSAGES
FROM
THE WORD OF TRUTH MINISTRY
339 South Orange Drive, Los Angeles, Cal. 90036

Otis Q. Sellers, Bible Teacher

LESSONS FROM NICODEMUS

Nicodemus was the wealthy, powerful Pharisee who came to Jesus by night (John 3:1-9). As to why he came at night has caused much speculation and discussion. Christians often like this type of discussion, as it is one that you can keep going on and on, but can never be settled. And even if we could settle why this man came at this time, it would not cause us to change our beliefs or our lives, the doing of which can cause us great trouble.

He is identified as being a man of the Pharisees, a small, powerful, and very exclusive sect in Israel. They were meticulously correct in all their actions; they were moral, zealous, and righteous. Their place in society and their sectarianism led some of them to do much that was contrary to the will and word of God. Nicodemus must be considered as one whose life was exemplary among them. He is also described as being one of the rulers (a chief) of the Jews. This indicates that he was a member of the Sanhedrin, those seventy men who made up the governing body in Judea.

One can easily imagine the prolonged and intense discussions that went on in this governing body and among the Pharisees concerning the person, the words, and the works of the Lord Jesus Christ. There were many good men among the Pharisees, such as Nicodemus and Joseph of Arimathea, and in the beginning of His ministry, before all the rancor and bitterness arose, the discussions in the Sanhedrin and among the Pharisees were probably conducted on a high plane of propriety. However, we know nothing of what went on, especially in the closed meetings of the Sanhedrin, but Nicodemus in his nighttime visit to Jesus made known the outcome of these discussions. His statement when amplified was: "Rabbi, we understand and appreciate by the facts we have observed and considered that you are an authoritative teacher come from God, for no man can do these attesting miracles that you are constantly performing except God be with him" (John 3:2).

The pronoun "we" here can refer only to "the rulers of the Jews," that is, the Sanhedrin, as there is no other antecedent. And it is wrong to imagine one, such as certain others who may have accompanied him on this visit. His statement reveals that seventy of the best minds in Israel, men in a position to make a judgment based upon information not readily available to others, had considered the person and works of the man Jesus and knew and comprehended that the miracles of Jesus accredited Him as a teacher sent from God.

Since all the miracles of Jesus Christ were performed to let men know what could be expected when God governed the world, each one being a foretaste of the kingdom of God (See Issue No. 67), and since a vast amount of truth was contained in each one of them, the declaration of Nicodemus revealed that the rulers in Israel had apprehended and comprehended much truth concerning the kingdom of God.

The word Nicodemus used which is translated "know" is *eideō*, a word that means to get knowledge by means of any or all of the senses. Note this in Luke 5:24. His declaration brought forth from the Lord an answer that must be regarded both as a commendation and a warning to him and to all the rulers of the Jews. "Jesus answered and said unto him, Verily, Verily, I say unto you, Except a man be generated from above he cannot see (*eideō*) the kingdom of God" (John 3:3).

What these rulers had perceived, and Nicodemus confessed that they knew and comprehended, was the outcome of divine generation. Nicodemus had said: "We know" (*eideō*) and the Lord used his exact word in His reply, saying, "Except a man be generated from above he cannot see (*eideō*) the kingdom of God." Thus, only one conclusion is possible. If Nicodemus spoke the truth, then these rulers had been generated of God, otherwise they would not have known the message of His miracles. Our Lord declared that a divine work had been done in the lives of all of these, an enabling work that had made it possible for them to know and comprehend. This had brought upon them a new responsibility and accountability to God, one that could not be ignored or treated lightly. Words that have a bearing on this are found in John 9:41: "Jesus said unto them (the Pharisees), If you were blind you would have no sin: but now ye say, We see; therefore your sin remaineth."

The outcome of neglecting to respond to the generating work of God is set forth in a later passage: "If I had not come and spoken unto them, they had not had sin: but now they have no cloke for their sin. If I had not done among them the works which none other man did, they had not had sin: but now they have both seen and hated both Me and My Father" (John 15:22,24).

From this we know that if they had heard His words and seen His works, and had lacked the ability to recognize and appreciate the truths that these words and works were declaring, then they would not have been condemned. And since there was nothing in human ability that could bring an understanding of the things of God (1 Cor. 2:11), they had to be given divine ability. This, the rulers had enjoyed, for God had performed in them a generating work that made this understanding possible. Thus their condemnation was just.

Jesus Christ was not demanding of Nicodemus that he be generated of God. This Pharisee stood before Him as one who had been generated from above. He said, "We know" (*eideō*), and the Lord had informed him that this was evidence of a divine activity in his life, since apart from generation from above, no one can know.

The Lord's answer put Nicodemus on the spot, one that demanded decisive action. It must have surprised him, so as a delaying tactic he asked a question. "How can a man be generated when he is old? Can he enter the second time into his mother's womb and be generated?" (John 3:4).

This question was asked in order to draw more information from the Lord about this strange matter of being "generated from above." He infers that the only generating he knows anything about is that which takes place in the mother's womb, and that once this was complete, nothing could be added to it, neither could it be done the second time. He certainly knew, even as we do today, that one's capabilities and possibilities are inborn, and that these are fixed in us when we come forth. It is the genes of the father combined with the genes of the mother as developed over a nine-month period that makes us what we are.

In his question Nicodemus toyed with the idea that the imperative generating work the Lord spoke about was somewhat like and maybe related to the human generative process that produces in the end a child. But the Lord quickly set him straight by declaring in answer: "Verily, verily, I say unto thee, Except a man be generated of water and of the Spirit, he cannot enter into the kingdom of God." (John 3:5).

Quite a bit of confusion exists in regard to this passage due to the failure of most translators to properly render two figures of speech. I have done this deliberately in my rendering above in order to get the problem before the reader. Two metaphors are used here. Something is called *hudōr*, which literally translated means "water," but actual water is not meant. Water never generated anyone, no matter how solemn the ceremony or what words were spoken when it was applied. Something else is called *pneuma*, which literally means "wind," but actual wind is not meant here. In most versions we get translation of the first metaphor and interpretation of the second. If we had a literal translation of both words it would read: "Except a man be generated of water and of wind," just as *pneuma* is literally translated "wind" in verse eight. And if we had interpretation of the figures in both places it would read: "Except a man be generated of the Word, even of the Spirit, he cannot enter into the knowledge of the kingdom of God."

Inasmuch as the Lord later declared, "The words that I speak unto you, they are Spirit" (John 6:63), I have translated *kai* as "even" to show that only one thing is meant. The Lord combined these two under the word Spirit in verses six and eight. And since knowledge and comprehension are so dominant in the context, I have amplified the translation by adding the word "knowledge" in my version.

All this fits in with the next statement of our Lord: "That which is generated of the flesh is flesh; and that which is generated of the Spirit is Spirit. Marvel not that I said unto you. You must be generated from above" (John 3:6,7).

In these words the Lord further clarifies the truth for Nicodemus. That which the flesh generates is always flesh, but it generates nothing that will make it possible for a man to know and comprehend God's truth concerning the kingdom of God. Since Nicodemus has said "we know," then, if this be true, there had to be the generating work of God that produced this knowledge and made it possible. They are now faced with the divine judgment that: "Unto whomsoever much is given, of him shall much be required" (Luke 12:48).

Following this our Lord added an illustration applicable to all who have enjoyed the generating work of God, saying: "The wind blows where it wills, and you hear the sound of it, but you do not know where it came from or where it is going. So is everyone that is generated by the Spirit" (John 3:8).

Since this illustration is of those who are "generated by the Spirit," let us be honest interpreters and keep it that way. When men are generated by God's Spirit, there is no way that we can know what caused this to be done, what the divine purpose is, or what the result will be. Generation only makes things possible for us. It does not make them positive. We know from His Word that God generates, and that this makes possible among men such things as love, works of righteousness, perception of truth, and, most important of all, belief that the man Jesus is the Christ, the Son of God. Apart from divine generation, faith in Jesus Christ would disappear from the earth.

This fact is sure to cause us to ask if this generating work, this enabling work is one that God does for every man. And if I were able to determine the source and destiny of the wind, I would try to answer this. However, of this I am sure: Whenever and wherever Jesus Christ is faithfully presented, when the record God gave of His Son is declared, God will provide the ability for the hearer to comprehend and believe. If the herald does what he should do, God will do what He alone can do. But the hearer still has a part that he must also do. God does not do the believing for anyone.

The SEED and BREAD Bible-Study leaflets are published as often as time and means permit and are sent free to all names on THE WORD OF TRUTH MINISTRY mailing list. Send us your name. There will be no obligation, solicitation, or visitation. Additional copies of any issue available on request.   ISSUE NO. 95

SEED & BREAD

FOR THE SOWER ISA. 55:10 FOR THE EATER

BRIEF BIBLICAL MESSAGES
FROM
THE WORD OF TRUTH MINISTRY
339 South Orange Drive, Los Angeles, Cal. 90036

Otis Q. Sellers, Bible Teacher

GOD'S PRESENTATION OF CHRIST

In all languages there are commonplace words that seem to be of no great importance, yet when they are used in certain contexts they take on a great significance and deliver an important message. The Greek word *agō* is one of these — a word so simple that it is often used when one is being taught to conjugate the verb forms. It means "to lead forth" or "to bring forth" and is used of such ordinary actions as a shepherd leading or bringing forth his sheep from the sheep-fold in order for them to drink or to graze. It is used of "Elymas the sorcerer" who, when smitten by blindness went about seeking for someone to lead (*agō*) him by the hand (Acts 13:11).

It can be readily seen how this word takes on a new and enlarged significance, when in Acts 9 the newly converted Saul (Paul) sought to attach himself to the disciples. They wanted nothing to do with him because of his notorious past conduct, and did not believe he was a disciple. They took him to be an infiltrator, seeking to identify the followers of Jesus Christ. However, Barnabas, who knew that Paul had truly become a disciple of the Lord Jesus, took him and brought (*agō*) him to the apostles and declared the facts of his conversion and subsequent bold proclamation of Christ (Acts 9:27). In other words, Barnabas took him and presented him to the apostles so that they would truly know the facts concerning him. Thus we see that *agō* when used in certain contexts means not simply to bring forth but to present. This presentation of Paul by Barnabas changed the whole picture, so that he found fellowship with the apostles and labored as a bold proclaimer of Jesus Christ.

In John 19 we find the word *agō* used in a different context that is highly informative. There is here a presentation of the Lord Jesus Christ, but He is presented in the worst possible light. It was when Pilate went forth before those who were demanding the death of Jesus and said: "Behold I bring Him forth to you, that ye may know that I find no fault in Him." (John 19:4). In this passage "bring forth" is *agō*, and since Pilate did not physically lead Him forth or bring Him forth (He came forth Himself, 19:5), this was Pilate saying, "I now present Him to you so that you may see for yourself what an abject, helpless, and harmless person He is."

So Jesus came forth, wearing the dreadful crown of thorns, hair matted with blood, clothed in the ridiculous, cast-off, purple robe: "And Pilate said unto them, 'Behold the man!'"

This was Pilate's presentation of Jesus Christ to His enemies, a presentation that should cause every believer to long and pray for that day when God will present Jesus Christ to the world, and every man on this earth will know Who Christ is in the sight of God.

This presentation of Jesus Christ by God to every man on earth is a plain truth of Scripture that has been absent from all theologies. Men have emphasized His incarnation, His ascension, His coming, His unveiling, and His manifestation, and rightly so, but they should not have missed altogether the great truth of His presentation. Even now as I write, I wonder if many will understand it. Will they accuse me of teaching that the time will come when God will give Christ to every man on earth? Well, if they do, then: "They say what they say so let them say it.

We can best advance our knowledge of this great truth by carefully considering Paul's inspired words in 1 Thess. 4:14: "For if we believe that Jesus died and rose again, even so them also which sleep in Jesus will God bring (*agō*) with Him."

Two great facts stand out in the last half of this passage. Jesus Christ is going to be presented, and those who are sleeping in Jesus are going to be presented with Him. This guarantees their resurrection from among the dead; otherwise there could be no presentation of His own to the world. Thus, this passage marks the time of their resurrection, which makes it to be one of great importance in the prophetic program.

Bible students have long struggled with this passage, not knowing just what to do with it. As a rule they have added to the confusion by failing to see that this passage speaks of God's presentation of Christ to all mankind and of our presentation with Him. Once this has taken place it can never again be said: "Therefore the world knoweth us not, because it knows Him not" (1 John 3:1). This passage is not dealing with His second coming or with His parousia (personal presence) that follows His coming. We need to clearly understand that there is a time gap between 1 Thess. 4:14 and 4:15, and this gap covers the entire period of the kingdom of God. The kingdom begins with His presentation and it ends with His parousia. We should not confuse these two events. There is a resurrection in 4:14 and another in verse 15 and these are centuries apart. A consideration of the outstanding facts will show this.

Paul did not want the Thessalonians "to be ignorant concerning them which are asleep" (1 Thess. 4:13). And to this we reply — very good. We do not want to be ignorant concerning those who have died and now "sleep in Jesus." Yes, we would like some concrete word from God's spokesman (1 Thess. 2:13) concerning them. Give us something solid to believe and to tell to others. Otherwise, we too will be sorrowing as those who have no hope.

So, in answer, Paul continues: "If we believe that Jesus died and rose again. . ." Very good, but permit us to interrupt and declare that we do believe, we most certainly do. This is fundamental with us and we cannot walk in fellowship with anyone who denies it. Jesus died, Jesus was buried, and Jesus rose again on the third day in harmony with the Scriptures (1 Cor. 15:3,4). And this was because God raised Him up (Acts 2:32). He who was dead became alive again (Rev. 2:8). However, speak on, Paul, and tell us about those who have fallen asleep and are now in the state of death. His declaration is brief: "Even so them also which sleep in Jesus will God present (agō) with Him."

What else can this mean but what it says? There is to be a bringing forth, that is a presentation of Jesus Christ, and all who sleep in Jesus are to be presented with Him. This presentation of Christ and His own is beyond all doubt to mankind as a whole, so that for the first time in the history of the human race the world will know Who Christ is in the sight of God and also what the children of God mean to Him.

God's presentation of Christ to mankind as set forth by Paul is not a new revelation. The Old Testament declared that this was to be, and reveals it to be the initial act of God when He assumes sovereignty and brings His government upon the earth. In Isaiah 40:5 we are told, "The glory of the LORD shall be revealed, and all flesh shall see it together: for the mouth of the LORD has spoken *it*." It should be noted here that it is the glory of the LORD (Jehovah) that is to be revealed, and this comes about as a result of the mouth of the LORD declaring that it shall so be. The word *glory* has to do with *esteem*, so much so that it would make a better translation in most occurrences. Thus this passage tells us that suddenly, universally, and miraculously the whole of mankind (all flesh) is going to be informed by God of the esteem in which He holds Jesus Christ. Every living man will then know Who Christ is and What Christ is in God's sight, and all will know it in the same amount and at the same time.

How else can "the earth be filled with the knowledge of the glory of the LORD, as the waters cover the sea" (Hab. 2:14), unless God makes a universal and official presentation and declaration concerning Jesus Christ?

In 1 Corinthians 1:7 we find that the Corinthian believers were waiting for this grand presentation of the Lord Jesus. The translators of the KJV not knowing what to do with this simple declaration, they having no place in their theology for a future unveiling of

Jesus Christ to mankind, used the word "coming" as a translation of *apokalupsin*, something that it could not possibly mean, as its elements clearly show. The prefix *apo* means "from," and *kalupsin* (from *kaluptō*) means a covering or veil. And yet this egregious error of translation is often cited as proof positive that the first century believers expected Christ to return during their lifetime. This idea is totally false. What they were waiting for was the unveiling of Jesus Christ. This is identical with His presentation, but a different word is used in order to emphasize another aspect of this many-faceted event.

In Titus 2:12, 13 we are exhorted to live: "Awaiting that blessed expectation, even the blazing forth (*epiphaneia*) of the glory of the great God, even our Savior, Christ Jesus" (TRV). This event is identical with that set forth in Isa. 40:5 and 1 Thess. 4:14.

This same glorious truth is set forth in other words in Colossians 3:4: "When the Christ, Who is our life, shall be manifested (*phaneroō*) then shall ye also be manifested with Him in glory." This corresponds to 1 Thess 4:14. Thus, whether it is called presentation, unveiling, or manifestation, it is the same event. If we are among the dead when this takes place, we will need to be raised to participate in it. If we are living we will need to be changed. But this presents no problem to the one familiar with the secret revealed in 1 Cor. 15:51,52.

There has been a struggle by some students to make the words "in glory" in Col. 3:4 refer to a place, a very special and exclusive place, far above all heavens, for those who are now believers. But all one needs to do is to check out all occurrences of the Greek phrase *en doxē*, and he will find that trying to hold this idea is about the same as trying to carry water in a sieve. It simply will not work.

Thank God that when we are presented with Christ, when we are manifested with Him, it will not be in shame, disgrace, or humiliation, but in the esteem in which God holds the believer in the Lord Jesus Christ.

Finally, it needs to be noted that all such events as the divine presentation, the unveiling, the manifestation, the blazing forth of His glory are all aspects of a still greater all-encompassing event, the divine assumption of sovereignty. So we pray, "Thy kingdom come."

The SEED and BREAD Bible-Study leaflets are published as often as time and means permit and are sent free to all names on THE WORD OF TRUTH MINISTRY mailing list. Send us your name. There will be no obligation, solicitation, or visitation. Additional copies of any issue available on request.   ISSUE NO. 96

SEED & BREAD

FOR THE SOWER   ISA. 55:10   FOR THE EATER

BRIEF BIBLICAL MESSAGES

FROM

THE WORD OF TRUTH MINISTRY

339 South Orange Drive, Los Angeles, Cal. 90036

Otis Q. Sellers, Bible Teacher

WHAT DOES "EKKLĒSIA" MEAN?

The presentation of this study demands that the ground be cleared at once. I refuse to plant this seed in a weed patch, and most certainly not on top of a boulder. The Greek word *ekklēsia* does not mean "church," no matter what definition is given to this term. If anyone thinks he can stamp his foot or pound the pulpit and this will become true, then he will have to take his place with the Red Queen in *Through the Looking-Glass,* whose sanity was somewhat questionable.

Every student of the reformation is familiar with Martin Luther's strong aversion to the word *church* (*kirche* in German) as a translation of the word *ekklēsia.* But Luther was unable to prevail in this and in the end a denomination was named after him called *The Lutheran Church.* The acceptance of the word *church* was due to Calvin's influence.

In a previous study (No. 87) we saw how the Greek verb *kaleō* primarily means to name, to designate, to position, to appoint, or to establish. In the history of this word it seems that at first *kaleō* meant only to call or to summon in the sense of an invitation. But in the prevailing governmental systems that existed in those times, the invitation by a sovereign for a man to serve was equal to an appointment which could not be refused, so *kaleō* came to mean to position, to name, or to appoint, and this soon became its predominant usage. A consideration of all occurrences of *kaleō* in the New Testament will demonstrate the truth of this.

The Greek word *ekklēsia* is formed from the descriptive adjective *kletōs,* a word that described all who had been named to serve in some position designated by the sovereign. These were designated ones, appointed ones, not merely invited ones. When the prefix *ek,* which means "out," is added to the word *kletōs,* it gives us *ekklēsia* which means out-called ones, or, to make it more clear, out-positioned ones.

These are facts that are generally known, but they have been misconstrued by many, and probably will continue to be until

His lightnings enlighten the world (Psa. 97:4). The exalted meaning of "out-called' is degraded and stultified so that it can be used to signify something that we are today. They say that since the followers of Christ have been called out of the world, this makes us the out-called ones. All this is in spite of the fact that Jesus Christ said of His own, "I pray not that Thou shouldest take them out of the world, but that thou shouldest keep them from the evil" (John 17:15). They illustrate this by saying that Israel is called "the *ekklēsia* in the wilderness" (Acts 7:38), declaring that this was because they had been called out of Egypt. These are not the facts in the case of Stephen's declaration, as will be shown later.

I suppose that the most prevalent error in Christendom today is the idea that when the Lord Jesus said: "Upon this rock I will build My *ekklēsia*" (Matt. 16:18), that He was speaking of the great mixture of organized religion that travels under the canopy which today is called "the church." Quite a few men of God, seeing the utter fallacy and impossibility of this being true, limit the privilege of being the *ekklēsia* to the true believers in the Lord Jesus, that we are "the church." In regard to this, let it be said that if *ekklēsia*, means little or nothing, then we can all claim to be the *ekklēsia*, but if this grand word does have a meaning of great significance, then we should be careful about applying such an exalted title to ourselves.

In spite of the attempts to prove otherwise, the word *church* comes from the Latin word for circle, and it is from this that we get our English word *circus*. So today when we see the pretentious parades and the religious extravaganzas that are put on display for all to see, we are convinced that the word *circus* fits it to quite a degree of exactitude. If I were any part of this great three-ring American religious circus, I would hang my head in shame. But, thank God, from all this I have been delivered and separated. I consider all of this highly successful religious activity to be little more than men putting on the "form of Godliness, but denying the power thereof," as Paul said would characterize men in the concluding days of this dispensation of grace (2 Tim. 3:5).

The subject of the New Testament is the kingdom of God (Issue No. 27), and it has been shown in previous studies that "kingdom" means "government" (Issue No. 29). One thing that is essential to any government, even absolute monarchies, is that men shall be given positions that are out of the sovereign. In the United States we insist that the sovereignty belongs to the people; therefore, our President has a position which is out of the people. He is an out-called or out-positioned one in the true meaning of *ekklēsia*. However, let none think that I am saying that our Presidents are the out-called of God. Not in the least! Their position is not out of God; it is out of the people.

Since no man is able to do everything, even if it is his right and duty to do certain things, he gives positions to others, and these then become out-positioned ones, their position being out of the President. However, there must be no thought of severance in the word "out" as used here, no more than when we say the arm is out of the body — not severed from it but projected.

When one gives a position to another, the place given must first be inherent in the one who gives it. It was the declared purpose of Jesus Christ to give many a position out of Himself. These would be a projection of Him, and individually and collectively they would be His out-called, that is, His *ekklēsia*. Therefore, Jesus Christ being the Son of God could give others this position so that they might be sons of God. He was God's apostle, and He could give others out of what He was and they too became apostles. He was God's prophet, and He gave of Himself to others and they became prophets. All such had a position out of Him, and were the out-called of God. We could go on through a long list, for He was Shepherd, Teacher, Governor, Miracle-worker, Healer, Evangelist. He was one who could scatter and yet increase (Prov. 11:24).

Thus as the Lord Jesus gave of Himself so that others could become in a measure what He was, He built up His own body (substance) upon the earth (Eph. 4:12). See my version and notes on Ephesians 4 in Issue No. 61. And we need to note that no man could ever be anything in the sight of God unless this position is first found in Jesus Christ. Truly, Jesus Christ loved the *ekklēsia* and gave Himself for it that it might become in a measure what He is.

An illuminating illustration of all this is found in Stephen's message in Acts 7, where in speaking of Moses he declared: "This is he that was in the *ekklēsia* in the wilderness." This is usually taken to mean that Stephen was telling these Israelites that Moses was in Israel. If so, this would have been a bit of gratuitous and useless information, about the same as if I should tell a Britisher that Queen Victoria was a citizen of Great Britain. The *ekklēsia* spoken of here was not Israel, and we will miss important truth if we think so.

The man Moses had a position out of God. He was *ekklēsia*, an out-called man. He was Israel's Chief Executive, Supreme Judge, and Lawgiver. But let no one choke on the idea of one man being out-called of God. This is one truth that all must learn. As Karl Ludwig Schmidt, the renowned Greek scholar, puts it: "To put the matter in a nutshell — a single individual could be, — would have to be — the *ekklēsia* if he has communion with Christ."

Moses was the monarch in Isarel. He ruled alone, but when at the suggestion of Jethro (Exo. 18:23), he chose able men out of all Israel and made them "heads over the people, rulers of thousands, rulers of hundreds, rulers of fifties, and rulers of tens," an enormous *ekklēsia* was produced that numbered about 80,000, all of whom had a position out of Moses. And it was a position that he could take back to himself at any time.

However, at a later date, a more important event took place.

The burdens that Moses still had to bear became so heavy that he took his complaint to God (Numbers 11:10-15). The Lord responded by telling him to gather seventy men out of the elders of Israel and bring them unto the tabernacle of the congregation that they might stand with him there. Furthermore, the LORD declared: "And I will come down and talk with thee there: AND I WILL TAKE OF THE SPIRIT THAT IS UPON THEE, AND WILL PUT IT ON THEM: and they shall bear the burden of the people with thee, that thou bear it not thyself alone" (Num. 11:17).

So it was that these seventy men had a position which was out of Moses. He was in them. They partook of what he was — his position, his substance, his very essence. This is what Stephen was talking about when He said of Moses: "This is he, that was in the *ekklēsia* in the wilderness" (Acts 7:38). He was telling them that Moses was in the seventy, for in fact they were the body of Moses, or his substance, which is what the word *body* means. And it is my understanding that this is what the dispute was about when Michael the archangel contended with Satan over "the body of Moses" (Jude 1:9). Satan was most eager to seize control of the seventy men.

My belief is that in the famous and familiar passage in Matt. 16:18 the Lord speaking through Peter to the ten other apostles (Judas excluded) declared, "And I say also unto you, that you are rock, even as I am rock, and upon this rock I will build of Me the out-called ones, and not even the power of the state of death shall prevail against them." Indeed, His out-called ones must be built out of Him.

It is my belief and conviction that no man upon the earth today can truthfully say that he has a position out of God, that he is an out-called one. He can claim certain blessings, yes, but position, no. The chief characteristic of all out-called men is that they mediate between God and men. There were many of these in the thirty-three years of the Acts period, but not one in this the dispensation of God's grace. All anyone can claim today is that he is a sinner saved by grace. But, I also belive that in view of the service we will perform when God governs, we will need to have a position out of Him, and we will need to mediate between God and men. Then we will be units in that great *ekklēsia* Jesus Christ said He would build out of Himself.

The SEED and BREAD Bible-Study leaflets are published as often as time and means permit and are sent free to all names on THE WORD OF TRUTH MINISTRY mailing list. Send us your name. There will be no obligation, solicitation, or visitation. Additional copies of any issue available on request.   ISSUE NO. 97

SEED & BREAD

FOR THE SOWER   ISA. 55:10   FOR THE EATER

BRIEF BIBLICAL MESSAGES

FROM

THE WORD OF TRUTH MINISTRY

339 South Orange Drive, Los Angeles, Cal. 90036

Otis Q. Sellers, Bible Teacher

WHAT DOES "TA PANTA" MEAN?

In the *King James Version* of Ephesians 1:11 we read of the purpose of God "who worketh all things after the counsel of His own will." This statement naturally raises the question as to what is meant by "all things." Just what does this take in, what does it include? Does it include all evil as well as all good? This passage is constantly being cited by many as an impregnable proof text that every detail of life in this universe has been determined in advance by God, the good as well as the evil. Those who hold this idea do not hesitate to claim that every move of man, his thoughts, his motives, and his acts are all predetermined by God and that they must come to pass according as He has already willed.

I came upon this doctrine in the first year of my Christian life. My father and I had greatly benefited at that time by reading certain small pamphlets written by Arthur W. Pink, and we had sought out more of his writings. One of these was *The Sovereignty of God*, which my father happened to read first, and he was somewhat disturbed by it. After I read it, I suggested to him that we did not need to be in any hurry about either accepting or rejecting his teaching — that we had only recently become students of God's Word and we had better wait until we knew more about the Bible. He agreed, but we did not drop the subject as I went on to examine with care other writings by Mr. Pink along this same line.

In one study he made use of 1 Cor. 11:12 which says:

"For as the woman is of the man, even so is the man also by the woman, but all things of God." Concerning this he said: "All is according to His eternal purpose which He purposed in Himself before the foundation of the world. My friends, it was predestined by God before the world began that I should occupy this pulpit tonight, and that you should sit in those chairs tonight, and that I should speak on the subject I am speaking on tonight, and that you should hear it. It was all fixed by God before this world began, and if any of you question that, I bring you back to the Scriptures, 'All things are of God.'"

The utter fallacy of Mr. Pink's reasoning was easy for me to see.

There must have been many meetings going on that Sunday in Sydney, Australia, where the words set forth above were spoken: High Church, Low Church, Christian Science, Catholic, Baptist, Methodist, Presbyterian, and even spiritistic seances. If Pink's teaching were true, then it must have been predestined by God before the world began that every preacher, priest, rabbi, and medium should also stand in their pulpits that day and give a message that had been predetermined by God. This of course could only lead to great confusion, but I suppose it was held that the confusion was also predestined by God, which would make God the author of this confusion, something which I knew was denied in Scripture (1 Cor. 14:33). Therefore, I rejected Mr. Pink's ideas and determined that before I ever assented to any such teaching, I would need to have unimpeachable proof that it was in complete harmony with everything declared in the Word of God; especially such passages as God's word in Jer. 23:21: "I have not sent these prophets, yet they ran: I have not spoken to them, yet they prophesied;" and the words of our Lord to the Pharisees, "You are out of your father the devil, and the lusts of your father ye will do" (John 8:44).

Some years later I came upon the writings of Mr. A. E. Knoch, the translator of *The Concordant Version,* and found in them such statements as: "All is out of God. The bad as well as the good," and "There are many passages in God's Word that bear the truth that all things — the evil as well as the good — find their source in the one and only God, Who alone can originate." Upon careful examination of these "many passages" I found that they all contained the peculiar Greek phrase *ta panta,* a phrase concerning which Mr. Knoch showed both ambivalence and confusion. In the sublinear of his version, for which he claimed exquisite accuracy, he sometimes translated it "the all" and in other occurrences "the universe." Then in his version he would render it "all these." This started me on a study of *ta panta,* as I determined to know what this phrase meant when used by the Spirit of God. This study has now continued for more than forty years and has been profitable to many.

In consideration of this phrase a few simple facts need to be recognized. The Greek word for "all" is *pas.* The neuter form is *pan,* and the accusative is *panta.* The form *panta* is found 269 times in the Greek New Testament, but in thirty-seven of these occurrences it is preceded by the definite article *ta.* This gives us *ta panta,* the subject of our study.

A cursory review of the thirty-seven occurrences will show that to a certain extent, this is a Pauline phrase. Mark uses it but once, and John uses it twice in Revelation, but all other occurrences are found in the writings of Paul.

Out of all occurrences of *ta panta* the first effort of the student should be to find one passage in which the meaning is so clear that even "wayfaring men, though fools, shall not err therein," then apply this meaning to all other places where the same phrase is found. As we trace down the list, Colossians 3:8 stands out at once. Here Paul says: "But now ye also put off all these (*ta panta*); anger, wrath, malice, blasphemy, filthy communication out of your mouth."

This passage shows clearly what Paul meant when he used the phrase *ta panta*. Here, the translator is almost forced to translate it correctly by rendering it "all these," which is about the only way it could be translated unless one deliberately ignores the Greek. This passage shows it does not mean "the universe," and that it cannot mean "everything without exception or distinction." Even A. E. Knoch translates it "all these" in this occurrence, although he has already translated it "the universe" in three other occurrences in the first chapter.

On the basis of this one passage, when considered in the light of all other occurrences, we can say that *ta panta* is a demonstrative expression, idiomatic in character, referring back to something which has just been said or pointing forward to something about to be mentioned. By "demonstrative" I mean serving to point out or identify, and by "idiomatic" I mean an expression that is peculiar to itself in grammatical construction, the meaning of which cannot be derived from the conjoined meaning of its elements. It can be best rendered in English by using "all this" or "all these" depending upon whether the subject requires a singular or plural construction. It always points to what it set forth in the context. This can be seen in every passage where it is found. We will note some of these.

Mark 4:11. In the first occurrence it has been translated correctly — "all these things (*ta panta*) are done in parables."

Rom. 8:32. This should read "with Him also freely give us all these" (*ta panta*), referring to the various blessings set forth in the context.

Rom. 11:36. "For out of Him, and through Him, and to Him are all these" (*ta panta*), pointing to the works and ways of God set forth in chapters 9, 10, and 11. I refuse to divorce this statement from its subject matter.

1 Cor. 8:6. This should read: "Nevertheless, to us there is one God, the Father, out of whom is all this (*ta panta*) and we for Him, even one Lord Jesus Christ, through whom is all this (*ta panta*), and we through Him." The reference is to the position and the knowledge of the Corinthian believers. All this was out of God, the Father.

1 Cor 11:12. The last part of this verse should be translated, "Yet all this (*ta panta*) is out of God." In the context of this passage Paul has stated ten details of the divine arrangement God has established in regard to men and women. Then, following this, lest any should think that this is a human arrangement, imposed by the males upon the females and standing only in social custom,

Paul declares, "Yet all this (*ta panta*) is out of God."

1 Cor. 12:19. Read here: "Now if all these (*ta panta*) were one member, where the body?"

1 Cor. 15:27,28. Here we have a passage in which *panta* is found three times, *ta panta* three times, and *en pasin* once. I would translate this as follows: "For He has subjected all (*panta*) under His feet. But when it says 'All (*panta*) is subject, it is evident that this does not include Him who subjects all these (*ta panta*) to Him. Now, whenever all these (*ta panta*) are subjected to Him, then the Son Himself will be subject to Him who subjected all these (*ta panta*) to Him that God may be everything (*panta*) in everyone (*en pasin*)." When this passage is examined with care, it provides an excellent demonstration that *ta panta* is a demonstrative term, idiomatic in character, referring to something which has just been mentioned.

Eph. 1:11. I would translate the final part of this passage "according to the purpose of the One who is executing all this (*ta panta*) according to the counsel of His own will." This is the passage which is constantly used as the supreme proof text by those who insist that everything that has ever happened in the history of the universe has been determined in advance by God. Scripture denies this and this passage does not declare it. It has to do with the present operations of God. Men of good will who read these lines should pause and give thanks to God that they no longer need to believe an erroneous translation that makes the awful, ugly, realities of life to be out of God.

To examine in full all passages where *ta panta* is found would require about forty times the space I have used here. The best I can do now is furnish the student with a complete list of passages where this phrase is found and he can take it from there. These are Mark 4:11; Rom. 8:32, 11:36; 1 Cor. 8:6(2), 11:12, 12:6, 12:19, 15:27, 15:28(2); 2 Cor. 4:15, 5:18; Gal. 3:22; Eph. 1:10, 1:11, 1:23, 3:9, 4:10, 4:15, 5:13, Phil. 3:8, 3:21; Col. 1:16 (2), 1:17, 1:20, 3:8, 3:11; 1 Tim. 6:13; Heb. 1:3, 2:8, 2:10 (2); Rev. 4:11, 5:13.

The student will find that to understand the true meaning of *ta panta* will shed light on every passage in which it is found. He may also find an overlay of traditional interpretations that do nothing more than obscure the true meaning. These will need to be removed and set aside. And let all remember that if any one thing in Scripture can be found which is declared not to be of God, or not to be out of God, none can say that everything is out of Him.

The SEED and BREAD Bible-Study leaflets are published as often as time and means permit and are sent free to all names on THE WORD OF TRUTH MINISTRY mailing list. Send us your name. There will be no obligation, solicitation, or visitation. Additional copies of any issue available on request.   ISSUE NO. 98

SEED & BREAD

FOR THE SOWER   ISA. 55:10   FOR THE EATER

BRIEF BIBLICAL MESSAGES
FROM
THE WORD OF TRUTH MINISTRY
339 South Orange Drive, Los Angeles, Cal. 90036

Otis Q. Sellers, Bible Teacher

POSITIVE BIBLICAL THEOLOGY

Let no one be afraid of the word *theology* or hesitate to read this leaflet because this term is found in its title. There have been so many putrid theologies, some of them spun out of the corrupt minds of men, that the word that describes the bad as well as the good has fallen into disrepute. However, let it be recognized and admitted that every Christian has a theology. In fact, if he did not have one, he could not claim to be a Christian. For one to say he has no theology is the same as saying, "I believe nothing." If he says, as some do, "I have the Bible, and I need no theology," then let him understand that anything he gets out of the Bible becomes his theology. Others will say, "I have Christ, and I need nothing more," but the brief statement that Christ is all he needs is a declaration of his theology. Any declaration that anyone makes concerning God, His works, His words, or His ways is a declaration of his theology.

The proclamation of a bumper sticker that says "Jesus is coming" expresses one facet of the person's theology who placed it there. This is a declaration related to God, and since it is well attested to by plain statements in the Bible, it declares a Biblical fact or truth, yes, a Biblical theology. But when he adds to this statement, as some do, "It may be today," then he has added an erroneous, human, unscriptural declaration to his theology and it is no longer Biblical. According to the Bible, Jesus Christ is not coming today or tomorrow, there being too many events that must come to pass before Jesus Christ comes again. All one needs to do is ask the question: "Who comes first, Christ or antichrist?" and he will see what I mean.

So to all who may be unsure about the word "theology," let him face the fact that theology becomes the occupation of every Christian the moment he begins to think about, to develop, and then to communicate his Christian faith and principles. If his faith began with some truth from God's Word, as it should, then let him remember that Jesus Christ declared, "If ye continue in My word (*logos*), then are ye My disciples indeed" (John 8:31). These words were spoken to those Jews who believed on Him, and to this He added, "And ye shall know the truth, and the truth shall make you free." Therefore, if we continue in His word, we will be constantly adding to our theology, and thus we will know the truth and find freedom from all the satanic, fleshly, and human lies that pass for Biblical theology today. Again I say, no Christian can avoid being a theologian.

The challenge to "define your terms" is usually a fair one, and it certainly is in regard to the title of this study. In this leaflet the word *theology* is used to designate a body of knowledge related to God. It comes into the English language from *Theos* which means God, and *logos* which means a word or an expression — not a single word, which may say nothing if it has no context, but a statement or declaration that says something. Thus when these two Greek words are put together they form the word *theology*, which means any statement or declaration that is made concerning God, His person, His works, His words, and His ways.

The word "Biblical" needs no definition in this study, and the word "positive" means that one has done the work that is necessary to know what the Bible says concerning the subject so that he can speak from a "thus saith the Word of God" standpoint, and know that he is not misrepresenting the sacred scriptures.

Of course there are many who feel that in order for one to be a theologian he must have certain qualifications and be well-versed in all the million and one opinions that so-called theologians have declared as their understanding of all matters related to God. It is held that we must consider all of this, strain out the unacceptable, add a few ideas of our own, and then hold and present this as being divine truth in regard to all matters of faith and practice. This, to me, is somewhat ridiculous, since most of these theologians do not believe the Bible is the inspired Word of God, and they reject its authority. So before we can accept the witness of any man we must examine his words in the light of the law and the testimony, for "if they speak not according to this Word, it is because there is no light in them." (Isa. 8:20).

Very early in my Christian experience (which began fifty-nine years ago) I became disillusioned, dissatisfied, and even disgusted with that great mass of opinions, ideas, and views that made up the greater part of "church theology." The confusion that existed even within a single denomination was ridiculous. Out of this condition of mind there came to be within me a deep desire to establish for myself a positive Biblical theology in regard to all matters set forth in the Word of God. I determined to be a personal student of the Word in my own right, and to seek out diligently what the Bible had to say in regard to any matter that was related to God. I would come to my own conclusions after considering all the Biblical material that was available. Even if I could do this on only one subject, at least on that subject I could be positive and say, "Thus saith the Word of God."

This does not mean that I set aside or ignored the findings of all those men who had gone to the Bible for truth in times past. But I have ever kept in mind the divine directive, "Put to the test all things, hold fast to that which is good" (1 Thess. 5:21). However, in doing this my opinion was confirmed all the more that the theology of Christendom is not only an incongruous mixture, it is also an unholy mess, and very little of it is actually Biblical. Furthermore, I found that professing Christians everywhere were making statements concerning the God whom I honor, love, and serve that were libelous, degrading, and debasing, and the theology of Christendom did nothing to denounce and correct these falsehoods. Everyone was, and still is, afraid of "disturbing the flock." These facts have done much to set the course of my life and work, a course from which I have never veered, one of perpetual and progressive Bible study.

The truth set forth in God's Word is made up of an innumerable number of individual truths, all of which are in some manner related one to another. The only way to get "the truth" is to gather up one by one the actual facts of God's Word: "For precept must be upon precept, precept upon precept; line upon line, line upon line; here a little and there a little" (Isa. 28:10). Even facts that seem to be insignificant and unimportant must be embraced and stored away in the God-given computer bank of our memory to wait for that day when suddenly we will need them in order to understand related truths that can then be added to our positive, Biblical theology.

The active believer in the Lord Jesus Christ who continues in the truth is bound to meet up with matters that challenge him in regard to what the Bible says about the problem he faces. The more active he is in study or service, the more he will be confronted with these matters. Most ministers display great skill in avoiding coming to grips with these, inasmuch as their efforts will provide them with no material for their Sunday morning message. "My people are not interested in doctrine, so why should I bother with Biblical problems." These were the words of one minister to me. Another said, "My congregation is composed of simple people, and I give them only the simplest things." Such men as these will never possess or speak a positive Biblical theology, even when they speak on simple matters. They will not do the work that brings it forth.

A much better spirit, even a spirit of truth, is revealed by a missionary in a personal letter to me. He works among the Indians in South America and is pushed to the limit of his strength every day by his labors among these people. He says in part: "In my ministry to these people, nothing is more important in my teaching than conveying the TRUTH. I want only to teach what is true. I have a fever to know the Word in all its truth and power. It is not easy when you deal with primitive people and uneducated people to be motivated to serious Bible study. These people have to be taught the basic, simple things first. However, I have discovered that the more one knows and understands the Bible, the easier it is to simplify and explain."

I am not personally acquainted with the writer of the letter quoted above, but I am sure we are kindred spirits. And I know from long experience that he will find even as I have found that when one comes upon a Biblical matter that demands study, and if he carefully searches out for himself all the clues, bits, and pieces that pertain to it, even if it be only a simple truth, and when he has pieced all this information together, it will remain for the rest of his life in some way truer than anything he has simply read or has been merely taught. Furthermore, it will be more free from the onslaughts of doubt and attacks that come from the spiritual forces of wickedness among the most elevated.

Of course many will insist that such research and study is the work of scholars. This is true, but the scholars are not doing it. Bible study is the work of all believers, especially those who feel within themselves the deep urge to establish in their lives a positive, Biblical theology, and thus glorify God by holding, speaking, and walking in the truth that He has so freely given.

In view of the times in which we live, and the future which lies ahead as evil men and seducers wax worse and worse, before God assumes sovereignty, we who believe in the Lord Jesus Christ need a positive, Biblical theology. We need to lay hold of orderly statements in regard to the record God has given of His Son, past, present, and future. This is what I am laboring to establish in my own life, and to pass it on to others who can check it out and make it their own if they wish to do so. This has been my impelling desire for over a half century. It is one that I can never get away from. And, of course, when one feels such an impelling desire, and also is sure it is from the Lord, he will not think of his shortcomings or his lack of ability to perform the task that God has laid upon his heart.

As I look at God's Word, I know of no sentence that describes it better than the one spoken by the Samaritan woman when she spoke of Jacob's well and said: "The well is deep." With this I agree. But not for one moment will I admit that I have "nothing to draw with." As a believer in the Lord Jesus Christ, I have God's holy Spirit as the earnest of my inheritance (Eph. 1:14). Since He is given so that I might "know the things that are freely given to us of God" (1 Cor. 2:12), I will put my hand in His and let Him lead me into the deep things of God (1 Cor. 2:10).

The SEED and BREAD Bible-Study leaflets are published as often as time and means permit and are sent free to all names on THE WORD OF TRUTH MINISTRY mailing list. Send us your name. There will be no obligation, solicitation, or visitation. Additional copies of any issue available on request.　　ISSUE NO. 99

SEED & BREAD

FOR THE SOWER   ISA. 55:10   FOR THE EATER

BRIEF BIBLICAL MESSAGES

FROM

THE WORD OF TRUTH MINISTRY

339 South Orange Drive, Los Angeles, Cal. 90036

Otis Q. Sellers, Bible Teacher

THE GLORY OF BELIEVING

Of all the words to be found in the Word of God there is none that is more important than the word *believe*. This one word represents all that a sinner must do, all that he can do, and all that he is expected to do in order to be saved. This is a truth that is easily demonstrated by the Word of God. In it we are told: "He that believeth on Him is not condemned: but he that believeth not is condemned already, because he has not believed in the name of the only begotten Son of God" (John 3:18). In the time period in which we live, and under the administration of God that establishes His present gracious method of dealing with us, there is no act that we can do in relationship to Him that is greater or more important than the act which is indicated by the word *believe*.

If we desire complete forgiveness, if we would lay hold of the blessing of redemption and justification, if we would possess the guarantee of a life in the eon to come and a place and portion in the kingdom of God, then the one thing we must do is believe. If we have not done this and if we are not continuing to do it, we may as well forget about ever being a member of God's redeemed family and enjoying the many blessings that come as the result of being so positioned.

In view of these facts it is a tragedy indeed that throughout Christendom, in all its multifarious branches, the word *believe* and the act of believing is misunderstood, misinterpreted, misused, and abused. Any little religious act or ritual is equated with believing, and no one seems to be making any serious attempt to expose, denounce, or correct all the errors that have arisen out of this.

One of the chief errors that has come out of the misuse and abuse of this word is exhibited in the practices of those who call themselves evangelistic and evangelical. With them, anything and everything is equated with believing. If one has bowed his head, closed his eyes, raised his hand, walked down the aisle, shook hands with the evangelist, gone into the inquiry room, been worked on and over by some personal worker, prayed what is called "the sinners prayer," signed a card, indicated the church of his choice, been baptized, united with some church, and confessed to four points of faith — any three, four, or five of these actions are considered as "belief" in Jesus Christ, and all of them together are held to constitute him a true believer, yes, even a "born-again believer" which is supposed to be something much better than the ordinary believer.

I repudiate this entire human, fleshly ritual in its totality, so far as having anything to do with one becoming a believer is concerned. It is all orchestrated to produce visible results, and it is quite successful in doing it. All may go through it who care to do so, but they deceive themselves if they think that any of it or all of it together qualifies one as a believer in the Lord Jesus Christ.

The above words are not spoken in any spirit of carping criticism. They are spoken in order to let all readers know that this writer is no part of those practices which are now being rightfully described as being "cheap and easy believism."

Certain facts in the Word of God when carefully considered will reveal at once the great importance of believing. There was a time in the earthly ministry of the Lord Jesus when a great multitude traveled a long distance in the hope that they would again be miraculously fed as they had been the day before. They were chided by the Lord for this, and He exhorted them saying that they should not put forth such great effort for that food that perished so soon after the eating, but labor for that food which would endure unto everlasting life which He, the Son of Man, would give to them (John 6:26, 27). This caused them to ask a question that was uppermost in their minds — a question which should always be uppermost in the minds of every one of us: "Then said they unto Him, What shall we do that we might work the works of God" (John 6:28).

In asking this question, since they spoke of "works," they may have had in mind that He would give them a new set of ten commandments, even as Moses had given Israel 1500 years before. Or, they may have expected He would give them a revised and shortened set of the 600 commandments that the Pharisees and scribes had laid upon the people (Matt. 23:4,5). But nothing like this happened. In one of the plainest and most direct statements to be found in the Bible, the Lord Jesus answered and said unto them: "This is the work of God, that ye believe on Him Whom God hath sent" (John 6:29).

I can never read this passage without giving thanks to God that this question was asked, and that our Lord gave such a direct and specific answer. They had asked about the "works" of God. He told them of the "work" of God, one work that they could do and lay claim to having done "the work of God." Those who have done this have climbed the Mount Everest of God's works. There is nothing greater, and there is nothing higher. Part of the glory of believing is to know and rest in the assurance of having done that of which Jesus Christ said: "This is the work of God."

However, let no one think from anything said so far that belief is a cheap and easy matter. As a believer, I know it is not. But let it be understood that one becomes a believer by believing the truth that is at hand, the truth that God has set before him, the truth that the Spirit of God has applied to his heart and mind. This could be something as simple as the divine pronouncement that, "This is the work of God, that ye believe on Him Whom God hath sent." In fact this is an excellent truth to start with, for it brings us face to face with the fact of what must be done if we would work the work of God. The reader might do well to start with this one truth, for let him be well assured that if he denies it, rejects it, or even neglects it, he will then stand in the sight of God as an unbeliever, one who has failed to respond to a direct statement from the mouth of the Lord Jesus Christ.

Of course to believe the truth declared by Jesus Christ in John 6:29 would be only a start, but one must start with something that is out of the mouth of God. From this beginning he can continue in God's Word, and if he does continue, then he is a disciple (learner) indeed (John 8:31). Furthermore, he shall know the truth, and the truth will make him free (John 8:32). Remember, one cannot be a believer unless he believes something, and he will never be charged with unbelief until he has rejected something that God has declared.

Exactly what it is that one must believe in order to qualify as a believer is set forth in an important declaration found in the first chapter of John's Gospel. There the beloved Apostle states: "He came unto His own, and His own received Him not. But as many as received Him, to them gave He authority to become the children of God, even to them that believe on His name" (John 1:11-12).

We have reason to rejoice here that the truth is stated in two different ways, which the Spirit of God has done so as to preclude any misinterpretation. First, the promise is "to as many as received Him." To all such He gives the authority to say: "God is my Father, I am His child, and, therefore, a member of His family." And since the right to make these claims is based entirely on "receiving Him," we need to ask how He is received, what one does to obtain Him so as to be able to truthfully say, "He is mine!" The Spirit of God anticipated these questions and provides the answer. "Receiving Him" is explained in an appositional statement as being "Even to them that believe on His name."

Thus by the authority of the Word of God we can say that there is no ceremony, ordinance, or ritual that has anything to do with receiving Him. Jesus Christ is received when we "believe on His name." Men sin against God when they try to make a religious rite or ceremony of this.

But what does it mean to "believe on His name"? some are sure to ask. Is it enough to simply say, "I believe in Jesus," as some teach in their "easy believism."? No, it is not enough to say some such words as these, words which are usually placed on the lips by some prompter.

Shakespeare asked, "What's in a name?" but the question we need to ask is, "What IS a name?" We all know that a name is the distinguishing term by which a person or thing is called, and by means of which it can be distinguished or identified. However, this complex word has a host of meanings, one of which is the reputed character, that is, a good or bad reputation. Thus the name of God or the name of the Lord Jesus Christ is His character as declared in the Word of God. This is succinctly stated in 1 John 5:10 as being "the record God gave of His Son." This record established Who He is and What He is, and it is what we must believe if we believe in His name.

Thus it is my conviction that anyone who ever faces a group of people to present things that pertain to God should if it is at all possible get something into his words that is a definite part of the record that God has given of His Son. If he does this, what he says may be taken by the Spirit of God and used to start someone out as a believer.

The angel of the Lord instructed Joseph before the birth of our Lord that he should "call His NAME Jesus: for He shall save His people from their sins" (Matt. 1:21). Very few know that "Jesus" is the English spelling of the Greek word "Iesous," and that "Iesous" is the Greek form of the Hebrew word "Yeshua," which comes to us in our Bibles as "Joshua." The word "Yeshua" means "Jehovah the Savior." Many male children in Israel were given this name so that all through life they would proclaim that "Jehovah saves." But the babe born in Bethlehem was not given it for this reason. He was to be called "Jehovah the Savior" because He would save His people from their sins. Thus, the distinguishing term by which He was called becomes a part of God's record as to Who He is and What He is. I believe on this name. The Jehovah of the Old Testament is the Lord Jesus Christ of the New Testament. And to this record God added the name "EMMANUEL," which being interpreted means "God with us" (Matt. 1:23).

The SEED and BREAD Bible-Study leaflets are published as often as time and means permit and are sent free to all names on THE WORD OF TRUTH MINISTRY mailing list. Send us your name. There will be no obligation, solicitation, or visitation. Additional copies of any issue available on request.   ISSUE NO. 100